CPD FOR TEAC[HERS'] LEARNING IN P[HYSICAL] EDUCATION

Drawing on best practice for the continuing professional development (CPD) of practising physical education teachers, this book encourages teachers to reflect on their own practices and how these can be developed as they continue their professional journey to support student learning. The book covers three main themes: improving students' learning and supporting student progress; the teacher as learner – developing your expertise as a teacher; and supporting professional development – how as a teacher you can lead and own your continuing learning in a sustainable manner.

Throughout the book, teachers are encouraged not just to reflect on where they are now, but also what changes they INTEND to make to their practice, how they IMPLEMENT those changes and then to review the IMPACT this has had on students' learning. Each chapter includes tasks embedded within the content to encourage the reader to reflect on how they could apply the new knowledge they are acquiring from reading and engaging with the chapter.

Written for a global audience, the book brings together examples from the Singapore Physical Education and Sports Teacher Academy (PESTA), which provides CPD to teachers in the high-performing Singaporean system. Offering high quality research and practice, this book is a pivotal resource for physical education teachers undertaking CPD all over the world.

Susan Capel is Emeritus Professor of Physical Education at Brunel University, London, UK.

Julia Lawrence is Senior Lecturer in Education at Northumbria University, Newcastle-upon-Tyne, UK.

Melanie Martens is Academy Principal at the Physical Education and Sports Teacher Academy, Ministry of Education, Singapore.

Hanif Abdul Rahman is Principal Master Teacher at the Physical Education and Sports Teacher Academy, Ministry of Education, Singapore.

Each chapter in the book is designed to provide a springboard to help teachers expand their pedagogical skills. They are designed to be used both as independent reading for both teachers and professional development personnel but also as a focus for shared professional development experiences. They will be an invaluable resource for both.

Dr Judith Rink, Emeritus Professor, University of South Carolina, USA

Overall, this is an insightful and comprehensive book that suits CPD providers of in-service teacher training and in-service teachers. Although the topics were drawn from Singapore's educational context, the practices are applicable worldwide as they are guided by good practices globally. Hence, I strongly recommend you have a read!

Koh Koon Teck, Head, Physical Education & Sports Science, National Institute of Education, Nanyang Technological University, Singapore

CPD FOR TEACHING AND LEARNING IN PHYSICAL EDUCATION

Global Lessons from Singapore

Edited by
Susan Capel,
Julia Lawrence,
Melanie Martens, and
Hanif Abdul Rahman

LONDON AND NEW YORK

Cover image: Sarah Hoyle

First published 2022
by Routledge
4 Park Square, Milton Park, Abingdon, Oxon OX14 4RN

and by Routledge
605 Third Avenue, New York, NY 10158

Routledge is an imprint of the Taylor & Francis Group, an informa business

© 2022 selection and editorial matter, Susan Capel, Julia Lawrence, and Melanie Martens and Hanif Abdul Rahman c/o the Government of the Republic of Singapore; individual chapters, Susan Capel, Julia Lawrence, and Melanie Martens and Hanif Abdul Rahman c/o the Government of the Republic of Singapore.

The right of Susan Capel, Julia Lawrence, and Melanie Martens and Hanif Abdul Rahman c/o the Government of the Republic of Singapore to be identified as the author of the editorial material, and of the authors for their individual chapters, has been asserted in accordance with sections 77 and 78 of the Copyright, Designs and Patents Act 1988.

All rights reserved. No part of this book may be reprinted or reproduced or utilised in any form or by any electronic, mechanical, or other means, now known or hereafter invented, including photocopying and recording, or in any information storage or retrieval system, without permission in writing from the publishers.

Trademark notice: Product or corporate names may be trademarks or registered trademarks, and are used only for identification and explanation without intent to infringe.

British Library Cataloguing-in-Publication Data
A catalogue record for this book is available from the British Library

Library of Congress Cataloging-in-Publication Data
Names: Capel, Susan Anne, 1953- editor.
Title: CPD for teaching and learning in physical education : global lessons from Singapore / edited by Susan Capel, Julia Lawrence, Melanie Martens, and Hanif Abdul Rahman.
Description: Abingdon, Oxon ; New York, NY : Routledge, 2022. | Includes bibliographical references and index. |
Identifiers: LCCN 2021052151 (print) | LCCN 2021052152 (ebook) | ISBN 9780367775889 (hardback) | ISBN 9780367775896 (paperback) | ISBN 9781003171973 (ebook)
Subjects: LCSH: Physical education and training—Singapore. | Physical education teachers—In-service training—Singapore. | Physical education teachers—Professional relationships—Singapore.
Classification: LCC GV303.S5 C74 2022 (print) | LCC GV303.S5 (ebook) | DDC 796.071—dc23/eng/20211222
LC record available at https://lccn.loc.gov/2021052151
LC ebook record available at https://lccn.loc.gov/2021052152

ISBN: 978-0-367-77588-9 (hbk)
ISBN: 978-0-367-77589-6 (pbk)
ISBN: 978-1-003-17197-3 (ebk)

DOI: 10.4324/9781003171973

Typeset in Interstate
by Apex CoVantage, LLC

CONTENTS

List of Figures	ix
List of Tables	xi
List of Tasks	xiv
List of Case Studies	xvii
Foreword	xix
Why You Should Read This Book	xxi
Acknowledgements	xxiii

1 Continuing Professional Development in Physical Education: Doing It Our Way 1
FATHUL RAHMAN KAMSANI AND MELANIE MARTENS

■ CPD Is Central to Better Teaching and Learning
■ The Singapore Context ■ CPD in Physical Education
■ How the Book Is Designed ■

I SUPPORTING STUDENT PROGRESS 7

2 Continuity and Progression: What Do My Students Need to Know and Understand to Make Progress? 9
KAREN LOW LAI FONG

■ Understanding the Physical Education Curriculum
■ Planning for Progress by Individual Students ■

3 Knowing Students as Individuals and Understanding Their Needs 27
TAN SECK HEONG

■ Developmental Differences in Your Students
■ Motivation ■

4 Learners and Learning in Physical Education: Games-Centred Approaches and Nonlinear Pedagogy — 45
TAN WEE KEAT CLARA

■ Games-Centred Approaches (GCA)/Teaching Games for Understanding (TGfU) ■ Pedagogical Principles of TGfU and Its Implications in Physical Education ■ Research for GCA/TGfU ■ Nonlinear Pedagogy (NLP) ■ Pedagogical Principles of NLP and Its Implications in Physical Education ■ Research in NLP in Physical Education ■

5 Identifying and Developing Students' Readiness to Learn — 64
JUSTIN WAKEFIELD AND JULIA LAWRENCE

■ Introduction ■ Understanding the Concept of Readiness to Learn ■ Conditions for Effective Learning ■ Characteristics of Effective Learning Environments ■ Learning Personalisation ■

6 Inclusive Physical Education — 86
HUI MIN KWOK

■ What Is Inclusive Physical Education? ■ Embedding Inclusive Practices in Your Teaching ■ Understanding Students ■ Importance of Teachers' Perceptions Towards Inclusion ■ Inclusion Is Holistic in Nature ■ Realising Inclusivity ■

7 Assessing Student's Progress Formatively — 110
MABEL YONG

■ Formative Assessment and Its Role in Physical Education ■ How Do You Know That Learning Has Taken Place? ■ Assessing the Psychomotor Domain for Learning ■ Assessing the Cognitive Domain for Learning ■ Assessing the Affective Domain for Learning ■

8 Intentionality: The Key to Effective Affective Learning — 130
HANIF ABDUL RAHMAN

■ Learning in the Affective Domain in Physical Education ■ Guiding Pedagogical Principles and Teacher Practices That Contribute to the Effective Development of Social and Emotional Competencies ■ Putting the Concepts Into Practice ■

II DEVELOPING AS A TEACHER — 147

9 You as the Teacher: Teacher Identity and How It Relates to Your Philosophy of Teaching — 149
TENG TSE SHENG

■ Why Are Teacher Beliefs Important? ■ How Can You Uncover and Reflect Upon Your Beliefs? ■ Closing Thoughts ■

10 **Teaching Approaches** 169
BENJAMIN S.J. TAN

■ Why Mosston's Spectrum of Teaching Styles Was Developed ■ What Is Mosston's Spectrum of Teaching Styles? ■ Reproduction Cluster (Styles A-E) The Production Cluster (Styles F- I) ■ Style F: Guided Discovery ■ Style G: Convergent Discovery Style ■

11 **Enhancing Physical Education Using Digital Technologies** 189
JASON ZHUO GENSHENG AND GOH MING MING KELVIN

■ Objective 1: Pedagogy First, Digital Technology Supports Objective 2: Leverage Technology to Enact Effective Assessment ■ Objective 3: Strategies to Support Learning in the Implementation of Digital Technologies in Physical Education ■

12 **Being a Reflective Teacher: Using Narrative Inquiry as Professional Development in Physical Education** 209
NASRUN BIN MIZZY

■ Reflective Practice ■ What Is Narrative Inquiry? Why Narrative Inquiry? ■ How Do Narratives Contribute to Professional Growth? ■ Supplementing the Narrative Process ■ From Narratives to Professional Insight ■

III ORGANISING CONTINUING PROFESSIONAL DEVELOPMENT 233

13 **Professional Development: What Is It and How Can It Work for Me?** 235
JOANNA PHAN SWEE LEE

■ What Is Professional Development? ■ The Role of Professional Development and the Adult Learner ■ Effective Professional Development ■ Continued Learning After the Professional Development Session - Integration of Learning ■ Your Professional Development Journey ■

14 **Being a Mentor** 250
FAZLIN JAYA INDRA

■ What Do You Need to Know Before You Start Mentoring? ■ Definition of Mentoring ■ Benefits of Mentoring ■ Developing Your Knowledge and Skills as a Mentor Understanding the Roles and Responsibilities of a Mentor ■ Learning Gaps ■ Commencing the Mentoring Cycle ■ Challenges of Mentoring ■

15 **Leading and Managing for Effective Continuing Professional Development in Physical Education** 273
MARK CHAN AND KIRAN KUMAR GOSIAN

■ Defining Effective Continuing Professional Development ■ The Role of the Principal ■ Monitoring and Evaluating Continuing Professional Development for Progress and Sustainability ■

16 **Continuing Professional Development (CPD): Supporting the Delivery of Quality Teaching in Physical Education** 289
WENDY KOH

■ What the Research Says About Effective CPD ■ An Overview of Singapore's CPD for Physical Education ■ The Nuts and Bolts of Delivering the CPD ■ Evaluating CPD for Physical Education ■ Improvements to CPD for Physical Education ■

17 **And Finally... Would You Like to Be Taught by You?** 307
HANIF ABDUL RAHMAN

Biographies 310
Author Index 318
Subject Index 326

FIGURES

3.1	An example of locomotor skills teaching progression	31
3.2	The self-determination continuum	40
5.1	Conditions for learning	68
5.2	Characteristics of effective learning environments	72
5.3	Rules and routines	73
5.4	Essential lesson information	73
5.5	Some possible differences in approach and application during learning, based on student mindset	76
5.6	Structuring strategy-based feedback	78
6.1	Adaptation of Bronfenbrenner and Morris' (1998) EF	91
6.2	A completed EF for a student	92
6.3	The Inclusion Spectrum incorporating TREE (Teaching style, Rules and regulations, Equipment, and Environment)	98
6.4	Example of a modification by adaptation task for Y	102
6.5	Elaboration of TREE modifications for Y with reference to Figure 6.4	103
6.6	FBA for Y	105
7.1	Formative assessment in gymnastics	119
9.1	TPI results of Teacher X	156
10.1	Mosston's Spectrum of Teaching Styles	170
10.2	Decision-making by teachers and students in Mosston's Spectrum of Teaching Styles	173
10.3	Sample criteria worksheet	178
10.4	Guided questioning in stages	184
11.1	Outcome/s-Approach-Features-Plan-Evaluation (OAFPE) process	193
11.2	An example of a set of routines for video recording pasted on the wall to remind students when they are recording a video of their peers	198
12.1a	Single-loop learning	212
12.1b	Double-loop learning	213

12.2	Practical theory	215
12.3	A three-dimensional narrative space	217
12.4	A shared educational space	218
12.5	Samples of mood graphs (reproduced with permission)	223
12.6	Examples of metaphors – kite, onion, weather (reproduced with permission)	224
14.1	The three phases of mentoring cycle	265
16.1	*The LeARN Approach*	294

TABLES

2.1	Goals of physical education in Singapore	11
2.2	What students are expected to achieve by the end of each educational level in physical education in Singapore with examples from basketball	13
2.3	Example of a goal and learning outcomes in P3 Gymnastics	15
2.4	The STEP principle	22
2.5	Examples of making activities more or less challenging	23
3.1	A summary of phases of motor development	30
3.2	Examples of the three general classifications of fundamental movement skills	30
3.3	Summary of levels of skill proficiency	32
3.4	Piaget's (1963) stages of cognitive development and associated characteristics	33
3.5	Erikson's stages of identity development	36
4.1	TGfU pedagogical principles and its key ideas	47
4.2	The three key constraints of CLA, together with descriptions and examples	52
5.1	Independent behaviours supporting learning	66
5.2	Rosenshine's (2012) principles of instruction	68
5.3	Strategies that can be used to support the development of a growth mindset	76
5.4	Key terminology associated with stretch and challenge	80
5.5	How Lead Learners can support learning	81
5.6	Examples of retrieval practices within physical education	82
6.1	Examples of specific needs within SEN groupings	87
6.2	A summary of Universal Design for Learning	96
6.3	The TREE model for adaptation	99
6.4	The STEP model for adaptation	99
6.5	Examples of the functions of behaviour exhibited by SEN students in physical education lessons	104

7.1	Example of assessment rubric for gymnastics with tasks to guide students on how to improve	112
7.2	Example of assessing a concept in a game play situation	113
7.3	Summary of indicators that show that learning is taking place	114
7.4	Rubrics for hanging from overhead apparatus	115
7.5	Learning log (DIRT): to hang from overhead apparatus and travel over a distance	117
7.6	Success criteria	119
7.7	Third graders' thoughts and puzzles about "Attacking space in a net-barrier game"	123
7.8	Learning taxonomy of Krathwohl, Bloom, and Masia's (1964) affective domain	126
7.9	Choice chart (sportsmanship, respect, integrity)	127
7.10	Student reflection of 'respect'	128
8.1	Key domains of social and emotional competencies	131
8.2	Guiding pedagogical principles and teacher practice for affective learning	134
8.3	Opportunities for affective learning	140
9.1	Summary of five perspectives on teaching	154
9.2	Beliefs, intention, action	156
10.1	A summary of the key roles of teacher and students in the Styles in the Spectrum	173
10.2	Some examples of decisions that students can make in using the Practice Style in a basketball lesson on dribbling	176
10.3	An example criteria worksheet	181
11.1	Guiding questions for OAFPE process	194
11.2	Examples of apps and software for physical education	195
11.3	Seeing the affordance of technology through issues in assessment	201
11.4	Seeing the affordance of technology through issues in assessment	202
11.5	Seeing the affordance of technology through issues in assessment	204
11.6	Possible limitations and recommendation of integrating digital technologies in relation to students	206
12.1	Types of reflection	214
13.1	Knowles (1990) principles of adult learning	242
13.2	Five essential principles for professional development to be effective	243
13.3	Six factors that affect learning in the workplace	245
14.1	Differences between mentoring and coaching in physical education	253
14.2	The Mind the Gap framework	262

14.3	Examples of mentoring work at the orientation phase for mentoring beginning teachers	266
14.4	Examples of mentoring work at the development phase	266
14.5	Examples of mentoring work at the separation phase	267
14.6	Examples of mentoring challenges for the mentor in the workplace	269
14.7	Examples of mentoring challenges due to conflicting beliefs between mentor and mentee	269
15.1	Professional development evaluation model involving five levels of data	276
15.2	CPD evaluation model	286
16.1	Sample analysis of data from CPD	297
16.2	*Rubrics for Level of Change: Orientation of Reflection*	300

TASKS

2.1	Understanding of the purpose and goals of the national curriculum	12
2.2	The aims of your physical education curriculum	14
2.3	Key learning outcomes in your national curriculum	17
2.4	Providing clarity in the intended lesson outcomes to help students learn and make progress	20
2.5	Understanding individual differences	21
2.6	Using the STEP principle to differentiate within your lesson	23
3.1	Identifying differences in the classes you teach	28
3.2	Planning for skill development	32
3.3	Planning for skill acquisition	35
3.4	Pause to reflect	38
3.5	Providing for the competence, autonomy, and relatedness needs of your students	41
3.6	Creating a positive learning environment	42
4.1	Pedagogical approach/approaches	46
4.2	Application of the pedagogical principles of TGfU	51
4.3	Theory to practice	59
5.1	Factors affecting students' readiness to learn	65
5.2	Embedding conditions for learning and principles of instruction in my own teaching	71
5.3	Creating your own expectations and routines	74
5.4	Developing a growth mindset culture	78
5.5	Planning for stretch and challenge	79
5.6	Supporting metacognition in your lessons	81
6.1	Inclusion policy	88
6.2	What does inclusive physical education mean to me?	89
6.3	Identifying support in school	90
6.4	Understanding your students	93
6.5	How do you talk about your students?	95

6.6	How do you support students with SEN to participate in your lessons?	103
6.7	Employing FBA	106
7.1	Reflections of your experiences of assessment	111
7.2	Reflections of an assessment tool you have used	113
7.3	Using indicators of learning in your own lessons	114
7.4	Applying tiered activities to your own practice	121
7.5	Applying Think-Puzzle-Explore strategy to your own practice	124
7.6	Assessing in the cognitive domain in your own practice	126
7.7	Assessing in the affective domain	128
8.1	Reflecting on your current practice in relation to students' development in the affective domain	133
8.2	How do I embed the four guiding pedagogical principles for developing the affective domain in my current practice?	139
8.3	Embedding affective learning opportunities in my planning	144
9.1	Knowing yourself	151
9.2	Your beliefs	153
9.3	Completing the TPI	156
9.4	Analysing your TPI profile	159
9.5	Consolidating your thoughts on beliefs	166
10.1	Plan a Style A lesson activity and record students' behaviour	175
10.2	Identify potential decision-making opportunities for students	177
10.3	Design a Peer Observation Worksheet	179
10.4	Application of Self-Check Style	180
10.5	Design tasks with different levels of difficulties/complexities	182
10.6	Design a set of questions and possible answers	184
10.7	Questions and possible answers for the Convergent Discovery Style	186
10.8	Experiment with different subject matter using Style H	186
11.1	Reflecting on teaching and learning in lessons in which digital technology is integrated	193
11.2	Selecting an appropriate digital tool	197
11.3	Routines for implementation of selected digital tool	197
11.4	How do you assess every last student if there is only one mode of assessment?	199
11.5	Overcoming limitations in integrating digital technologies	207
12.1	A reflection on growth and change	211
12.2	Am I reflective enough?	222
12.3	Enhancing your narrative	227
13.1	What kind of professional development have I been involved with?	237
13.2	Reflecting on my own professional development experiences and learning in relation to the six principles for adult learning	242

13.3	Reflecting on my own professional experiences and level of learning in relation to the five principles for effective instructional strategies	244
13.4	Identifying school supporters and inhibitors of professional development	246
13.5	My professional development journey as a physical education teacher	247
14.1	What does mentoring mean to you?	252
14.2	What benefits have you and your students gained from being mentored?	256
14.3	How have you developed as a mentor?	259
14.4	Identify roles of a mentor	261
14.5	What is your process of identifying your mentee's learning gap?	263
14.6	Reflect on your best mentoring moment	268
15.1	Effective CPD from a principal's perspective	276
15.2	Reflecting on roles of a principal in CPD	283
15.3	School's efforts to monitor and evaluate CPD	286
16.1	Planning for CPD	293
16.2	Evaluating the impact of CPD	299

CASE STUDIES

2.1	Share intended lesson outcomes with students	18
4.1	Applying theory to practice	57
5.1	Managing learning conditions to develop readiness to learn	71
5.2	Creating learning routines to develop student engagement	74
5.3	Managing the characteristics of effective learning environments to enhance students' learning within examination physical education	83
6.1	Adapting Bronfenbrenner and Morris' (1998) EF to engage a child with autism in physical education	93
6.2	Working with a student with low IQ/low intellectual ability	97
6.3	Using Black and Stevenson's Inclusion Spectrum and EF for inclusion in a lesson	101
7.1	Using assessment criteria to support formative assessment	115
7.2	Qualitative analytic rubrics	119
7.3	Physical education grade 1 tiered activities on rope skipping	120
7.4	Example of Think-Puzzle-Explore (TPE)	122
7.5	Differentiated assessment (cognitive)	125
7.6	Affective domain in physical education	127
8.1	Planning and teaching for affective outcomes	141
9.1	Teacher X	157
9.2	Students' voice and its impact on teaching beliefs	162
10.1	An example of the teacher guiding a student to discover the snapping of the wrist in the badminton overhead drive	183
10.2	An example of the use of Style G for a netball lesson	185
11.1	Use of Google Classroom for flipped learning	191
11.2	Using OnForm: Video Analysis App (formerly known as Hudl Technique to support game-centred approach (GCA)	191
11.3	Enhancing cooperative learning with videos	192
13.1	Aarifa's professional development journey	238
13.2	Banu's professional development journey	239

13.3	Chris's professional development journey	240
14.1a	What's the difference?	251
14.1b	Preparing, being, and developing as a mentor	256
14.1c	Identifying learning gaps in the mentoring process	261
14.1d	Addressing a learning gap	264
14.1e	Performing mentoring work in phases	264
14.1f	A challenge of mentoring	268

FOREWORD

Continuing Professional Development for Teaching and Learning in Physical Education: Global Lessons from Singapore

This book is written by practitioners with a wide range of experience and knowledge; most of whom are currently serving or have served as professional development officers for the Physical Education and Sports Teachers Academy (PESTA) of the Ministry of Education Singapore.

It has been ten years since the inception of PESTA and during that time, the PESTA team has benefitted from the vast learning they have experienced in providing continuing professional development (CPD) in Singapore. This book is their effort to share what they have learned in Singapore in delivering effective CPD. The different chapters share their structures and processes, the thinking behind the design of their CPD programmes, and the improvements that they have made as part of this continuous pursuit of excellence and transformation.

What readers will get by reading the book are new ideas, knowledge, and understanding to help them develop and refresh their skills as a physical education teacher to enhance students' learning. It will enable them to develop their teaching and demonstrate that physical education focuses on student learning, and is not just recreation. It is written in a style that mirrors a CPD session that combines both theory and practice as well as application of theory in real-life examples from physical education lessons.

This book is interesting for a number of reasons. Firstly, there is a strong focus on CPD instead on initial teacher preparation. Secondly, it is written by practitioners involved with CPD for physical education teachers on a daily basis and who, over time, have developed effective ways of delivery to support teachers' learning. Thirdly, the range of topics are identified by teachers in Singapore, and are the areas that they would like to deepen their subject content and pedagogical knowledge in, and understand how to apply this in their lessons.

Finally, the focus of the chapters shows how physical education develops the individual across domains of learning, offers examples of how traditionally academic-based teaching strategies can be applied within a more practical based subject – as such it can act as a resource for teachers across schools and across contexts.

Most importantly, readers are encouraged to reflect on their current practice and apply the learning from the chapters to their practice.

This book also serves to acknowledge the work of the physical education fraternity in the past, pay tribute to and celebrate those involved in CPD. Our teachers have indeed lived up to our philosophy of Teacher Ownership and Teacher Leadership.

Mrs Chua Yen Ching
Deputy Director General of Education
(Professional Development)
Ministry of Education

WHY YOU SHOULD READ THIS BOOK

As PESTA celebrates ten years of service to the development of physical education in Singapore, I consider myself fortunate to have worked with the PESTA group in their early years. I was and continue to be impressed with the level of professionalism and total dedication of this group to improving practice in the schools. They have developed one of the most comprehensive and successful professional development programs for physical education that can and should serve as a model for the rest of the world. *CPD Teaching and Learning in Physical Education* will make a major contribution to this effort.

The premise of the book is well stated by Kamsani and Martens:

> Teaching is a complex activity and is both an art and a science; teaching is not a mechanical process and there is no one correct way of teaching. An effective teacher puts students' learning first, is interested in and can motivate students, is able to adapt their teaching to the needs of students in their lessons, is able to integrate theory with practice, uses evidence to underpin their practice, and uses structured reflection to improve their pedagogical practice.

The book is consistent with this premise. Each chapter in the book, written by members of the PESTA team, is designed to provide a springboard to help teachers expand their pedagogical skills. Understanding the curriculum and students, choosing appropriate instructional methods that are appropriate for psychomotor, affective, and cognitive content for all students and assessing instruction, all developed throughout the text are designed to lead the teacher to reflective practice. Chapters are written to provide the reader with updated theories and to lead the reader through these theories to practice. The chapters focusing on professional development are particularly unique and should provide professionals who both receive and are responsible for developing professional development experiences a good understanding of the need for professional development experiences and how to provide effective professional development experiences.

The chapters in *CPD Teaching and Learning in Physical Education* are designed to be used both as independent reading for both teachers and professional development personnel but also as a focus for shared professional development experiences. They will be an invaluable resource for both.

Dr Judith Rink
Emeritus Professor, University of South Carolina

ACKNOWLEDGEMENTS

This book would not have been possible if not for the physical education teachers of Singapore whose desire and dedication to their vocation drives them to partner with us to improve the quality of the teaching and learning that takes place in their physical education lessons. Often the impact of what you do can only be seen when the young have graduated from the school system and demonstrate what they have learned in their adult life. We are inspired by your deep sense of mission and commitment to the holistic education of the child. May you find inspiration from the work presented in this book and continue to be the inspiration to the many lives you touch daily.

We owe a deep sense of gratitude to the pioneering work of our colleagues who in 2011 set up the Physical Education and Sports Teacher Academy. In particular Tan Teck Hock, its first Academy Principal whose vision for the academy and unwavering belief in the impact of quality teaching on student learning set the strong foundations of passion, innovation and professionalism that characterise the work of PESTA today.

We also wish to thank Emeritus Professor Judith Rink of the University of South Carolina, who we first consulted when setting up the academy and who continued to work with our team of PESTA officers in our early years contributing her expertise particularly to the development of the Physical Education Lesson Observation Tool (PELOT) that is used in all our schools today, and leading the international panel involved in the Physical Education, Art and Music Research project (referenced in Chapter 8). Thank you for nurturing and bringing out the best in us as we navigated the very new domain of providing continuing professional development.

We would also like to acknowledge the strong support we have received from colleagues at the Physical Education, Sports and Outdoor Education Branch (PSOEB), our curriculum partners at the Ministry of Education, the National Institute of Education Physical Education and Sports Science Academic Group, and SportSG, the national governing body for Sports in Singapore. Your generosity in sharing your specialist knowledge and expertise in physical education and sports has enabled us to continue to improve on the quality subject content knowledge and pedagogical content knowledge of the professional development programmes we deliver.

Finally, to our Director General of Education, Mr Wong Siew Hoong, and our Deputy Director General of Education (Professional Development), Mrs Chua Yen Ching, thank you for always encouraging and supporting us in our endeavours to deliver quality continuing professional development.

To all we have acknowledged, this book is a testament to your steadfast belief that every child deserves the best quality of teaching possible, and the responsibility of the teacher is to do everything in their power to bring that quality to the classroom every time they are in it. Thank you for journeying with us as we strive to support teachers in delivering that quality.

With deepest gratitude
The Team of Authors

1 Continuing Professional Development in Physical Education
Doing It Our Way

Fathul Rahman Kamsani and Melanie Martens

CPD Is Central to Better Teaching and Learning

> Teacher ownership and leadership is when teachers, driven by a sense of mission, individually or collectively, exert intentional influence to achieve an enhanced state of professional excellence within a climate of trust and supportive relationships.
>
> (Ministry of Education (MOE), 2019, p. 55)

Continuing professional development (CPD) is important for teachers to hone their teaching skills and to remain relevant in an ever-changing education landscape. All teachers, including physical education teachers, should be learning continuously throughout their teaching career. This is our commitment to self, to our colleagues, and, most importantly, the many students that come under our guidance over the years.

The focus of teaching in physical education should be on students' learning and development of their skills and knowledge in physical activity so that they can achieve and sustain a lifetime of healthy active living. The aim of this book is therefore to support your development as a physical education teacher to enable and empower your students to achieve this outcome in school and carry it into adulthood.

Teaching is a complex activity and is both an art and a science; teaching is not a mechanical process and there is no one correct way of teaching. An effective teacher puts students' learning first, is interested in and can motivate students, is able to adapt their teaching to the needs of students in their lessons, is able to integrate theory with practice, uses evidence to underpin their practice, and uses structured reflection to improve their pedagogical practice.

This book looks at various aspects of CPD which physical education teachers in Singapore have found useful in helping them improve the effectiveness of their teaching so as to enhance student learning.

DOI: 10.4324/9781003171973-1

The Singapore Context

Singapore is known to have one of the best education systems in the world according to different International Benchmarking studies – Progress in International Reading Literacy Study (PIRLS), Trends in International Mathematics and Science Study (TIMSS), and the Organisation for Economic Co-operation and Development's (OECD) Programme for International Student Assessment (PISA) and the Teaching and Learning International Survey (TALIS). This success can be attributed to sound educational policies that are complemented by good infrastructure and a strong teaching workforce built on a deliberate approach of attracting, developing, and retaining the best talent in education.

In developing the best teacher-talent, CPD policies and practices have had to evolve to meet the shifts in focus in an ever-changing global, economic, and education landscape. These CPD policies recognise that there cannot be a one-size-fits-all approach to CPD for all teachers and call upon teachers to take greater ownership and leadership of their professional learning and growth in various ways.

Firstly, CPD in Singapore is designed to facilitate learning through multiple platforms – at the individual level through face-to-face, blended, or online learning workshops; at the school level through school support or partnership programmes; and when teachers come together to learn and collaborate as either Networked Learning Communities or Communities of Practice. This allows teachers to identify the most appropriate learning platform and attend relevant CPD based on their self-assessed needs.

Secondly, CPD is positioned to cater to the different teacher segments in the Singapore system. One example is the introduction of three career advancement tracks with the objective of greater teacher retention in the service. The three tracks are: the Teaching Track, the Leadership Track, and the Senior Specialist Track. With these three career tracks, CPD is designed to better match the career profiles of teachers in the respective tracks. For example, CPD for teachers in the Teaching Track focuses on deepening teaching mastery and pedagogical excellence, while CPD for those on the Leadership Track focuses on skills and competencies needed in leading and managing a team or department of teachers.

Thirdly, teachers are encouraged to remain current and equip themselves with the necessary competencies to develop in students a diversity of skill sets that will prepare them well for the future. As such, CPD opportunities are offered through providing a Professional Development Leave (PDL) scheme where teachers are allowed to take paid leave for continual upgrading of their professional skills and qualifications, and through a Teacher Work Attachment (TWA) scheme where teachers take on short-term local or overseas attachments in external organisations. These opportunities help teachers broaden their perspectives and contribute to their skill set to shape new learning experiences for students.

More recently, MOE as part of the 'Learn for Life' movement in schools introduced the Skills Future for Educators (SFEd) initiative which serves as a CPD roadmap to guide teachers to be learners for life and support them to continually deepen their beliefs and further strengthen their classroom practice. CPD activities are now aligned to the six prioritised SFEd areas of practice (i.e. Assessment Literacy, Differentiated Instruction, Inquiry-Based Learning, e-Pedagogy, Character and Citizenship Education, and Special Educational Needs).

CPD in Physical Education

A dedicated teacher academy, Physical Education and Sports Teacher Academy (PESTA) was set up in 2011 to enhance the quality of teaching in physical education. Its purpose is to raise the pedagogical expertise of teachers to ensure quality delivery of physical education in our schools. PESTA has developed a range of practice-oriented professional development programmes in the areas of Subject Content Knowledge (SCK), Pedagogical Content Knowledge (PCK), and Professional Practice. These programmes are intended to deepen the professional knowledge, hone the professional practice, and enhance the professional engagement of physical education teachers.

With its mission to 'Empower, Inspire, Transform Lives', PESTA has sought to improve its CPD efforts to inspire physical education teachers to embark on CPD to elevate the quality of their physical education lessons and sports activities in and outside schools with the intention to bring about transformation in the lives of people who are impacted – students, teachers, and the wider community. In the ten years since the inception of PESTA, we have learned and are still learning about what effective CPD is and how to deliver it. We are coming to grips with how to encourage and support the motivation for CPD among physical education teachers, and have learned that effective CPD for our physical education teachers must be aligned to the five principles for effective CPD that research supports. Namely,

1. Coherence to the standards and outcomes of education in Singapore;
2. Focus on Subject Content Knowledge (SCK) and Pedagogical Content Knowledge (PCK);
3. Provision of opportunities for active learning;
4. Ensuring collaborative learning; and
5. Supporting sustained learning.

(MOE, 2015, cited in Chapter 16)

From our regular internal reviews, surveys, and focus group discussions, we have learned that teachers want authenticity in the content of the workshops and programmes. They didn't want workshops that showcased the 'perfect' lesson. They wanted to learn how to teach and cope with "the day to day complexities of teaching" (Armour and Yelling, 2003, p. 2) that emerge in a classroom.

We learned that situating a workshop in a school and with a teacher participant (from that school) and a PESTA CPD officer demonstrating how theory translates into practice in a real classroom setting produced not just impactful learning but generated deep discussion and reflection long after the workshop ended.

In providing authentic experiences and settings, we learned we needed to partner stakeholders such as schools, the National Institute of Education (NIE), and the national governing body for sports in Singapore (Sport Singapore (SportSG)). We recognised that for us to achieve what we set out to do we could not do this alone. We needed to include everyone in this collaborative and collective effort, who we feel has a stake in the development of our young.

In order to ensure the learning didn't end with the last day of a workshop or programme, PESTA CPD officers continue to support workshop participants in the application of their learning back in their schools with a variety of approaches that include face-to-face lesson observations or co-teaching with physical education teachers in schools using digital platforms to enable all workshop participants to observe and discuss (synchronously and asynchronously) a fellow participant's video of a lesson using newly acquired SCK or PCK. We use digital technology and technological hardware such as wearables (electronic devices that can be worn as accessories like Apple watches and Fitbit) and cameras with video-analysis applications, and software using interactive and online application tools that offer virtual and augmented reality, to deliver our programmes as well as support the application and reinforcement of learning by participants. This is especially significant during the COVID-19 pandemic where PESTA has had to pivot its many face-to-face CPD programmes to online and virtual platforms by converting the face-to-face content to e-pedagogy with synchronous and asynchronous learning via Zoom and the creation of Micro Learning Units which deliver short, bite-sized content for learners to study at their own convenience. In using this approach we have found that creating opportunities for like-minded participants to come together to discuss their learning, not just their successes, leads to greater engagement and desire to continue with CPD. PESTA CPD officers supporting physical education teachers' efforts to form networked learning communities and/or communities of practice have become either a 'knowledgeable other' to these communities or are able to provide access to other knowledgeable others, either within the school system or connecting with our key partners like NIE and SportSG.

How the Book Is Designed

The book is designed more for you to dip in and out of, to look up a specific problem or issue that you want to consider, rather than for it to be read from cover to cover although you may want to read it that way too. The chapters in the book cover both the theory and practice of various aspects of teaching and learning of physical education. The reader will find that each chapter has its objectives stated at the beginning. Embedded in the body of the chapters are case studies from the Singapore context that apply theory to practice and/or examples from physical education, and tasks based on the content of the chapter for the reader to engage in, in relation to their own context. At the end of each chapter, the reader will also find a summary and the key points raised in the chapter, followed by a weblink to lists of further resources for each chapter that the reader can turn to as a start, if they want to deepen their understanding of what they have read. There are, of course, a whole wealth of other resources on each topic.

The book is loosely grouped into three sections:

Section 1 provides an overview on supporting student progress. In any good teaching, students will always be at the core of what you do. Chapter 2 covers topics of continuity and progression, and Chapter 3 starts with the fundamentals of knowing the students as individuals and recognising that every student is unique with different needs. It focuses largely on student development. This is followed by a chapter on games-centred approaches and nonlinear pedagogy that emphasise students as active learners and teachers as facilitators in the teaching-learning experiences. Chapter 5 of the book explores student readiness and how to create a positive climate to support student learning. Chapter 6 offers the reader insight into inclusive practices in physical education and how to plan for and manage it to benefit both students and teacher. The reader is introduced to Bronfenbrenner and Morris' (1998) Ecological Framework, and how it can be adapted to better understand the needs of students, particularly those with special needs. To conclude this section, the next two chapters dive into the use of formative assessment to measure students' learning and progress, and understanding affective processes and how to be deliberate in planning for them in physical education lessons.

Section 2 focuses on the teacher as a learner and the various competencies you need to be equipped with to better support students to learn and to prepare them for the future. The first chapter in this section (Chapter 9) is devoted to who you are as a teacher - your identity and how that relates to your philosophy of teaching and the learning experiences you want to achieve for your students. The remaining three chapters are related to teaching competencies, starting with teaching approaches you can adopt in physical education, the use of digital technologies, reflective practice and classroom inquiry to enhance the quality of learning.

Section 3 outlines/describes what goes into the organising of CPD and how as a teacher you can lead and own your continuing learning in a sustainable manner. It helps you to have a better understanding of the importance of CPD; what is involved when you take on the role of being a mentor; how you and school leadership can take on a leading role in the management of your colleagues' CPD; and how to deliver effective CPD at an organisational level (whether it be in-house school CPD, or at a zonal/district/national level) and sustain the motivation of teachers to be involved in continuing CPD for themselves. This section ends with a concluding chapter that bring the contents of the book together and leaves the reader to ponder three pertinent questions: "Would you like to be taught by *you*?", "Have you been the best teacher you can be?", and, crucially, "So what now? Where do you go from here?"

In summary, this book is intended to support your professional learning and growth and serve as a stimulus for you to want to continue to learn and develop throughout your career as a physical education teacher. We encourage you to use this book in a manner that best fits your learning needs and for you to reflect on practices suited to your own context. We also encourage you to use the book for professional reading at the department level to support the development of physical education teachers in your department. Lastly, we encourage you to complement the reading of this book with the wealth of resources available in print and online, and to attend professional CPD activities that are available to you as part of your commitment to lifelong learning. We hope that this book provides a stimulus for you to want to continue to learn and develop throughout your career as a physical education teacher.

It is only teachers who can make a difference to students' learning. It is not possible to say exactly what to do to be that perfect teacher. All a book such as this can do is share experience of what has worked elsewhere and provide guidance in order for teachers to develop their knowledge, understanding, and skill in enhancing students' learning in the subject. It is up to teachers to decide what aspects of the content are relevant to them, and use and adapt the information as appropriate in the context in which they are working.

If we teach today as we taught yesterday, we rob our children of tomorrow.

(John Dewey, 1916)

References

Armour, K.M. and Yelling, M. (2003) 'Physical education departments as learning organisations: The foundation for effective professional development', Paper presented at the annual meeting of the British Education Research Association, Edinburgh, September 2003.

Bronfenbrenner, U. and Morris, P.A. (1998) 'The ecology of developmental processes', in W. Damon and R.M. Lerner (eds.) *Handbook of Child Psychology: Theoretical Models of Human Development*, Hoboken, NJ: John Wiley & Sons Inc., pp. 993-1028.

Dewey, J. (1916) *Democracy and Education: An Introduction to the Philosophy of Education*, New York: Macmillan.

MOE (Ministry of Education) (2015) *Guide to Effective Professional Development - Workshops and Learning Programmes*, Volume 1, Singapore: Ministry of Education.

MOE (Ministry of Education) (2019) *History of Professional Development of Education Officers in Singapore*, Singapore: Ministry of Education.

I Supporting Student Progress

2 Continuity and Progression
What Do My Students Need to Know and Understand to Make Progress?

Karen Low Lai Fong

Note: Within this chapter, specific reference is made to the national curriculum in Singapore. As you read the chapter you need to consider terminology used in your own context and are encouraged to reflect on your own national curriculum.

Introduction

The aim of this chapter is to identify and demonstrate, through practical examples, the knowledge and understanding required by you, as a physical education teacher, to support continuity and progression in your students' learning. Continuity has been defined as "The nature of the curriculum experienced by children as they transfer from one setting to another" (Department of Education and Science (DES), 1991, p.13). It is reflected in how you structure your teaching, to build students' learning on existing knowledge and understanding in a logical and progressive way. Progression has been defined as "The sequence built into children's learning through curriculum policies and schemes of work so that later learning builds on skills, knowledge and understandings and attitudes learned previously" (DES, 1991, p.13). Thus, progress is reflected in growth, development, and continuous improvement (Dictionary.com). As continuity and progression are interlinked, continuity in learning brings about progress, and vice versa.

To achieve continuity and progression in learning, you need to know and understand in detail the physical education curriculum within which you are teaching. Embedded within the curriculum will be the purpose; that is, why you are teaching the subject. In order to achieve the purpose of the curriculum, you have specific goals against which progress and achievement are measured. In order to support your students to take ownership of their own continual learning and improvement, they too need to know what they are trying to achieve, where to go next, and find ways to get there through realistic goal setting strategies. As all students have different needs, you will need to adapt the curriculum and

DOI: 10.4324/9781003171973-3

differentiate the tasks for students to complete in order to challenge students and enable them to be successful. This, in turn, will contribute to their motivation to learn.

> **OBJECTIVES**
>
> At the end of the chapter you should be able to:
>
> - understand and plan for continuity and progress in student learning
> - help students make meaning of the physical education curriculum to promote their interest in and motivation for learning
> - empower students to make progress in learning with clear intended lesson outcomes.

Understanding the Physical Education Curriculum

Before you can help students make progress in their learning, you need to understand the physical education curriculum. The following sections review the purpose, goals, aims, and learning outcomes of the national curriculum for physical education in Singapore, to enable you to reflect on the impact this may have on how you support students' understanding and progression in the subject. However, while considering the national curriculum in Singapore you are also encouraged to reflect on the national curriculum in which you are teaching (if there is no national curriculum in the country in which you work, refer to the relevant curriculum materials that guide your teaching).

Purpose and Goals of Physical Education

Any curriculum needs to support the initial development of strong foundations and a breadth of skills, knowledge, and understanding, with a degree of specialisation introduced at later stages (Siraj-Blatchford, 2008). This is reflected in the purpose of the curriculum. In Singapore, "the purpose of physical education is to enable students to demonstrate individually and with others, the physical skills, practices and values to enjoy a lifetime of active healthy living" (Ministry of Education (MOE), 2016, p.1). In practice, as a teacher of physical education you are looking to develop in your students the knowledge, skills, and understanding across a range of physical activities that will allow your students to be able to make informed choices about maintaining a healthy and active lifestyle throughout their life.

It is important for teachers to be clear about the purpose of the curriculum. However, the purpose should also be communicated and explained to students to provide them with an understanding of why they are doing or learning what they do. Being able to see connections between the big ideas and learning content serves as a cognitive hook to trigger students' learning interest and motivation. For example, a clear communication of the purpose would lead students to understand the inclusion of different physical activities as being necessary and important to help them develop skills and interests in at least one of them and to be able to participate and enjoy physical activity in the future. Students who understand the overall intentions and know the value and importance of what they are trying to learn are likely to exhibit higher levels of interest and increased motivation (Chen et al., 2008).

With a clear purpose for the subject identified, goals of the curriculum serve as a guide to the skills, knowledge and understanding, and values students are expected to achieve in physical education across compulsory schooling (Lund and Tannehill, 2014; Rovegno and Bandhauer, 2016). Table 2.1 provides a summary of the goals of physical education as written in the national curriculum in Singapore. These goals focus on the development of physical competency, knowledge and understanding and appreciation of physically active and healthy lifestyles, alongside the development of students' affective/social and emotional competences, in order for students to develop a deeper understanding of being active and healthy.

Having introduced the purpose and goals of the Singapore curriculum, Task 2.1 encourages you to explore your understanding of the purpose and goals of the national curriculum within which you teach.

Table 2.1 Goals of physical education in Singapore

Singapore Physical Education Teaching and Learning Curriculum
Goal 1 Acquire a range of movement skills to participate in a variety of physical activities.
Goal 2 Understand and apply movement concepts, principles and strategies in a range of physical activities.
Goal 3 Demonstrate safe practices during physical and daily activities with respect to themselves, others and the environment.
Goal 4 Display positive personal and social behaviour across different experiences.
Goal 5 Acquire and maintain health-enhancing fitness through regular participation in physical activities.
Goal 6 Enjoy and value the benefits of living a physically active and healthy life.

Source: MOE (2016, p. 6)

> **Task 2.1 Understanding of the purpose and goals of the national curriculum**
>
> 1 How would you articulate the overall purpose and goals of your curriculum?
> 2 Do the purpose and goals of the curriculum align with what you feel to be the purpose and goals of physical education?
> 3 What would you identify as the core skills, knowledge and understanding, and values your students are expected to learn/develop?

Being clear about the purpose and goals of physical education allows you to articulate them in order that your students understand the desired skills, knowledge and understanding, and values they are expected to learn/develop to become a physically educated person by the time they leave compulsory schooling. Such an understanding is necessary if you seek to enable and empower your students to learn to take responsibility for their own learning in working towards achieving the curriculum goals. However, whilst you might be able to articulate the purpose and goals of the curriculum, you must also look at how these are reflected and achieved within the different age levels in which you teach. One obvious example is to consider how your expectations of primary and secondary students would differ.

Aims of Physical Education Curriculum

To enable students to achieve the purpose and goals of physical education, the aims of physical education at the primary (ages 7-12 years), secondary (ages 13-16 years), and pre-university (ages 17-18 years) levels need to be made explicit to support smooth continuity and progression in the development of skills, knowledge and understanding at the different educational levels (primary, secondary, and pre-university). Developing a clear understanding of the skills, knowledge and understanding expected in each level not only allows you to become more versatile and comprehensive in planning and delivering lessons, but also helps students thrive in physical education by knowing what they are expected to achieve. Table 2.2 shows what students are expected to achieve by the end of primary, secondary, and pre-university levels in Singapore, with an example of what this might look like in basketball.

Table 2.2 shows progression in the physical education curriculum from competence (possession of fundamental movement skills) to confidence (being able to apply skill and knowledge) to commitment (where the student takes greater ownership for their continued participation). During the primary level, the focus is on the acquisition of fundamental movement skills and knowledge associated with physical education (see Chapter 3 for an overview of these). By focusing on

Table 2.2 What students are expected to achieve by the end of each educational level in physical education in Singapore with examples from basketball

Educational Level	What Students Are Expected to Achieve	How Students Might Demonstrate Achievement
Primary Level	"Competent movers who demonstrate efficiency, effectiveness and versatility in movement competencies" (MOE, 2016, p. 23). "They develop efficiency in the correct performance of discrete fundamental motor skills and in combination with other skills" (p. 23). "Students refine their effectiveness by being consistent and successful in their performance, in relation to the different movement concepts and settings. Concurrently, students' versatility is developed through the ability to transfer and apply these skills and movement" (p. 23).	A student who is a competent mover *will be able to* execute fundamental movement skills and apply the concepts effectively in any invasion game with modified conditions (e.g. 2-v-2 game, with 4 scoring targets). Some examples include: ■ Combine skills of locomotor movements and dribbling with hands ■ Execute appropriate and successful throws to moving teammates who are defended ■ Move into open space to receive passes, and attempt to score at targets ■ Stay close to opponent during defence and make attempt to intercept or block a pass
Secondary Level	"Confident participants with positive self-efficacy who value the need for sustainability in an active, healthy lifestyle" (MOE, 2016, p. 143). Their understanding and capacity are deepened and enriched "through the application of skills and concepts strategically across a variety of authentic physical activity settings such as an individual and team recreational game of their choice with confidence" (MOE, 2016, p. 143).	A student who is a confident participant *will be able to* execute the skills and apply the concepts effectively required of a 3-v-3 basketball game. Some examples include: ■ Understand and play according to the rules of the game ■ Execute combined skills of passing, dribbling and set shot or jump shot under the basket ■ Execute good footwork specific to the rules of the game ■ Use of available space to penetrate the defence and support teammates to score ■ Work with teammates to slow down an attack by guarding the attackers, denying attacking space, and preventing scoring ■ Enjoy the competition experience

(Continued)

Table 2.2 (Continued)

Educational Level	What Students Are Expected to Achieve	How Students Might Demonstrate Achievement
Pre-university Level	"Committed advocates who demonstrate a conscious decision and action to pursue personal excellence and are an inspiration to their family and friends in leading an active, healthy lifestyle" (MOE, 2016, p.179). They will achieve a "higher level of performance excellence as set against the self-established standards in physical activities" (MOE, 2016, p.179).	A student who is a committed advocate will work on improving existing skill and knowledge about basketball and organise games with others outside physical education classes. Some examples include: ■ Refine skills and improve game tactics ■ Add in more variety and effectiveness to the game by learning new skills like lay-up shots ■ Read up about 5-v-5 basketball game and its rules to understand the game ■ Value the game as a form of exercise and socialisation in and out of school

Source: Adapted from MOE (2016, pp.23, 143, 179)

developing fundamental movement skills and knowledge, you are able to build the foundations and develop the qualities required by your students by exposing them to a wide range of motor skills, concepts, and knowledge that they can apply later in their education and throughout their lives. This can be achieved by learning experiences across different activities such as gymnastics, dance, and games. At the secondary level, students build on these skills and knowledge by developing more mature movement patterns. By the pre-university level students are taking on more ownership of their learning. Whilst the syllabi identify what students are expected to achieve in relation to physical skill development, it also identifies expected achievement in relation to students' cognitive and affective outcomes.

Now look at your own curriculum to identify the specific aims and how progression is embedded within the expectations of student achievement. Task 2.2 will help you to do this.

 Task 2.2 The aims of your physical education curriculum

Drawing on the physical education curriculum in your school designed to meet the purpose of the national curriculum, think about the following questions:

1. What is the aim of the physical education curriculum you are delivering?
2. Are you able to describe it in terms of the knowledge, skills, understanding, and values that your students are expected to possess at the end of each physical education level?
3. How can you support your students to understand the development and progressions in the skills, knowledge and understanding and values they are expected to achieve?

In summary, it is important for you to have a detailed understanding of what students are expected to be able to do, know, and understand in physical education at the end of each educational level so you can plan lessons to ensure continuity and progression in learning. One way to reflect this is through key learning outcomes.

Key Learning Outcomes in Physical Education

Key learning outcomes are measurable outcomes that specify what students at a particular age should be expected to do that lead them towards the goals (Rink, 2014). In some countries, key learning outcomes are specified in the physical education curriculum. In the Singapore curriculum, the learning outcomes specify minimally what students should be able to do, know, and understand in all the learning areas (Athletics, Dance, Games and Sports, Gymnastics, Outdoor Education, Swimming, Physical Health and Fitness) and specific physical activities by the end of each academic year. They provide details about the progression in learning that is expected of students, and an overview of how each year builds towards the attainment of the goals of the curriculum as a whole. Thus, they serve to guide teachers in the planning units of work and lessons, and make it easy for teachers to assess and track student progress across the different years. Table 2.3

Table 2.3 Example of a goal and learning outcomes in P3 Gymnastics

Goal 1	Primary 3 Gymnastics Learning Outcomes
Acquire a range of movement skills to participate in a variety of physical activities	Travelling, Jumping, and Climbing 1. Travel in relation to position (e.g. over/under, beside, on/off, alongside) with a variety of low, medium-height, and high apparatuses (e.g. bench, vaulting box, bar); 2. Jump over a self-turned rope several times in succession.

Source: MOE (2016, p. 118)

provides an example of goal and learning outcomes in Travelling, Jumping, and Climbing in Primary (P) 3 (age 9 to 9+) in Gymnastics in the Singapore Curriculum.

While the learning outcomes provide more specific direction for teachers in planning a unit of work and teaching lessons; these outcomes also need to be communicated to students so they are clear about what they should be able to do, know, and understand for each skill in each learning area by the end of the year. This will allow them to develop an understanding of how what they have learned will be built upon to allow them to demonstrate progression. Although the learning outcome may require a few lessons to be achieved, it is important to help students understand and visualise what each learning outcome will look like. For example, this can be done by showing examples at the beginning of the unit of work, such as videos and images of travelling on different body parts and positions in relationship with a variety of apparatuses/equipment. In order to reflect the readiness to learn (see Chapter 5) of your students, opportunities to be creative and travel differently at varied heights need to be planned for. With a variety of apparatuses of different heights set up in the physical education venue, students will be able to progress from the lowest to highest height when asked to travel on/off an apparatus. Once students are able to use dynamic balance and safe dismounting off low apparatuses with different body parts, they will be ready for the next height. The planning of such learning experiences can help students to make better self-assessment of their readiness based on the success criteria at each juncture and make progress at their own pace (see also Chapter 7 on assessment).

Whilst this example focuses on a specific skill in the gymnastics learning area, Tomlinson, Moon, and Imbeau (2015) suggest that a quality curriculum should also enable students to make sense of what they learn so they can apply their learning in different situations. Using the examples in Table 2.3, developing students' understanding of the importance and acquisition of different travelling skills not only allows them to apply the skills to navigate around objects or apparatuses confidently at the next stage of their learning (e.g. next academic year or educational level), but also to transfer the learning to other areas like games, where they need to be able to use a range of travelling skills in dynamic situations. For example, an attacking player running fast while dribbling the ball with the floorball stick, and having to leap over an opponent's stick as the opponent attempts to get the ball. Thus, progression is not just about improving a specific skill, it is also about being able to use that skill in more challenging contexts, as well applying the principles of that skill or knowledge across different activities. Task 2.3 encourages you to think through and draw deeper understanding of the progression in skill and knowledge in your national curriculum.

> **Task 2.3 Key learning outcomes in your national curriculum**
>
> With reference to the goals in your national curriculum, how would the key learning outcomes differ for a student aged 8 years compared with a student aged 11 years, in sending and receiving an object? What would it look like for any other goals and key learning outcomes you are currently teaching? If your curriculum does not include key learning outcomes, you may wish to consider what progression towards the goals might look like for the age groups identified (or other age groups).

Being clear about the outcomes expected at each educational level allows you and your students to identify gaps between their current level of skill, knowledge, and understanding and the expected level of achievement for each learning area or specific physical activity. This allows both you and your students to identify what needs to be learned next (what the next progression should be), supporting opportunities for students to take ownership of their learning through target setting.

From your reading of the chapter thus far, you should be starting to see how the purpose and goals of the curriculum (the skills, knowledge, and understanding students are expected to achieve) are reflected in the aims of the curriculum (what is expected at each educational level) are then reflected in the key learning outcomes (what students are expected to achieve at the end of each academic year). These reflect the continuity and progression expected of students. The next section considers how this can be reflected at the lesson level.

Clear Intended Lesson Outcomes

When the goals of a physical education curriculum and the objectives of units of work are being broken down into 'operational' segments, they become the intended lesson outcomes for individual lessons (Whitehead, 2021). These outcomes specify what students should achieve by the end of a lesson. The design and crafting of lesson outcomes is fundamental to planning a lesson. Clarity of lesson outcomes enables you to create progressive learning activities, generate key teaching points, and identify key success criteria for assessing students' learning.

As mentioned earlier in the chapter, it is important for students to know what they are learning and why they need to learn it. When the intended lesson outcomes are shared with students, they can be actively involved in assessment for learning and in using assessment information to evaluate their own performances against the outcomes. This creates opportunities for students to plan for their progression and support their own learning and development by reflecting on their own work against those outcomes, setting goals and timelines for their learning, and providing meaningful feedback to one another (Tomlinson, Moon and Imbeau, 2015). All of these help to develop students' accountability and ownership for their learning and associated progress.

How you share the intended lesson outcomes with students is important. Some strategies that you can use are outlined here:

- Present the intended lesson outcomes visually
  Before the start of the lesson, write the lesson outcomes as specifically as you can on a whiteboard (or equivalent), so that students can see what they will *Know*, *Understand*, and *Be Able to Do* by the end of the lesson. For example, students will be able to pass the ball successfully to a moving partner. Highlighting the keywords in terms of the skills and concepts and adjusting the vocabulary appropriately for the students in your class also helps to clarify these outcomes. Rink (2014) suggests that the greater the specificity in writing the lesson outcomes, the clearer the intent for the lesson.
- Share the intended lesson outcomes verbally
  Talk through the intended lesson outcomes with students at the start of the lesson or right after the warm-up routine. Gather students together as a class or sit them down in their own personal space, and present what they will *Know*, *Understand*, and *Be Able to Do* in a short and concise manner. This helps to focus both you and your students' attention on the learning and targeted achievements.
- Review the intended lesson outcomes with the class throughout the lesson
  Remind students to make reference to the intended lesson outcomes throughout the lesson, thus allowing assessment for learning to take place by students gauging their current level and working hard in the tasks/practices to progress and achieve the learning outcomes. This, of course, should be accompanied by a set of success criteria for students to assess themselves against. It will also help students develop their skills over time in observing and giving constructive feedback to self and others (see Chapter 7 for more information on assessment and feedback strategies).

Having looked at how intended lesson outcomes can be shared, Case study 2.1 provides an example of how a teacher can help students to learn and make progress through good planning and delivery of lesson with clear intended lesson outcomes.

Case study 2.1 Share intended lesson outcomes with students

Teacher Z is going to conduct the second Ultimate Frisbee lesson for a class of 40 students in Secondary 1 (aged 12 to 12+ years). The first lesson was a diagnostic lesson to find out about students' interest in the game, their knowledge about the game in terms of the skills, tactics, and rules, as well as their skill level in throwing and catching the disc. Students were excited to learn the game after Teacher Z showed them a video of an Ultimate Frisbee competition to provide them with an idea of the learning outcomes. While students showed that they are able to transfer some of their existing knowledge from other invasion games, specifically in relation to attacking and defending moves like moving into open space and marking an opponent tightly, they were not familiar with the disc throw and catch or the rules of the game, as they had not been introduced to the game in primary school.

At the start of the lesson, Teacher Z pushed a big movable whiteboard onto the field. On the board, he had written the lesson outcomes clearly. These stated: Students should be able to:

- Execute backhand throws accurately to a stationary partner at increasing distances
- Catch the disc successfully most of the time
- Keep possession of the disc with at least three successful passes in the modified games
- Identify three types of catches (i.e. two-handed rim catch, one-handed rim catch, and pancake catch)
- Care for friends' learning by giving feedback on the backhand throws based on the learning cues in the task card

Students walked onto the field, and Teacher Z instructed them to get into groups of three and pick up a disc to start throwing and catching in triangular formation while waiting for full attendance. A few minutes later, Teacher Z signalled for all students to stop and gather in front of the whiteboard. Immediately after the greeting, he went through the lesson outcomes and success criteria. Students became aware and excited that they would get to work on throws and catches as well as an attacking strategy that day. Teacher Z then demonstrated the backhand throw and catch with a student (coupled with cues), followed by explaining the role of a student observer in their groups of three. Students then went back to their practice areas to start their learning experiences for the first task. Teacher Z moved around to watch the throws and listen to the feedback given by the student observers on the preparation phase of the throw. Once the students were able to demonstrate that they could throw accurately to each other, they were allowed to increase the distance between each other so that they were throwing over a longer distance. Ten minutes later, Teachers Z signalled for the students to gather and be ready to move onto concentrating on catching.

This case study identifies some of the key aspects of continuity and progression at a unit and lesson level that support students to make progress. By undertaking an initial diagnostic lesson, the teacher is able to identify what students already know and can do – therefore subsequent lessons will build on this knowledge. Whilst the students might not have refined skills yet to play a game, they are showing competence in aspects of game play like moving into open space to receive a pass. By sharing the lesson outcomes, the teacher is providing a clear overview of what students are expected to achieve, and this appears to be acting in such a way as to motivate the student. By sharing the key learning cues to perform the skill, the teacher is encouraging students to start to take greater ownership of their learning by allowing them to self- and peer assess each other's progress, thereby supporting students in assessing their progress.

With a set of clear intended lesson outcomes and planned activities to structure the learning, you will need to provide time for students to reflect on their own learning and review their progress. It helps the students further if you provide questions to scaffold their assessment of their progress and to aid self-assessment and reflection. Examples of questions to ask, based on the criteria for making successful passes to keep possession of the disc, can be:

- What were you able to do well?
- What could have caused any unsuccessful passes?
- What do you want to work on to increase the number of successful passes to your moving partner?

Task 2.4 asks you to reflect on your practice in terms of intended lesson outcomes in your physical education lessons.

Task 2.4 Providing clarity in the intended lesson outcomes to help students learn and make progress

1. Among the strategies you have used to communicate intended lesson outcomes, what has worked well for you? What were some observations you have made on students' learning and progression when they were clear about the intended lesson outcomes?
2. What does the assessment for learning approach look like in your physical education lessons currently? What can be developed or improved further to enable students to assess their own progress against lesson outcomes, to empower students to take ownership of their own learning, and to enable them to set goals and make progress based on where they are at?

Planning and teaching for continuity and progression in learning is the core business of teachers. So far this chapter has focused on understanding the continuity and progression in your physical education national curriculum and in planning generally. Although a progressive curriculum and progressive lessons are important, they should not be viewed as fixed and to be delivered without appropriate adaptation. You need to plan and teach for continuity and progression for each student's learning; the needs of students must always supersede a pre-planned fixed curriculum. Attention in this chapter now turns to planning for progress by individual students.

Planning for Progress by Individual Students

In order to plan for progression in students' learning, teachers must *know* their students (see Chapter 3). Not all children of the same age are the same. Every student is different as a result of, for example, different rates of growth and development in the physical, cognitive, and affective domains of a child, their background and experiences, the environment they grow up in, and amount of practice. For example, there may be a tendency to believe that older boys will jump further than younger boys and larger children may be stronger than smaller children of the same age. However, this is not the case for all skills. For example, a larger boy may not be able to jump further than a smaller boy of the same age due to a heavier weight. Being aware of differences in, and factors affecting, students in physical education is important because it helps you plan progressive tasks for the range of students in your lessons. Task 2.5 asks you to put some observation skills into practice to focus on differences between students in your lessons.

 Task 2.5   Understanding individual differences

1. Observe students of different ages perform jumps. Watch their movement patterns (e.g. arm and leg actions, flight, and consistency). Take note of how the movement patterns differ by age (note children of the same age might be at different stages of motor development). With reference to the related curriculum key learning outcomes for children at these different ages, how would you plan for progression in jumps?
2. Make another observation of students of the same age but having different weights. Watch their movement patterns and performance and take note of any differences in the performance. Are you able to explain your observations to a colleague?

Bearing in mind that students of the same age may be at different stages of development and in their learning, differentiated tasks are needed to cater for the range of student learning needs in a class to enable all students to succeed. Differentiation is a means of planning and organising all aspects of teaching and managing learning to enable each student to progress. It involves taking account of differences between students, such as their different learning needs, abilities, levels of achievement, personal interests, motivation in order to design learning that challenges and interests students but, at the same time, is achievable and ensures a large measure of success - and progress, by giving the right amount of challenge and support to every student.

Generally, lesson outcomes are the same for all students, but there are differences in the way students work towards these and hence make progress. In order to achieve this, you need to consider, for example, how students are grouped, the learning environment, content, tasks set, teaching approaches, assessment, and classroom leadership/management to help all students meet the lesson outcomes. Additionally, formative assessment (see Chapter 7) enables you to determine the best teaching approach or modification needed for each student.

There are a number of different ways to differentiate to enable all students to progress in physical education. The Youth Sport Trust (YST, 2004) identified the 'STEP' principle as shown in Table 2.4.

Task 2.6 encourages you to consider how you could use the STEP principle to differentiate within your lessons.

Table 2.4 The STEP principle

STEP	Description	Example
S = Space	the space in which a student works is increased or reduced to make the task more challenging or easier to achieve	e.g. changing the distance between the starting point and the goal.
T = Task	a task is changed in order to make it more complex or to simplify it	e.g. changing the number of the variables in a task or giving less or more time to solve a problem before putting it into practice
E = Equipment	the type of equipment students use to achieve a task is changed so it makes it more difficult or easier	e.g. changing the size of the racquet head in badminton to increase or decrease the surface area that makes contact with the shuttle
P = People	how students work together with others to make the activity more difficult or easier	e.g. an active defender is removed to increase chance of success

Source: Adapted from Youth Sport Trust (2004)

CONTINUITY AND PROGRESSION

 Task 2.6 Using the STEP principle to differentiate within your lesson

Using a lesson you will be teaching, review your planning and identify where activities could be adapted in relation to space, task, equipment, and people to make them more or less challenging to enable all students to progress.

Identify specifically what adaptations you will make, for example,

- Changing the amount of space in which students work
- Providing a range of targets for students to aim at to score a point
- Allowing students to choose the equipment they are going to use
- Changing how students will work with other people

After teaching the lesson, consider

- What impact did these adaptations have on the progress your students made towards meeting the lesson outcomes?

Examples of other ways in which activities can be adapted to make them more or less challenging in order to enable each student to progress are listed in Table 2.5.

Table 2.5 Examples of making activities more or less challenging

Lesson Outcome	More Challenging	Less Challenging
Students will perform over and underarm throws at a target with accuracy.	Student is given smaller object to throw. Size of the target to aim at is made smaller. Distance from the target is increased.	Student is given larger object to throw. Size of target to aim at is made larger. Distance from the target is reduced.
Students will perform a gymnastics sequence containing, rotation, flight and balance	Student includes more than one example of rotation, flight and balance. Student includes balances that require using small body parts (hands, head) or no more than two body parts	Student includes a minimum of one example of rotation, balance and flight. Student uses larger body parts to balance on (shoulders, back, side) or can use two or more body parts to balance on.
Students will play a 3 v 3 game focusing on accuracy of passing.	Student must pass the ball at least 5 times before a point can be scored. All students in the team must receive the ball at least once before a point can be scored.	Student must pass the ball 3 times before a point can be scored.

From Table 2.5 you can start to see that whilst the lesson outcome remains the same, how the students might progress towards achieving this might vary according to the adaptations that are made. What is important is that students need to feel that they are successful in achieving the lesson outcome. Based on Rovegno and Bandhauer (2016) and my own practices, some strategies to help students feel successful and competent could involve:

- Teaching students to make decisions about the level of task difficulty so they are challenged and successful. For example, providing clear success criteria for self-assessment to make appropriate choice of level.
- Teaching students how to modify tasks and games to ensure challenge and success for all students. For example, in a game, enlarging the leading team's goal area to create greater scoring opportunities for the other team.
- Praise students for their effort and persistence in desiring to improve, and not praise just their successful outcome. It is important to reinforce to students that making a mistake is part of the learning process and it just means they need to try harder and practise more.

So, how can progression by students be evidenced? Where progress is being made, students are more able to, for example,

- Increase the difficulty, complexity, or quality of existing skills, knowledge, and understanding (e.g. they show a greater level of precision and accuracy when shooting or passing)
- Modify and adapt skills, knowledge, and understanding appropriate for the situation (e.g. they are able to modify an initial take-off in high jump or to execute their jump to perform a lay-up shot in basketball)
- Combine a number of different skills (e.g. they are better able to combine the hop, skip, and jump in triple jump)
- Transfer learning from one context or situation to a new/different context or situation (e.g. they are able to apply the principles of using space to attack in football to attacking in hockey)
- Work in different or unpredictable environments or in a different relationship with people (e.g. working to solve problem in outdoor education)
- Engage in a range of activities (e.g. are confident to participate in both team and individual activities)
- Reflect on, and evaluate, skills (e.g. are able to engage in effective self and peer feedback to support progress)
- Act independently (e.g. are able to take increasing levels of ownership for their own learning and progression through focused target setting)

Thus, although continuity and progression in the curriculum are important, it is equally important to modify the curriculum to enable all students to make progress.

SUMMARY AND KEY POINTS

Having read this chapter you should have developed your understanding around the following objectives:

- understand and plan for continuity and progress in student learning
- help students make meaning of the physical education curriculum to promote their interest in learning
- empower students to make progress in learning with clear intended lesson outcomes.

The broad purpose and goals of physical education identify the critical skills, knowledge, and understanding that students should work towards achieving during their education, and throughout their lifetime. These must be communicated to all students to give them a reason and focus for engagement in the physical education class. Once they know what they need to do in order to achieve success in physical education, they will inevitably find more meaning and be more engaged in the tasks, and this will lead to more effective learning.

However, although continuity and progression encompass the 'what' of a lesson, the 'why' and the 'how' of teaching it is vital in making the learning more effective. Knowing your students is key, and using that knowledge to adapt and differentiate the tasks and activities in your lessons, will enable *all* your students to show progression with their learning.

Students who are successful learners enjoy their learning, make progress, achieve and realise their potential, and are intrinsically motivated to learn (Isen and Reeve, 2005; Lemos and Veríssimo, 2014; Rantala and Maatta, 2012). The planning and teaching of your lessons is critical in ensuring that your students progress and feel successful in and after the lessons.

Note: A list of further resources to help you take your learning forward is available on the PESTA website: https://academyofsingaporeteachers.moe.edu.sg/pesta/professional-development/book-chapters-by-the-pesta-team

References

Chen, A., Martin, R., Ennis, C.D. and Sun, H. (2008) 'Content specificity of expectancy beliefs and task values in elementary physical education', *Research Quarterly for Exercise and Sport*, 79 (2), 195-208.

DES (Department of Education and Science) (1991) *Physical Education for Ages 5-16. Proposals of the Secretary of State for Education and Science and the Secretary of State for Wales*, London: HMSO.

Isen, A.M. and Reeve, J. (2005) 'The influence of positive affect on intrinsic and extrinsic motivation: Facilitating enjoyment of play, responsible work behavior, and self-control', *Motivation and Emotion*, 29 (4), 295-323.

Lemos, M.S. and Veríssimo, L. (2014) 'The relationships between intrinsic motivation, extrinsic motivation, and achievement, along elementary school', *Procedia-Social and Behavioral Sciences*, 112, 930-938.

Lund, J. and Tannehill, D. (2014) *Standards-based Physical Education Curriculum Development*, New York: Jones and Bartlett Publishers.

MOE (Ministry of Education) (2016) *Physical Education Teaching and Learning Curriculum: Primary, Secondary & Pre-University*, Singapore: Student Development Curriculum Division.

Rantala, T. and Maatta, K. (2012) 'Ten theses of the joy of learning at primary schools', *Early Child Development and Care*, 182 (1), 87-105.

Rink, J. (2014) *Teaching Physical Education for Learning*, Boston, MA: McGraw-Hill Higher Education.

Rovegno, I. and Bandhauer, D. (2016) *Elementary Physical Education*, New York: Jones and Bartlett Learning.

Siraj-Blatchford, I. (2008) 'Understanding the relationship between curriculum, pedagogy and progression in learning in early childhood', *Hong Kong Journal of Early Childhood*, 7 (2), 6-13.

Tomlinson, C.A., Moon, T.R. and Imbeau, M.B. (2015) *Assessment and Student Success in a Differentiated Classroom*, Alexandria, Virginia: ASCD.

Whitehead, M. (2021) 'Aims of PE', in S. Capel, J. Cliffe and J. Lawrence (eds.) *Learning to Teach Physical Education in the Secondary School: A Companion to School Experience* (5th edn), Abingdon: Routledge, pp. 20-35.

YST (Youth Sport Trust) (2004) *TOP Play and TOP Sport Student Handbook: Using TOP Play and TOP Sport in Higher Education Institutions*, Loughborough: YST.

Knowing Students as Individuals and Understanding Their Needs

Tan Seck Heong

Introduction

As a teacher, if you are to provide meaningful learning opportunities in your lessons, a key question to ask yourself is what do you need to know and understand about your students to improve their learning? This question refers to knowing students as a group but also, because each student is unique, knowing each individual student.

One of the first observations you make as you teach a typical class is that it is comprised of students who vary widely, even within the 'normal' range in the psychomotor, cognitive, and affective domains of learning, for example, in size, strength, motor, language, or social-emotional abilities. An awareness of these differences enables you to develop a deeper knowledge and understanding of your students, and to design lessons and learning experiences that cater for these differences and bring about more effective teaching and student learning in your lessons.

Thus, as a teacher, you first need to be a student of your students, so that you are able to pitch lessons at the right level of challenge that is just beyond their current competence, that is, in their zone of proximal development (Vygotsky, 1978). This supports the learning of all students and enables them to experience greater success.

By adopting a developmental perspective in your teaching you will be able to adapt, for example, the content, task designs, equipment selection, group size, feedback, to cater for the differential development of the students within a class thereby enabling you to design lessons and learning experiences that facilitate and support their learning. This, in turn, can prevent a mismatch in expectations which may result in students struggling to learn that which is beyond their level of readiness to learn (see Chapter 5), or students who are bored and disengaged because they are under-challenged.

This chapter provides an introduction to some of the frameworks/theories of development in the psychomotor, cognitive, and affective domains. However, the chapter cannot do justice to these. Some of the content is followed up in other

DOI: 10.4324/9781003171973-4

chapters in this book (Chapter 5 addresses cognition and readiness, Chapter 8 looks at the affective domain). However, there is a considerable amount of material on each of these in libraries and online, to which you should refer for further information. Further, the chapter focuses largely on development (nature). However, it is important to recognise that the environment (nurture) also contributes to individual differences. Although the environment is not the focus of the chapter, mention is made of it in this chapter on occasion, in other chapters and in other sources, to which reference should be made. The chapter concludes by looking at motivation - an essential underpinning for all students to learn.

> **OBJECTIVES**
>
> At the end of this chapter, you should be able to:
>
> - identify different stages of growth and development of students in the psychomotor, cognitive, and affective domains
> - develop an understanding of appropriate frameworks/theories for different domains of development
> - recognise teaching strategies that are appropriate for students at different developmental stages to support students' learning.

Developmental Differences in Your Students

Individuals develop at different rates. If, for example, you look at class of 12-year-olds, you will see that they vary in height and weight. Some will be able to perform basic skills, whilst other will be more advanced. Some will be able to work together whilst others will struggle. Whilst all children go through the same stages of development, the speed at which they develop is influenced by their biological make-up as well as their experiences.

Before continuing, Task 3.1 asks you to take a closer look at the classes you teach.

> **Task 3.1 Identifying differences in the classes you teach**
>
> Observe a range of classes that you teach - for example different age groups, different activities.
>   As you observe, make a note of differences you see in the students - for example are there any differences in their level of skill development, how they work together?

> What factors might impact on these differences?
> How do these factors affect their learning in the lesson?
> How might you adapt your teaching to cater for these differences and to support the learning of all students?

Having completed Task 3.1, the range of differences you have identified might include, for example, differences in size of the students, their strength, whether or not students are able to achieve a motor skill, their language abilities, what their level of knowledge is, their attitudes towards physical education, differing levels of engagement, their social-emotional abilities, how they work with each other, amongst others.

As a physical education teacher, it is important that you understand development in the psychomotor, cognitive, and affective domains and how individual students vary within these in order to provide your students with a developmentally appropriate physical education programme. As the psychomotor, cognitive, and affective domains are explored later, it is also important to bear in mind that, given that human beings are holistic, there is a constant interplay amongst these domains. Each domain influences all of the others and is likewise influenced by all others. For example, ability to participate effectively in a game of hockey is affected by, among other things, the person's muscular strength (psychomotor domain), their ability to read the game play accurately (cognitive domain), and their emotional state (affective domain).

The next three sections take a closer look at development in the psychomotor, cognitive, and affective domains, respectively and provide examples of how you need to take account of this in your teaching.

Psychomotor Development

The psychomotor domain refers to motor development, motor skills and the ability to coordinate them.

The development of motor skills is governed by general principles of:

1 Motor skills progress through a similar sequence – for example students need to develop fundamental movement skills before they can move to more complex movement patterns; and
2 The rate of progress through the sequence of motor development varies; it is age-related, not age-dependent.

The phases through which motor development occurs can be broken down into a number of phases. A summary of those identified by Gallahue, Ozmun, and Goodway (2012) can be seen in Table 3.1.

Table 3.1 A summary of phases of motor development

	Phase of Motor Development	Approximate Age Range	Examples of Movements
1	Reflexive movement	birth to 1 year old	Palmar grasp reflex and sucking reflex
2	Rudimentary movement	birth to 2 years old	Reaching to grasp and releasing objects, crawling, walking
3	Fundamental movement	2 to 7 years old	Running, jumping, throwing, catching
4	Specialised movement	7 years old onwards	Rope jumping, basketball dribbling, forehand tennis serve

Source: Gallahue, Ozmun, and Goodway (2012)

Table 3.2 Examples of the three general classifications of fundamental movement skills

Locomotor	Non-Locomotor	Manipulative
Walking, running, leaping, jumping, hopping, skipping, galloping, sliding, crawling, climbing, rolling	Curling, stretching, twisting, turning, spinning, pushing, pulling, rocking, swinging, pivoting, balancing, counter-balancing, counter-tension	Rolling a ball, throwing, catching, bouncing, dribbling with foot, hand, implement, trapping, kicking, volleying, striking

Source: Adapted from Ministry of Education (MOE) (2016, p. 25)

For early years or primary school teachers, the first interaction with students is likely to be at the fundament movement phase (see Gallahue, Ozmun and Goodway, 2012, for more details of all four phases). In this phase, students explore and experiment with different types of locomotor, non-locomotor, and manipulative movements (summarised in Table 3.2), enabling them to develop an understanding of how the body moves, how it can be controlled and their movement potential. These are often referred to as the fundamental or basic movement skills, as they provide the foundational movement vocabulary for building a repertoire of activity-related specific psychomotor skills (e.g. in athletics, dance, gymnastics, games, outdoor activities, and swimming) students learn as they progress through the different grade levels in physical education.

When teaching the skills outlined in Table 3.2, you need to be aware that students gradually develop each skill, and also that any skill combines aspects from different categories. For example a student in the early stages of running will lack coordination of their limbs; therefore their ability to run in a straight line will be limited. As a student becomes more confident and balanced, their movement will become more efficient; thus, when running, a student uses both locomotor and non-locomotor skills.

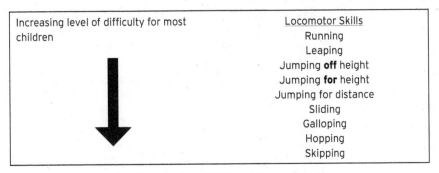

Figure 3.1 An example of locomotor skills teaching progression

Fundamental movement skills should be taught in a general progression from simple to more complex skills. An example is shown in Figure 3.1 in relation to teaching progressions of locomotor skills.

As students start to master fundamental movement skills, their ability to combine movements increases. As an example, a leap involves a combination of aspects of running (to provide the power needed to perform a leap) and the understanding of how to jump (for example from one foot to the other foot).

In summary, students' fundamental movement skills develop over time. This development is linked to their age and level of maturation, as well as to the amount of practice of the skill. Once fundamental movement skills have become established, students can be encouraged to combine these skills (for example a run and a jump for distance – and later as a long jump). Lessons should then be planned to ensure that there are opportunities for students to select and apply their skills in different situations. This allows students to consolidate their skills and improve their levels of competence before they start to specialise in specific activity areas.

To date, the chapter has focused on the development of fundamental movement skills and hence largely on primary physical education. Secondary-aged students should have developed their fundamental movement skills. However, it is important that secondary teachers identify where any fundamental movement skills have not matured and take steps to help students to develop these skills so that they are able to learn the specialised skills which are the focus of secondary physical education.

Students develop their proficiency in all (fundamental or new specialised) movement skills in a series of identifiable stages known as generic levels of skill proficiency (Graham et al., 2010). The four generic levels of skill proficiency are: Pre-control, Control, Utilisation, and Proficiency levels (see Table 3.3). Students' levels of proficiency differ from that of other students and also the same student will have different levels of proficiency in different skills.

Having a clear understanding of the progression in motor skill development, knowledge about the motor skills students are learning, and the ability to identify students' levels of proficiency, allows you to gauge the overall ability level of your

Table 3.3 Summary of levels of skill proficiency

Level of Skill Proficiency	Observable Characteristics	Example
Pre-control	Lack of ability to control the body or an object Each attempt of a movement/skill is different	Student learning to dribble a basketball spends more time chasing after the ball than bouncing it.
Control	Ability to repeat movement/skill is more consistent Performance is carried out with intense concentration	Student can repeatedly bounce the basketball to dribble but eyes are focused on the ball.
Utilisation	Movement/skill becomes more automatic Ability to perform movement/skill in combination with other skills	Student can dribble the ball to move to a desired court location or can dribble and change speed and direction to outwit an opponent.
Proficiency	Performance of movement/skill becomes automatic and effortless Ability to perform the skill/movement intended while making required adjustments to the demands of the environmental situation	Student is able to dribble the ball without focusing on it to keep away from the opponent or is able to dribble using both hands, allowing them to guide the ball away from the defender more effectively.

Source: Graham et al. (2010, pp.103–104)

class and therefore what their next steps in learning should be. This enables you to plan developmentally appropriate activities that challenge your students to move forward with their learning, but does not over-challenge them which may result in them becoming frustrated and reluctant to engage. Thus, you plan tasks and activities that work best for the class overall and modify the tasks for those students who fall outside the generic level of the class (both those working above and those working below this level). To support your understanding of this framework, Task 3.2 asks you to consider how you might plan to deliver a new skill to your class.

 Task 3.2   Planning for skill development

Select a skill for a class you teach.

Plan a progression of differentiated learning experiences/tasks that enable all students to be challenged, but successful in achieving the task.

Now teach the progressions.

■   As you teach the progression take notice of the learning taking place – for example,

> ☐ Are students able to perform the tasks you have planned?
> ☐ Are all students making progress at the same rate? If not, what are some of the reasons students are not progressing at the same rate?

The next section focuses on cognitive development.

Cognitive Development

Cognitive development refers to the development of thinking, knowledge, and understanding. According to Payne and Isaacs (2012), "Cognitive and motor development interact continually throughout the lifespan as they reciprocally inhibit or facilitate each other" (p. 32).

One popular developmental theory among educators is Jean Piaget's Stages of Cognitive Development. According to Piaget (1963), there are four major stages of cognitive development: sensorimotor, preoperational, concrete operational, and formal operational. These are outlined in Table 3.4. Each stage is defined by the emergence of new intellectual abilities that enable the individual to understand the world in increasingly complex ways.

Table 3.4 Piaget's (1963) stages of cognitive development and associated characteristics

Stage	Approximate Ages	Characteristics
1 Sensorimotor	Birth to 2 years	Infants explore the world by using their senses and reflexive motor skills, eventually learning to self-initiate movements. Evidence of achievement: ■ Progress from reflexive to goal-directed behaviour such as hitting a musical toy to produce a sound ■ Developing object permanence such as looking for a lost ball ■ Deferred imitation such as infant repeating an action observed previously
2 Preoperational	2 to 7 years	Children develop language and begin to use gestures, sounds, and words to represent and convey meaning. Tend to be egocentric in thinking, that is, unable to view the world from another perspective. Evidence of achievement: Symbolic thought and language

(Continued)

Table 3.4 (Continued)

Stage	Approximate Ages	Characteristics
3 Concrete Operational	7 to 11 years	Children develop logical reasoning about concrete events. Able to mentally organise or modify their thought processes and use rules in thinking. Evidence of achievement: ■ Understanding conservation such as the amount of water remains unchanged when it is poured into containers of different sizes and/or shapes ■ Reversibility – ability to reverse one's thinking to mentally 'undo' actions
4 Formal Operational	11 years onwards	Adolescents are capable of abstract and purely symbolic thinking. Able to systematically problem solve, make predictions and plan. Evidence of achievement: ■ The capacity to use propositional and hypothetical-deductive reasoning

As the individual moves through the stages of cognitive development, they build on the knowledge and understanding they already possess and use this to underpin the development of new knowledge. According to Piaget and Inhelder (2000), they do this through assimilation and accommodation. In assimilation, learners modify or change new information to fit into their existing knowledge (also known as schemas). For accommodation, learners adjust their schemas so that new information can fit better. Usually, assimilation and accommodation occur at the same time, creating a state of balance or equilibrium which leads to a stable understanding of the world around them. Therefore, according to Driscoll (2014), Piaget asserted that humans are active meaning-makers who construct rather than passively receive knowledge.

If learning is constructed, as a teacher it is important to consider how to plan for this and adopt constructivist approaches and learner-centred pedagogies in teaching physical education. For example, how do you ensure that the students you are teaching are actively learning? Do they have the opportunity to explore and experiment, allowing them to learn what works and what does not work through trial and error? Theorists such as Piaget (1963) and Vygotsky (1978) promote the adoption of a student-centred approach where students take increasing ownership over their own learning (Chapter 10 provides information on how teachers can help students realise this). Further, Bruner (1961) argues that the teacher becomes a facilitator providing opportunities for students to experiment, explain and select and apply their learning and understanding. Within your lessons you should therefore provide opportunities for your students to work individually, in pairs and in groups to explore, analyse, and construct movement content such as designing a gymnastics or dance routine using a movement education approach or finding tactical solutions to a given game situation using an inquiry approach to games teaching, like Teaching Games for Understanding (Bunker and Thorpe, 1982) and its variations- game sense (den Duyn, 1996), Tactical Games Approach (Griffin, Mitchell and Oslin, 1997), play practice (Launder, 2001), and games concept approach (Fry et al., 2010; Tan et al., 2002) (see Chapter 4).

In summary, understanding students' level of cognitive development/functioning enables teachers to choose appropriate teaching and assessment strategies that encourage students to think and to use their knowledge and understanding. For example, using age-appropriate language that is easier for your students to understand and limiting the number of instructions given at a time so that they do not become overloaded with too much information. Chapters 5 and 7 look in more detail the aspects of cognitive development. Now complete Task 3.3 which encourages you to apply your learning from this section.

 Task 3.3   Planning for skill acquisition

Using the overarm throw as an example, design a resource card (to include learning cues) for each of the following age phases:

1   Students being introduced to the skill for the first time;
2   Students developing their skill in a games situation;
3   Students transferring the skill to other activities, for example, athletics, badminton, softball.

Now use the resource cards in your teaching and reflect on how they have supported students' learning. Further, you may want to undertake the same exercise with another skill you are teaching.

The next section focuses on how students develop in the affective domain.

Affective Development

The affective domain refers to how students develop and experience feelings and emotions and how they interact with the world around them socially. Erikson (1963) developed a theory of stages of identity development, in which each successive stage is influenced by the earlier stages. Table 3.5 provides a summary of those most relevant to teachers (further details of all stages can be found in Gallahue, Ozmun, and Goodway, 2012).

As a teacher, you can help your students to overcome difficulties presented by stages 1 to 3 of identity development by being a reliable source of support in order to build trust. You should give students age-appropriate opportunities to work

Table 3.5 Erikson's stages of identity development

Stage	Age	Stage of Development	Overview	Links to Physical Education
3	3–6 years	Initiative vs. guilt	Students become more independent. They begin to make choices about activities to pursue. Where support and guidance is provided they develop initiative, that is, independence in planning and undertaking activities. If they are discouraged in pursuing independent activities or dismissed as being silly and bothersome, they develop guilt about their needs and desires.	Plan opportunities for students to ■ Practise the fundamental movement skills in different situations to allow them to become confident ■ To share their ideas through individual and paired work Feedback to students should focus on what they are doing well and what they need to do next to make progress.
4	6–12 years	Industry vs. inferiority	The focus moves to learning new cognitive, physical, and social skills. Students begin to work and gain recognition by producing artefacts such as artwork and videoed movement performance. Students need to experience success in order to learn that they are competent and can master skills. If they are encouraged to achieve and are praised for their	Plan activities that ■ Develop students' ability to work cooperatively and competitively ■ Allow students to evaluate their own and others' performances ■ Allow students to experience a range of different areas of activity ■ Continue to develop students' confidence and competence

Stage	Age	Stage of Development	Overview	Links to Physical Education
			accomplishments, students have a feeling of competence and belief in their abilities. If they are unsuccessful, or if they are punished for their efforts, they develop a sense of inferiority and helplessness. Students develop the ability to cooperate with peers and a sense of responsibility.	
5	12-19 years	Identity vs. identity confusion	In their attempt to gain independence and identity, peer approval and acceptance is very important at this stage. Adolescents seek out people who mean the most to them as significant others and role models in their lives. They begin to develop a sense of who they are, what they believe in, and what they want to become. Successfully negotiating this stage leads to a sense of identity; otherwise it leads to an identity crisis. Many students at adolescence are prone to experience this	Provide opportunities for students to: ■ Specialise in a smaller range of activities ■ Engage in more competitive activities

(Continued)

Table 3.5 (Continued)

Stage	Age	Stage of Development	Overview	Links to Physical Education
			confusion, hence they may experiment with different behaviours and activities (e.g. risk-taking behaviours like smoking/vaping, binge drinking, thrill seeking, etc.).	

independently, allowing them to build autonomy and take on self-initiated activities. Adolescents can be helped in their search for identity by providing opportunities to engage in meaningful tasks to promote a sense of competence and accomplishment and to explore their areas of strength so that they can identify their possible adult roles in society. Physical education lessons should therefore be focused beyond learning objectives in psychomotor and cognitive domains, to include the affective domain.

The affective domain is not always as obvious as the psychomotor and cognitive domains in either students themselves or in teachers' thinking and lesson planning. However, Laker (2000) contends that physical education is perhaps the most social of school subjects; therefore, teachers need to deliberately plan and teach affective learning goals during each physical education lesson so that students are taught not just to become skilful and thinking performers but also to have a positive attitude, be motivated and confident to participate and develop as caring and sharing individuals (Chapter 8 looks at the affective domain). Therefore, understanding how students develop emotionally and socially allows teachers to provide learning experiences that can help to develop students' positive sense of self and positive interaction skills as well as a positive attitude towards physical education and physical activity.

Task 3.4 encourages you to reflect on how you embed the affective stages of development in your teaching (Chapter 8 provides more examples of this).

 Task 3.4 Pause to reflect

In view of your students' stage of affective development, what learning activities can you plan that will support them to:

- Work with a range of different students within the class to develop their awareness of how to work with others
- Develop their ability to provide feedback on their own and others' performances with consideration of how this feedback is presented

It is also important to remember that all three domains are linked. So, for example in adolescence, rapid body growth may result in a student experiencing periods of motor incoordination and feelings of awkwardness. Other bodily changes due to hormone surge bring about sexual maturation and changes in the body such as increased body fat for many girls and increased muscle development for boys. Such changes may result in negative attitudes towards participating in physical education. Thus, it can be seen that students' development in the psychomotor, cognitive, and affective domains, along with their experiences, impact their motivation towards participating in physical education and physical activity. The next section focuses on motivation in physical education.

Motivation

In order to learn, students have to be motivated to participate and engage in lessons. In physical education "pupils' bodies and physical abilities are uniquely visible and pupils are made vulnerable as they demonstrate their abilities and skills (or lack of them) to classmates" (Bailey et al., 2009, p.14). As a result, some students find physical education embarrassing or frightening, or on occasion, humiliating. Research suggests that such negative experiences – if accompanied by, for example, differential development in any of the three domains or perceived or real lack of competency – are a strong barrier to being motivated to participate and learn in physical education or to habitual participation of physical activity outside lessons or school or after completing school (Ladwig, Vazou and Ekkekakis, 2018; Sallis, Prochaska and Taylor, 2000; Sterdt, Liersch and Walter, 2014). As a physical education teacher your aim is to plan and teach lessons which motivate students within the lesson and to participate in physical activities throughout their life.

So how can a joy and passion for learning be cultivated so that students are motivated to be resilient to keep practising? The task of motivating students to learn is difficult. Students at different ages are motivated in different ways and what is motivating for one student may not be motivating to another student.

As a teacher, recognising these challenges is important. A useful theory of motivation that can provide guidance in all aspects of lessons, including lesson planning and enactment, creating a positive learning environment, monitoring and feedback is Ryan and Deci's (2000) Self-Determination Theory.

Self-Determination Theory

Self-Determination Theory of motivation asserts that there are several kinds of motivation that shape thinking and behaviour. These are arranged in a continuum from the absence of motivation, named amotivation, to intrinsic motivation (see Figure 3.2).

Self-Determination Motivation Continuum					
Increasing level of autonomy in task engagement Increasing value and relevance of task Increasing sense of ownership					
Amotivation	External Motivation	Introjected Motivation	Identified Motivation	Integrated Motivation	Intrinsic Motivation
Low perceived competence Non-valuing Non-intentionality	Rewards Punishment Compliance	Approval Ego Avoidance of guilt/shame	Value Endorsement	Synthesis Congruence	Interest Enjoyment Pleasure Satisfaction
"I take part in physical education but I can't see what I am getting out of it"	"I take part in physical education because that is what I am supposed to do"	"I take part in physical education because I want the teacher to think I am a good student"	"I take part in physical education because I want to learn skills to participate in physical activities"	"I take part in physical education because I want to improve my skills"	"I take part in physical education because I enjoy it"

Figure 3.2 The self-determination continuum

Source: Ryan and Deci (2000)

It also posits that every individual has three innate psychological needs: the need for autonomy, need for competence, and need for relatedness to others. These needs are identified by Deci and Ryan (2000) as follows:

Autonomy   Need to self-organise and regulate one's own behaviour
Competence   Need to engage optimal challenges and experience mastery
Relatedness Need to seek attachments and experience feelings of security, belongingness, and intimacy with others

Motivation resides in the fulfilment of autonomy, competence, and relatedness, therefore people seek out activities that satisfy these three needs (Deci and Ryan, 2000). Satisfaction of these needs can be a strong motivator for students' achievement in school, including in physical education. Promoting autonomy, competence, and relatedness facilitate more self-determined forms of motivation in students.

Research (de Bruijn, Mombarg and Timmermans, 2021; Van den Berghe et al., 2014) has revealed that when students' motivation is more autonomous, it leads to more positive learning outcomes (e.g. greater concentration, enjoyment, activity levels, and well-being). One way for teachers to motivate students is to provide them with choices and opportunities for self-direction (Chapters 4, 5, 6, 7, and 10 offer ways to provide this choice) because this satisfies the need for autonomy. How can you give students choices when you have a prescribed curriculum to cover? What about students' choices that impact on safety to self or/ and others? Many teachers are already providing their students choices within limitations to address such concerns. For example, in a net-barrier game like tennis, students are allowed to choose equipment such as rackets that are more suited to their development and playing ability like a short racket instead of a regular size racket, tennis balls with different levels of compression for varying level of bounce or even sponge/foam balls instead of tennis balls, etc. in order to facilitate a greater degree of success. This success develops a positive perception of competence in students, which motivates them further. Sun and Chen (2010) maintained that helping students satisfy the need for competence should be the first priority of physical education. Therefore you need to ensure that you focus on developing and acknowledging the competence of all students in the class.

Research has shown that students' relationship and interactions with parents, teachers, and peers is correlated to their motivation, interest, and performance in school (Wentzel and Watkins, 2011 and Wentzel, 1998). Hence, you should provide a learning environment that enhances social interactions, promotes a sense of belonging, and establishes relatedness in the classroom, because such an environment encourages students to adopt adaptive instead of maladaptive behaviours during learning. As an example, students come to an agreement before playing a game whether the rally is to be cooperative, rather than cooperative-competitive or competitive. This will allow students of different abilities to maintain a decent rally to practise and develop their skills rather than being unable to sustain a rally due to differences in skill level of the two players. This helps to serve the need for relatedness.

An example of how the need for autonomy, need for competence, and need for relatedness to others can be achieved is the use of the Sport Education Model (Siedentop, 1994) to teach games in physical education. The key features of affiliation, formal competition, keeping records, culminating event and festivity in the model provides avenues for these needs to be met.

Task 3.5 asks you to consider how you provide for the need for competence, autonomy, and relatedness in lessons.

 Task 3.5 Providing for the competence, autonomy, and relatedness needs of your students

Focusing on one class you teach, plan a series of activities that allow students to self-organise (autonomy), experience mastery (competence), and work with others (relatedness).

Once you have taught the activities, reflect on any changes you have observed in relation to students' engagement and motivation.

Think about how you might now apply such approaches to a future lesson with this class and to lessons with other classes you teach.

Now complete Task 3.6 that encourages you to think about how you can create a positive learning environment.

 Task 3.6 Creating a positive learning environment

Observe different teachers for several lessons. Focus on how they establish and maintain a positive learning environment. Record their actions and dispositions, along with their students' responses toward them. Classify how these actions/dispositions satisfy the three basic needs – autonomy, competence, and relatedness – proposed by self-determination theory.

Now apply what you have seen and learned to your own teaching over a number of lessons.

How have the responses of your students changed?

How have the changes you have implemented impacted on the progress of the students in your class?

SUMMARY AND KEY POINTS

Human beings are complex creatures. This chapter has attempted to provide lenses for you to understand your students' stages of development in the psychomotor, cognitive, and affective domains. In order for students to learn in lessons, they need to be motivated. Hence, the chapter also focused on motivation. A number of frameworks/theories have been introduced to which you should look in greater depth; it is important to remember that no single framework/theory can adequately or completely explain a student or a class. As a teacher, you need to consider how the different frameworks/theories can be used to meet the needs of your students. Thus, the frameworks/theories form the basis that guide you to plan developmentally based lessons that incorporate not only age-appropriate, but developmentally appropriate learning experiences that make learning effective and fun (Gallahue, Ozmun and Goodway, 2012).

Note: A list of further resources to help you take your learning forward is available on the PESTA website: https://academyofsingaporeteachers.moe.edu.sg/pesta/professional-development/book-chapters-by-the-pesta-team

References

Bailey, R., Armour, K., Kirk, D., Jess, M., Pickup, I., Sanford, R. and BERA Physical Education and Sport Pedagogy Special Interest Group (2009) 'The educational benefits claimed for physical education and school sport: An academic review', *Research Papers in Education*, 24 (1), 1–27.

Bruner, J. (1961) 'The act of discovery', *Harvard Educational Review*, 31, 21–32.

Bunker, D. and Thorpe, R. (1982) 'A model for the teaching of games in secondary schools', *Bulletin of Physical Education*, 18 (1), 5–8.

De Bruijn, A.G.M., Mombarg, R. and Timmermans, A.C. (2021) 'The importance of satisfying children's basic psychological needs in primary school physical education for PE-motivation, and its relations with fundamental motor and PE-related skills', *Physical Education and Sport Pedagogy*, published online: 30 March 2021, https://doi.org/10.1080/17408989.2021.1906217

Deci, E.L. and Ryan, R.M. (2000) 'The "what" and "why" of goal pursuits: Human needs and the self-determination of behavior', *Psychological Inquiry*, 11 (4), 227–268.

den Duyn, N. (1996) 'Game sense: Why it makes sense to play games', *Sports Coach*, 19 (3), 6–9.

Driscoll, M.P. (2014) *Psychology of Learning for Instruction: Pearson New International Edition* (3rd edn), Harlow: Pearson Education UK.

Erikson, E.H. (1963) *Childhood and Society* (2nd edn), New York: Norton.

Fry, J.M., Tan, W.K.C., McNeill, M. and Wright, S. (2010) 'Children's perspectives on conceptual games teaching: A value-adding experience', *Physical Education and Sport Pedagogy*, 15 (2), 139–158.

Gallahue, D.L., Ozmun, J.C. and Goodway, J.D. (2012) *Understanding Motor Development: Infants, Children, Adolescents, Adults* (7th edn), New York: McGraw-Hill.

Graham, G., Holt/Hale, S.A. and Parker, M. (2010) *Children Moving: A Reflective Approach to Teaching Physical Education* (8th edn), New York: McGraw-Hill.

Griffin, L.L., Mitchell, S.A. and Oslin, J.L. (1997) *Teaching Sport Concepts and Skills: A Tactical Games Approach*, Champaign, IL: Human Kinetics.

Ladwig, M.A., Vazou, S. and Ekkekakis, P. (2018) '"My best memory is when I was done with it": PE memories are associated with adult sedentary behaviour', *Translational Journal of the American College of Sport Medicine*, 3 (16), 119–129.

Laker, A. (2000) *Beyond the Boundaries of Physical Education: Educating Young People for Citizenship and Social Responsibility*, Abingdon: Routledge.

Launder, A. (2001) *Play Practice: The Games Approach to Teaching and Coaching Sports*, Champaign, IL: Human Kinetics.

MOE (Ministry of Education) (2016) *Physical Education Teaching & Learning Syllabus: Primary, Secondary & Pre-University*, Singapore: Student Development Curriculum Division, MOE, viewed 26 August 2021, www.moe.gov.sg/-/media/files/primary/physical_education_syllabus_2014.pdf

Payne, V.G. and Isaacs, L.D. (2012) *Human Development: A Lifespan Approach* (8th edn), New York: McGraw-Hill.

Piaget, J. (1963) *The Origins of Intelligence in Children*, New York: Norton.

Piaget, J. and Inhelder, B. (2000) *The Psychology of the Child* (2nd edn) (H. Weaver, Trans.), New York: Basic Books.

Ryan, R.M. and Deci, E.L. (2000) 'Self-determination theory and the facilitation of intrinsic motivation, social development, and well-being', *American Psychologist*, 55 (1), 68–78.

Sallis, J.F., Prochaska, J.J. and Taylor, W.C. (2000) 'A review of correlates of physical activity of children and adolescents', *Medicine and Science in Sports and Exercise*, 32, 963–975.

Siedentop, D. (1994) *Sport Education: Quality PE through Positive Sport Experience*, Champaign, IL: Human Kinetics.

Sterdt, E., Liersch, S. and Walter, U. (2014) 'Correlates of physical activity of children and adolescents: A systematic review of reviews', *Health Education Journal*, 73 (1), 72–89.

Sun, H. and Chen, A. (2010) 'A pedagogical understanding of the self-determination theory in physical education', *Quest*, 62, 364–384.

Tan, S., Wright, S., McNeill, M., Fry, J. and Tan, C. (2002) 'Implementing the games concept approach in Singapore schools: A preliminary report', *REACT*, 1, 77–84, viewed 26 August 2021, https://repository.nie.edu.sg/bitstream/10497/3853/1/REACT-2002-1-77.pdf

Van den Berghe, L., Vansteenkiste, M., Cardon, G., Kirk, D. and Haerens, L. (2014) 'Research on self-determination in physical education: Key findings and proposals for future research', *Physical Education and Sport Pedagogy*, 19 (1), 97–121.

Vygotsky, L.S. (1978) *Mind in Society: The Development of Higher Psychological Processes*, Cambridge, MA: Harvard University Press.

Wentzel, K.R. (1998) 'Social relationships and motivation in middle school: The role of parents, teachers, and peers', *Journal of Educational Psychology*, 90 (2), 202–209.

Wentzel, K.R. and Watkins, D.E. (2011) 'Instruction based on peer interactions', in R.E. Mayer and P.A. Alexander (eds.) *Handbook of Research on Learning and Instruction*, New York: Routledge, pp. 322–343.

4 Learners and Learning in Physical Education
Games-Centred Approaches and Nonlinear Pedagogy

Tan Wee Keat Clara

Introduction

In the last few decades, the perspective of the teaching-learning process has evolved from a teacher-centred approach to a more student-centred approach where students are active learners, and teachers as facilitators in physical education (Lee, 2003). Advances in theory and practice in physical education in the last decade have also provided strong support for more constructivist approaches that consider individual needs (Chow et al., 2016). Constructivist approaches emphasise the importance of students being actively engaged in constructing knowledge and learning (Rovegno and Dolly, 2006). In physical education, these approaches have focused on how students as active learners are encouraged to develop problem-solving skills, critical thinking, and autonomy of thought (Chow et al., 2016; Lee, 2003; Richard and Wallian, 2005) and how they individually construct their knowledge in relation to their learning environment (Richard and Wallian, 2005).

This chapter highlights two constructivist approaches in physical education, namely Games-Centred Approach es (i.e. approaches) (GCA), which is based on the Teaching Games for Understanding (TGfU) (Bunker and Thorpe, 1982; Thorpe and Bunker, 1989; Thorpe, Bunker and Almond, 1984), and the Nonlinear Pedagogy (NLP) approach (Chow et al., 2006; Davids, Chow and Shuttleworth, 2005), which have become popular, attracting widespread attention.

OBJECTIVES

At the end of this chapter, you should be able to:

- have an overview of TGfU/GCA and its pedagogical principles and theoretical underpinnings
- have an overview of NLP and its pedagogical principles and theoretical underpinnings
- understand and consider how to apply the pedagogical principles of both approaches in your planning and teaching to enhance student learning.

DOI: 10.4324/9781003171973-5

As noted by Chow et al. (2016), when we fully understand why we are doing the things that we do, we can apply the principles to better adapt to different practice contexts, resolve challenging questions, and make adjustments to our practice depending on the unexpected changes of specific teaching and learning contexts.

At this point, think about the pedagogical approach/approaches that you are already using in your planning and teaching in physical education by undertaking Task 4.1.

> **Task 4.1   Pedagogical approach/approaches**
>
> - What pedagogical approach/approaches are you using in your planning and teaching?
> - Are there pedagogical principles that guide you in your planning and teaching to help students learn in physical education? If so, what are they? How have you applied them?
> - What are the student outcomes as a result of using the pedagogical approach/approaches and its principles?

Games-Centred Approaches (GCA)/Teaching Games for Understanding (TGfU)

GCA is based on TGfU (Hastie and Mesquita, 2016; Oslin and Mitchell, 2006). TGfU is a learner- and game-centred approach to learning games (Thorpe, Bunker and Almond, 1986). The approach shifted learning of games from a teacher-centred approach with an emphasis on technical development or knowledge content, to a more student-based approach which focuses on both tactics and skills in small game learning contexts. It aims to address concerns that children were not experiencing the excitement associated with games, and had little understanding of games (Thorpe and Bunker, 1989). The original six-step TGfU, which places emphasis on understanding the logic of play imposed by the rules of the game and helping students develop appreciation of the tactical structure of play, was presented as a curriculum model for developing decision-making and skill performance in games (Thorpe and Bunker, 1989; Thorpe, Bunker and Almond, 1984).

A number of variations of TGfU, known as GCA, have developed over the years (Harvey and Jarrett, 2014; Hastie and Mesquita, 2016). For example, TGfU has been simplified to three stages, known as the Tactical Games Approach, by Griffin, Mitchell, and Oslin (1997). The Tactical Games Approach, which focuses on three essential lesson components for practitioners, includes modified game forms which highlight tactical problems, tactical awareness, and decision-making developed through questioning, and the development of skill execution. Other examples of GCA include Play Practice (Launder, 2001), Tactical-Decision Learning (Gréhaigne, Wallian and Godbout, 2005), and Games Concept Approach

(Tan et al., 2002). As noted by Stolz and Pill (2014), while the variations of TGfU may look different, they are defined by subtle rather than distinctive differences. In the next section, the pedagogical principles of TGfU, which influenced the development of other GCA, are discussed in relation to teaching and learning of games in physical education to help students develop problem-solving skills, critical thinking, and autonomy of thought.

Pedagogical Principles of TGfU and Its Implications in Physical Education

The pedagogical principles of TGfU enable physical education teachers to design learning tasks to enhance student learning in games. Table 4.1 briefly presents the TGfU pedagogical principles and its key ideas before addressing each principle in greater detail.

Representation

Representation refers to developing modified mini-games with a similar tactical structure to the adult formal game (Thorpe and Bunker, 1989; Thorpe, Bunker and Almond, 1984). It aims to provide students with opportunities to experience and develop tactical awareness, make appropriate decisions, and practise skills in simplified, manageable practice environments adapted to suit

Table 4.1 TGfU pedagogical principles and its key ideas

TGfU Pedagogical Principles	Description/Key Ideas
Representation	■ Modified, mini-games with similar tactical structure to the adult formal game
Exaggeration	■ Modified elements or rules to exaggerate a tactical idea to be explored and discovered by students
Sampling	■ Selecting different types of games with similar tactical characteristics; the tactical elements and strategies, when understood by students, can be transferred from one game to another within the same games category
Tactical Complexity	■ Designing and matching game forms to the ability level of the student so that the tactical problems presented are appropriate
Modification by Adaptation*	■ Modifying the game to increase the challenge to the player who was successful in the previous game encounter so as to ensure the game outcome is close

* Note: proposed as another pedagogical principle for TGfU by Hopper, Sanford, and Clarke (2009) and Hopper (2011).

the students' profile (e.g. ability, size, age). An example is a simplified 1-v-1 modified tennis game using a shorter, lighter racket and a sponge ball instead of an adult 1-v-1 game.

Exaggeration

Closely related to the principle of representation, the principle of exaggeration suggests that representative modified mini-games should have modified elements to exaggerate a tactical idea to be explored and discovered by students (Thorpe and Bunker, 1989; Thorpe, Bunker and Almond, 1984). It involves modifying the rules of the game to emphasise a specific tactical problem by making the concept to be taught obvious to the students, thus guiding them towards exploring and learning about the intended game concept. For example, in net games, a well-established example of exaggeration is the use of a long and narrow court which makes it obvious for students to play to the front and back of the court. Exaggeration can also be through adjustments to game rules such as scoring. For example, in a modified game of netball, awarding more points for consecutive passes than scoring a goal would encourage the team in possession to explore the tactical concept related to maintaining possession of the ball.

Sampling

The principle of sampling is based on the premise that games selected for learning should provide a variety of experiences to show similarities and differences between apparently similar and dissimilar games, respectively (Thorpe and Bunker, 1989; Thorpe, Bunker and Almond, 1984). Systems of games classification (e.g. Almond, 1986; Ellis, 1983) highlight that games within the same category have common tactical elements and strategies to achieve similar goals. The principle of sampling suggests that these tactical elements and strategies, when experienced and understood by students, can be transferred from one game to another within the same games category. For example, in invasion/territorial games such as netball, students who understand the concepts related to maintaining possession (e.g. running into space to provide options for a pass in a 3-v-3 modified game) are likely to be able to transfer that understanding to football. Similarly, modified games in tennis where students explore playing into space and positioning can also allow positive transfer to net games such as badminton or volleyball. Thus, sampling from different types of games can expose students to similar tactical characteristics within different games. This helps them learn to transfer their learning from one game to another and enhance their understanding of game play in general (Thorpe, Bunker and Almond, 1984; Thorpe and Bunker, 1989).

The principle of sampling can result in educational advantages for both teachers and students (Butler and Robson, 2013). For teachers, designing curricula around common tactical themes can allow them to teach more deeply and systematically for understanding as they focus on tactical play, game concepts, decision-making, and movement competencies that will support play in the variety of games within each game category. For example, teachers who focus on teaching tactical themes related to invasion/territorial games (e.g. maintaining possession by running into space to provide options for a pass or regaining possession by interception, etc.) will allow for transfer of understanding and support play in a variety of invasion games such as netball, basketball, and football. For students, instead of becoming skilful at a series of unrelated movement patterns or techniques of specific games, they can gain better conceptual understanding as they learn to transfer tactical elements and strategies from one game within the category to others (Butler and Robson, 2013).

Tactical Complexity

According to the principle of tactical complexity, there are certain tactics that are more complex than others. This principle highlights the importance of designing and matching game forms to the ability level of the student, so that the tactical problems presented are not too complex for them (Thorpe, Bunker and Almond, 1984; Thorpe and Bunker, 1989). Applying the principle in designing a progression of game forms to support the ability level of students can take place both within and across different game categories (Butler et al., 2003; Tan, Chow and Davids, 2012). The former involves planning levels of games complexity within each category of games, with increasing tactical complexities. For example, Mitchell, Oslin, and Griffin (2003, 2006) proposed three levels of game complexity, namely levels I, II, and III. Applying their levels II and III of game complexity for tactical goals and problems linked to defending space (see Mitchell, Oslin and Griffin, 2003, 2006), teachers can teach guarding or marking at level II and clearing the ball and quick outlet pass at level III. Tactical complexity can also take place across different games categories. Planning progressions of games based on the four game categories involves teaching less complex games such as target games first, followed by net/barrier or fielding games, and then invasion/territorial games (e.g. Thorpe, Bunker and Almond, 1984; Thorpe and Bunker, 1989; Werner, Thorpe and Bunker, 1996).

Modification by Adaptation

In recent years, modification by adaptation has been proposed as another pedagogical principle for TGfU (Hopper, Sanford and Clarke, 2009; Hopper, 2011). Drawing on game-based learning in video games, modification by adaptation involves modifying the game to increase the challenge to the player who was successful in the previous game encounter. Hopper (2011) proposes that modification may be made to different aspects of the game (e.g. number of players, space, scoring, or rules conditioning play) to ensure the game outcome is close and the unanticipated can happen during game play. For example, in badminton, the court space could increase from quarter to half-court and so on as each player gains a point. As such, the game structure adapts to the varied ability of students; students are presented with appropriate levels of challenge as they progress in their game play (Hopper, 2011; Richardson, Sheehy and Hopper, 2013). Modification by adaptation shows how the video-gaming concept of game-as-teacher can be applied to games teaching in physical education to include and engage players of different abilities in meaningful, yet unpredictable game play (Hopper, 2011). It can provide challenge, engagement, and enjoyment for all students (Hopper, 2011; Richardson, Sheehy and Hopper, 2013).

The key pedagogical principles of TGfU/GCA have several key practical implications for teaching games in physical education. As physical education teachers, you can facilitate students' learning and performance by providing opportunities for them to experience representative tasks with similar tactical characteristics within different games in the same category. By sampling key common features within specific categories based on the games classification systems, you can also allow positive transfer of students' learning from one game to another (e.g. running into space to provide options for a pass in netball and football). To adequately challenge your students to achieve success, you can plan for developmentally appropriate tasks by adjusting the complexity of the task (e.g. by changing space, target area, equipment, and number of players involved, etc.). And finally, by applying the video-gaming concept of game-as-teacher to games teaching, you can allow all your students to engage in and enjoy game play at an appropriate level of complexity as they progress through a series of appropriate challenges in game play.

To gain greater insight into how the pedagogical principles and related ideas have been incorporated in the teaching of games, physical education teachers may refer to various GCA literature that has provided practical activities (e.g. see Launder and Piltz, 2013; Mitchell, Oslin and Griffin, 2020).

Research for GCA/TGfU

Research has provided support for GCA/TGfU and the application of its pedagogical principles in the teaching of games. For example, studies have shown that the GCA can effectively engage students regardless of their skill level (e.g. Jones, Marshall and Peters, 2010), teachers believe students can improve game play and understanding, students report enjoyment in developing the tactical aspects of game play (e.g. Fry et al., 2010; Mandigo et al., 2008), there is transfer of tactical understanding from one game to another within the same games category (e.g. Martin, 2004; Mitchell and Oslin, 1999), and the game-as-teacher approach can accommodate, challenge, and engage players of different abilities in game play (e.g. Richardson, Sheehy and Hopper, 2013). Such findings, together with the various GCA work that has provided practical activities, strongly encourage physical education teachers to consider the use of GCA/TGfU and its pedagogical principles in the teaching of games.

Now complete Task 4.2 which encourages you to reflect on how TGfU and its pedagogical principles may be applied to enhance your teaching of games.

> **Task 4.2   Application of the pedagogical principles of TGfU**
>
> - In your teaching of games, what are your desired student outcomes? Do you focus on tactics and/or skills?
> - What pedagogical principles have you used to inform/guide you in your lesson planning and implementation?
> - Considering the TGfU pedagogical principles presented, how might you apply these principles to enhance the teaching and learning of games in your own practice?

Nonlinear Pedagogy (NLP)

NLP is a student-centred approach which encourages exploratory learning and variability in practice (Chow et al., 2016). In NLP, the student is an active participant who is empowered with the autonomy to search, explore, and discover individualised movement solutions in the learning process while the teacher assumes the role of facilitator in enhancing students' movement coordination and decision-making skills during practice and play. It has provided a theoretical grounding to advance understanding of the learning processes and pedagogical principles to help understand how functional movement behaviours can be taught to students in physical education and sports (e.g. see Chow et al., 2011; Chow et al., 2007; Renshaw et al., 2010).

A constraints-led approach (CLA) has been proposed for understanding skill acquisition and game play and how it provides a basis for NLP. CLA describes how a student's acquisition of movement and decision-making skill is based on the interaction of three key constraints, namely performer, environmental, and task constraints (Newell, 1986, 1996). The three key constraints, together with descriptions and examples, are presented in Table 4.2.

As a result of the dynamic interactions among these three constraints in the learning situation, students adapt their movements/behaviours to the unique set of constraints that is acting on them and search for functional behaviours that are likely to achieve the behavioural goals (e.g. to catch or hit a ball) (Chow et al., 2007; Renshaw et al., 2010). Thus, although students can potentially move in many varied ways, constraints acting on them (e.g. task constraints such as the weight/length of racket used) can shape the ways that they can possibly move.

Recent work in NLP has demonstrated that the theoretical principles underlying NLP can provide relevant information on how to design activities and practices, assess performance, and provide instructions and feedback during delivery of lessons for effective teaching and learning (Chow et al., 2009; Chow et al., 2013).

Table 4.2 The three key constraints of CLA, together with descriptions and examples

Key Constraints	Description/Examples
Performer Constraints	■ Refer to the structural and functional characteristics or features that relate to the physical, physiological, emotive, and psychological disposition of the learner (Newell, 1986) ■ Examples include individual's fitness levels, cognitions, motivations, prior experiences and knowledge, technical abilities, etc.
Environmental Constraints	■ Refer to physical factors such as practice surfaces, the visual (e.g. amount of light) and auditory information (e.g. noise level) surrounding the performer ■ Also includes sociocultural factors such as presence of peer groups or teachers, societal and cultural expectations, etc.
Task Constraints	■ Refer to the goal or intent of the task, equipment used, playing areas, number of players, rules of the game or activity during the learning experience, etc.

Practitioners have been called to take on the role of designers of practices and facilitators of learning (Correia et al., 2019; Roberts, Newcombe and Davids, 2019). NLP and its pedagogical principles are indeed useful in equipping physical education teachers to assume the role of designers of practices and facilitators of learning. In the planning and implementation of lessons, physical education teachers should consider both quantity and quality of practice that incorporate the pedagogical principles of NLP to maximise learning opportunities (e.g. Chow et al., 2009).

The next section addresses the pedagogical principles of NLP (also referred to as design principles) and how you, as learning designers and facilitators of learning, can incorporate them in your planning and teaching. The pedagogical principles are representativeness, task simplification, exploratory learning, constraints manipulation, and attentional focus (Button et al., 2020; Chow, 2013).

Pedagogical Principles of NLP and Its Implications in Physical Education

Representativeness

The principle of representativeness, similar to that of TGfU, proposes that practice tasks, games, and/or learning contexts should be designed to capture the essence of the actual performance environments as much as possible (Atencio et al., 2014). In physical education classes, teachers should design tasks and activities where there is representativeness to help students better transfer the learning to other movement contexts and actual performance environments (Chow et al., 2009). For example, in invasion games such as field hockey, a representative activity for maintaining possession could be a modified 3-v-3 or 4-v-3 possession game where students learn to pass the ball to a teammate in a supporting position rather than passing practices where students are stationary. Rules and equipment can be modified to design representative learning contexts that are developmentally appropriate for students in physical education (e.g. depending on the skills, capacities, and experience levels of the students) (Tan, Chow and Davids, 2012). For example, in net games such as volleyball, a modified 3-v-3 game which allows for an additional bounce between volley passes by the same team may be more appropriate for students with lower skill levels, while maintaining the tactical structure of the adult game.

Task Simplification

Closely linked to the principle of representativeness is the principle of task simplification (Chow et al., 2006, 2007). In physical education, providing meaningful representative activities appropriate for students' skill level may require teachers to consider simplifying representative tasks or games for students. Task simplification is a principle that allows students to seek, explore, and maintain information and action relationships in modified tasks/games. In the process of task simplification, physical education teachers should modify tasks/games that still present relevant information and affordances (opportunities or invitations for actions) for the students to perceive and use. It allows students to recognise or become familiar with critical sources of information during practice (e.g. the relative position of teammates or opponents) so they learn to couple appropriate responses.

With practice such as skill practice or game play, a student will increasingly be able to couple the information available in the practice environment to the actions required to achieve a specific task goal; this allows students to form relevant 'information-movement couplings' (Chow et al., 2016; Chow et al., 2013; Renshaw et al., 2016). This has great relevance for designing tasks in physical education. For example, in invasion games such as football, simplified tasks with fewer defenders and/or passive defenders who become increasingly more active as learning increases would allow students to develop relevant information-movement relationships between attackers and defenders. Such task simplifications enable students to practise in a simplified representative environment with all key information sources present, so that students' perceptual and action processes can become appropriately coupled during practice. In the process of task simplification, NLP cautions physical educators on the error of separating information and movement in order to simplify tasks for students; this is known as task decomposition (Davids, Button and Bennett, 2008). For example, in physical education, teaching the run-up separately from an action like long jumping or the tennis serving action separately from the toss are examples of task decomposition. In modified small-sided invasion games where students learn to develop concepts related to maintaining possession of ball, a practice without defenders would be an example of task decomposition. Thus, as designers of practices, you can consider designing tasks and modified games which maintain the functional information-movement couplings of the structured game or practice task such that it is still representative of the actual performance environment.

Exploratory Learning

NLP embraces individual differences and encourages providing students with opportunities to explore and search for movement solutions (Chow et al., 2009). In NLP, it is important to introduce variability during the learning process to provide students with multiple opportunities to explore and search solutions for themselves (Chow and Atencio, 2014; Chow et al., 2011). This is in accordance with Bernstein's (1967) phrase "repetition without repetition", which refers to having students repeat the outcome without necessarily repeating the process to achieve the outcome (Hopper, Butler and Storey, 2009). Thus, unlike the more traditional approach of 'one-size-fits-all' where movement variability is linked to inconsistency or 'noise' and perceived as undesirable and detrimental to performance, variability in practice is viewed as helping the student to explore and find movement solutions that meet the needs of his/her own performer constraints, as well as the specific objectives of the task (e.g. Chow et al., 2013; Chow et al., 2009; Davids, Button and Bennett, 2008; Tan, Chow and Davids, 2012). For example, a student can make refinements and acquire new movements (e.g. kicking for distance or height) through executing a skill in different ways (e.g. kicking a ball with different parts of the foot). Movement variability in practice can also encourage students to adapt their behaviour to different situations. For example, in ball games, variability in practice may be infused by changing the characteristics of the ball (e.g. size, bounce, shape), thereby inviting different solutions to emerge (Lee et al., 2017). An example beyond games, such as in hurdles in athletics, variability within practice can be infused by presenting students with a range of possibilities such as variation in start timing and different distances between hurdles (Atencio et al., 2014). Such movement variability can help students deal with unexpected changes in the performance environment and enhance their flexibility and adaptability to complex dynamic sport environments (Davids, Bennett and Newell, 2006; Davids, Button and Bennett, 2008; Renshaw et al., 2010; Tan, Chow and Davids, 2012). Creating supportive learning environments to encourage movement variability in practice however does not simply mean allowing free play during lessons, but rather through careful manipulation of task constraints (Tan, Chow and Davids, 2012), which is discussed next.

Task Constraints

While there are three key constraints as previously mentioned (i.e. performer, environment, and task), it is task constraints that physical education teachers have most direct control to manipulate (Lee et al., 2017). The manipulation of task constraints, which underlies and supports many of the other pedagogical principles, is a very powerful aspect of NLP in encouraging transitions and acquisition of new preferred stable movement behaviours (Chow, 2013; Davids, Button and Bennett, 2008). For example, creating a representative learning environment or enhancing information-movement coupling through task simplification, as mentioned earlier, requires the well-thought manipulation of task constraints such as equipment, space, number of players, rules, and task goals. In task simplification, for example, the complexity of tasks can be adjusted by manipulating appropriate task constraints to help different students progress, and succeed at different rates. An example in tennis is by shortening racket handles and increasing racket head area.

Task constraints (e.g. changes to instructions, space, player numbers, rules of the activity, playing area, or equipment) are usually manipulated to guide students towards certain movement solutions without the presentation of explicit instructions on how to solve a problem (Chow and Atencio, 2014; Chow et al., 2009; Tan, Chow and Davids, 2012). For example, using balls of different sizes can encourage different throw and catch behaviours in students using one or both hands. In games, task constraints can be manipulated to provide exaggeration without the presentation of explicit instructions on how to solve the tactical problem (Tan, Chow and Davids, 2012); this is similar to the principle of exaggeration highlighted in TGfU earlier. For example, the earlier badminton example of using a long narrow court to exaggerate long and short play in badminton. In invasion games, exaggeration through task manipulation can be in the form of game rules, for example, having a rule which requires players to make minimally five passes between teammates before scoring would challenge students to explore, search, and learn to move into space to create passing options and encourage quick passing among teammates. In practice or game play, having a higher net in badminton can force students to execute overhead clears rather than smashes without providing explicit instructions to do so. Through such exaggeration, students can be provided with more opportunities to search for functional movement solutions within a practice or game scenario. Thus, by manipulating task constraints such as rules of the activity and equipment (e.g. rackets balls, court size), developmentally appropriate tasks can be planned by adjusting the complexity of the task to adequately challenge students to achieve success and encourage them to explore various movements solutions most suitable for themselves.

Attentional Focus

In NLP, verbal information given by you (e.g. instructions, feedback, teaching cues, etc.) is seen as a temporarily imposed information constraint that can result in positive or negative effects on performance (Chow et al., 2009). NLP suggests that such verbal information can focus students' attention on the movement form (also known as internal focus of attention) or movement outcome or effects (referred to as external focus of attention) (Chow, 2013; Peh, Chow and Davids, 2011). Positive effect on performance could be elicited by directing students to focus their attention externally on outcomes of movements rather than on internal control processes (Passos et al., 2008). This is because verbal information that focuses on internal focus of attention are likely to lead to an overly conscious control. This, in turn, can lead to performance disruption and lead to less successful learning (Chow, 2013; Peh, Chow and Davids, 2011). An example of an internal focus of attention on body parts would be to focus on cues such as locked ankles, bent knees, and body lean, in kicking a ball in football. Conversely, instructions that are focused on an external focus of attention seem to reduce conscious and explicit control of movement (Chow, 2013). An external focus on movement effects could be on ball trajectory or targets. For example, students can be tasked to kick a ball over a height barrier such that it lands accurately and comfortably at their partner's feet, without any specific, prescriptive technical instructions on the kicking action.

As NLP suggests, verbal information that focuses on movement outcomes can also account for differences in individual constraints and allow individual students to explore new and different solutions to achieve the same movement outcome (Chow, 2013). As such, you should focus attention on the movement outcome/effect of a movement when presenting verbal information such as instructions, teaching cues, feedback, and even questioning. For example, in football, teaching cues and feedback can be on movement outcomes (e.g. a firm and accurate pass in football) instead of movement forms (e.g. to kick the football at a specific angle by using a specific part of the foot). Analogies can be used effectively as an external attentional focus (Peh, Chow and Davids, 2011). In invasion games, an example of an analogy for teaching the concept of moving into space for a clear line of pass can be asking students to explore and create a 'laser beam' between passer and receiver. This analogy, used with a laser pointer, can be an effective visual tool to help younger students understand better. The 'laser beam' analogy can also be used to teach concepts related to defence, for example, where students are asked to 'cut/block the laser beam' so as to block or prevent a clear line of pass. In net games, for example, in executing a badminton serve, the analogy of a 'rainbow' or 'inverted U' could be given to get students to focus on the flight trajectory rather than cues for how the arms and body should move. As students explore their individualised movement solutions, teachers can facilitate students' learning by asking questions that focus on the task goal (e.g. "can you create a bigger rainbow?", "can you do it in another way?", "can you show it again?" etc.) instead of telling them how to do it. The use of questioning to guide the search process has been considered an important strategy for developing thinking, autonomous performers (Chow et al., 2009).

As facilitators of learning, you may consider providing relevant and meaningful teaching cues, instructions, feedback, analogies, and the like as well as use of questioning to influence student learning by guiding them to focus on movement outcomes rather than movement form. This allows them to find movement solutions that are sensitive and appropriate to their own performer constraints, thus helping students develop greater individual movement competencies.

Case Study of NLP: Theory to Practice

Case study 4.1 illustrates how a physical education teacher, Mishel, applied 'theory to practice' and the impact of the approach on her upper primary students' learning in a unit of invasion games.

Case study 4.1   Applying theory to practice

Mishel, together with a colleague and a Continuing Professional Development (CPD) officer, embarked on an NLP project. It focused on how the pedagogical principles of NLP could be applied in the design and delivery of the tasks/practices in invasion games to enhance students' joy of learning, success, and confidence in game play. Meeting on a weekly basis over five weeks, the process was based on a co-building and co-learning process. It included lesson planning, observations, co-teaching, reflections, and post-lesson discussions. Mishel found the post-lesson discussions, which involved bouncing off ideas with the project team and allowing them to learn from one another, to be one of the most fruitful parts of learning. Assuming the role of learning designers, the team collaborated to apply the NLP pedagogical principles in (re)designing their tasks for the unit on invasion games.

Mishel highlighted some of her key learning, successes, and pedagogical practices in the application of NLP and its pedagogical principles. She shared that she usually started the lessons with exploratory learning, to provide opportunities for her students to discover for themselves the rationale of the 'what', 'why', and 'how' in problem-solving. This allowed her students to better understand and relate to the practice task(s) as they knew what they were practising for. In the application of task constraints, an example of an appropriate manipulation was having the rule of 'no overhead passes' for a small-sided possession game. She observed that this added rule seemed to 'force' the students to look and move into space for passes, without which they were often observed to be just very stationary and relied on high passes. Other appropriate manipulations of task constraints with rules included having a minimum or maximum of five passes before scoring, which resulted in different movement patterns and decisions by the students. As students learned to move into space with passing and scoring, dribbling was introduced next as part of a progression. In her first dribbling lesson, Mishel noticed that her students were very comfortable just passing to score; they did not seem to want to dribble or see the need to do so in the game. However, as the lesson objective was on dribbling, she wanted them to have more dribbling practices. Her initial attempt to 'invite' students to dribble more was to manipulate the task constraint by awarding more points for dribbling to score. This, however, resulted in another situation where only the higher skilled students would dribble to score. The post-lesson discussion surfaced different possible solutions/situations. The team asked themselves, 'what other rules can we add, or what can we do to exaggerate dribbling and to encourage students of various abilities to dribble?' The synergistic discussion resulted in a differential scoring system, termed 'first-time freebie'. Specifically, it offered 3 points for any player scoring for the first time and only 1 point for subsequent scoring by the same player. The goal of the game was to see which team reaches 9 points first. This rule, intended to encourage the better-skilled students to pass to other team members, created more dribbling opportunities for different students. It was observed that different students dribbled more with the manipulation of the scoring system.

For external attentional focus, Mishel used analogies of a laser and a triangle to help her students visualise and apply the concept of 'moving to space'. As she noted, the use of analogies was different to the more traditional repetition of cues such as 'drop shoulder, push off with outside foot for movement form', which she had previously used in her lessons to help her students move to space. The laser beam analogy, done through questioning and feedback, allowed the students to understand quickly the concept of moving into space and moving further from opponents to allow the laser to last longer for a more successful pass. This laser beam analogy was also useful for teaching a defence concept, where the students learned to block/cut the beam as they prevented/intercepted the pass.

Mishel shared that in addition to her personal positive experience of applying the pedagogical principles in her teaching, her observation and her students' positive feedback through student surveys and interviews also supported the useful application of NLP's principles in their learning; many students expressed having fun and achieving personal improvement in their practices and game play. The application of NLP in her learning designs, instructions, and feedback helped her students develop movement competency and better decision-making skills in a challenging, safe, and fun learning environment. She shared that the collaboration has helped her to think deeper about the purpose and intent of task design and shaped how she teaches her students. The reflections and discussions with the team on the application of the pedagogical principles have allowed her to explore more effective ways to teach better.

Using Case study 4.1, complete Task 4.3.

> **Task 4.3 Theory to practice**
>
> - What challenges have you faced when designing tasks to achieve your lesson objectives in teaching invasion games? Consider how you may use/adapt some of the task designs presented earlier to enhance your students' learning.
> - What pedagogical principles can you use and/or how can you apply the pedagogical principles to (re)design tasks to meet the profile of your students?
> - How can you apply the pedagogical principles beyond the teaching of games?

To further enhance your application of NLP and its pedagogical principles, some work in NLP has provided examples of practical activities from different sports commonly taught in physical education (e.g. net-barrier games (tennis), invasion games (netball and basketball), striking and fielding games (cricket) and track and field) to demonstrate how aspects of NLP can be applicable for teachers and students (see Atencio et al., 2014; see Chow et al., 2016).

Research in NLP in Physical Education

In recent years, there has been significant interest and effort to understand and support the application of NLP and its pedagogical principles in teaching and learning in physical education (e.g. Chow et al., 2021; Lee et al., 2014; Lee et al., 2017; Roberts, Newcombe and Davids, 2019) and research has provided support for the pedagogical principles (e.g. Bootsma and van Wieringen, 1990; Chow et al., 2008; Lee et al., 2014; Wulf et al., 2002). Notably, in a study conducted within a school physical education setting to examine how teaching and learning occurs with NLP, Lee et al. (2017) provided insights into the pedagogical principles and learning processes of students. They reported that in the NLP approach which used representative modified games, with emphasis on exploration and problem-solving, autonomy, the freedom to choose (e.g. preferred equipment and playing courts), and less prescription from the teacher as a facilitator, both student and teacher interviews suggested that the NLP approach created a learning environment that facilitated students' perceived competence, autonomy, and enhanced their enjoyment during practice. On the other hand, the interviews from the traditional prescriptive and repetitive approach group (referred to as Linear Pedagogy in the study) indicated that students' perceptions of competence and autonomy were threatened by being told how to perform the 'correct' movement pattern. These students also expressed a lack of enthusiasm with the boring repetitive drills and they wished they had more play time. More recently, Chow (2020) and Lew and Tan (2020) presented findings on the application of NLP in the teaching and learning of fundamental movement skill and invasion games, respectively; they reported similar findings on student learning process (e.g. use of analogies, manipulation of task constraints, variability), skills improvement, and enjoyment through the application of NLP pedagogical principles from interviews with students and teachers.

While GCA/TGfU and NLP have been addressed and discussed separately in this chapter, it should be noted that there has been recent work to discuss the relationship between TGfU and NLP. For example, NLP has been proposed as a theoretical framework to account for how TGfU might work in games teaching (see Chow et al., 2009; see Tan, Chow and Davids, 2012), and similarities and differences between the two approaches have also been discussed (see Renshaw et al., 2016).

SUMMARY AND KEY POINTS

This chapter discussed how GCA/TGfU and NLP and their respective pedagogical principles can be incorporated in physical education to help teachers design learning environments so that students learn to explore, search, and adapt to different practice contexts as they develop problem-solving skills, critical thinking, and autonomy of thought. The two student-centred approaches, together with their pedagogical principles, provide us with insights into why we are doing the things that we do and how we can apply the pedagogical principles to positively impact student learning and development in physical education. This also provides us with good understanding to better adapt to practice contexts, resolve challenging questions, and make relevant and meaningful adjustments to our practice to meet the different needs of students in our specific teaching and learning contexts. Adopting TGfU/GCA and NLP in physical education to enhance learning tasks and practice for students may create a more functional and supportive learning and an intrinsically motivating environment. The approaches are likely to facilitate students' development of problem-solving, decision-making, movement and games skills and enjoyment for all students in the physical education contexts.

Note: A list of further resources to help you take your learning forward is available on the PESTA website: https://academyofsingaporeteachers.moe.edu.sg/pesta/professional-development/book-chapters-by-the-pesta-team

References

Almond, L. (1986) 'Reflecting on themes: A games classification', in R. Thorpe, D. Bunker and L. Almond (eds.) *Rethinking Games Teaching*, Loughborough, England: Loughborough University of Technology, pp. 71-72.

Atencio, M., Chow, J.Y., Tan, W.K.C. and Lee, C.Y.M. (2014) 'Using a complex and nonlinear pedagogical approach to design practical primary physical education lessons', *European Physical Education Review*, 20 (2), 244-263.

Bernstein, N.A. (1967) *The Control and Regulation of Movements*, London: Pergamon Press.

Bootsma, R.J. and van Wieringen, P.C. (1990) 'Timing an attacking forehand drive in table tennis', *Journal of Experimental Psychology: Human Perception and Performance*, 16 (1), 21-29.

Bunker, D. and Thorpe, R. (1982) 'A model for the teaching of games in secondary schools', *Bulletin of Physical Education*, 18 (1), 5-8.

Butler, J. and Robson, C. (2013) 'Enabling constraints: Co-creating situated learning in inventing games', in A. Ovens, T. Hopper and J. Butler (eds.) *Complexity Thinking in Physical Education: Reframing Curriculum, Pedagogy and Research*, Abingdon: Routledge, pp. 107-120.

Butler, J., Griffin, L., Lombardo, B. and Nastasi, R. (2003) *Teaching Games for Understanding in Physical Education and Sport*, Reston, VA: National Association for Sport and Physical Education.

Button, C., Seifert, L., Chow, J.Y., Araujo, D. and Davids, K. (2020) *Dynamics of Skill Acquisition: An Ecological Dynamics Approach*, Champaign, IL: Human Kinetics.

Chow, J.Y. (2013) 'Nonlinear learning underpinning pedagogy: Evidence, challenges, and implications', *Quest*, 65 (4), 469-484.

Chow, J.Y. (2020, November 11) 'Implications of nonlinear pedagogy on teaching and learning', Paper presented at the 2020 Physical and Sports Education Virtual Conference, Singapore.

Chow, J.Y. and Atencio, M. (2014) 'Complex and nonlinear pedagogy and the implications for physical education', *Sport, Education and Society*, 19 (8), 1034-1054.

Chow, J.Y., Davids, K., Button, C. and Rein, R. (2008) 'Dynamics of movement patterning in learning a discrete multiarticular action', *Motor Control*, 12 (3), 219-240.

Chow, J.Y., Davids, K., Button, C. and Renshaw, I. (2016) *Nonlinear Pedagogy in Skill Acquisition: An Introduction*, Abingdon: Routledge.

Chow, J.Y., Davids, K.W., Button, C., Renshaw, I., Shuttleworth, R. and Uehara, L.A. (2009) 'Nonlinear pedagogy: Implications for teaching games for understanding (TGfU)', in T. Hopper, J. Butler and B. Storey (eds.) *TGfU: Simply Good Pedagogy: Understanding a Complex Challenge*, Vancouver: University of British Columbia/Physical and Health Education (PHE) Canada, pp. 131-143.

Chow, J.Y., Davids, K., Button, C., Shuttleworth, R., Renshaw, I. and Araújo, D. (2006) 'Nonlinear pedagogy: A constraints-led framework for understanding emergence of game play and movement skills', *Nonlinear Dynamics, Psychology, and Life Sciences*, 10 (1), 71-103.

Chow, J.Y., Davids, K., Hristovski, R., Araújo, D. and Passos, P. (2011) 'Nonlinear pedagogy: Learning design for self-organizing neurobiological systems', *New Ideas in Psychology*, 29 (2), 189-200.

Chow, J.Y., Davids, K., Shuttleworth, R., Button, C., Renshaw, I. and Araújo, D. (2007) 'From processes to principles: A constraints-led approach to teaching games for understanding (TGFU)', *Review of Educational Research*, 77 (3), 251-278.

Chow, J.Y., Komar, J., Davids, K. and Tan, C.W.K. (2021) 'Nonlinear pedagogy and its implications for practice in the Singapore PE context', *Physical Education and Sport Pedagogy*, 26 (3), 230-241.

Chow, J.Y., Renshaw, I., Button, C., Davids, K. and Tan, C.W.K. (2013) 'Effective learning design for the individual: A nonlinear pedagogy approach in physical education', in A. Ovens, T. Hopper and J. Butler (eds.) *Complexity Thinking in Physical Education: Reframing Curriculum, Pedagogy and Research*, Abingdon: Routledge, pp. 121-134.

Correia, V., Carvalho, J., Araújo, D., Pereira, E. and Davids, K. (2019) 'Principles of nonlinear pedagogy in sport practice', *Physical Education and Sport Pedagogy*, 24 (2), 117-132.

Davids, K., Bennett, S. and Newell, K.M. (2006) *Movement System Variability*, Champaign, IL: Human Kinetics.

Davids, K., Chow, J.Y. and Shuttleworth, R. (2005) 'A constraints-based framework for nonlinear pedagogy in physical education', *Journal of Physical Education New Zealand*, 38 (1), 17-29.

Davids, K.W., Button, C. and Bennett, S.J. (2008) *Dynamics of Skill Acquisition: A Constraints-led Approach*, Champaign, IL: Human Kinetics.

Ellis, M. (1983) 'Similarities and differences in games: A system for classification', Paper presented at the AIESEP conference, Rome, Italy.

Fry, J.M., Tan, C.W.K., McNeill, M. and Wright, S. (2010) 'Children's perspectives on conceptual games teaching: A value-adding experience', *Physical Education and Sport Pedagogy*, 15 (2), 139-158.

Gréhaigne, J.F., Wallian, N. and Godbout, P. (2005) 'Tactical-decision learning model and students' practices', *Physical Education and Sport Pedagogy*, 10 (3), 255-269.

Griffin, L.L., Mitchell, S.A. and Oslin, J.L. (1997) *Teaching Sports Concepts and Skills: A Tactical Games Approach*, Leeds: Human Kinetics Publishers (UK) Ltd.

Harvey, S. and Jarrett, K. (2014) 'A review of the game-centred approaches to teaching and coaching literature since 2006', *Physical Education and Sport Pedagogy*, 19 (3), 278-300.

Hastie, P. and Mesquita, I. (2016) 'Sport-based physical education', in C. Ennis (ed.) *Routledge Handbook of Physical Education Pedagogies*, Abingdon: Routledge, pp. 68-84.

Hopper, T. (2011) 'Game-as-teacher: Modification by adaptation in learning through gameplay', *Asia-Pacific Journal of Health, Sport and Physical Education*, 2 (2), 3-21.

Hopper, T., Butler, J. and Storey, B. (2009) *TGfU… Simply Good Pedagogy: Understanding a Complex Challenge*, Ottawa, Canada: Physical Health Education (PHE) Canada.

Hopper, T., Sanford, K. and Clarke, A. (2009) 'Game-as-teacher and game-play: Complex learning in TGfU and videogames', in T. Hopper, J. Butler and B. Storey (eds.) *TGfU… Simply Good Pedagogy: Understanding a Complex Challenge*, Ottawa, Canada: Physical Health Education (Canada), pp. 201-212.

Jones, R., Marshall, S. and Peters, D.M. (2010) 'Can we play a game now? The intrinsic benefits of TGfU', *European Journal of Physical and Health Education: Social Humanistic Perspective*, 4, 57-64.

Launder, A. and Piltz, W. (2013) *Play Practice: Engaging and Developing Skilled Players from Beginner to Elite* (2nd edn), Champaign, IL: Human Kinetics.

Launder, A.G. (2001) *Play Practice: The Games Approach to Teaching and Coaching Sports*, Champaign, IL: Human Kinetics.

Lee, A.M. (2003) 'How the field evolved', in S.J. Silverman and C.D. Ennis (eds.) *Student Learning in Physical Education: Applying Research to Enhance Instruction*, Champaign, IL: Human Kinetics, pp. 9-25.

Lee, M.C.Y., Chow, J.Y., Button, C. and Tan, C.W.K. (2017) 'Nonlinear pedagogy and its role in encouraging twenty-first century competencies through physical education: A Singapore experience', *Asia Pacific Journal of Education*, 37 (4), 483-499.

Lee, M.C.Y., Chow, J.Y., Komar, J., Tan, C.W.K. and Button, C. (2014) 'Nonlinear pedagogy: An effective approach to cater for individual differences in learning a sports skill', *PloS one*, 9 (8), e104744.

Lew, K.E.M. and Tan, C. (2020, November 11) 'Nonlinear pedagogy: Teaching and learning of invasion games', Paper presented at the 2020 Physical and Sports Education Virtual Conference, Singapore.

Mandigo, J., Holt, N., Anderson, A. and Sheppard, J. (2008) 'Children's motivational experiences following autonomy-supportive games lessons', *European Physical Education Review*, 14 (3), 407-425.

Martin, R.J. (2004) 'An investigation of tactical transfer in invasion/territorial games', *Research Quarterly for Exercise and Sport*, 75 (1), A73-A74.

Mitchell, S.A. and Oslin, J.L. (1999) 'An investigation of tactical transfer in net games', *European Journal of Physical Education*, 4 (2), 162-172.

Mitchell, S.A., Oslin, J.L. and Griffin, L.L. (2003) *Sport Foundations for Elementary Physical Education: A Tactical Games Approach*, Champaign, IL: Human Kinetics.

Mitchell, S.A., Oslin, J.L. and Griffin, L.L. (2006) *Teaching Sport Skills: A Tactical Games Approach*, Champaign, IL: Human Kinetics.

Mitchell, S.A., Oslin, J. and Griffin, L. (2020) *Teaching Sport Concepts and Skills: A Tactical Games Approach*, Champaign, IL: Human Kinetics Publishers.

Newell, K.M. (1986) 'Constraints on the development of coordination', in M.G. Wade and H.T.A. Whiting (eds.) *Motor Development in Children: Aspects of Coordination and Control*, Dordrecht, The Netherlands: Martinus Nijhoff, pp. 341–360.

Newell, K.M. (1996) 'Change in movement and skill: Learning, retention and transfer', in M.L. Latash and M.T. Turvey (eds.) *Dexterity and Its Development*, Mahwah, NJ: Erlbaum, pp. 393–429.

Oslin, J. and Mitchell, S. (2006) 'Game-centered approaches to teaching physical education', in D. Kirk, D. MacDonald and M. O'Sullivan, *The Handbook of Physical Education*, London: Sage pp. 627–651.

Passos, P., Araújo, D., Davids, K., Gouveia, L., Milho, J. and Serpa, S. (2008) 'Information -governing dynamics of attacker – defender interactions in youth rugby union', *Journal of Sports Sciences*, 26 (13), 1421–1429.

Peh, S.Y.C., Chow, J.Y. and Davids, K. (2011) 'Focus of attention and its impact on movement behaviour', *Journal of Science and Medicine in Sport*, 14 (1), 70–78.

Renshaw, I., Araújo, D., Button, C., Chow, J.Y., Davids, K. and Moy, B. (2016) 'Why the constraints-led approach is not teaching games for understanding: A clarification', *Physical Education and Sport Pedagogy*, 21 (5), 459–480.

Renshaw, I., Chow, J.Y., Davids, K. and Hammond, J. (2010) 'A constraints-led perspective to understanding skill acquisition and game play: A basis for integration of motor learning theory and physical education praxis?' *Physical Education and Sport Pedagogy*, 15 (2), 117–137.

Richard, J.F. and Wallian, N. (2005) 'Emphasizing student engagement in the construction of game performance, in, L. Griffin and J. Butler (eds.) *Teaching Games for Understanding: Theory, Research, and Practice*, Champaign, IL: Human Kinetics, pp. 19–32.

Richardson, K.P., Sheehy, D. and Hopper, T. (2013) 'Modification by adaptation: Proposing another pedagogical principle for TGfU', in *Complexity Thinking in Physical Education: Reframing Curriculum, Pedagogy and Research*, Abingdon: Routledge, pp. 181–193.

Roberts, W.M., Newcombe, D.J. and Davids, K. (2019) 'Application of a constraints-led approach to pedagogy in schools: Embarking on a journey to nurture physical literacy in primary physical education', *Physical Education and Sport Pedagogy*, 24 (2), 162–175.

Rovegno, I. and Dolly, J.P. (2006) 'Constructivist perspectives on learning', in D. Kirk, D. MacDonald and M. O'Sullivan (eds.) *The Handbook of Physical Education*, London: Sage, pp. 242–261.

Stolz, S. and Pill, S. (2014) 'Teaching games and sport for understanding: Exploring and reconsidering its relevance in physical education', *European Physical Education Review*, 20 (1), 36–71.

Tan, C.W.K., Chow, J.Y. and Davids, K. (2012) "How does TGfU work?' examining the relationship between learning design in TGfU and a nonlinear pedagogy', *Physical Education and Sport Pedagogy*, 17 (4), 331–348.

Tan, S.K.S., Wright, S.C., McNeill, M.C., Fry, J.M. and Tan, C.W.K. (2002) 'Implementing the games concept approach in Singapore schools: A preliminary report', *REACT*, 21 (1), 77–84

Thorpe, R. and Bunker, D. (1989) 'A changing focus in games education', in L. Almond (ed.) *The Place of Physical Education in Schools*, London: Kogan/Page, pp. 42–71.

Thorpe, R., Bunker, D. and Almond, L. (1984) 'A change in focus for the teaching of games', in M. Pieron and G. Graham (eds.) *Sport Pedagogy* (Olympic Scientific Congress Proceedings), Champaign, IL: Human Kinetics, pp. 163–169.

Thorpe, R., Bunker, D. and Almond, L. (1986) 'Rethinking games teaching', Loughborough: Department of Physical Education and Sports Science, Loughborough University of Technology.

Werner, P., Thorpe, R. and Bunker, D. (1996) 'Teaching games for understanding: Evolution of a model', *Journal of Physical Education, Recreation and Dance*, 67 (1), 28–33.

Wulf, G., McConnel, N., Gärtner, M. and Schwarz, A. (2002) 'Enhancing the learning of sport skills through external-focus feedback', *Journal of Motor Behavior*, 34 (2), 171–182.

5 Identifying and Developing Students' Readiness to Learn

Justin Wakefield and Julia Lawrence

Introduction

Readiness to learn is "a prerequisite to effective learning" (Schindler, 1948, p.301) and "is viewed as the amount of previous learning that can be transferred to new learning" (Jensen, 1969, p.1). Schindler (1948) suggests that readiness is associated with levels of physical, mental, social, and emotional maturity, coupled with the foundations of the learning to take place having been attained. Jensen (1969) supports this premise, identifying that "certain kinds of learning take place more readily at one age than another" (p.1). In many respects you can see this reflected in the curricula on which your teaching is based. However, have you ever considered that following a prescriptive curriculum might actual be a limiting factor in supporting students' progression in learning?

The principles of readiness to learn encourage teachers to consider the most appropriate strategies to support and guide learning. Your role as a teacher is to both instruct and inspire students, enabling them to develop knowledge and skills and provide a platform for future learning. Students' engagement and willingness to learn are key contributors to any teacher achieving an effective and impactful learning environment. Within a physical education lesson this could be determined by, for example, the level of meaningful interactions a student has, time spent on task(s), or on the level of effort that each student applies to the task. Being able to adapt your teaching to take account of the readiness of the students you teach is an important skill if you are to ensure that they remain motivated to engage with the learning process. Failure to do so may result in students who are not ready for the particular learning becoming confused and frustrated. In turn this may result in disengagement, distracted behaviour, and demotivation. But how do you know whether your students are ready to learn, and what the most appropriate strategies are to support students' learning?

This chapter explores how readiness to learn is linked to conditions for learning and how these might be reflected in the characteristics of effective pedagogy and the construction of an effective learning environment that provides a platform for success both inside and outside lessons. It encourages you to consider

DOI: 10.4324/9781003171973-6

how different strategies impact on levels of engagement, and how mindset and motivation can contribute to successful learning and teaching. Throughout this chapter you are encouraged to reflect on your own practice and consider how you could apply the key themes explored to your own teaching.

> **OBJECTIVES**
>
> At the end of this chapter you should be able to:
>
> - understand the concept of readiness to learn
> - identify key characteristics and conditions for successful learning
> - construct impactful learning environments that are grounded in high expectations and aspirations
> - reflect upon and apply evidence-informed practice to your own teaching to enhance students' learning.

Understanding the Concept of Readiness to Learn

Readiness to learn is a concept dating back to Schindler (1948), with further development of the concept by Jensen (1969), Gagne (1972), Rosenshine (2012), and Sherrington (2019). Readiness is not age specific. It is based on the cognitive development of students and their ability to apply previous learning to new contexts. Jensen (1969) suggests that readiness to learn can also be linked to the concept of learning to learn, whereby students develop independent behaviours that allow them to take greater ownership of their own learning and become a learning resource for one another to support each other's learning (Wiliam and Thompson, 2007) (see Table 5.1). More recently, parallels between readiness to learn, learning to learn, metacognition, and self-regulated learning (Muijs and Bokhove, 2020; Quigley, Muijs and Stringer, 2018) have become established.

Whilst you might be beginning to develop an understanding of what readiness to learn is, Task 5.1 asks you to consider what factors might impact on a student's readiness to learn.

> **Task 5.1 Factors affecting students' readiness to learn**
>
> Reflecting on your own learning journey consider the following:
>
> - What factors impacted on your ability to learn?
> - When did you find some learning easy?
> - Why did you find this learning easy?
> - What made some learning difficult?
> - When you found learning difficult what made you keep going?

Table 5.1 Independent behaviours supporting learning

Behaviour	Example in Physical Education
Cognitive "the mental process involved in knowing, understanding, and learning" (Quigley, Muijs and Stringer, 2018, p.9)	A student identifies how to improve their technique, deconstructing a skill into smaller segments they can refine and improve through deliberate practice, for example, **Badminton** smash ■ **Preparation** ☐ Assessing the flight of the shuttle (body behind and in line with the shuttle) ☐ Moving body into the correct position (sideways) ☐ Racquet high ☐ Flexible and fluid grip ■ **Execution** ☐ Play the shot quickly ☐ Connect with the shuttle at the highest point (before it starts to drop) ☐ Whipping action of racquet (starting high, finishing low) ■ **Result and reflection** ☐ How did the shot feel? ☐ How accurate was the shot (did it go to its intended target)? ☐ Could a better action be performed? If so why/how? Based on this feedback, students work in pairs to enable the student to practise an aspect(s) of 'preparation' or 'execution', for example, **Focus of development:** 'grip and racquet action' ■ Partner plays a 'passive' feed ■ The student practising/developing their skill tries to execute the smash repeatedly, with target zones to aim for.
Social (working with others)	Student provides clear and well-structured feedback to a peer(s) on an area of development, so that they/the team can further improve, for example, **Rugby Union** safeguarding possession A student(s) is assigned a role of 'scout' The scout (peer) notices that the team are successfully performing a high percentage of 'rucks' but are poor at 'clearing out of the line' and handling which results in the opposition gaining an advantage by moving closer to their opponent's try line. The scout identifies that a kick to touch temporarily relieves pressure on the defence and moves the kicking team closer to the opposition's try line.
Emotional (management of own feelings)	During invasion games, a student acknowledges an official's decision, accepts the decision (regardless of whether or not they agree with it) and diffuses any conflict from teammates, as they understand the impact this will have on the team, for example, **Basketball** technical foul The 'coach' (a peer) identifies that any challenge towards an official will result in a technical foul being awarded, reducing the number of players on the court.

Behaviour	Example in Physical Education
Motivation "willingness to engage" (Quigley, Muijs and Stringer, 2018, p.9)	A student reflects whilst performing required learning tasks. They recognise the worth of applying effort into practices to achieve longer term gains, for example, **Handball** footwork/movement that creates opportunities *The student playing the role of 'circle runner' (pivot) regularly practises footwork and movement skills in isolation over a number of scenarios with increased pressure and difficulty. This builds up their portfolio of skill, meaning they can react and adapt quickly within a competitive game situation. The player recognises the merit for their team and their own individual development.*

Having reflected on your own learning journey, you can start to identify some of the factors that helped you to learn and reasons why you may not have learned. For example, you might have learned best when you paid full attention and were interested in the activity you were learning; you might have seen the effort you were putting in being rewarded by the progress you made; or you could have continued to persist in the activity even though you found it challenging because you knew you needed to complete it to move onto the next step. In essence, you were showing characteristics such as attention, effort, resilience, and self-direction. These are all associated with readiness to learn which in its simplest form means how well equipped the individual is to cope with processes and apply knowledge at a particular moment in time. Other factors that may affect this may include, for example, home life, the students' interest in the subject, the lesson before and peer relationships. However, your role as a teacher is to provide effective provision from the moment that each student enters your lesson, that is, the point of entry into the changing room/working space.

So how can students' readiness to learn be improved?

A starting point is perhaps to consider what conditions for effective learning are.

Conditions for Effective Learning

Figure 5.1 provides an overview of three key conditions for effective learning and associated questions for you to consider when planning and teaching your lessons. Three core aspects of the lesson – **engagement**, **delivery**, and **assessment** – are based on the work of Gagne (1985), which focuses on how theory of instruction is linked to conditions for learning.

This work has been more recently developed through the work of Rosenshine (2012) who identified principles of instruction (see Table 5.2 and Lawrence (2021, pp.161–162), for a more detailed explanation). Central to the process is that in designing, managing, and evaluating learning, conditions must be

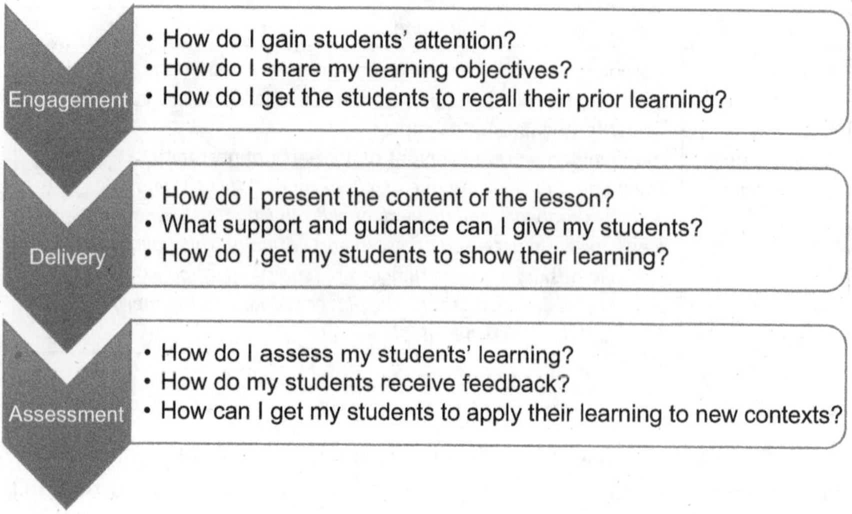

Engagement
- How do I gain students' attention?
- How do I share my learning objectives?
- How do I get the students to recall their prior learning?

Delivery
- How do I present the content of the lesson?
- What support and guidance can I give my students?
- How do I get my students to show their learning?

Assessment
- How do I assess my students' learning?
- How do my students receive feedback?
- How can I get my students to apply their learning to new contexts?

Figure 5.1 Conditions for learning

Source: Adapted from Bates (2016)

Table 5.2 Rosenshine's (2012) principles of instruction

Principle of Instruction	Physical Education Example: Basketball Lay-Up
Perform Daily Review	At the start of each basketball lesson students practise shooting as part of their warm up routine, for example, ■ Set/jump shot and rebound ■ *Uncontested* (with no pressure from another student) ■ *Contested* (pressure from a student) ■ Open lay-up ■ *Left hand* ■ *Right hand* ■ Reverse lay-up ■ *Left hand* ■ *Right hand* ■ Perimeter shooting ■ *Left of 'key'* ■ *Centre of 'key'* ■ *Right of 'key'*

Present New Material Using Small Steps	The skill (lay-up) can be broken down into smaller steps practised in isolation before combining them together:
	
	■ **Approach** (dribble into the key)
	   ■ *Drive towards the basket from a wide position*
	   ■ *Dribble and hold the ball (with two hands)*
	■ **Footwork**
	   ■ *No more than two steps once ball held*
	   ■ *Stride towards the basket*
	■ **Jump**

Principle of Instruction	Physical Education Example: Basketball Lay-Up
	■ **Jump** 　■ *Ball raised high (above head upon the start of the jump)* 　■ *Maximum height on jump, inside leg raised (to guard body/ball)* ■ **Action** 　■ *Aiming to place the ball in the top corner of the backboard (smaller rectangle above hoop)* 　■ *Pushing and flicking of arm and wrist* 　■ *Ball released at its highest point* ■ **Rebound** (if required) 　■ *Land* 　■ *Keep eye contact on the ball* 　■ *Jump (maximum height) with both arms raised* 　■ *Retrieve the ball at its highest point.*
Provide Scaffolds for Difficult Tasks	The skill of a lay-up is broken down into smaller steps. The instructions for each step are simple to understand and may include visual guidance. The teacher also provides developmental feedback during the learning process. For example, guidance sheets are issued to support instruction with visual images to model technique. ■ *Approach* ■ *Footwork* ■ *Jump* ■ *Action* ■ *Rebound* Example questions: ■ *Which part of the process do you think you could develop further? How can you overcome this challenge?* ■ *You are releasing the ball too low; remind me what height you release the ball and why this is important?*
Obtain a High Success Rate	The teacher does not set tasks that are too challenging, especially during early skill development and learning rehearsal. The lay-up practice is modified to focus on a step-by-step approach to mastering the skill. Feedback and praise is given by the teacher often, for example, the skill practice has an associated points system: ■ *Approach* +1 point ■ *Footwork* + 2 points ■ *Jump* + 3 points ■ *Action* + 4 points ■ *Full action* performed with no errors + 5 points (must be peer reviewed)
Ask Questions	Intrinsic and extrinsic feedback gained through instruction, circulation, monitoring, and questioning of the group. ■ *How did that feel?* ■ *Could you have improved on that?* ■ *Why was your lay-up successful?* ■ *Would you change any part of your technique? If so, why?*

(Continued)

Table 5.2 (Continued)

Principle of Instruction	Physical Education Example: Basketball Lay-Up
Provide Models	The teacher provides verbal instruction, a visual model, and supportive materials (checklists for skill rehearsal).
Guide Student Practice	Concurrent (whilst the student is doing the action/skill) and terminal (once the movement has been completed) feedback is provided by the teacher during practice, for example, - Why was your lay-up not as successful? - How could you improve next time? - If you were to adjust your starting approach, do you think this would help?
Check for Student Understanding	The teacher is inquisitive and checks for understanding regularly. This could be undertaken through, for example, group circulation, group voting system (thumbs up, thumbs down), 1-1 feedback or questioning, for example, - What are you required to do for this task? - What are the benefits of performing a lay-up? - Why is raising your leg (in the jump phase) important? - How might angle of release affect the shot's outcome?
Independent Practice	Students are given time to rehearse in unpressurised environments. Lay-up tasks are practised in isolation with opportunities to regularly reflect on their ability to perform the skill (based on feedback). Learning aids may be used to assist with this, for example, **Dedicated Improvement and Reflection Time** (DIRT) Working in pairs - *Student A: Assesses Student B (scaffold sheet if required)* - *Student B: Performs a lay-up* - *Student A: Provides feedback to Student B* - *Process repeats with reverse roles* - *Student A and B practise independently (based on feedback gained)* - *Process repeats*
Weekly and Monthly Review	Structure lay-up practices as part of a selection of skills reviewed during ongoing teacher assessments within the unit of work. The data gained from this can be used to compare and track progress which could improve student motivation.

managed to "support pupils to maximise their working memory" (Quigley, Muijs and Stringer, 2018, p.19).

(See Chapter 11 for digital technologies which can support teachers' efforts in enacting the principles of instruction identified in Table 5.2).

Case study 5.1 Managing learning conditions to develop readiness to learn

Daisy (the teacher) had observed that the progress of each student in a class of 26 13-year-old students was not maximised. Students seemed capable of identifying the learning objective the class were aiming for, but not their own area of development. It was apparent the class had limited transfer of their previous learning, inhibiting the acquisition of new skill(s) and overall progress.

Following Rosenshine's (2012) principles, Daisy restructured the learning approach placing greater emphasis on the use of independent practice that incorporated daily review and questioning. Daisy routinely referenced previous learning, skill acquisition, and supported students to develop improvement strategies (providing less teacher involvement as time passed). Over the next 12 lessons, student engagement improved and self- and peer reflections became more detailed and useful. Feedback had more depth and regular rehearsal improved students' learning of skills. When questioned, students were able to discuss what had gone well, what they needed to improve upon in future practice and appeared more resilient when difficulty of learning tasks increased.

This case study highlights how the management of learning can yield significant student development. A simple shift in emphasis and routine structure enabled students to develop skills to achieve better progress and become more ready to learn. Considering this, Task 5.2 asks you to reflect on how you might embed conditions for learning and Rosenshine's (2012) principles of instruction to your own teaching.

Task 5.2 Embedding conditions for learning and principles of instruction in my own teaching

Using an area of activity that you are about to teach, review your planning to identify:

1 What strategies will you use to engage your students?
2 How will you teach your lessons to ensure that there are opportunities for students to show their learning?
3 How will you work with your students to review the learning that has taken place and plan the next steps in their learning?

Having given some consideration to the conditions for learning, the next section focuses on how these can be embedded in the learning environments you create, to allow students to feel confident and ready to learn.

Characteristics of Effective Learning Environments

Your ability as a teacher to deconstruct and connect learning materials is critical to enable students to achieve sustained learning. The development of impactful learning environments is therefore a significant part of effective teaching and learning.

Figure 5.2 provides an overview of important characteristics that may help construct meaningful and progress-driven learning environments. As a teacher you should reflect on these areas when planning and sequencing learning.

These characteristics are now considered in more detail.

High Expectations and Learning Routines

When constructing and planning for highly impactful lessons, time should be taken during planning, and embedded within lessons, to frame your expectations, routines, and non-negotiables. Simplicity, associated importance and consistency of teacher input (for content and expected behaviours) result in sustained progress over time. But why do they matter so much and how can they be used to prepare your students' readiness to learn?

Rosenthal and Babad (1985) stated, "When we expect certain behaviors of others, we are likely to act in ways that make the expected behavior more likely to occur" (p. 36). Rosenthal and Jacobson (1968) and Bennett (2017) conclude that progress and learning habits can become established if the teacher places significance on specific values and traits within the learning environment. Thus

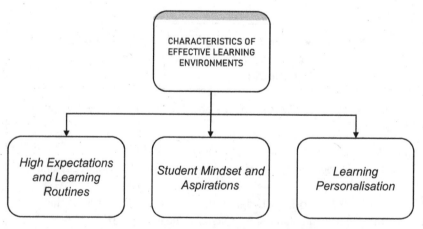

Figure 5.2 Characteristics of effective learning environments

by promoting and embodying high expectations you are encouraging students to develop and demonstrate independent behaviours, as introduced earlier in the chapter.

Effective learning environments also aid the successful retention of information by students. Table 5.1 identified that developing cognitive behaviours was a key aspect of readiness to learn. To support this, Cognitive Load Theory (Atkinson and Shiffrin, 1968) proposes that humans have limited short-term working memory capacity, and an unlimited long-term memory capable of building 'schema' (mental representations of the world). It is important not to overload the working memory as this may result in students becoming frustrated that they do not understand or cannot achieve a task. As such they are not 'ready' to learn. Therefore, when introducing your expectations to students, connect the language you use to actions, and to students personally, so that they can visualise and interpret what these expectations mean for their learning. Explicit instruction and guidance assists you in providing clear, concise expectations that are embraced and understood by all. Figures 5.3 and 5.4 provide examples of this.

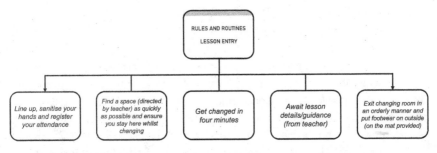

Figure 5.3 Rules and routines

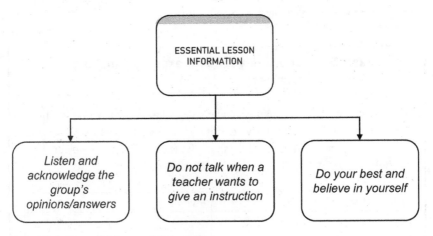

Figure 5.4 Essential lesson information

> **Case study 5.2 Creating learning routines to develop student engagement**
>
> Teacher Helen regularly reflects and annotates her lesson plans following a lesson. She noted that for one group of 32 11-year-old students, progress was limited and this group had a relatively high level of behaviour incidents. The majority of behaviour incidents were low level and occurred predominantly at the start and end of lessons (whilst students were changing into and out of their physical education kit). As part of her lesson's routine, Helen started to include a PowerPoint (displayed on an interactive white board) that used icons to display behaviours she expected, together with a lesson summary (previous lesson) and learning objective (for that lesson). Hard copies of these were also placed in and around the changing facilities and space(s) used for her physical education lessons. Over time, engagement increased and behaviour incidents reduced. Students stated they understood learning expectations and that the teacher reminded them of lesson standards through visual cues (interactive white board and posters). They also described how the teacher had used icons in their discussions and demonstrations, and that this, and regular reminders of what they had already learned, helped them improve.

Case study 5.2 and Figures 5.3 and 5.4 provide practical examples that demonstrate how clarity of instruction develops readiness to learn by minimising the likelihood of cognitive overload occurring through the use of visual aids to clarify instructions. This is supported by Cavigioli (2019) who suggests that they can be very powerful in conveying a message to the class you teach. They should be simple and well thought out instructions that set a benchmark for what you expect in your lessons, as discussed in Case study 5.2, to ensure that learning is timely, focused, and impactful. Task 5.3 asks you to use Figures 5.3 and 5.4 to start creating your own expectations and routines.

> **Task 5.3 Creating your own expectations and routines**
>
> Maintaining student engagement in lessons is key to supporting learning. For a class you teach regularly, identify your expectations for that class, and what routines you have established (list these using the following proforma), then reflect on these using the questions.
>
> | Expectations | Routines |
> | --- | --- |
> | | |

> **Reflection**
> - How did you share these expectations and routines with your class?
> - How did you work with students to co-create these?
> - How effective are they? Is there anything you should change?

Whilst establishing high expectations and routines creates clear guidance around expected behaviour to support learning, it is also important to consider the readiness of students themselves to learn, in relation to how they think about learning (their mindset), what they value and are looking to achieve (aspirations).

Student Aspiration and Mindset

A student's readiness to learn can be affected by their aspirations, which may be reflected in their work ethic or mindset. As a teacher, you should attempt to develop a learning environment that raises both aspiration and attainment. The learning environment must encourage students to not only reflect on their achievements, but also on errors and failures that occur during the process of learning. This has the potential to support the student to identify areas for development and how this might be addressed, resulting in the student becoming successful. However, one potential barrier to engagement, application, and achievement may well be how the student thinks about and believes in themselves. Therefore, when developing students' readiness to learn, you must seek to develop their ability to become self-directed and intrinsically motivated (Jensen, 1969).

Whilst theories around motivation are not new (see, for example, Ames's (1992) self-determination theory), over recent years, the application of Mindset theory has become more prevalent. Dweck (2006) argues that what you believe you are able to do has a significant impact on how you engage in the learning. The work of Mueller and Dweck (1998) identify two different (and opposing) mindsets evident in individuals; a growth mindset, which is grounded in the belief that ability is something that can be developed, in contrast to a fixed mindset, which is grounded in the belief that talent and ability are unchangeable traits. In relation to readiness to learn, students with a fixed mindset may be perceived as less ready to learn than those with a growth mindset due to their approach to learning. Figure 5.5 highlights some key differences and traits for both mindsets you may encounter when introducing new learning to students.

As a teacher, you should seek to get students to move towards a growth mindset so that learning is maximised due to these students wanting to gain feedback and continually improve. However, changing students' mindset and beliefs can be difficult. Growth mindset is not merely about the continual, routine praise for students' effort regardless of outcome. Attainment and progress gaps need to be narrowed. Table 5.3 provides some examples of how you can enrich your lesson and students with a more ambitious and positive growth mindset.

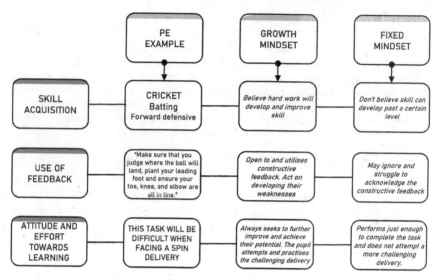

Figure 5.5 Some possible differences in approach and application during learning, based on student mindset

Source: Adapted from Smith (2020)

Table 5.3 Strategies that can be used to support the development of a growth mindset

Area	Explanation	Example in Physical Education
Language for Learning	Choose words that encourage, routinely challenge, and develop resilience. Encourage persistent engagement by stating, "you haven't fully mastered this skill **yet**", opposed to, "you haven't achieved this skill". A change of emphasis affects the connotations on delivery.	**Tennis** **Teacher feedback:** "Fantastic shot. You got into the 'check step' quickly, assessed where the ball would land, and played a forehand groundstroke with direction." Teacher then asks, "how do you think you can make that shot even more difficult for your opponent to return?"
Learning Approach	Make regular connections to prior and future learning, showing the student the purpose of content and drive towards achieving and surpassing the intended outcomes.	**Basketball** ■ In a lesson you may be focusing on 'shooting' but make links to the assessment criteria and other skills/strategies that help students develop further. (See Chapter 7 that looks in more detail at assessment in physical education.) Such as ■ discussing how this skill combines with the previous 'passing lesson'

Area	Explanation	Example in Physical Education
		■ discussing how practising a '3 player weave' and analysing the game/selecting relevant strategy result in the player and team being more unpredictable and harder to penetrate. Even if some of the learning phases have not been covered, it helps students connect what they are practising currently to something they will in the future.
Use of Feedback (Teacher and Student)	Welcome and encourage the use of feedback often. Discuss the importance of using this feedback to make the next steps in learning (strategy).	When circulating around a group observing students performing skills in isolation, ask questions such as ■ 'how does this feel?' ■ 'how can you develop accuracy when you are performing the skill?' ■ 'why do you think you played that shot so successfully?' ■ 'when you played that shot, it landed off court, why do you think that happened? What can you do to keep on improving?'

By implementing and routinely reflecting on the teaching strategies you adopt, you should soon form highly effective learning environments that strengthen meaningful teacher-student working relationships and impact students' learning. If students understand that skill mastery comprises regular practice, review, and further practice, they know that learning can be challenging but they are supported to work through these challenges (by the teacher and how their learning is structured) and scaffolded and they develop their readiness to learn.

Changing student beliefs and developing a growth mindset to learning is a big step in achieving effective readiness to learn, but these beliefs need to be mirrored and embodied by the teacher themselves. Research by Rattan, Good, and Dweck (2012) highlights how growth mindset teachers utilise more strategy-focused approaches, explaining how learning will be supported and the types of tasks that are to be practised (to improve). This strategy-based practice of providing clear instruction of what learning needs to happen and how this will be structured, alongside the maintenance of a growth mindset, could support further student progress through sustained guidance and practice. Figure 5.6 provides a practical example of how you may structure strategy feedback within your teaching.

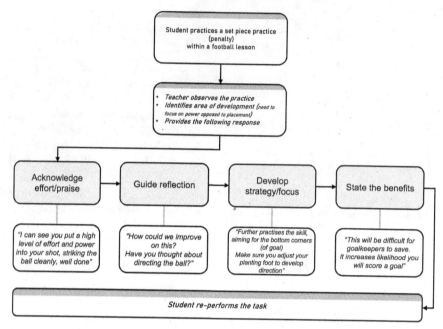

Figure 5.6 Structuring strategy-based feedback

Task 5.4 asks you to consider what you have read and apply it to some of your recent planning.

> **Task 5.4   Developing a growth mindset culture**
>
> Review and reflect on the research of Mueller and Dweck (1998) on growth mindset. Then, annotate a lesson plan that you have taught using the three following points.
>   Could you develop and improve the:
>
> ■ Language for learning
> ■ Learning approach
> ■ Use of feedback
>
> so that growth mindset is improved within your learning environment.

Learning Personalisation

This condition of learning is comprised of the following components:

■ Stretch and challenge
■ Self-regulation and metacognition
■ Retrieval

Stretch and Challenge

Repeatedly developing and broadening the learning of students is vital for successful outcomes. Lessons should be planned to enable many opportunities for students to be 'stretched' and 'challenged', leading to wider progress and impact. But what does 'stretch' and 'challenge' mean? Table 5.4 identifies words you could use to define both key terms.

When looking to stretch and challenge students' boundaries, you should try to structure and build practices and tasks to operate within the 'zone of proximal development' (ZPD). This is defined as "the distance between the actual developmental level as determined by independent problem solving and the level of potential development as determined through problem-solving under adult guidance, or in collaboration with more capable peers" (Vygotsky, 1978, p. 86). Simply, you need to ensure that the pitch of the lesson/task(s) is not too comfortable nor too difficult (resulting in a sustained lack of success).

However, when working to stretch and challenge your students, it is important that you introduce the right level of scaffolding to support their learning. Scaffolding can be defined as the "role of teachers and others in supporting the learner's development and providing support structures to get to that next stage or level" (Raymond, 2000, p. 176). Without adequate support, some students' engagement, confidence, and readiness to learn may suffer. Task 5.5 asks you to consider how you might apply stretch and challenge in your own teaching.

 Task 5.5   Planning for stretch and challenge

Ask another teacher to observe one of your lessons, with a specific focus on stretch and challenge. Once you have taught the lesson, gain the views of students within the group about whether they felt that they were sufficiently stretched and challenged. This could be performed by doing a straw poll (thumbs up, thumbs down, red, amber, green (traffic lights). (Chapter 11 also offers you digital alternatives to do this during/post lesson.) Use this knowledge to inform future planning for the class, and for individual students, especially when designing the level of stretch and challenge pitch of the lesson.

Activity	Possible Learning Challenges

Table 5.4 Key terminology associated with stretch and challenge

Term	Definitions
Stretch	■ Extending ability ■ Developing knowledge/skills ■ Driving progression ■ Improving capability ■ Surpassing expectations
Challenge	■ Demanding more ■ Testing one's ability and determination ■ Exciting activity ■ Inspiring, enthusing, and motivating to succeed

Self-Regulation and Metacognition

One approach that may achieve an appropriate level of challenge whilst fostering sufficient scaffolding is the use of metacognition and self-regulated learning. Muijs and Bokhove (2020) define the terms as follows:

Term	Definition
Self-Regulation	"self-regulation is about the extent to which learners are aware of their strengths and weaknesses, the strategies they use to learn, can motivate themselves to engage in learning, and can develop strategies and tactics to enhance learning" (p. 5)
Metacognition	"the ways learners can monitor and purposefully direct their learning, for example, by deciding that a particular strategy for memorisation is likely to be successful, monitor whether it has indeed been successful, and then deliberately change (or not change) their memorisation method based on that evidence" (p. 5)

For students to be ready to learn, they must be able to take ownership of their learning, knowing coping strategies for when they become 'stuck'. Learning can be improved if metacognitive skills are developed (Nietfeld and Shraw, 2002, Thiede, Anderson and Therriault, 2003). Without adequate support, some students' engagement, confidence, and readiness to learn may suffer. The work of Fogarty (1994) and Muijs and Bokhove (2020) advises that teachers can develop such opportunities within their lessons by teaching and supporting the planning, monitoring, and evaluation of the learning sequence, setting an appropriate level of challenge to develop students' self-regulation and metacognition, promoting and developing metacognitive talk in the lesson, and explicitly teaching students how to organise and effectively manage their learning independently.

One possible way of achieving this could be to use 'Lead Learners' in lessons. In short, the main objective for a Lead Learner is to support the teacher to develop learning within the lesson. These students are selected based on their readiness

Table 5.5 How Lead Learners can support learning

Lead Learner Responsibilities		
Role	Description	Skills and Qualities Developed
Scout	Responsible for identifying learning/achievement within the group and evaluating where improvements can be made.	■ Communication ■ Observation ■ Reflection ■ Analysis ■ Evaluation ■ Leadership
Coach	Responsible for assisting with practices, game-based strategy and leading the development of the group.	
Official	Responsible for officiating games and helping other students develop their knowledge and understanding of the rules.	
Feedback Finder	Responsible for questioning the group, gathering group opinions and feeding this back to the teacher.	

to learn and then supported to make further progress. Their role within a lesson can take many forms, depending on the individual student. Table 5.5 highlights possible learning support roles that a Lead Learner can undertake in a lesson.

Task 5.6 looks at developing metacognition in your lessons.

Task 5.6 Supporting metacognition in your lessons

Using the example question listed as a guide, consider metacognitive questions you could use in your lessons.

Stage	Example Question	Your Example
Plan	■ What is the best way to approach this task?	
Monitor	■ How is the task going? What parts of your approach are most effective?	
Evaluate	■ How could you improve your work next time?	

Retrieval

In the pursuit of learning and development through regular practice, lessons should regularly provide opportunities for students to recall prior learning and apply it within another lesson. To develop and successfully implement self-regulation within your learning environment, as discussed earlier within the chapter, adopting Rosenshine's principles of instruction (2012) and embedding distributed, retrieval practices, provides sufficient opportunities for students to consolidate and progress their learning. Cepeda et al. (2008) among others, also advocate the use of distributed and retrieval practice to support learning development. Such practices allow students to trigger their prior knowledge, manage cognitive load, and increase both their motivation and working memory. Table 5.5 shows how retrieval practices might be applied to a physical education context.

Table 5.6 Examples of retrieval practices within physical education

Retrieval Examples in Physical Education			
Activity	Learning Activity	Benefit	Example Questions
Athletics Field Event: Jumps	Lessons begin with four low-stakes questions requiring active recall from memory. The questions are based on knowledge over time (e.g. asking two questions from previous topics and two from the most recent topic).	Instant feedback is provided which can be used to inform the explicit teaching of a concept or process before moving on or planning for future lessons.	(During discussion) ■ Why is the 'run up' important for a jump? ■ What phases are involved in triple jump? ■ How might an athlete be disqualified in Long Jump/Triple Jump/High Jump? ■ List two learning points required for the long jump ■ What rules are associated with this activity? ■ How can you apply Newton's laws of motion?
Netball	Students are given five minutes to discuss/list on a whiteboard everything they can remember about a topic or concept.	Once the time is up, instant feedback can be given through peer discussion. This forms the basis of a re-review of learning (re-questioning students before the lesson ends).	■ Teacher highlights key information through discussion ■ X student has stated 'pivot' – can we expand on this any further? ■ I can see X student has listed 'chest pass' – is this an important skill? Why? How might you coach this skill? ■ Some positions have been listed. Can you plot which zones they operate within and key roles and responsibilities for each position?

Case study 5.3 Managing the characteristics of effective learning environments to enhance students' learning within examination physical education

Jenson (teacher) has responsibility for examination physical education for 25 16-year-old students. When completing their first end-of-term assessment that included all exam specification content currently taught, he found that students were not able to access higher level marks (6–8 marks), with students generally achieving a maximum of 3 marks. He concluded that students could not structure their answers adequately and did not always use correct terminology nor link to other examination syllabus content. To address this problem of underachievement, Jenson refined his lesson delivery to include more metacognition, retrieval, and self-regulation opportunities. Jenson assigned aspirational target grades and repeatedly reinforced his belief that each student would achieve. Students were given a wealth of support that consisted of explicit instructions on approach to study, what a typical exam paper consists of, the style of questions, subject verb responses, statistical analysis of exam papers (linked to exam specification) shown how to structure 6–8 mark answers (which linked to the English department's extended writing structure), and regularly revised the many areas of the exam specification (a five question quiz) every lesson.

Students' progress increased significantly with their final grades showing a 30%+ rise on the previous years' cohort. Students reported an increased level of confidence and motivation when completing tasks. They felt well equipped to guide their own learning (with minimal teacher input), ready to learn, and could approach tasks with a reduced fear of failure.

It is clear within Case study 5.3 that the structure of the learning environment provided effective conditions for learning to take place. Fostering a growth mindset (through implementation of aspirational target grades and approach) and established routines that regularly reinforce and connect student learning (through regular metacognitive, self-regulated, retrieval practices) resulted in a significant rise in student progress. By diagnosing shortfalls in student learning and skilfully managing the learning conditions and environment, students' readiness to learn was successfully developed.

SUMMARY AND KEY POINTS

The aim of this chapter was to try and develop your knowledge and understanding of the concept of readiness to learn. In order to help you explore key contributing factors that affect successful learning and teaching, the chapter has explored factors impacting on readiness to learn as well as some of the key conditions for learning that can be embedded within your lesson planning and delivery. During this journey you have looked at what high-functioning learning environments possess, specifically focusing on expectations, routines, mindset, aspirations, and scaffolding learning. Having read the chapter you should now have developed an understanding that:

- Readiness to learn has many elements that act as a conduit for successful learning. Independent behaviours and the conditions for learning help shape effective learning environments.
- Teachers should seek to develop student mindset and aspirations. Encouraging a growth mindset can result in students becoming more self-directed and intrinsically motivated due to their approaches to task and value placed on feedback.
- Personalising learning helps create impactful learning environments. Promoting the use of regular learning routines, such as retrieval, metacognition, and self-regulated approaches to learning, helps develop students' readiness to learn, allowing for greater depth, understanding, and the embedding of learning.

Note: A list of further resources to help you take your learning forward is available on the PESTA website: https://academyofsingaporeteachers.moe.edu.sg/pesta/professional-development/book-chapters-by-the-pesta-team

References

Ames, C. (1992) 'Classrooms: Goals, structures, and student motivation', *Journal of Educational Psychology*, 84, 261-271.

Atkinson, R. and Shiffrin, R. (1968) 'Human memory: A proposed system and its control processes', in K. Spence and J. Spence (eds.) *The Psychology of Learning and Motivation*, Vol. 2. New York: Academic Press, pp. 89-195.

Bates, B. (2016) *Learning Theories Simplified*, London: Sage.

Bennett, T. (2017) *Creating a Culture: How School Leaders Can Optimise Behaviour, Independent Review of Behaviour in Schools*, London: Crown, viewed 2 May 2021, www.gov.uk/government/uploads/system/uploads/attachment_data/file/602487/Tom_Bennett_Independent_Review_of_Behaviour_in_Schools.pdf

Cavigioli, O. (2019) *Dual Coding with Teachers*, Woodbridge: John Catt Educational Ltd.

Cepeda, N.J., Vul, E., Rohrer, D., Wixted, J.T. and Pashler, H. (2008) 'Spacing effects in learning a temporal ridgeline of optimal retention', *Psychological Science*, 19 (11), 1095-1102.

Dweck, C.S. (2006) *Mindset*, New York: Random House.

Fogarty, R. (1994) *How to Teach for Metacognition*, Palatine, IL: IRI/Skylight Publishing.

Gagne, R.M. (1972) 'Domains of learning', *Interchange*, 3, 1-8.

Gagne, R.M. (1985) *The Conditions of Learning and Theory of Instruction* (4th edn), New York: Holt, Rinehart and Winston.

Jensen, A.R. (1969) 'How much can we boost IQ and scholastic achievement?' *Harvard Educational Review*, 39 (1), 1–123.

Lawrence, J. (2021) 'Creating an effective learning environment', in S. Capel, J. Cliffe and J. Lawrence (eds.) *A Practical Guide to Teaching Physical Education in the Secondary School* (3rd edn), Abingdon: Routledge, pp. 160–173.

Mueller, C.M. and Dweck, C.S. (1998) 'Praise for intelligence can undermine children's motivation and performance', *Journal of Personality and Social Psychology*, 75 (1) 33–52.

Muijs, D. and Bokhove, C. (2020) *Metacognition and Self-regulation: Evidence Review*, London: Education Endowment Foundation, viewed 2 May 2021, https://educationendowmentfoundation.org.uk/public/files/Metacognition_and_self-regulation_review.pdf

Nietfeld, J.L. and Shraw, G. (2002) 'The effect of knowledge and strategy explanation on monitoring accuracy', *Journal of Educational Research*, 95, 131–142.

Quigley, A., Muijs, D. and Stringer, E. (2018) *Metacognition and Self-regulated Learning: Guidance Report*, London: Education Endowment Foundation, viewed 2 May 2021, https://educationendowmentfoundation.org.uk/tools/guidance-reports/metacognition-and-self-regulated-learning/

Rattan, A., Good, C. and Dweck, C.S. (2012) ' "It's ok – Not everyone can be good at math": Instructors with an entity theory comfort (and demotivate) students', *Journal of Experimental Social Psychology*, 48 (3), 731–737.

Raymond, E. (2000) *Cognitive Characteristics: Learners with Mild Disabilities*, Needham Heights, MA: Allyn & Bacon, pp. 169-201.

Rosenshine, B. (2012) 'Principles of instruction: Research-based strategies that all teachers should know', *American Educator*, 36 (1), 12–20.

Rosenthal, R. and Babad, E.Y (1985) 'Pygmalion in the gymnasium', *Educational Leadership*, 43 (1), 36–39.

Rosenthal, R. and Jacobson, L. (1968) 'Pygmalion in the classroom', *Urban Review* 3, 16–20.

Schindler, A.W. (1948) 'Readiness for learning', *Childhood Education*, 24 (7), 301–304.

Sherrington, T. (2019) *Rosenshine's Principles in Action*, Woodbridge: John Catt Educational Ltd.

Smith, J. (2020) 'Growth mindset vs fixed mindset: How what you think affects what you achieve', viewed 2 May 2021, www.mindsethealth.com/matter/growth-vs-fixed-mindset

Thiede, K.W., Anderson, M.C. and Therriault, D. (2003) 'Accuracy of metacognitive monitoring affects learning of texts', *Journal of Educational Psychology*, 95, 66–73.

Vygotsky, L.S. (1978) *Mind in Society: The Development of Higher Psychological Processes*, Cambridge, MA: Harvard University Press.

Wiliam, D. and Thompson, M. (2007) 'Integrating assessment with instruction: What will it take to make it work?' in C.A. Dwyer (ed.) *The Future of Assessment: Shaping Teaching and Learning*, Mahwah, NJ: Lawrence Erlbaum Associates, pp. 53–82.

6 Inclusive Physical Education

Hui Min Kwok

Introduction

The Salamanca Statement of 1994 (United Nations Educational, Scientific, and Cultural Organisation [UNESCO], 1994) advocated that all children should be enrolled in regular schools unless there are compelling reasons to prevent this. As a result, inclusive practices have emerged, with many students with special educational needs (SEN) being educated in mainstream or regular schools. Inclusive practice is a process whereby systematic barriers to learning and participation are minimised, where every student is accepted, valued for their individuality and supported, and in which intentional fostering of meaningful peer relationships are fostered (Booth and Ainscow, 2002). In essence, it is about "creating meaningful learning opportunities within supportive environments where all students feel they belong" (Wrench and Carrett, 2018, p.135).

Understanding the needs of the students in the classes you teach is vital if you are to create 'meaningful learning opportunities'. Whilst there is broad range of SEN within the school environment most can be grouped as follows:

- Speech/language and literacy
- Social, emotional, and behavioural
- Physical and sensory (see Table 6.1)

As part of your professional development, seeking out opportunities to equip yourself with skills and strategies to address inclusion in your teaching is important. With some modifications and special attention to students with SEN, physical education affords endless possibilities for inclusion, benefitting both students with SEN and their peers. The skills and strategies employed require you, as a teacher, to reflect on your own teaching beliefs (Chapter 9 provides an in-depth look at this) and how the heart of teaching seeds an environment for inclusive physical education to flourish.

This chapter looks at inclusive practices in physical education. It draws on the inclusive physical education (IPE) programme delivered via the Physical and

Table 6.1 Examples of specific needs within SEN groupings

Speech/Language and Literacy	Social, Emotional, and Behavioural	Physical and Sensory
■ Verbal expression ■ Understanding spoken language ■ Articulation ■ Reading accuracy/fluency ■ Spelling/writing (e.g. dyslexia)	■ Peer relationships/friendships ■ Emotional regulation/anger outbursts ■ Difficulties with changes in routines ■ Understanding social cues (e.g. Attention Deficit Hyperactivity Disorder (ADHD), Autism Spectrum Disorder (ASD))	■ Visual ■ Hearing ■ Mobility (e.g. cerebral palsy)

Sports Teacher Academy (PESTA), which oversees the professional development needs of physical education teachers in Singapore. Case studies cover students diagnosed with the following learning difficulties: Autism Spectrum Disorder (ASD), Attention Deficit Hyperactivity Disorder (ADHD), and lower intellectual ability, as these reflect the most commonly diagnosed learning difficulties in mainstream Singapore Schools (Lim, Wong and Tan, 2014; Poon et al., 2016). As you work through the chapter, you are encouraged to reflect on your existing practices and how other skills and strategies may impact student learning in your lessons.

OBJECTIVES

At the end of this chapter, you should be able to:

- define what is meant by inclusive physical education
- rationalise the value inclusive physical education has for your students and you as the teacher
- identify skills and strategies to support the adoption of inclusive practice in your physical education lessons and
- consider how strategies can be applied within your teaching to support students' learning.

Before focusing on these objectives, special education provision in Singapore is explained briefly in order to put the discussion into context.

Special Educational Provision in Singapore

Singapore is one of the few Asian countries whose special educational provisions typify a dual system in which children are placed in an appropriate educational setting according to their needs. In this dual system, children with moderate to severe SEN attend Special Education Schools (SPED) whilst children with mild SEN (those that have the cognitive ability to access the national curriculum and learn in large group settings (Ministry of Education (MOE), 2021) attend general education schools (Yeo et al., 2014). An estimated 2.1% of school-going children in Singapore are reported to have disabilities (Ministry of Community Development, Youth and Sports, 2017), equating to more than 25,000 students with SEN in mainstream schools (MOE, 2019). While MOE does not provide a definitive definition of 'special educational needs', it does cite a range of student learning difficulties, including students of lower academic or intellectual ability as well as diagnosed learning needs and behavioural issues such as ASD, ADHD, dyslexia, and emotional and behavioural disorders (Lim, Wong and Tan, 2014). Note: In Singapore children with moderate to severe physical and sensory difficulties are educated in special schools. Examples/case studies in this chapter relate to students with speech/language and literacy, social, emotional and behavioural difficulties being educated in mainstream schools. These examples/case studies should help you in your work with students with mild physical and sensory difficulties or different speech/language and literacy or social, emotional, and behavioural difficulties to those identified in this chapter.

The Singapore Curriculum Philosophy states that "we believe in holistic education, centred on values, social and emotional well-being and character development" and that "every child wants to, and can learn. When children find meaning in learning, they are motivated and challenged, and take ownership of their learning" (MOE, 2018). In practice, this requires the creation of a learning environment (see Chapter 3) that allows students to develop in the physical, cognitive, affective, and social domains. Task 6.1 encourages you to review your own governmental policy on inclusion.

> **Task 6.1 Inclusion policy**
>
> Review your own governmental policy on inclusion.
>   How do they define inclusion?
>   What provision is in place to support students with SEN?

What Is Inclusive Physical Education?

Inclusive education has been defined as "a diverse, continual process that takes into account individual needs, abilities, traits and learning outcomes for all students" (UNESCO, 2012, p. 4). Inclusion is more than children with SEN receiving education in a mainstream school setting. Rather, it means adapting mainstream settings/lessons to accommodate the needs of all students in order to bring about deeper participation in normal learning activities so each student fulfils their potential, for example, modifying instructional strategies and learning tasks

(Yeo and Tan, 2018). Inclusion benefits all students. In its broadest sense, inclusion promotes learning and personal development in students with and without SEN (Martin and Smith, 2002; Tapasak and Walther-Thomas, 1999), for example, by providing opportunities for leadership (Lieberman, Arndt and Daggett, 2007), like when students take on various roles in working together in the course of their lessons, leveraging one another's strengths to accomplish a goal. Further, inclusion allows opportunities for students with SEN to learn/develop and practise social skills in an integrated, natural environment, and helps to forge new friendships with typically developing peers, which in turn can result in the child having an age-appropriate role model. On the other hand, students without SEN can gain a new perspective and appreciation for challenges in life, as well as learn to appreciate individual differences (Block, 2016).

In the context of physical education, inclusion aims to create a sense of belonging and meaningfulness for all students during a lesson. It compels teachers to embrace student diversity as an expected and valued attribute (Bunker, 1994). Instead of isolating a student with SEN from their peers, inclusive physical education looks to integrating the student in a mainstream setting, allowing them access to a holistic education, which supports learning, improvements in social skills (Suomi, Collier and Brown, 2003), and positive attitudes toward peers and teachers as a result of inclusion (Obrusnikova, Valkova and Block, 2003).

Having read the first section of this chapter, take some time to reflect on how you define inclusion in physical education and what strategies you use to support it in your teaching. Task 6.2 helps you do this.

 Task 6.2 What does inclusive physical education mean to me?

Take time to consider if your physical education lessons are inclusive and how that came about. Use that experience to answer the following questions:

1 Why is inclusion important in your own teaching?
2 What would you identify as important when creating an inclusive environment in your lessons?
3 How do you develop inclusive practices in your lessons?

Embedding Inclusive Practices in Your Teaching

Teachers who believe that their students can learn given the right conditions, who are willing to reconceptualise their roles as teachers if needed, and who can diversify their teaching to match the different students in their lessons, are more likely to ensure learning takes place in their lessons (Saphier, Haley-Speca and

Gower, 2008). In Poon et al.'s (2016) study of staff perceptions towards inclusive education in Singapore, it was reported that teachers' receptiveness towards inclusion was dependent on the amount of success or issues they had experienced teaching students with SEN (Thaver and Lim, 2014; Yeo et al., 2014; Yeo and Tan, 2018). This suggests that your mindset towards inclusive practice impacts your ability to plan and manage positive and successful learning environments (Lavay, French and Henderson, 2006). Internationally, studies have shown that the right to a quality inclusive education is matched by staff readiness and competence (Coates and Vickerman, 2013; O'Connor and McNabb, 2020; Vickerman, 2012), as well as the support available. Task 6.3 encourages you to consider what support is available for students and for you within your own school context.

> **Task 6.3   Identifying support in school**
>
> Make sure you are clear about your school inclusion policy, if necessary, discussing this with the member of staff responsible for inclusion in your school. Address the following questions:
>
> 1 How are students with SEN in school supported?
> 2 How are staff supported to develop their knowledge, skills, and understanding of students with SEN?

Understanding Students

It is imperative that you consider the entire class before planning your lessons (see Chapters 2 and 4 for further guidance on getting to know your students). Research (Yeo et al., 2014) suggests that teachers' concerns are usually associated with the challenges of engaging all their students while managing the student(s) with SEN. At times, this can result in the teacher feeling alone in trying to achieve inclusivity. However, inclusive practices can be achieved through school-wide collaboration (Yeo et al., 2014). For example, within school(s), there will be teachers who have a deeper understanding of those students with SEN and be able to provide more detail(s) about their specific learning needs.

As well as drawing on existing knowledge, Bronfenbrenner and Morris' (1998) Ecological Framework (EF) offers a model that can help you better understand your students (an example of the application of the framework is provided later in the chapter) (see Figures 6.1 and 6.2). The framework identifies that a child's development is affected by six key factors:

1 School/external factors;
2 The student themselves;
3 Physical setting;

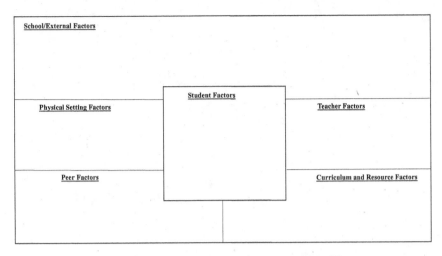

Figure 6.1 Adaptation of Bronfenbrenner and Morris' (1998) EF

4   The teacher;
5   Peers;
6   The curriculum and resources.

Using this information allows you to look at existing practices that have worked for your students and which help you to connect with them, thus fostering your teacher-student relationship. Using existing information about your students is a stepping stone for you to enact 'educating communities', where you consciously help students to integrate and live out the values, attitudes, and skills necessary to include diverse individuals, particularly their peers with SEN (Tharp and Gallimore, 1988, as cited in Thaver and Lim, 2014). Figure 6.1 is a document adapted from Bronfenbrenner and Morris' (1998) EF. When completed, it provides an overview of the range of factors relevant to one student with SEN, in a single document, which makes it easy to use. Completion of the document is best undertaken in collaboration with as many stakeholders as possible. Stakeholders in this aspect refer to the adults and peers who are constantly in contact and communication with the student (e.g. parents, siblings, caregivers, classmates, other subject teachers). For example, if a document is shared between staff, they can work together to support each other in making learning experiences more meaningful for the student.

Figure 6.2 provides an example of a completed EF.

If there is no document already in existence within the school, developing a document similar to that in Figure 6.1 allows you to draw up a more detailed profile of students with SEN. (Figure 6.2 shows you what a completed document could look like). With the information gathered, you then have a better sense of what a student is capable of, allowing you to make the necessary provisions to help the student learn. Case study 6.1 looks at this in greater detail.

School/External Factors

- Living with mother and younger sister
- Father is based overseas. However he does communicate regularly with the boy and his family via video calls
- Grandmother used to look after him and his sister after school before mother got them a place of their own. He now waits in the school library until the mum knocks off work to pick him and his younger sister
- Mother goes through his misbehaviour with him at home and updates form and co-form teachers
- School has been trying to get his mother to diagnose him since lower primary. Mum has always used the lack of time and the reasoning that he will 'outgrow' the behaviour
- Only in Term 1 did the mother finally consent to sending him for a diagnosis when he had a meltdown during EL class (during dictation)

Physical Setting Factors

- Sits with a student (this student changes every term or every month) who is patient with him
- Seated in front of the class
- Special single seat for him should he become disruptive during lessons
- *regardless of who he sits with, he is always near the teacher's table

Peer Factors

- Gets along well with the boys in the class whom he plays with during recess. Unfortunately, they take advantage of him and are impatient with him. He is forgiving towards them
- Classmates give him the space should he act up and when he does things that are inappropriate, like the touching of friend's hair and chewing on his stationary and collar, they will remind him that he is not to do so
- Has a ready peer to partner him whenever necessary.

Student Factors

- Diagnosed with ADHD and sensory processing disorder
- Touches peers
- Chews on collar and stationary
- Intelligent (likes Maths and Science and reads a lot)
- Flustered when he is in a hurry
- Unable to process his thoughts in a coherent manner when he has to explain or converse in sustained conversations
- Unable to control his excitement when playing with his peers or when he is excited about a task
- Talks unnecessarily during lesson (makes comments that make his peers look bad)
- Active boy who likes moving about. He participates actively during physical education lessons but needs reminders to be safe
- Likes Floorball and participates in that in co-curricular activities

Teacher Factors

- All his subject teachers update one another on his progress
- Form (Maths and Science Teacher) and co-form (English) teachers see him most. They are both firm and engaging teachers with a good rapport with students
- Form and co-form teachers are the ones who communicate with his mother about his behaviour
- His form and co-form teachers have spoken to the class before about the boy and how the class can collectively do their best to help a fellow classmate who has proven his capabilities on more than one occasion

Curriculum and Resource Factors

- Has a log book to capture his merits and demerits
- Should he have more than three demerits in a class, he is to be sent to the General Office. Teachers do not adhere to this strictly and do give him chances when his misbehaviour does not disrupt the lesson
- He is allowed to hand in work later than his peers. No differentiation in teaching required for he is intelligent. However, for certain pieces of work, he is allowed to not hand it in especially if he has shown comprehension of the objective

Figure 6.2 A completed EF for a student

Case study 6.1 Adapting Bronfenbrenner and Morris' (1998) EF to engage a child with autism in physical education

Teacher K is a new physical education teacher for a Primary 5 class (11-years-old). One of the students in the class is M, who has autism. From Primary 1 to 4 (6 to 10 years), M has had a teacher aide with him. The school and M's parents have come to an agreement that it is time for M to try to be more independent and less reliant on the teacher aide. In the first few weeks of implementing this, M would either run away from the physical education lesson or would exhibit disruptive behaviours during the lessons he attended. Despite K's attempts to engage M before the lesson to set boundaries with him and to better understand his needs, they proved futile.

K called M's mother and asked for assistance to better engage M during lessons. Through the conversation with M's mother, K learned of M's aversion towards perspiring and learned about a unique rewards system employed at home. Together with M's mother and his other subject teachers, K leveraged the existing rewards system used by M's parents to get him to participate during physical education lessons. To allow M to experience success during physical education lessons and to engage with his peers meaningfully, equipment was loaned to M's family so the family could bond with M over activities using that equipment, which would then seem less alien to M during physical education lessons. Over time M became more confident in his lessons and started to fully participate.

Task 6.4 asks you to reflect on what you need to take into account when working with students with SEN. The guiding questions in Task 6.4 allow you to analyse how well you know your students with SEN and what you actually need to know in order to be a step closer to realising inclusivity in your lessons.

 Task 6.4 Understanding your students

Focusing on one student in one of the classes you teach, use the six factors within the EF (see Figure 6.1 and 6.2) to identify how the factors might affect their learning.

1. What is their home/external environment like?
2. What do you know about the student themselves? For instance, how does the student engage with the teacher?
3. What is their relationship like with their peers?
4. What is their relationship like with their other teachers?

> 5 What are the expectations of the student in the lesson?
> 6 What do you know about the student themselves?
>
> Reflecting on your responses to these questions, what adaptations might you consider to ensure that the student is included fully in your lessons?

Importance of Teachers' Perceptions Towards Inclusion

The number of students diagnosed with SEN attending mainstream schools is increasing. In 2016, the Straits Times (an English-language daily broadsheet newspaper in Singapore) reported that there was a 60% increase (from 2,500 new cases in 2010) of children diagnosed with developmental problems (The Straits Times, 2016). Thus, teachers need a wider repertoire of instructional strategies to support the learning of students with SEN (MOE, 2020). Studies conducted by Poon et al. (2016) and Yeo et al. (2014) highlighted that teachers from Canada, Australia, Hong Kong, and Singapore were least positive about including students who were verbally or physically aggressive, or disruptive (Loreman, Forlin and Sharma, 2007, as cited in Yeo et al., 2014). Similarly, students with emotional and behavioural difficulties were least tolerated as compared to students with learning, physical, and sensory difficulties (Poon et al., 2016; Yeo et al., 2014). This indicates that the extent to which inclusion successfully fulfils the needs of all students in lessons is dependent on the attitudes of teachers towards inclusion and their willingness to create optimal learning environments (Ang, Lipponen and May Yin, 2021; Yeo and Tan, 2018).

A positive mindset, the creation of a positive learning environment and the links between school and home are key to realising inclusivity. As a teacher, you need to look beyond a diagnosis or a label. Instead, you need to foster a positive learning environment, in which you lead by example and use people first language. People first language is a form of linguistic etiquette in which the trait or diagnosis is described as something a person has, rather than who a person is (Foley and Graff, 2018). For example, rather than saying that you have an autistic boy in your lesson, the respectful and sensitive thing to do would be to describe his diagnosis or SEN by saying, "a boy with autism". This change in language simply states the child's SEN as something he has but does not define who he is. As a teacher, the emphasis should always be on the child first; their SEN should not define them. The use of people first language helps to avoid making unwarranted generalisations and perpetuating stereotypes, resulting in a compassionate and empathic environment for children to learn and grow in. It also helps break down attitudinal barriers such as ill-informed stereotypical views of SEN and prejudiced behaviours which have a significant negative impact on the emotional development of children with SEN (De Boer et al., 2010, as cited in Wong et al., 2015). In some of my conversations with teachers, they shared that expressing what a student could do, as opposed to what the student could not do allowed the student to set goals for themselves and work towards them. For example, "Student X can throw and catch if a bigger ball is used", as opposed to "Student X has problems or needs to work on her throw and catch". This change in mindset and language demonstrates respect for what the student can do, dignity in what the student has done and an understanding of the student's effort by focusing on each student as an individual and not their SEN.

When you take the lead in using positive language, students can also start to recognise the power of their words. Bit by bit, they can role model use of words, verbalising the strengths of their peers, instead of focusing on weaknesses. This helps in creating a positive learning environment where language is used to make students with SEN feel comfortable and confident enough to receive feedback from their peers, enabling them to recognise that any suggestions made by their peers is a means to help them improve their skills, allowing inclusivity to thrive. To help you clarify your perceptions towards inclusion, Task 6.5 helps you to reflect on how you communicate about your students with SEN to your colleagues and their peers.

Task 6.5   How do you talk about your students?

Reflect on your communication processes in relation to a student with SEN. Consider the following questions:

1   How do you talk about that student to your colleagues and their parents?
2   What do you normally share about that student when in conversation with colleagues?
3   How do their classmates react when asked to work or be placed in group settings with them?

Having considered your experiences and perceptions of inclusion, the next section looks at inclusion in relation to planning.

Inclusion Is Holistic in Nature

When planning for inclusion, the use of Universal Design for Learning (UDL), which considers the physical, social, and learning needs of students, can be applied to support teaching and learning (Thousand, Villa and Nevin, 2007). UDL is a research-based model for curricular design that ensures participation in mainstream schools for all students, including those with SEN. It is based on the philosophy that the physical environment and the activities within that environment should be accessible to all students without adaptations or specially designed equipment. The range of students' abilities are considered at the design stage of curriculum making and accommodations are incorporated at that point. This built-in access for a wide range of students – with and without SEN – is the underlying principle of UDL (Lieberman, Lytle and Clarcq, 2008). Leveraging UDL allows you to devise tasks that best meet the learning needs of your students.

UDL is an approach to designing instructional materials and activities that allow learning goals to be attained by individuals with different abilities. It is an approach that accommodates the various ways a student accesses and displays understanding of what is presented in a lesson. Hence, each student has access to the learning materials without adaptations having to be made to the curriculum repeatedly to meet needs. Tools and materials deployed by the teacher support student motivation as they offer multiple pathways for students to engage with the task at hand, enabling students with different learning needs to find pathways that suits them (Meyer and O'Neill, 2000). UDL encompasses three components which are summarised in Table 6.2.

If UDL is linked with Bronfenbrenner and Morris' (1998) EF (see earlier), you will be able to use the information about each student to include all students. Hence, knowledge of the different factors enables you to use an approach that is comprehensive, holistic, and inclusive. Case study 6.2 provides an example of all factors coming together for a student to meaningfully participate in physical education lessons.

Table 6.2 A summary of Universal Design for Learning

Component	Summary	Example
Multiple means of representation	Provides students with various ways of acquiring information.	Other than a demonstration of an activity on dribbling past a defender, a video recording of it is also made available to students for reference
Multiple means of engagement	Encourages teachers to delve deeper into student's interests to better arm them with more information about the student to appropriately challenge them.	Instead of having students work in fixed groups for a dribbling task, plan activities that allow students to first work on a dribbling task on their own, before going into pair or group work in which each takes on different roles (coach, defender, on-the-ball and off-the-ball attacker)
Multiple means of expression	Affords the student alternative means to demonstrate what they know.	Students demonstrate their dribbling skills through group demonstration, a portfolio capturing their progress over a period of time (to track their initial skills entry point at the beginning of the unit vs. their final skills acquired at the end of the unit) or a presentation (verbal explanation/physical demonstration) on how they can improve their dribbling

Case study 6.2 Working with a student with low IQ/low intellectual ability

S is a 12 year-old student with a low intelligence quotient (low intellectual ability). In Singapore, this indicates scoring less than 70 on intelligence tests to determine intellectual readiness for a mainstream school. Based on her score (less than 70), S could have enrolled in a SPED school in Singapore. However, her parents preferred that she attend a mainstream school.

One of S's characteristics is that she takes longer to process information and often needs instructions to be broken down before she is able to comprehend aspects of what is expected of her. During physical education lessons, she could not understand the teacher's instructions when her peers could. Nonetheless, she was always happy to be participating in the lesson.

S struggled to communicate her thoughts and often stayed silent. This resulted in her having low self-esteem and being sensitive when placed in group work, often worried that she would upset her peers when she did not demonstrate the same competency they did.

S's physical education teacher communicated regularly with the family and other teachers. The teacher surrounded S with a positive learning environment where her peers encouraged her to work with them and offered her plenty of encouragement and support during lessons. As S was given ample opportunities to work with different groups of peers who accepted her and focused on her strengths, she began to enjoy physical education lessons.

Recently, for one of the physical education assessments, S worked with some fellow students on a group gymnastics sequence. The culminating move in the sequence was a pyramid and S was hoisted to the top from the back by her peers. As that movement played out, the smile on S's face was indescribable, and spoke volumes. It was a genuine smile of happiness from within, an acknowledgement of her being part of something, that she had played her part in performing certain skills she was comfortable with and capable of doing, for the group sequence.

As a result of the changes adopted in physical education, S's other subject teachers are planning to rotate the groups she works with during group work so she can expand her social circle in school.

In this case study, S's teacher worked with parents, peers, and other teachers to allow S to develop a sense of belonging in school. By working in this way, S's teacher was able to realise inclusivity in lessons. By better understanding S and sharing with S's family and teachers what worked for S, the teacher enabled S to experience success. In S's teacher's words, "[S's classmates] step[ped] up to be [her] teacher aides so that I can continue teaching."

Realising Inclusivity

The section before identified one strategy used to support inclusivity could be that of considering who your students work with, thus allowing you to adapt your teaching to meet the needs of all students. But what are adaptations? According to Sport Australia (2020), adaptations are changes made to the teaching method, rules and regulation, equipment and environment (TREE) to ensure each student learns (see Table 6.3). Similar models on adaptations include the STEP process of modifying and adapting the physical education curriculum by looking at space, task, equipment, and people (Training and Development Agency for Schools (2009) (see Table 6.4) and Black and Stevenson's Inclusion Spectrum (Black and Stevenson, 2011) (see Figure 6.3).

Adaptations include accommodations and modifications. Accommodations do not substantially alter the learning objectives in a curriculum. Instead, they simply change the manner in which students learn. For example, using visual aids like task cards and checklists, extending the time students have to complete the task, shorter practices, or providing more scaffolds to learning. On the other hand, modifications are adaptations made to the curriculum, instruction, or environment that change the learning objectives. Simply put, modifications change what students are taught and are expected to learn while working towards the same learning objectives. These changes are necessary to allow students to learn and progress at their own pace, taking into account what they can and cannot do. This goes back to the premise that every child wants to and can learn. Examples of modifications include changing the size/length/width of a court, changing the size/weight/make of the ball/bat/racket or changing the rules to a game. While a teacher might think that they need to modify all activities/components of an activity, it is important to note that modifications do not need to apply to every component of the activity. Instead, the modified activity should mirror the original activity as much as

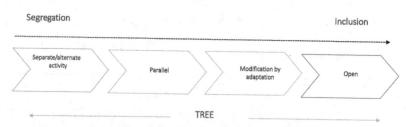

Figure 6.3 The Inclusion Spectrum incorporating TREE (Teaching style, Rules and regulations, Equipment, and Environment)

Source: Adapted from Black and Stevenson (2011)

Table 6.3 The TREE model for adaptation

TREE Stands for		What Can I Adapt	Example
T	Teaching Method/ Coaching Style	How instructions are communicated?	Holding the student's hand to demonstrate a follow-through movement pattern when throwing a tennis ball using the overhead throw
R	Rules and Regulation	The way the game is played?	All players to receive a pass before an attempt at goal is allowed
E	Equipment	What sports manipulatives/ equipment is being used?	Beach balls used in place of volleyballs
E	Environment	Where it takes place and who is involved?	Students are grouped according to their skill proficiency in a game of basketball

Table 6.4 The STEP model for adaptation

STEP Stands For		What Can I Change?	Example
S	Space	Where is the activity happening?	In a game of softball, students have different space (in terms of zone or size of space) to bat the ball to challenge the better skilled
T	Task	What is happening?	In a game of volleyball, students can either catch the ball or allow it to bounce once before the player sends the ball
E	Equipment	What is being used?	In a game of floorball, players can use a bigger air flo ball for easier control
P	People	Who is involved?	In a game of football, students can make use of a safety zone to advance the ball towards the goal according to their proficiency

possible, only making changes needed to meet individual needs. In short, modifications should be customised to the needs of the student with SEN.

Adaptations such as these help to make lessons more inclusive. The Inclusion Spectrum (Black, 1996), adapted by Black and Stevenson (2011), acts as a guide to the different types of activities that cater to the readiness of the student. The Inclusion Spectrum considers the range of options available in the different categories of activities and how to adapt aspects of these to suit the individual needs of students. The different activities will also show how integrated the student is in a lesson and provide a structure for teachers to work towards integrating the student(s) in the lesson. Crucially, the Inclusion Spectrum considers the different ways categories of activities can be presented and integration achieved, by modifying a combination of things (teaching style, rules and regulations, equipment and environment) (TREE) (see earlier). Although Black and Stevenson (2011) do not explicitly use TREE, their examples of modifications can be grouped under the TREE headings to help teachers consider possible changes when creating, for example, a parallel activity.

The four types of activities in Black and Stevenson's Inclusion Spectrum (2011) are as follows:

- Separate/alternate activity: Students do an activity that is deliberately planned differently (e.g. student with ASD practises throw and catch with a buddy at a separate area and upon completing the planned throw and catch activity, joins the rest of the class)
- Parallel activity: Students are grouped according to ability; each group does the same activity but at a level appropriate to their ability, skill, and fitness. The rules, equipment, and playing area can be different for different groups to suit the requirements of that group (e.g. students with intellectual difficulties can be placed in a group with students who are less athletic or, in a passing activity, the defenders are passive defenders)
- Modification by adaptation: Each student does the same activity with adaptations to challenge the more able, and support the inclusion of those with SEN, for example, changes to rules, area, or equipment (e.g. in badminton, allow students with physical difficulties to use a racket with a wider surface and a bigger shuttlecock)
- Open activity: A simple activity based on what the whole class can do with little or no modification. Each student does the same thing, without adaptation or modification, regardless of impairment (e.g. during a warm-up all students engage in stretching activities)

So how can this be reflected in practice? With knowledge of the different types of activities you are teaching, you can plan your lessons around the needs of different students in your class. You can use one or have a mix of the four types of activities (separate, parallel, modification by adaptation, open) during the course of a lesson. Ideally, you should avoid activities that result in segregation, and aim to integrate and include each student within the lesson. As much as possible, you want to integrate students doing separate activities into either doing a parallel or modification by adaption activity so that they are interacting with their peers. Keeping students in separate activities gives them little interaction time with their peers. By continually referring back to Bronfenbrenner and Morris' (1998) EF, you can plan activities that optimise learning for each student. Case study 6.3 looks at how the Inclusion Spectrum (Black and Stevenson, 2011) can be used with a student diagnosed with ADHD.

Use Black and Stevenson's (2011) Inclusion Spectrum and EF (refer to Figure 6.1) together to allow inclusion in a lesson.

Case study 6.3 Using Black and Stevenson's Inclusion Spectrum and EF for inclusion in a lesson

Y is an 11-year-old student diagnosed with ADHD and Sensory Processing Disorder. As Y gets excited easily, he tends to lose control and ends up dominating conversations and group work, resulting in his peers finding it difficult to work with him. Additionally, Y has difficulties staying on task and is easily distracted by his surroundings. This often results in him being off-task, leaving his groupmates to complete the work without his input. Y also has a tendency to bite and touch things around him and this has resulted in a few uncomfortable situations between him and his classmates.

Y's teachers got together with the school counsellor and profiled Y, sharing with one another information about him in their respective classes. Additionally, Y's form and co-form teachers met with his mother to learn more about the family and how Y was managed at home. Leveraging Y's strength and willingness to keep trying and Y's caring and forgiving nature towards his peers, Y's teachers came together to create opportunities in lessons for Y's peers to see more of his strengths. This common strategy deployed by Y's teachers soon allowed them to identify a group of classmates whom Y could work with in different subjects and settings, to allow him to stay on task during lessons.

For physical education lessons, Y's teacher recognised that he liked sports but tended to get overly excited and easily distracted. A parallel activity in floorball dribbling (three graded zones with a different number of defenders in each zone – see Figure 6.4 and Figure 6.5) was planned for Y to allow him to see how he could progress from one activity to another. Y had buddies who would go first to allow him to get a sense of the requirement of the activity. Video instructions were also provided for Y to refer to if he needed more explanation. The different zones allowed Y to work with different peers, thus providing him with greater social mingling. By the end of the semester, Y had made a couple of close friends in the class who spent time with him after school. Y's classmates also acknowledged that Y was a sensitive classmate who always asked about their well-being. More importantly, Y was much happier in lessons. He no longer felt like no one understood him or that he did not have friends.

Case study 6.3 demonstrates that the EF document provided Y's teachers with the information they needed to create a positive learning environment for both Y and his peers. Black and Stevenson's (2011) Inclusion Spectrum allowed Y to actively participate in lessons while having a goal to work towards.

Task Description

Graded zone activity (Invasion game with feet)
Each zone will be divided into thirds.

Red Court - One defender
Yellow Court - Two defenders
Green Court - Three defenders

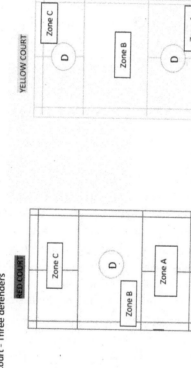

Task 1
Each pair will work together to dribble the ball from one end of the zone to the other successfully before taking a shot at goal found at the end of Zone C. The aim is for them to achieve a personal best in terms of the time taken for them to travel from one end of the zone to the other.

Task 2
As an extension to the above task, each pair must now make between 3 and 5 passes (with at least a pass in each zone) before either can take a shot at goal. This forces students to think about when and where they want to make the passes (in which zone)

Figure 6.4 Example of a modification by adaptation task for Y

INCLUSIVE PHYSICAL EDUCATION 103

Modifications	
*It is not necessary to fill in all four segments; fill in what is appropriate for your student	
Teaching style	Other than a teacher demonstration, YH will buddy with a boy who will model the requirements of the activity for him. An iPad containing a recording of two other peers carrying out the activity will also be placed near the benches for YH or other students to refer to as and when necessary.
Rules & regulations	As YH is easily excited, defender(s) will be reminded to not rush at him. Also, the defenders can start off with a lower level of defending (shadowing to pressure him to dribble faster/make a pass).
Equipment	YH also has the option of not using the floorball stick and other long handled implements instead to add variability to the task. On the other hand, these variabilities will be made available to the class in the last 15 min of the lesson. This allows for a class discussion on how the different implements allowed them better control. YH will have the option of using an implement to propel the ball. This can then be switched with other forms of manipulatives (different sized objects) to allow both YH and his peers to see the different types of equipment they can choose from so they get better. At the same time, there is greater variability to the activity.
Environment	When it comes to Task 2, he will deliberately be given opportunities to pair with a boy and a girl. This is to allow him to work with members of the opposite gender and for the girls to see that he too is trying to work with different peers.

Figure 6.5 Elaboration of TREE modifications for Y with reference to Figure 6.4

Source: Drawn by and carried out in the lesson by chapter author

Task 6.6 asks you to reflect on what you currently do to support students with SEN.

 Task 6.6 How do you support students with SEN to participate in your lessons?

As you reflect on the question, are you able to categorise your response to the following:

1. What was/were the teaching method(s) deployed? Did you use visual aids or the likes?
2. What were the changes to rules/regulations/equipment that you made?
3. What was the environment for the task like?

Having knowledge of why your students behave in a certain way allows you to make your lessons more inclusive. One way of approaching this is through the use of Functional Behavioural Analysis (FBA) (MOE, 2016). This helps teachers to understand why certain behaviours are exhibited or present themselves in a physical education lesson. For example, student A is identified as having ADHD and during physical education lessons, she wants to move from one station to another every few seconds. Efforts to get her to stay on task often result in her staring blankly at the teacher. Student B has autism and rarely speaks. When it is time for physical education he starts running around the school hall. Student C has anger management issues. During a game of badminton, when she loses a point, she is so upset that she smashes the racket and runs to her classmate, yelling at her for being competitive. When C presents these behaviours, they usually result in a consequence, for example the teacher needing to step in to defuse the situation or to remove student C from the activity so as to not endanger the other students. Socially, the other students may not want to work with student C and that would leave her without willing groupmates. With an understanding of the story behind the behaviour which impedes student C's participation in lesson(s), for example what causes the behaviour to happen, strategies can be put in place to replace or manage the behaviour, allowing her to participate meaningfully in

Table 6.5 Examples of the functions of behaviour exhibited by SEN students in physical education lessons

Function	Examples
Tangible (when child wants access to items or activities)	- Student snatches the ball from teammates during a game of basketball - During a toss and catch activity, the student refuses to exchange a ball for a beanbag
Automatic (sensory stimulation and can happen anytime)	- When a student's pass is intercepted, he hits the defender - When the opponent follows the student closely to defend, the student pushes the opponent
Attention (when child wants to socially interact)	- When the teacher calls for a volunteer, the student is always shouting to be chosen - When the teacher highlights positive behaviours during lesson, the student is always interrupting the teacher and making comments that are unwarranted
Escape (when child wants to avoid or get away from something)	- During a warm-up which includes running, the student always asks for permission to use the washroom - A student who prefers individual skills practice tasks to game play always informs the teacher of giddiness and a need to rest and sit out small-sided games, activities.

lessons. A trigger (or antecedent), causes the behaviour, which results in a consequence. By understanding the function behind the behaviour, a teacher can then identify possible triggers to prevent the behaviour from taking place. Alternatively, measures can be put in place to replace or manage the behaviour. Table 6.6 shows examples of the functions behind the behaviours exhibited that can present in physical education lessons.

We now return to Case study 6.3.

Case study 6.3 (continued) Functional Behavioural Analysis for student Y

Y is a physically active student. He is easily distracted and often chews on his collar and things around him. When excited, he is unable to control himself in his excitement and ends up behaving in a manner that can hurt his peers (e.g. rushing at them/rough play). During modified game play, Y gets upset when he feels he is being excluded or that his peers are ganging up on him. When placed in stressful situations (e.g. when pressed for time or when everyone is telling him to hurry), Y cries out in frustration and flails his arms or hits out at those around him. When that happens, Y needs to be isolated. Due to such outbursts, many of his classmates are cautious about having Y in their group during physical education especially when it is modified game play. Figure 6.6 shows the FBA for Y.

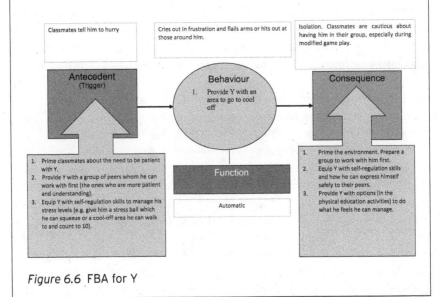

Figure 6.6 FBA for Y

Task 6.7 asks you to reflect on how you would employ FBA to manage student behaviour in your lessons.

> **Task 6.7 Employing FBA**
>
> Identify one student in one of the classes you teach who does not participate in your lesson or behaves in a manner that limits their participation. What behaviour(s) does the student show (action)?
>
> 1. What does the student get from behaving in that manner (e.g. getting attention from the teacher, using the equipment of their choice, or not having to participate in the lesson)?
> 2. When does the behaviour happen (when the class is placed in groups, when the students have to change equipment or get started on a different task)?
> 3. What is the consequence of the behaviour?
> 4. What strategies can you employ to get the student to now participate positively?

Discussion

The examples in these case studies show that inclusivity can happen in physical education settings when the necessary effort and coordination are put in place to create an environment that aids learning. Teachers are more willing to support inclusion when they have opportunities to experience success. This change in attitude is consistent with Woolfson and Brady's (2009) perception that mastery experiences are instrumental in fostering positive teacher beliefs about inclusion.

As a teacher you should look to promote a positive learning environment where inclusion goes beyond physical placement to social acceptance and a sense of belonging in the class and, hence, school (Booth and Ainscow, 2002; Lieberman and Houston-Wilson, 2009; Warnock, 2005). For that to happen, teachers need to model inclusive behaviours and use people first language (Ang, Lipponen and May Yin, 2021; Foley and Graft, 2018). This way, students in the class will also role model the teachers' behaviours and language, helping to create an inclusive learning environment for students with SEN. After all, when a teacher believes that inclusion allows all students opportunities to learn and practise social skills in an integrated, natural environment, students without additional learning needs can gain new perspectives and appreciation for challenges in life and learn to appreciate individual differences (Block, 2016). Such activities allow teachers to reflect critically on their 'heart-ware' of educating children in equitable ways (Lim, Wong and Tan, 2014).

SUMMARY AND KEY POINTS

The aim of this chapter has been to develop your understanding of inclusion and the role you play in realising inclusivity in your lessons. Specifically you should now be able to:

- define what is meant by inclusive physical education
- rationalise the value inclusive physical education accords to your students
- identify skills and strategies to support the adoption of inclusive practice in your physical education lessons and
- consider how strategies can be applied within your teaching to support students' learning.

An understanding of your role as a teacher allows you to see value in seeding aspects of inclusivity in your lessons and to make a concerted effort in doing so. It is imperative that you work to ensure meaningful learning experiences for all your students and that students with SEN are warmly embraced and valued. As research has shown, teachers' competence in including all students grows as they gain more experience in working with students with SEN (Hardin, 2005). There is also no denying that students tend to model teachers' behaviours. The more inclusive practices a teacher deploys, the likelier students will follow suit.

Note: A list of further resources to help you take your learning forward is available on the PESTA website: https://academyofsingaporeteachers.moe.edu.sg/pesta/professional-development/book-chapters-by-the-pesta-team

 References

Ang, L., Lipponen, L. and May Yin, S. (2021) 'Critical reflections of early childhood care and education in Singapore to build an inclusive society', *Policy Futures in Education*, 19 (2), 139-154, https://doi.org/10.1177/1478210320971103

Black, K. (1996) *TOP Play/BT TOP Sport: Including Young Disabled People*, Loughborough: Youth Sport Trust.

Black, K. and Stevenson, P. (2011) *The Inclusion Spectrum*, Australia: Theinclusionclub.com.

Block, M.E. (2016) *A Teacher's Guide to Adapted Physical Education* (4th edn), Baltimore, MD: Paul H. Brookes.

Booth, T. and Ainscow, M. (2002) *Index for Inclusion: Developing Learning and Participation in Schools*, Bristol: CISE.

Bronfenbrenner, U. and Morris, P.A. (1998) 'The ecology of developmental processes', in W. Damon and R.M. Lerner (eds.), *Handbook of Child Psychology: Theoretical Models of Human Development*, Hoboken, NJ: John Wiley & Sons Inc., pp. 993-1028.

Bunker, L.K. (1994) 'Virtual reality: Movement's centrality', *Quest*, 46 (4), 456-474, doi: 10.1080/00336297.1994.10484139

Coates, J. and Vickerman, P. (2013) 'A review of methodological strategies for consulting children with special educational needs in physical education', *European Journal of Special Needs Education*, 28 (3), 333-347, https://doi.org/10.1080/08856257.2013.797705

De Boer, A.A., Pijl, S.J. and Minnaert, A. (2010) 'Attitudes of parents towards inclusive education: A review of the literature', *European Journal of Disabilities Education*, 25 (2), 165-181, https://doi.org/10.1080/08856251003658694

Foley, M. and Graff, C. (2018) 'Getting started with person-first language', viewed 6 August 2021, www.edutopia.org/article/getting-started-person-first-language

Hardin, B. (2005) 'Physical education teachers' reflections on preparing for inclusion', *The Physical Educator*, 62 (1), 44-56.

Lavay, B., French, R. and Henderson, H. (2006) *Positive Behavior Management in Physical Activity Settings* (2nd edn), Champaign, IL: Human Kinetics.

Lieberman, L.J., Arndt, K.L. and Daggett, S. (2007) 'Promoting leadership in physical education and recreation', *Journal of Physical Education, Recreation and Dance*, 78 (3), 46-50.

Lieberman, L.J. and Houston-Wilson, C. (2009) *Strategies for Inclusion: A Handbook for Physical Educators* (2nd edn), Champaign, IL: Human Kinetics.

Lieberman, L.J., Lytle, R. and Clarcq, J. (2008) 'Getting it right from the start: Employing the Universal Design for Learning approach to your curriculum', *Journal of Physical Education, Recreation and Dance*, 79 (2), 32-39.

Lim, S., Wong, M. and Tan, D. (2014) 'Allied educators (learning and behavioural support) in Singapore's mainstream schools: First steps towards inclusivity?' *International Journal of Inclusive Education*, 18 (2), 123-139, https://doi.org/10.1080/13603116.2012.758321

Loreman, T., Forlin, C. and Sharma, U. (2007) 'An international comparison of pre-service teacher attitudes towards inclusive education', *Disability Studies Quarterly*, 27 (4), 1-13.

Martin, J. and Smith, K. (2002) 'Friendship quality in youth disability sport: Perceptions of a best friend', *Adapted Physical Activity Quarterly*, 19 (4), 472-282.

Meyer, A. and O'Neill, L.M. (2000) 'Supporting the motivation to learn: How Universal Design for Learning can help', *The Exceptional Parent*, 30 (6), 35.

Ministry of Community Development, Youth and Sports (2017) *3rd Enabling Masterplan 2017-2021; Caring Nation, Inclusive Society*, Singapore: Ministry of Community Development, Youth and Sports, viewed 6 August 2021, www.msf.gov.sg/policies/Disabilities-and-Special-Needs/Documents/Enabling%20Masterplan%203%20%28revised%2013%20Jan%202017%29.pdf

MOE (Ministry of Education) (2016) *Every Behaviour Serves a Function*, Singapore: Ministry of Education Psychological Services Branch.

MOE (Ministry of Education) (2018, October) *Singapore Curriculum Philosophy*, Singapore: Ministry of Education, viewed 6 August 2021, www.moe.gov.sg/education-in-sg/our-teachers/singapore-curriculum-philosophy

MOE (Ministry of Education) (2019, September) *Infosheet on Skillsfuture for Educators (SFEd)*, Singapore: Ministry of Education, viewed 6 August 2021, www.moe.gov.sg/news/press-releases/-/media/files/news/press/2020/infosheet-on-SFEd.pdf

MOE (Ministry of Education) (2020) *Professional Practice Guidelines: Developmental and Psycho-educational Assessments and Provisions for Preschool-aged Children*, Singapore: Ministry of Education, viewed 6 August 2021, www.ecda.gov.sg/Documents/Parents/Guidelines%20(For%20Professionals)%202021.pdf

MOE (Ministry of Education) (2021, January) *Frequently Asked Questions*, viewed 6 August 2021, www.moe.gov.sg/special-educational-needs/frequently-asked-questions#school

Obrusnikova, I., Valkova, H. and Block, M. (2003) 'Impact of inclusion in general physical education on students without disabilities', *Adapted Physical Activity Quarterly*, 20 (3), 230-245.

O'Connor, U. and McNabb, J. (2020) 'Improving the participation of students with special educational needs in mainstream physical education classes: A rights-based perspective', *Educational Studies*, https://doi.org/10.1080/03055698.2020.1719385

Poon, K.K., Ng, Z., Wong, M.E. and Kaur, S. (2016) 'Factors associated with staff perceptions towards inclusive education in Singapore', *Asia Pacific Journal of Education*, 36 (1), 84-96, https://doi.org/10.1080/02188791.2014.922047

Saphier, J., Haley-Speca, M.A. and Gower, R. (2008) *The Skillful Teacher: Building Your Teaching Skills* (6th edn), Acton, MA: Research for Better Teaching, Inc.

Sport Australia (2020) *Using Tree*, viewed 6 August 2021, www.sportaus.gov.au/sports_ability/using_tree

Suomi, J., Collier, D. and Brown, L. (2003) 'Factors affecting social experiences of students in elementary physical education classes', *Adapted Physical Activity Quarterly*, 22 (2), 186-202.

Tapasak, R. and Walther-Thomas, C. (1999) 'Evaluation of a first-year inclusion program', *Remedial and Special Education*, 20 (4), 216-225.

Tharp, R.G. and Gallimore, R. (1988) *Rousing Minds to Life: Teaching, Learning, and Schooling in the Social Context*, New York: Cambridge University Press.

Thaver, T. and Lim, L. (2014) 'Attitudes of pre-service mainstream teachers in Singapore towards people with disabilities and inclusive education', *International Journal of Inclusive Education*, 18 (10), 1038-1052, https://doi.org/10.1080/13603116.2012.693399

The Straits Times (2016, May) *More Children Diagnosed with Developmental Problems*, p.10, viewed 6 August 2021, www.straitstimes.com/singapore/more-children-diagnosed-with-developmental-problems

Thousand, J.S., Villa, R.A. and Nevin, A.I. (2007) *Differentiating Instruction: Collaborative Planning and Teaching for Universally Designed Learning*, Thousand Oaks, CA: Corwin Press.

Training and Development Agency for Schools (2009, December) *Including Pupils with SEN and/or Disabilities in Primary Education*, viewed 6 August 2021, https://dera.ioe.ac.uk/13804/1/physicaleducationpe.pdf

UNESCO (United Nations Educational Scientific and Cultural Organization) (1994) *The Salamanca Statement and Framework for Action on Special Education*, Paris: UNESCO.

UNESCO (United Nations Educational Scientific and Cultural Organization) (2012, June) *Addressing Exclusion in Education: A Guide to Addressing Education Systems Towards more Inclusive and Just Societies*, Paris: UNESCO, viewed 6 August 2021, https://unesdoc.unesco.org/ark:/48223/pf0000217073

Vickerman, P. (2012) 'Including children with special educational needs in physical education: Has entitlement and accessibility been realised?' *Disability and Society*, 27 (2), 249-262, https://doi.org/10.1080/09687599.2011.644934

Warnock, M. (2005) *Special Educational Needs: A New Look*, London: Philosophy of Education Society of Great Britain.

Wong, M., Poon, K., Kaur, S. and Ng, Z. (2015) 'Parental perspectives and challenges in inclusive education in Singapore', *Asia Pacific Journal of Education*, 35 (1), 85-97, https://doi.org/10.1080/02188791.2013.878309

Woolfson, L.M. and Brady, K. (2009) 'An investigation of factors impacting on mainstream teachers' belief about teaching students with learning difficulties', *Educational Psychology*, 29, 221-238, http://doi.org/10.1080/01443410802708895

Wrench, A. and Carrett, R. (2018) 'Diversity and inclusion', in G. Griggs and K. Petrie (eds.) *Routledge Handbook of Primary Physical Education*, London: Sage, pp.134-144.

Yeo, L., Chong, W., Neihart, M. and Huan, V. (2014) 'Teachers' experience with inclusive education in Singapore', *Asia Pacific Journal of Education*, 36 (sup 1), 69-83, https://doi.org/10.1080/02188791.2014.934781

Yeo, L. and Tan, S. (2018) 'Educational inclusion in Singapore for children with physical disabilities', *Asia Pacific Journal of Education*, 38 (2), 175-186, https://doi.org/10.1080/02188791.2018.1460253

7 Assessing Student's Progress Formatively

Mabel Yong

Introduction

This chapter focuses on formative assessment/assessment for learning (AfL), a common strategy used by teachers to evaluate the progress of students (note, in this chapter the term formative assessment is used). Nuthall (2007) stresses that in order to know if learning has taken place in a lesson (or unit), the teacher must know two things about each student;

1. What did each student know/was able to do before the lesson/unit?
2. What did each student know/was able to do at the end of the lesson/unit?

This information enables the teacher to know what each student has learned and also what they did not learn in the lesson/unit.

Physical education teachers play a critical role in helping to guide students in their journey toward becoming physically literate. According to Mandigo et al. (2012), a physically literate individual is able to move with competence and confidence in a wide variety of physical activities in a range of environments. While physical education is often deemed a performance subject, where achievement is seen as the ability to do or perform a specific skill, concept, or tactic, it is important that students learn in the psychomotor, cognitive, and affective domains. Thus, as a student learns skills/concepts/tactics in the psychomotor domain, it is also important to consider learning in the cognitive and affective domains concurrently (see Chapter 3 for more details).

Faced with a wide range of diverse individuals in a class, teachers must find ways to assess each individual student's learning and progress. By providing a range of differentiated assessments, teachers can assess students' progress, then use this information to enable students to be successful in their learning.

This chapter considers the why, how, and what to measure students' learning and progress in physical education. Most of the suggested formative assessment strategies identified in the chapter to differentiate assessment can be used across grade levels.

DOI: 10.4324/9781003171973-8

ASSESSING STUDENT'S PROGRESS FORMATIVELY

OBJECTIVES

At the end of this chapter, you should be able to:

- understand formative assessment and its role in physical education
- identify indicators of learning in physical education and different assessment strategies to meet the diverse learning needs of students and
- select forms of formative assessment appropriate for assessing student learning based on their needs.

Before looking in detail at assessment practices, take some time to consider your experiences of assessment. Task 7.1 helps you to do this.

 Task 7.1 Reflections of your experiences of assessment

Reflect on the following questions:

- How has the application of knowledge and skills of assessment influenced your practice in search of seeking evidence that your students have or have not learned?
- How can assessment be used to enhance learning, achievement, and self-regulation?

Formative Assessment and Its Role in Physical Education

Formative assessment/assessment *for* learning (AfL) is an integral part of the teaching and learning process. It allows teachers to collect information to inform them whether student learning has taken place and to use that information to inform their instructional decisions to facilitate learning.

According to (Schiemer, 2000) the methods of assessments, coupled with a well-organised and thought through system of assessment, can provide a range of information to

1. Measure progress of a student;
2. Determine competence on a particular aspect of learning;
3. Determine the need to remediate or accelerate the learning;
4. Determine the instructional needs for curriculum design.

Formative assessment refers to a wide variety of assessment methods that teachers use to conduct in-process evaluations of student learning, comprehension, and progress during a lesson or unit. It is used to consider students' learning needs and to make adjustments to the teaching and learning process. The information collected informs students and the teacher about their progress and status in relation to a desired goal. Formative assessment may occur as pre-, ongoing, or post-lesson/unit, to assess what students currently know, can do and feel they can do, and what they have learned. With clear goals and feedback as to how to get there, it should also motivate students to improve their levels of achievement. An example of how formative assessment and the use of learning experiences can help guide students to move to the next stage of learning in practice is shown in Table 7.1 (level four is the highest level of achievement).

Table 7.1 Example of assessment rubric for gymnastics with tasks to guide students on how to improve

Success Criteria:	Level One	Level Two	Level Three	Level Four
Success Criteria 1: Balance – weight bearing (momentary stillness)	My body is moving all the time when I bear my own or other's weight.	My body makes small/slight movements when I bear my own or other's weight.	My body is momentarily still when I bear my own or other's weight.	My body is able to sustain stillness when I bear my own or other's weight.
	\multicolumn{4}{l}{Learning experiences which guide students on how to get to the next level}			
<ul><li>Travel across a mat on hands and feet, on your front, on your back</li><li>Balance on like and unlike body parts</li><li>Balance in inverted positions</li><li>Overbalancing to new balance</li><li>Individual balance with stillness</li></ul>	To get to the next level, I can:<ul><li>Work on stillness and hold balance shape momentarily</li><li>Individual/Pair balance on like and unlike body parts</li><li>Individual/Pair balance in inverted positions</li><li>Overbalancing to new balance</li></ul>	To get to the next level, I can:<ul><li>Explore pair balances with reliance on each other's support, refine the balances for momentarily stillness.</li><li>Travel across a flat mat on hands and feet, on your front, on your back</li></ul>	To get to the next level, I can:<ul><li>Explore pair/group balances with reliance on each other's support, refine the balances for momentarily stillness.</li><li>Pair/group balances with reliance on each other's support.</li></ul>	To get to the next level, I can:<ul><li>Work on originality and variety of pair/group balances with reliance on each other's support, refine the balances for momentarily stillness.</li><li>Combine asymmetrical balances to enhance aesthetic feel.</li></ul>

Success Criteria:	Level One	Level Two	Level Three	Level Four
■ Pair/group balances with reliance on each other's support		■ Pair balances with reliance on each other's support.	■ Create symmetrical and asymmetrical balances to enhance aesthetic feel.	

Table 7.2 Example of assessing a concept in a game play situation

Dribbling past a defender towards goal in a 1v 1 situation in basketball			
Instruction: In a 1v 1 situation, dribble and shield the ball from the defender towards goal.			
Name	Level 1: head and eyes on ball Level 2: Head and eyes looking up	Level 1: Dribbles with dominant hand only Level 2: Dribbles with dominant and non-dominant hand (where appropriate)	Level 1: Has occasional control of ball Level 2: Has full control of ball

Source: Modified from Rovegno and Bandhauer (2017)

The mode of assessment should allow students to utilise authentic aptitudes and abilities. Formative assessment is authentic when students are required to problem solve and make decisions to achieve an objective that can be applied in a real-life setting (Schiemer, 2000). For example, a task which puts students in a situation that is evident during a game play (see Table 7.2). Task 7.2 asks you to reflect on assessments you have used.

Task 7.2 Reflections of an assessment tool you have used

Choose one assessment tool that you have recently used to formatively assess students learning.

- How has the information enabled your students to improve their learning?
- What adjustment/modification would you make to it so as to improve the quality of the information the assessment provides?
- How has the information influenced your decisions in planning and instructions?

How Do You Know That Learning Has Taken Place?

But how do you know you are assessing learning? In fact, what does learning look like? Many teachers use general observations of gains in knowledge, understanding, skills, and attitudes as evidence of learning. They may also look at comparisons between target and attainment grades for signs of progress. Hughes (2006) provides key indicators that suggest learning is taking place (see Table 7.3).

So what would this look like in practice? Task 7.3 provides an opportunity for you to reflect on how you have observed learning in your own classroom.

> **Task 7.3 Using indicators of learning in your own lessons**
>
> Using the gymnastics example, reflect on a different area of activity you have taught and consider what indicators of learning you have embedded within your teaching.
>
> Example: In a gymnastics lesson when students are learning the concept of smooth transition between movements they are encouraged to explore different ways their body movement can express an idea. The teacher then provides learning cues and guided questions to scaffold the discovery of those movements. Soon, students begin to create a series of movements using different body parts to illustrate the concepts.

Table 7.3 Summary of indicators that show that learning is taking place

	Indicator of Learning Taking Place When Students…	Example From Physical Education
1	Explain something in their own words.	"It means to connect the movements like a sentence without a comma in between the words."
2	Ask questions.	"Does it feel like taking a deep breath?"
3	Make connections.	With smooth transitions, the performance looks aesthetically pleasing to watch.
4	Recreate (rather than reproduce) information.	Students are able to apply their understanding of a tactic through their actions in a game situation.
5	Justify their decisions.	Link a low balance to a side roll in gymnastics to eliminate extra steps between movements as both actions are at a low level.
6	Explaining their thinking.	
7	Talking to each other.	Peer learning situation in gymnastics or dance when students are co-designing a sequence of movements with smooth transitions.
8	Active - doing something with the information.	

■ ■ ■ ■ **ASSESSING STUDENT'S PROGRESS FORMATIVELY**

To determine if students have made progress, it is important that students know their starting point as well as what they are aiming for. Clarity of the learning intentions and success criteria must be made known to, and understood by, students. A good formative assessment activity not only demonstrates the progress students make during a lesson(s) but also clearly indicates how students can improve further. Providing regular dedicated improvement and reflection time (DIRT) in response to formative assessment activities enables students to respond to feedback and make further progress. Case study 7.1 provides an example of how this might be applied within your own teaching.

Case study 7.1 Using assessment criteria to support formative assessment

This set of rubrics (see Table 7.4) and the DIRT template (see Table 7.5) were introduced to a class at the start of the unit. The descriptors were crafted using the students' input and experiences. The students indicated in lesson 1 the stage they felt they were at ("Where am I"). Over a series of lessons, they worked on the key learning experiences, focusing on the specific experiences that could facilitate their progress to the next stage. They logged their progress throughout the unit.

Table 7.4 Rubrics for hanging from overhead apparatus

Learning outcome: ■ Travel while hanging from overhead apparatus, bearing full body weight with the hands. ■ Come off the hanging apparatus safely with control.				
Where am I? Progress	Level 1	Level 2	Level 3	Level 4
Success Criteria				
1: Travel while hanging with hands bearing full body weight. Use different types of grip: forward/overgrip reverse/undergrip mixed, cross, cross/mixed	I am able to travel while hanging with hands across the bar for less than three steps.	I am able to travel while hanging with hands across the bar for more than three steps.	I am able to travel while hanging with hands bearing full body weight for half the distance of the bar.	I am able to travel while hanging with hands, across the bar using different types of grip.

Learning outcome:
- Travel while hanging from overhead apparatus, bearing full body weight with the hands.
- Come off the hanging apparatus safely with control.

2: Mount/ Dismount with control	I need someone to guide me to mount and dismount safely	Sometimes, I need someone to guide me to mount and dismount safely	Most of the time, I am able to mount and dismount safely on my own	Consistently, I am able to mount and dismount safely on my own
"I can improve by" Key Learning experiences:				
■ Revise types of grip. ■ Hands to hold body weight with feet off floor. ■ Travel for a distance while hanging with hands. ■ Dismount with control.	To get to the next level, I can work on medium height apparatus: ■ Jump to front support using forward/overgrip on the bar. ■ Travel using forward/overgrip on inclined pull-up bar level.	To get to the next level, I can work on overhead apparatus:[1] ■ Hang stationary, demonstrating a variety of symmetrical and asymmetrical body shapes. ■ Travel using forward/overgrip and/or reverse/undergrip on high apparatus level.	To get to the next level, I can work on overhead apparatus:[1] ■ Travel using forward/overgrip and/or reverse/undergrip on overhead apparatus level. ■ Travel across the bar with body control for a designated distance.	To get to the next level, I can work on a set of apparatus with a combination of heights: ■ Travel at various speeds, directions and use different grips (mixed, cross, cross/mixed, etc.) ■ Travel across the bar with body control, forming shapes with hanging feet or a designated distance.

1- Overhead apparatus is apparatus that is taller than the height of the student

Table 7.5 Learning log (DIRT): to hang from overhead apparatus and travel over a distance

Name: Class:		
Target: **Level 3** "Where do I want to go?"	What I did to improve myself (For example, skill level, activity type, time spent)	Dedicated improvement, reflection time (DIRT)
Lesson 1: "Where am I" **Level 2**	I practised on the monkey bar at the playground, started with just hanging stationary, then tried moving with a step then two.	I worked on my grip by jumping to front support using overgrip on the bar. Did that for 15 min over three days. I need to be stronger at my upper body and core to have more control when I swing from one step to another.
Lesson 2: "Where am I" **Level 3**	I practised daily on the monkey bar at the playground during recess. I have been doing push-ups daily over the days since Lesson 1, spending 15 min on the bar and 15 min on strengthening and core exercises.	I am able to travel for a few steps with better control of body swinging as I move from bar to bar. I think I am stronger because of my practice.
Lesson 3: "Where am I" **Level 4**	I practised daily on the monkey bar at the playground whenever I am free from class. I have been doing strengthening exercises and core exercises daily for 20 min.	I am able to travel while hanging with hands across the bar using different types of grip, mount and dismount safely on my own. Next, I want to work on forming shapes with my legs while hanging from the bar.

Assessing the Psychomotor Domain for Learning

According to Lund and Veal (2013), learning in the psychomotor domain has been defined as a permanent change in behaviour. Once a motor skill has been learned, it does not occur by chance or luck. This means that when a skill is learned, the change in behaviour can be repeated consistently over a period of time. In other words, consistent level in execution may be achieved though it may not be a perfect execution.

It has already been established that as teachers, you need to ensure that learning has taken place. In order to achieve this, you need to take into consideration the profiles of your students, including their needs and readiness. A one-size-fits-all assessment tool is therefore not appropriate. Differentiated assessment is a logical approach to ensure fair assessment. Here, the assessment is modified to match and respond to the varied learning needs of students in the class. This enables students to demonstrate their learning in ways that fit their needs and are effective for them. Differentiated assessment provides options and opportunities for students' learning to be assessed. By providing various assessment methods/activities appropriate for different students, you are able to help them be successful in their learning. The assessments described next are examples that can inform teachers and students on the progress that is being made.

Tiering

Tiering is a readiness-based and differentiation strategy. It is useful when you want to ensure that students work with the same essential ideas and use the same key skills (or knowledge and understanding) but at different levels. Using tiered activities allows all students to focus on essential skills/knowledge/understanding, but at different levels of complexity, abstractness, open-endedness, and independence. By keeping the focus of the activity the same but providing different tasks at varying degrees of difficulty, you can maximise the likelihood that each student learns pivotal skills/knowledge/understanding and all students are appropriately challenged.

Typically, students are provided with the criteria prior to the assessment via a rubric that is then used to evaluate student's achievement against the criteria (see Case study 7.1 for an example). According to Shanklin (2004), when students are aware of the success criteria, learning is more focused, and practice is more deliberate. The rubrics (see Tables 7.1 and 7.4) use verbal descriptions for various levels. The descriptions provide students with information of what they must do to get to the next level.

The process of learning, where students work towards the achievement of criteria through focused and deliberate practice, provides opportunities for students to develop traits of independent and self-directed learners as they self-evaluate their current skill level and become motivated to work on it to move to the next level (see Tables 7.4 and 7.5 in Case study 7.1). Working with your students, begin the unit by assessing the level they are currently at. The students then set the target level they aim to achieve by the end of the unit. Therefore, each student has an individualised target that they review as they move through the lesson series to reflect on the progress they are making. Case studies 7.2 and 7.3 explore examples of how this might work in practice.

Case study 7.2 Qualitative analytic rubrics

An example of a qualitative analytic rubrics in gymnastics used as formative assessment in a class of 10-year-olds is shown in Figure 7.1 and Table 7.6. Success criteria were made known to the students at the beginning of the unit. Over a series of ten lessons, students gauged their level of progression based on the descriptors identified in each criteria. Whilst students were assigned the same learning intention, they were able to select the level of difficulty of the movement and progress as they gained more skill competence and confidence.

> Learning Intentions:
>
> Jump from low apparatus to rebound on a springboard, to form gymnastics shapes of stretch, tuck, and straddle during flight, to land in a controlled finished position.
>
> Pre-requisites of students' competence on floorwork:
>
> - Able to form gymnastics shapes in flight
> - Able to perform 1-2-2 hurdle step
> - Able to land softly on feet after a jump

Figure 7.1 Formative assessment in gymnastics

Table 7.6 Success criteria

Criteria	Level 1	Level 2	Level 3	Level 4
Jump and land with control	■ Arms used for balance, not force. ■ Minimal extension of knees and ankles. ■ Landing is flat-footed and heavy.	■ Arms reach to side or partially up. ■ Partial extension of knees and ankles. ■ Landing is flat-footed.	■ Arms swing down then up but don't reach vertical. ■ Knees and ankles extend on take-off. ■ Bend knees to absorb force on landing.	■ Arms swing down then up to vertical. ■ Knees and ankles extend powerfully on take-off. ■ Bend knees to absorb force on landing.
Rebound off spring-board	■ Step off the low apparatus with two feet, land two feet on springboard and no rebound off to land.	■ Step off the low apparatus with two feet, land two feet on springboard and rebound off to land.	■ Step off the low apparatus with one foot, land two feet on springboard and rebound off to land.	■ Step off the low apparatus with one foot, land with power two feet on springboard and rebound off to land.

Criteria	Level 1	Level 2	Level 3	Level 4
Form gymnastics shapes in flight	■ Form one basic gymnastics shapes in flight.	■ Form two basic gymnastics shapes in flight.	■ Form three basic gymnastics shapes in flight.	■ Form more than three basic gymnastics shapes in flight.

Case study 7.3   Physical education grade 1 tiered activities on rope skipping

Teacher A's grade 1 students are learning to skip ropes held by others. As a whole class activity, they have had class discussions and viewed videos showing what the skill looks like. It is essential that all students are able to perform the skill and understand why it is important for body movement in physical education. Teacher A wants each student to create a foundation for constructing additional knowledge and understanding of rope skipping.

To develop a challenging tiered activity, teacher A matched different assessments to individual students. The three assessments all contained the same elements:

- All students had to have some individual and some group tasks to complete.
- All students received a set of material (in print or video) on what rope skipping meant, how to do it with learning cues, and why it was important. The language of the various materials was kept simple.
- All students were required to take notes on essential information in the set of materials provided. Some students had a note-taking matrix to guide their work; others, Teacher A simply asked to take careful notes on a list of key ideas observed. The teacher monitored all student notes for clarity and thoroughness.
- All students had to demonstrate understanding of what rope skipping was and why it was important. Each student had to work with someone to complete the same version of an activity.
- All students had to share their learning with an audience.

The following adjustments were made for the different groups:

Group Profile	Tasks
Have the most difficulty to coordinate jump over swinging rope	Version 1 ■ Students jump over lines/ropes marked on the floor, and walk over knee level swing of ropes

ASSESSING STUDENT'S PROGRESS FORMATIVELY

Group Profile	Tasks
	■ List learning cues that help them achieve the set goals ■ Share with an audience the challenges and solutions of the task and share how he/she overcame them
Able to jump slow turning ropes	**Version 2** ■ Jump over slow turning ropes and progress to jumping rope facing different directions ■ List possible challenges and solutions to jumping over a swinging rope held by others ■ Show a video clip of someone jumping over a skipping rope and its audience of elementary students
Competent to skip rope safely and confidently	**Version 3** ■ Perform three different ways to jump ropes held by others. ■ Conduct a survey of peer awareness and understanding of the importance of rope skipping to motor development. Survey is designed based on the parameters set by Teacher A (e.g. number of questions and students they can ask, information should cover essential safety and key learning cues.) ■ Present results as graphics, storyboards, or a series of charts. Whatever format students select, it has to convey both findings and implications.

Having read through Case studies 7.2 and 7.3, take some time to reflect on how you could use tiered assessment approaches in your own teaching using Task 7.4 to help you to do this.

Task 7.4 Applying tiered activities to your own practice

Using the example provided in Case study 7.3 undertake the following activities:

■ Plan how you might apply tiered activities to your own teaching and then use these activities in a lesson
■ Reflect on the impact of these assessment activities on the progress your students are making
■ Identify how you might apply tiered activities in other activities areas

Beyond assessment in the physical domain, it is important to assess learning in the cognitive domain. This is considered next.

Assessing the Cognitive Domain for Learning

Cognitive learning in physical education includes understanding of how the body benefits from activity. A student who can move proficiently has both skills and knowledge related to movement and values purposeful moving for life. Specific knowledge might include, for example, performance techniques, characteristics of movement quality, the application of movement concepts, tactics, elements of choreography, nutrition. To demonstrate learning, students make an intellectual connection between the activity and the physical benefit. This becomes evident through engaging in thinking activities.

In physical education, students can show what they have learned through using thinking routines. According to Ritchhart, Church, and Morrison (2011) these include:

1. Routines for introducing and exploring ideas;
2. Routines for synthesising and organising; and
3. Routines for digging deeper into ideas.

'Thinking' does not happen in a lockstep, sequential manner, systematically progressing from one level to the next (Ritchhart, Church and Morrison, 2011). It is much messier, complex, dynamic, and interconnected than that. It is intricately connected to content, and for every type or act of thinking, the levels of thinking can be discerned. In using thinking routines as tools for promoting thinking, you must first identify what kind of thinking you wish to elicit from students and then select the particular thinking routine as the tool for that job. Case study 7.4 provides an example of how a thinking routine can be applied in practice.

Think-Puzzle-Explore (TPE)

TPE is an inquiry and process-oriented routine which enables students' cognitive progress to be assessed as they reflect on their understanding of an activity through digging deeper into the ideas. It provides you with a sense of students' current understanding of a topic and thereby influences the shape and structure of subsequent teaching and learning. As such, it sets the stage for deeper inquiry and can be revisited throughout a unit.

Case study 7.4   Example of Think-Puzzle-Explore (TPE)

Teacher X introduced the topic of "Attacking Space" to her grade 3 class. She started the lesson with the question, "What do you think you know about attacking space in a net-barrier game?" In asking this question she used 'Think' to activate prior knowledge and curiosity about the concept of attacking space.

Prior to the practical lesson Teacher X got the class to access the school's student online learning platform to record individually their ideas and any thinking they had about keeping possession in the 'Think' section of a template (see Table 7.7) and questions they had of the topic in the 'Puzzle' column.

Before the practical lesson began, Teacher X collated the ideas and queries into a large piece of paper and hung it on a board. In the practical lesson, the ideas were shared with the whole class.

Next Teacher X directed the class to the 'Puzzle' column. Students' thinking was collectively made visible on the board, which helped trigger more responses from the students. Then, as a class, they discussed how they could explore the questions in groups or as individuals. Students' responses are displayed in Table 7.7.

Table 7.7 Third graders' thoughts and puzzles about "Attacking space in a net-barrier game"

Think *"What do you think you know?"*	Puzzle *"What puzzles you about this topic?"*
Attacking space to score a point. Attacking space means send object into place that opponent is not occupying. Put the object onto the ground in opponent's half of the court. Make opponent move all over their half of the court. Be quick with the attack. Guess where opponent will move and land object in the other end of the court. Win the game by scoring 11/15/21 points.	Who invented net-barrier game? How did the rules come about? Can the rules be different for players in the court? (For example the attacking area for players is different. Player A's space to attack is wider than Player B, because Player B has a higher skill level and so needs to be placed in a more pressured situation where there is less time to make decisions.) Can the height of the net be different? How was net-barrier created? Why were net-barrier games invented? How else can the object be sent to the opponent's half of the court besides using hand and racquet? How best to score points quickly in the game? What skills must I have to win the game? How can I improve my skills?
The students' thoughts and puzzles about "attacking space in net-barrier game" varied, both in content and levels of understanding. Topics raised included the origins of the game, the role and flexibility of rules, technical and tactical skills. Students' responses went far beyond acquiring technical skills related to "attacking space in net-barrier game" and questions of how to score points effectively and efficiently.	

(Continued)

Table 7.7 (Continued)

Think "What do you think you know?"	Puzzle "What puzzles you about this topic?"

As a result, Teacher X found herself thinking totally differently about the unit she was about to teach. After hearing and seeing the students' responses, she ensured that the planning for the unit addressed some of students' broader questions about the history, need, and importance of the concept as well as the standard objectives for net-barrier game. Consequently, there were rich discussions throughout the course of the unit. The students worked in small interest groups to explore some of the puzzles raised. These included designing a culminating competition for the class. While students still learned the basics of executing the fundamental skills and game play, their collective experiences with each other and appreciating the game increased.

Teacher X reflected that the process of using TPE gave her a good understanding about the student's conceptual level and how they could venture into a journey of deeper understanding about the content of the lesson. As the unit progressed, the students continued to review and refined their responses based on their learning in the 'Think', 'Puzzle', and 'Explore' sections via the school's online learning platform. From their responses, Teacher X was informed of the progress of students learning and planned her lessons for deeper inquiry throughout the unit.

Teacher X found that students' engagement in the unit was quite different than in the past. For example, by making their thinking visible, students were able to track their learning, with opportunities given to students to listen, interact, think, share, question, take risks, and value each other's thoughts. Further, students with learning difficulties enjoyed sharing their thoughts with others compared with being passive learners in the past. Their enthusiasm and engagement during the journey of thinking, exploring, and learning was evident.

Task 7.5 asks you to apply the Think-Puzzle-Explore strategy to your own practice.

 Task 7.5 Applying Think-Puzzle-Explore strategy to your own practice

Using the example provided in Case study 7.5 undertake the following activities:

- Plan how you might use Think-Puzzle-Explore strategy for formative assessment of your students and inform your own teaching
- Reflect on the impact of these assessment activities on the progress your students are making

- Identify how you might apply Think-Puzzle-Explore strategy in other activity areas

---

Case study 7.5 Differentiated assessment (cognitive)

A grade 5 class's profile ranged from students with a good background in net-barrier games to students with no exposure to playing net-barrier games. To gather information on students' progress, teacher P differentiated the assessment. She identified the following tasks for her students based on their readiness.

Focus Content: Net-Barrier Game

Grade: 5

Learning Outcomes: In order to assess students' understanding of attacking and defending space in a net-barrier game, students chose their group members and the task for the group to work on.

Same criteria for all groups: Based on the profile of the class,

- Groups' size between two to four persons
- Level of complexity: game to be inclusive
- Students decide the mode of presentation of their project of choice

Task (A): Modify/change the rules be inclusive for all group members

Task (B): Teach someone to play a net-barrier game. Record how you did it from start to end.

Evidence of learning included, for example,

- Suggesting three rules for the game that would ensure fair play
- Reflecting on self-contribution to group's quest for inclusivity
    - What was my contribution in the project?
    - What did I learn about myself?
- Collaboration in group to complete the project
    - How did the team come together to complete the project?
    - What did you learn about your teammates?
- Recordings of teaching someone to play the game
- Reflecting on individual contribution to group's quest for inclusivity
    - What was my contribution to the project?
    - What did I learn about myself?
- Collaboration to complete the project (if working in a group)
    - How did the team come together to complete the project?
    - What did you learn about your teammates?

Task 7.6 asks you to reflect on assessment in the cognitive domain.

> **Task 7.6 Assessing in the cognitive domain in your own practice**
>
> Using the example provided in Case study 7.5 undertake the following activities:
>
> - Plan how you might apply assessment of the cognitive domain to your own teaching
> - Reflect on the impact of these assessment activities on the progress your students are making

Assessing the Affective Domain for Learning

The affective domain deals with students' values, attitudes, and behaviours (see Chapter 8). Physical education contributes to the development of students' life-long learner traits; ability to work independently and with others, search for solutions, and stay focused during a task. This is a difficult domain to assess learning as it takes time and the right situation for values and behaviours to manifest.

According to Krathwohl, Bloom, and Masia's (1964) affective domain of learning taxonomy, the affective domain focuses on the attitudes, values, interests, and appreciation of learners. This taxonomy comprises of five levels (see Table 7.8), receiving and listening to information, responding to that information, internalising and organising values and consistently acting upon them, and developing characteristic behaviour based on the previous levels. This allows learners to understand what their own values are and how they have developed.

Table 7.8 Learning taxonomy of Krathwohl, Bloom, and Masia's (1964) affective domain

Level	Description
1 Receiving	Student's willingness to attend to particular phenomena of stimuli (classroom activities, textbook, music, etc.)
2 Responding	Active participation by the student. At this level the student not only attends to a particular phenomenon but also reacts to it in some way.
3 Valuing	The worth or value a student attaches to a particular object, phenomenon, or behaviour. This ranges in degree from the simple acceptance of a value (e.g. desire to improve group skills) to the more complex level of commitment (e.g. assumes responsibility for the effective functioning of the group). Valuing is based on the internalisation of a set of specified values, but clues to these values are expressed in the student's overt behaviour.

Level	Description
4 Organisation	Is concerned with bringing together different values, resolving conflicts between them, and beginning building an internally consistent value system.
5 Characterisation	Characterisation by a value or value set. A student has a value system that has controlled their behaviour for a sufficiently long time for them to develop a characteristic 'lifestyle'. Thus the behaviour is pervasive, consistent, and predictable.

Source: https://global.indiana.edu/documents/Learning-Taxonomy-Affective.pdf

Case study 7.6 looks at assessment of the affective domain in physical education.

Case Study 7.6 Affective domain in physical education

A grade 6 class was going to learn to play rugby over eight lessons. Besides learning the skills and concepts, they had to learn about the values of sportsmanship, respect, and integrity. Teacher Y invited students to co-construct evidence of each value into a choice of chart for their groups (refer to Table 7.9). In their groups of five, students were encouraged to practise at least one value across the lessons. After the unit, they were assigned to create a poster/video to promote sportsmanship, respect, and/or integrity within a physical education topic as educational material. Students had a choice to complete the assignment as an individual, pair, or group. They were also required to submit a reflection of their appreciation of 'Respect' (refer to Table 7.10). Students co-created the guidelines that included appropriate content and language for each of the values. Students were encouraged to be creative and original in presenting the intended messages.

From students' choices of actions over the lessons and submission of the poster/video assignment, Teacher Y referred to Krathwohl, Bloom, and Masia's (1964) affective domain learning taxonomy to assess students' understanding and learning of the values.

Table 7.9 Choice chart (sportsmanship, respect, integrity)

Name of student: _____			
Learning Taxonomy	Sportsmanship	Respect	Integrity
1 Receiving	Say 'sorry' for a foul I made	Referee's decision is final	I keep score accurately

(Continued)

Table 7.9 (Continued)

Name of student: _____			
Learning Taxonomy	Sportsmanship	Respect	Integrity
2 Responding	Describe to someone how a point is scored and lost	Present "How to play Rugby" to your class and answer questions from your peers about your presentation.	Play by the rules
3 Valuing	Help opponent who has fallen	I play my best in every game I participate in.	Include a rule that everyone touches the ball before a scoring attempt.
4 Organisation	Clap for opponents when they have done well (e.g. scored a goal)	Recognise and accept the different abilities of my team players by…	Own up when you caused the ball to be out of play.
5 Characterisation	#(Free)	#(Free)	#(Free)

#(Free) – students decide the actionable for the value.

Table 7.10 Student reflection of 'respect'

I used to think that being respectful is…	Now I think being respectful is…

Task 7.7 focuses on assessment of the affective domain.

Task 7.7 Assessing in the affective domain

Using the example provided in Case study 7.6 undertake the following activities:

- Plan how you might apply a choice chart and reflection strategy to assess how much your students' learning in the affective domain has progressed
- Reflect on the impact of these assessment activities on the progress your students are making
- Identify how you might apply student reflection strategies in other activity areas

SUMMARY AND KEY POINTS

Teachers often lament that assessing student learning in physical education lessons takes up curriculum time. They also question the accuracy of the information about student learning. For assessment to be administered effectively and efficiently, assessment must be integral to teaching and learning, routines need to be set in place, and teachers must teach and facilitate students' grasp of the purpose of assessment and how to use the assessment tools.

After working through this chapter, you should have a better understanding of formative assessment as a critical component of the physical education curriculum that provides information for both the student and teacher to focus on. This will inevitably support student learning and make for more effective teaching. It is important that you and your students both know students' starting points as well as what the aiming for. Clarity of the learning intentions and success criteria must be made known to students and be understood by them. Understanding the purpose of formative assessment, knowing your students and recognising them as individuals, enables you to be better able to select forms of assessment appropriate for assessing student learning.

Note: A list of further resources to help you take your learning forward is available on the PESTA website: https://academyofsingaporeteachers.moe.edu.sg/pesta/professional-development/book-chapters-by-the-pesta-team

References

Hughes, M. (2006) *And the Main Thing is... Learning: Keeping the Focus on Learning – for Pupils and Teachers No. 4 (Jigsaw Pieces) Paperback – 18 Dec. 2006*, Education Training and Support. https://www.amazon.co.uk/Main-Thing-Learning-Keeping-Teachers/dp/0954629035

Krathwohl, D.R., Bloom, B.S. and Masia, B.B. (1964) *Taxonomy of Educational Objectives, the Classification of Educational Goals. Handbook II: Affective Domain*, New York: David McKay Co., Inc.

Lund, J. and Veal, M.L. (2013) *Assessment-Driven Instruction in Physical Education: A Standards-based Approach to Promoting and Documenting Learning*, Champaign, IL: Human Kinetics.

Mandigo, J., Francis, N., Lodewyk, K. and Lopez, R. (2012) 'Physical literacy for educators', *Physical Education and Health Journal*, 75 (3), 27–30.

Nuthall, G. (2007) *The Hidden Lives of Learners*, Wellington: Nzcer Press.

Ritchhart, R., Church, M. and Morrison, K. (2011) *Making Thinking Visible: How to Promote Engagement, Understanding, and Independence for All Learners*, San Francisco, CA: Jossey-Bass.

Rovegno, I. and Bandhauer, D. (2017) *Elementary Physical Education: Curriculum and Instruction* (2nd edn), Burlington, MA: Jones and Bartlett Learning.

Schiemer, S. (2000) *Assessment Strategies for Elementary Physical Education*, Champaign, IL: Human Kinetics.

Shanklin, J. (2004) 'The impact of accountability on student response rate in a secondary physical education badminton unit', Unpublished master's thesis. Munice, IN: Ball State University.

Intentionality
The Key to Effective Affective Learning

Hanif Abdul Rahman

Introduction

Mention holistic development, and many teachers would immediately think of education that encompasses the cognitive, affective, and psychomotor domains. As Hansen (2008) stated, "the most effective physical education curriculums are those that incorporate all three domains (psychomotor, cognitive, and affective) of teaching and learning" (p. 9). Generally, the psychomotor domain is about physical movements, coordination, and the use of motor skills; the cognitive domain is predominantly related to mental and thinking processes; the affective domain refers to feelings, emotions, and attitudes (Hoque, 2016), or "student feelings, attitudes, values, and social behaviours" (Rink, 2014, p. 6).

This chapter is based on the premise that physical education is a subject that holds great potential for promoting students' affective development, specifically social and emotional competencies (SEC), as there are many opportunities for social interactions between students, and between students and the teacher, to occur in lessons (Bailey, 2006; Hellison, 2011; Theodoulides and Armour, 2001). With clearly defined affective outcomes that relate to the development of SEC, supported by an effective pedagogy, affective development fits naturally in a physical education setting. The impetus for developing students' SEC in an increasingly unpredictable, challenging, and complex world is unlikely to disappear. Therefore, as a physical education teacher, it is important that you understand how to effectively meet the affective learning needs of students in the 21st century without losing sight of the primary purpose of physical education, that of addressing students' psychomotor development.

Throughout this chapter, reference is made to the PAM (Physical Education, Art and Music) Research Report (Leow, Koh and Abdul Rahman, 2016) – a project undertaken from 2014–2016, designed to examine the impact of pedagogies in these subjects on student outcomes in relation to 21st century competencies.

OBJECTIVES

At the end of this chapter, you should be able to:

- define physical education learning outcomes for the affective domain with a focus on developing SEC
- recognise physical education pedagogical principles and practices that contribute to the effective development of SEC and
- use affective learning opportunities as a frame to explicitly infuse social and emotional learning (SEL) into your physical education lessons.

Learning in the Affective Domain in Physical Education

Due to the emphasis in education on the acquisition of academic skills, and the subjective, imprecise, and personal nature (Pope, 2005) of the affective domain, many teachers choose not to give attention to it due to its complexities (Adkins, 2004). Developing the affective learning of students in lessons is challenging but if physical education teachers look at affective learning as a specific skill set, they can use their knowledge of skill development in physical education to create opportunities for development of these skills in the affective domain.

A manageable way to codify the affective domain, is by unpacking the SEC that form part of learning in physical education. The Collaborative for Academic, Social and Emotional Learning (CASEL), works internationally to promote the development of social and emotional learning. It has identified five key domains of social and emotional competences (see Table 8.1) to support affective development. Certain SEC, which are better able to be developed by students in the context of physical education, can be identified and taught.

Table 8.1 Key domains of social and emotional competencies

Key Domains of Social and Emotional Competencies (SEC)	Description
Self-Awareness Students' ability to understand their own emotions, thoughts, and values and how they influence behaviour in various physical education settings.	This includes being able to recognise own strengths and limitations with a well-grounded sense of confidence and purpose. Behaviours include: ■ Identifying own emotions ■ Linking feelings and values ■ Experiencing self-efficacy ■ Demonstrating honesty and integrity ■ Integrating personal and social identities ■ Having a growth mindset ■ Developing interests and a sense of purpose

(Continued)

Table 8.1 (Continued)

Key Domains of Social and Emotional Competencies (SEC)	Description
Self-Management Students' ability to manage own emotions, thoughts, and behaviours effectively in different situations and to achieve goals in various physical education settings.	This includes being able to delay gratification, and motivation to accomplish personal and collective goals. Behaviours include: ■ Managing own emotions ■ Exhibiting self-discipline and self-motivation ■ Setting personal and collective goals ■ Using planning and organisational skills ■ Showing the courage to take initiative
Social Awareness Students' ability to understand the perspectives of, and empathise with, others in various physical education settings.	This includes being able to feel compassion for others and understand social norms. Behaviours include: ■ Demonstrating empathy and compassion ■ Showing concern for the feelings of others ■ Taking others' perspectives ■ Recognising strengths in others
Relationship Skills Students' ability to establish and maintain healthy and supportive relationships and to effectively navigate settings with diverse individuals and groups in various physical education settings.	This includes being able to communicate clearly, listen actively, cooperate, work collaboratively to problem solve and negotiate conflict constructively, provide leadership, and seek or offer help when needed. Behaviours include: ■ Communicating effectively ■ Developing positive relationships ■ Practising teamwork and collaborative problem-solving ■ Resolving conflicts constructively ■ Resisting negative social pressure ■ Showing leadership in groups ■ Seeking or offering support and help when needed
Responsible Decision-Making Students' ability to make caring and constructive choices about personal behaviour and social interactions in various physical education settings.	This includes being able to consider ethical standards and safety concerns, and to evaluate the benefits and consequences of various actions for personal, social, and collective well-being. Behaviours include: ■ Identifying solutions for personal and social problems ■ Anticipating and evaluating the consequences of own actions ■ Evaluating personal and interpersonal impacts ■ Making a reasoned judgement after analysing a situation

Source: Adapted from CASEL (2020)

Eccles and Roeser (1999) suggest that SEL is largely influenced by the teacher. Teachers who are socially and emotionally competent and aware of their own SEC are able to inculcate affective development in their students through means such as:

1 Development of a positive and supportive teacher-student relationship;
2 Establishment and implementation of guidelines for positive behaviour;
3 Promotion of intrinsic motivation;
4 Coaching students to navigate around conflicts;
5 Development of cooperation among students;
6 Modelling of respectful communication; and
7 Exhibition of positive behaviours.

(Jennings and Greenberg, 2009)

Where a teacher lacks social and emotional competencies, research by Marzano, Marzano, and Pickering (2003) suggests there are higher levels of disruptive behaviour and lower levels of on-task behaviour and learning exhibited by students. Thus, in order to effectively facilitate students' acquisition of SEC in physical education, the teacher must possess pre-requisite knowledge and skills (including subject content and pedagogical knowledge) to provide a foundation from which to effectively integrate and layer in the teaching of the affective domain in order to develop students' SEC. Task 8.1 provides an opportunity to reflect on your practices.

Task 8.1 Reflecting on your current practice in relation to students' development in the affective domain

Before reading further, reflect on your current physical education teaching practices in relation to students' development in the affective domain. List your approaches, and think of the reasons behind why you have adopted them. Two examples are provided to support you with this.

- I think I'm teaching fine. I'm doing fine because I believe in discipline; "No Discipline, No Learning". Hence, I instil discipline in my classes, so that my students are able to focus on the learning tasks without disruptions. A disciplined structured environment is the key to all learning. No noise, no chaos. I say, you the student, do. I will tell you if you are doing it right or wrong. Listen to me and do what I say and you will get the task right.
- *I* believe in being facilitative all the time, and attempt to talk to students when they are having difficulties learning and achieving the tasks I have given them, or, when they are behaviourally off-task. While talking to them, I try to get them to reflect on their actions and make their own decision to take appropriate actions to get back on task, or improve in achieving the task given. While showing them how to be confident in their own decision-making, I also hope to understand them better and develop a positive relationship with them.

Reflecting on the two examples in Task 8.1. In example 1, the teacher is demonstrating a very didactic teaching approach. Whilst minimising disruptive behaviours necessary to support student learning, what is not evident in this approach are the opportunities for students to develop their own self-awareness and management. In example 2, an approach focusing on engaging students with the learning process and giving them opportunities to take ownership of their learning is likely to build competencies such as personal relationships and responsible decision-making.

Guiding Pedagogical Principles and Teacher Practices That Contribute to the Effective Development of Social and Emotional Competencies

Drawing on previous research (CASEL, 2013; 2015; Hellison, 2011; Leow, Koh and Abdul Rahman, 2016; Rink, 2014; Rink and Hall, 2008; Saphier, Haley-Speca and Gower, 2008; Weare and Gray, 2003), Table 8.2 provides a set of pedagogical principles and examples of teacher practices that may help a teacher support student development in the affective domain in physical education. These were identified as part of the PAM Research Report (Leow, Koh and Abdul Rahman, 2016).

The next section looks as these four guiding pedagogical principles in detail.

Table 8.2 Guiding pedagogical principles and teacher practice for affective learning

Guiding Pedagogical Principles	Examples of Teacher Practice to Promote Learning in the Affective Domain
Positive Learning Environment Creating a caring and participatory learning environment	■ Developing positive teacher-student relationships, for example, referring to students by name, knowing their individual needs and interests, and engaging with them individually ■ Empowering students to make decisions by providing them with autonomy and choice, for example setting their own personal and group targets, such as allowing individuals or groups to choose movements for a gymnastics sequence or a group to choose tactics for playing a game ■ Creating a positive and supportive learning environment, for example, one that is motivating, encourages students to make an effort and persist in trying to achieve a new and challenging task
Effective Communication Giving clear instructions and useful feedback; modelling good behaviour	■ Modelling social and emotional competencies, for example modelling how to resolve a conflict when there is a disagreement among students during a lesson and explaining why you do so ■ Giving feedback appropriately, for example praising students for effort made and being specific about why the praise was given: "As the team captain, I liked the way you worked with

Guiding Pedagogical Principles	Examples of Teacher Practice to Promote Learning in the Affective Domain
	your team when that refereeing decision went against you. Rather than react, you spoke calmly to the team and were able to refocus them. You showed really good personal self-awareness. Well done" ■ Providing specific, clear, and concise instructions and learning cues for affective outcomes along with the behaviour expected, for example "Working in your groups, I want you to show each other the three balances you practised when you were working on your own. When you have seen and practised each others' balances, I want you decide on which three balances you are going to put into your group routine. Remember, you all need to be able to do the balances you have chosen, so listen before you decide"
Engaged Learning Engaging students meaningfully and guiding them in practice	■ Using appropriate psychomotor tasks to embed affective learning experiences, for example using a pair-work practice task on passing and receiving with peer feedback to encourage self and social awareness ■ Facilitating the achievement of learning outcomes by, for example, setting differentiated tasks which are appropriately scaffolded to adequately challenge all students, help them experience a sense of achievement, and enable them to develop self-awareness ■ Facilitating reflection, for example questioning students about affective learning instead telling them, providing opportunities and time for students to think about their actions, responses, and implications for themselves and others ■ Supporting students to transfer their learning within and beyond physical education, for example working with another person in the lesson or where the learning would be appropriate; or, they have exhibited the learning beyond the physical education lesson
Skilful Management Managing students with clear boundaries and routines	■ Having clear expectations of student behaviour, for example arriving at a lesson punctually and with physical education kit, encouraging students to support each others' learning ■ Establishing routines to encourage pro-social norms and respect for one another, for example respecting each other by enabling all students to voice an opinion, respecting equipment by collecting and returning it safely

Source: Adapted from Leow, Koh, and Abdul Rahman (2016)

Positive Learning Environment

CASEL (2013) states that a positive learning environment is vital to enhance students' affective development, including SEC. Through developing the ability to communicate and collaborate effectively, students will be able to show increased social awareness and sensitivity. The quality of the learning environment is dependent on the following:

1. Depth of teacher-student relationship;
   Beyond the relationship established between the teacher and the whole class, a teacher also needs to develop positive small-group and individual relationships with students. For example, during an activity a teacher can move around the class, address students by name, connect with them, and facilitate their learning. By being authentic in showing genuine concern for their well-being and needs, both physically and socio-emotionally, the teacher can further develop the relationship and support students in further internalising SEC.
2. Level of student autonomy and choice;
   Teachers should encourage students to take greater ownership of their learning by, for example, giving them autonomy and choice. For example, they can set goals individually, in pairs or groups, choose a partner or group with whom to work, select equipment that they feel most comfortable using for their particular ability or decide which differentiated task adequately challenges them (e.g. students choose to shoot at a goal from various distances).
3. Environment for student learning.
   The learning environment should be psychologically, socially, and emotionally safe and supportive and encouraging for all students to learn. For example, to be motivated to put effort into the planned tasks, persevere in overcoming the challenges of the lesson, develop an idea, and work collaboratively with others. For example, students' choice of distance from which to shoot at a goal can be used to enable students to use themselves as a point of reference for measuring their performance, focusing on their own ability, and motivating them to improve on their own previous learning, rather than comparing their achievements with other classmates.

Effective Communication

Three aspects of teachers' communication that influence students' affective development are:

1. The teacher as a role model for good behaviour;
   Teachers' management of students with respect, care, and concern are consistent with the promotion and expectation of student affective learning outcomes. If, for example, the value of teamwork is being emphasised in the lesson, as you move around to facilitate small-group activities, upon seeing students working well with each other, you can praise them, even 'high-five' them, and encourage them to do the same when they see one of their team doing something well.

2   Clear instructions and useful feedback by the teacher;
    Teacher effectiveness can be heightened through giving clear instructions on the management of activities and on student learning. Thereafter, feedback given to students needs to be task-specific, timely, and personal. In this respect, beyond addressing the psychomotor (and cognitive) domain, feedback should also be given on learning and attainment of SEC in the affective domain. For example, in addition to just the generic "good job!", "well done!", and "excellent!", which are encouraging, it is important to point out to students what was done exceptionally well. For example, "Good job! I love the way the both of you planned the gymnastic routine together. Just the way I had asked the class to do." Or, "Well done! I saw you persevere to beat the defender by trying all the moves we've practised before in class."
3   The teacher's use of appropriate learning cues for affective learning.
    As well as giving specific and appropriate learning cues in the psychomotor and cognitive domains, specific and appropriate learning cues for affective learning need to be provided. Verbal cue such as "say thank you" can be used, especially for younger students, to remind them to appreciate their classmates' help. Physical cues such as 'high-five' upon scoring a point or goal can be used to build the spirit of teamwork. Other reflective cues such as "step back and take a deep breath" can also be used to remind your students when they are facing high-anxiety situations.

Engaged Learning

Many physical education teachers perceive that affective development can be best achieved through pep talks and seizing casual and unpremeditated opportunities arising through certain situations, which are commonly termed *teachable moments* (Reuben, 1997). These situations can take many forms, for example, a pair of students cooperating very well in class, or a team which constantly encourages the opponents even when winning, or, when students disagree with each other during a lesson. While using teachable moments may not be wrong, it may result in the notion that affective development cannot be planned. However, failing to plan specifically for affective development can result in you failing to identify specific points within the lesson when the focus can be on an aspect of SEC. For example if you are planning for your students to lead their own warm-up, then you can consider how this will support their self-management skills. When using peer feedback you can work with your students to consider how to give feedback, thereby developing their self-awareness.

Engaged affective learning can be established through the following:

1   Using appropriate tasks to embed affective learning experiences;
    Pair and group work are ideal opportunities in physical education to promote affective development and should be incorporated in lessons, where appropriate. These need to be supplemented by facilitating the dynamics of

social awareness and relationship-building skills effectively when opportunities present themselves during the pair and group work, rather than at the end of the lesson. For example, both when students are cooperating or not working well together in a pair activity, this can be an opportunity for the teacher to observe, and then step in to facilitate students' self- and social awareness.

2   Facilitating success in learning;
    Task design and task development need to be appropriately pitched to promote student learning. A feeling of perceived success in physical education is important to engage students emotionally and develop them positively in the affective domain. The provision of differentiated tasks is an excellent way to empower students to practise tasks for which they perceive themselves to be physically and cognitively ready. The teacher's role in providing opportunities for them to experience success may well be to act as a facilitator in subsequent tasks.

3   Facilitating reflection;
    As well as asking students to reflect on their learning in the psychomotor domain, students should also be asked to reflect on their affective development. Beyond students thinking about ways to improve their runs, rolls, shots, or passes, a teacher should give students opportunities to reflect on their positive and negative personal and social behaviours.

4   Facilitating transfer in learning.
    Facilitating affective development could also include transfer of learning to other situations in physical education lessons, outside physical education lessons and to out-of-school contexts. Where possible, a teacher should also make connections on how positive behaviours, characteristics, and traits emphasised in physical education lessons are just as valid elsewhere. For example, teamwork is just as important in the students' science group project and playing in an orchestra. Perseverance, for example, is just as applicable in participating in sports and in academic and career pursuits.

Skilful Management

A teacher's ability to manage students well is a sign of having good management skills, and clear routines and expectations of behaviour are a hallmark of a good lesson. However, to enhance students' ownership of positive behaviour, autonomy and control needs to be transferred to the students through planned tasks that require them to exhibit sound reasoning, responsible decision-making, self-regulation, and conflict resolution. For example, while a teacher sets, and ensures students adhere to, organisational routines in lessons, depending on the maturity of the students, the teacher can also consider appointing leaders in the class to design and manage other routines such as the order for collecting and returning equipment, or organising an intra-class competition.

Task 8.2 asks you to reflect on how the principles explored earlier are embedded in your current practice.

 Task 8.2 How do I embed the four guiding pedagogical principles for developing the affective domain in my current practice?

Consider each of the four guiding pedagogical principles (earlier). As you do so, and using the table, consider how evident each of the principles is in your current practice. Do you enact any of the practices listed? If they are evident and/or you enact any of the practices, how else can you further strengthen the practice? If you do not enact any of the principles, what is preventing you from being able to enact them? An example is provided to help you.

Guiding Pedagogical Principle	Yes	No
Positive Learning Environment	*Example:* I often provide choice for my students, by letting them choose to practise a task in which they feel they can experience more success. I think I can further strengthen this practice by providing a scaffold for students to achieve and strive for more success in more challenging tasks. I can also try to get my students to set their own targets for tasks.	*Example:* I think I've not been establishing a positive learning environment by not developing positive teacher-student relationships. Because of my strong belief that, as a teacher, I should be in total control of the class, I often instruct and expect my students to practise tasks to my expectations. I should now try to understand their difficulties by connecting with them, for example, through talking to some students individually or in small groups.
Positive Learning Environment		
Effective Communication		
Engaged Learning		
Skilful Management		

Putting the Concepts Into Practice

The four guiding pedagogical principles and their corresponding teacher practices are essential in order to infuse affective learning into your physical education lessons. In planning a lesson you need to know the scope of the SEC you are aiming for students to develop and identify pertinent opportunities for affective learning. Infusing affective learning in your lessons should be seamless, and not compromise the achievement of psychomotor outcomes. Table 8.3 gives an overview of opportunities that may occur within a lesson for you to support affective learning. These opportunities were identified as part of the PAM Research Report (Leow, Koh and Abdul Rahman, 2016).

Table 8.3 Opportunities for affective learning

Affective Learning Opportunities	Description
Explicit Teaching The use of planned tasks, with a specific set of cues for the expected affective outcomes	■ Select an affective learning outcome and decide on the specific SEC objective(s) for the lesson ■ Define what the desired behaviour for the SEC should be ■ Design a task or tasks that create opportunities for students to practise the desired behaviour ■ Reinforce the desired behaviour through assessment, feedback, and while concluding the lesson ■ Facilitate the transfer of learning beyond physical education
Content Setting Settings occurring frequently or naturally in physical education with the potential for affective teaching	■ Student organisation (e.g. individually, in pairs, in groups) ■ Context of the setting (e.g. competitive with self, competitive with others, collaborative with others and in pairs) ■ The physical and psychosocial learning environment (e.g. well-spaced to explore movement, non-threatening, conducive, empowering with autonomy and choice)
Communication Styles The general disposition of a teacher's communication style that has an effect on the way students react and relate to the physical education tasks they do	■ Consider the tone you use to address students (e.g. firm yet approachable) ■ Consider the language used (e.g. words with positive nuances) ■ Consider role modelling the appropriate attitude, affective competencies, and expected behaviour through your actions
Didactic Interactions Specific approaches and interactions between the physical education teacher and a specific student or group of students	■ Establish a positive teacher-student relationship ■ Encourage positive student-student relationships ■ Facilitate reflection through questions that help students consider how they or others feel about the situation, the impact and appropriateness of their actions or the actions of others, and their next course of action ■ Give positive reinforcement of success in learning (e.g. be

Affective Learning Opportunities	Description
to act in a certain way; or, interactions between students that are structured by the teacher	specific when offering praise so students understand why they are receiving it and can maintain the behaviour; avoid using terms like "good job" or "that's fantastic" without elaborating why it is so good or fantastic)
Teachable Moments Anticipated positive or negative events the teacher takes advantage of to reinforce a certain aspect of affective teaching	■ Consider the planned tasks and predict possible teachable moments based on your experience so that you are better able to recognise and use them when they occur ■ While many teachers highlight negative teachable moments (e.g. upon noticing that a student was 'cutting-corners', the teacher stepped in and addressed the integrity issues), it is just as important to highlight positive ones (e.g. upon spotting a conflict resolved amicably between two students during a small-sided game, the teacher stepped in to address the situation by affirming and advocating pro-social behaviour) ■ Ensure that learning within a teachable moment is facilitated (e.g. draw attention to the expected behaviour, ask students to identify desired behaviour and state why it is desired, highlight links between skills and values within the moment and with application to real life)

Source: Adapted from Leow, Koh, and Abdul Rahman (2016)

Now that you have read the four guiding pedagogical principles and the five affective learning opportunities, read Case study 8.1. This case study looks to apply in practice the guidance provided in the chapter. It explores how you can start to think about opportunities within your lesson to develop students' learning in the affective domain and how this might be reflected in the activities you teach. It also considers how you can identify the impact on learning that is taking place.

Case study 8.1 Planning and teaching for affective outcomes

This case study is a narration of Misrun (*not his real name*), a primary school physical education teacher, planning and enacting a gymnastic lesson with the specific intentionality of layering and achieving the affective outcomes.

Part 1 – A little bit of background

Misrun has been teaching physical education in a primary school for 15 years. Whilst he developed a basic understanding of planning for learning in the psychomotor, cognitive, and affective domains during his initial teacher training, during his teaching career he has really only focused on developing his understanding of the psychomotor and cognitive domains of learning. His ability to plan for the development of the affective domain is therefore much less developed. In fact he freely admits that any learning in the affective domains is really by chance.

Following his attendance at a professional development course, he began to develop his understanding of social and emotional competencies (SEC), the concept of guiding pedagogical principles (GPP) relating to the affective domain, and the notion of affective learning opportunities. What started to become clear was that if he wanted to develop students' affective competencies within his teaching, he needed to ensure that they were planned for and that students needed to understand that it was an important part of their learning.

Part 2 - Identifying opportunities for developing students' learning in the affective domain

Following the course, Misrun started looking at how he might plan more intentionally to support the development of the affective domain. His first task was to identify within his planning what aspect of affective development he wanted his students to develop. He did this by focusing on what SEC he wanted to develop. From teaching the class previously, Misrun knew that the students were already able to work collaboratively and productively with a partner. He was confident that his students had started to develop *relationships skills*, specifically their ability to work together with others, and their *social awareness skills* in relation to understanding the need to show concern for others' feelings. He therefore identified that within his lesson he would look to develop students' ability to show cooperation by being aware of their own and partner's ability and showing care and concern for their partner when working together. This became his lesson objective.

Part 3- Planning for developing students' learning in the affective domain

Misrun included the following learning objective to his lesson plan: "Students will work cooperatively to develop and perform a gymnastic sequence and provide feedback on their own and their partner's performance". He looked again at what he would need to include in the lesson to allow his students the opportunity to develop in this area. As well as providing activities that would require his students to cooperate and work together, they would also need to develop their own *personal awareness* by thinking about their own performance as well as developing an *awareness of* others through their paired work. To achieve this, he planned a warm-up activity that required students to work cooperatively in a game of tag. To support students' ability to provide feedback on their own performance, he planned for them to video part of their sequence so that they could watch themselves and use cue cards to identify what was good about their performance and what they needed to improve upon. Finally, to allow students to provide feedback to others, he planned for groups to pair up to observe each other's sequences and provide feedback (in the same way as students had done when providing feedback on their own performance) to support improvement.

As well as looking at the SEC he wished to develop, Misrun also looked through his planning to ensure that he was embedding the general pedagogical principles when he was teaching. Key to the success of his lesson would be the establishment of a *positive learning environment* where the students felt confident to work together and both give each other feedback and receive feedback from a partner, as well as ensuring that the students remained *engaged in their learning*.

Part 4 – Teaching the lesson to support learning in the affective domain

At the start of the lesson, Misrun shared the lesson objectives with the students. Whilst he included psychomotor and cognitive objectives, he focused in more detail on the affective objective. He spent some time discussing with the students what it meant to work in a cooperative way and what to focus on when giving and receiving feedback on their/partner's performance. Misrun felt that by doing this he was able to set the tone for a *positive learning environment*. Misrun then introduced the warm-up activity, after which students moved on to working on their own to explore different ways of balancing, and then working with a partner to create a short routine using the different balances they had created. Throughout the lesson, Misrun observed different groups and listened to the feedback they either gave to themselves, or to others in the group.

Part 5 – The impact

During the lesson, Misrun took time to observe his students and how they were working with each other. As he watched, he saw that students frequently stopped the activity to talk with each other about what they could do to improve their performance. By providing cue cards that provided guidance for them to use to improve their feedback, the students appeared more engaged. Because they were listening to each other, their performances improved and towards the end of the lesson they were starting to challenge themselves to try some of the different balances they had seen other groups perform.

Cooperation (or indeed, any skill) is not developed in one lesson alone, so Misrun built on this initial work on cooperative learning in the next and future lessons.

When looking at developing students' learning in the affective domain, taking time to identify the key skills you wish to develop, providing planned opportunities within your lessons, and ensuring that students understand what skills they are developing are important. As the teacher, you also need to consider how you will assess the learning that has taken place (see Chapter 7 on assessment).

After reading Case study 8.1, Task 8.3 now asks you to reflect on and develop the use of affective learning opportunities within your lesson planning and delivery.

> **Task 8.3 Embedding affective learning opportunities in my planning**
>
> Using an existing lesson plan, identify any parts where you have leveraged on any of the five affective learning opportunities to develop students' SEC. Based on your reading of this chapter, find more affective learning opportunities in the lesson plan, and think of how you might further integrate affective learning if you were to teach the lesson again.

SUMMARY AND KEY POINTS

While physical education provides a natural conduit to promote affective learning, you must employ a range of teaching strategies that intentionally and purposefully address the affective domain and the development of students' SECs in your lessons.

Looking back at the three key objectives of this chapter:

- First, the chapter stressed the value of defining the affective domain by referencing students' SEC. To achieve this, you need to have a frame to define the affective learning outcomes for students to be able to demonstrate the expected behaviour in physical education lessons.
- Next, you need to demonstrate and model explicit expectations of students. As Gibbons et al. (2002) stated, "students ultimately take more responsibility for their actions and learning if they are aware of the expectations" (p. 31). Foregrounding affective expectations engenders a sense of accountability for students as they strive to achieve these expectations as well as for teachers as they facilitate students' affective development. The four guiding pedagogical principles and practices outlined present a compelling set of guidelines for professional practice. They define specific concepts that you can select in situating your teaching practices for student development of SEC in the affective domain.
- Finally, you need to understand and seek to assimilate affective learning opportunities into your pedagogical repertoire. The primary function of the five affective learning opportunities identified is to help

you to identify and plan pertinent opportunities for affective learning in planning and teaching a lesson. The five affective learning opportunities should help you plan and embed affective learning in your lessons without compromising the achievement of psychomotor (and cognitive) outcomes.

Researchers have identified that the achievement of affective learning goals is problematic, and adds to the range of skills and competencies required to be an effective physical education teacher (Bailey, 2006; Vidoni and Ward, 2009). However, as supported by Stenzel (2006), to navigate the complexities faced in developing students' competence in all the domains of physical education, this chapter stressed that the key to fostering effective affective learning within physical education lessons lies in the sheer intentionality of such efforts by the teacher.

Note: A list of further resources to help you take your learning forward is available on the PESTA website: https://academyofsingaporeteachers.moe.edu.sg/pesta/professional-development/book-chapters-by-the-pesta-team

References

Adkins, S. (2004) 'Beneath the tip of the iceberg', *American Society for Training and Development*, 58 (2), 28–33.

Bailey, R. (2006) 'Physical education and sport in schools: A review of benefits and outcomes', *Journal of School Health*, 76, 397–401.

Casel (Collaborative for Academic Social and Emotional Learning) (2013) *Effective Social and Emotional Learning Programs: Preschool and Elementary School Edition*, viewed 31 January 2021, https://casel.org/wp-content/uploads/2016/01/2013-casel-guide-1.pdf

Casel (Collaborative for Academic Social and Emotional Learning) (2015) *Effective Social and Emotional Learning Programs: Middle and High School Edition*, viewed 31 January 2021, https://casel.org/middle-and-high-school-edition-casel-guide/

Casel (Collaborative for Academic Social and Emotional Learning) (2020) *CASEL'S SEL Framework: What Are the Core Competence Areas and Where Are They Promoted?* viewed 31 January 2021, https://casel.org/wp-content/uploads/2020/12/CASEL-SEL-Framework-11.2020.pdf

Eccles, J.S. and Roeser, R. (1999) 'School and community influences on human development', in M.H. Bornstein and M.E. Lamb (eds.) *Developmental Psychology: An Advanced Textbook* (4th edn), Mahwah, NJ: Lawrence Erlbaum, pp. 566–638.

Gibbons, S.L., Robinson, B., Bruce, P., Bremen, K., Lundeen, L., Mouritzen, J., Perkins, J., Stogre, T. and Wejr, C. (2002) 'Using rubrics to support assessment and evaluation of personal and social outcomes in physical education', *Strategies: A Journal for Physical and Sport Educators*, 15 (4), 28–33.

Hansen, K. (2008) 'Teaching within all three domains to maximize student learning', *Strategies: A Journal for Physical and Sport Educators*, 21 (6), 9–13.

Hellison, D. (2011) *Teaching Personal and Social Responsibility through Physical Activity* (3rd edn), Champaign, IL: Human Kinetics.

Hoque, M.E. (2016) 'Three domains of learning: Cognitive, affective and psychomotor', *The Journal of EFL Education and Research*, 2 (2), 45–52.

Jennings, P.A. and Greenberg, M.T. (2009) 'The prosocial classroom: Teacher social and emotional competence in relation to student and classroom outcomes', *Review of Educational Research*, 79 (1), 491–525.

Leow, A., Koh, G.W. and Abdul Rahman, H. (2016) 'Effective affective learning: The case of physical education in Singapore', in S.L. Chua, K.B. Lim and H. Abdul Rahman (eds.) *Enhancing 21st Century Competencies in Physical Education, Art and Music: PAM Research Report*, Singapore: Ministry of Education, Singapore, pp.18–43.

Marzano, R.J., Marzano, J.S. and Pickering, D.J. (2003) *Classroom Management that Works*, Alexandria, VA: ASCD.

Pope, S. (2005) 'Once more with feeling: Affect and playing with the TGFU model', *Physical Education and Sport Pedagogy*, 19 (3), 271–286.

Reuben, S.C. (1997) 'Making the most of teachable moments', in C. Privisor and M. Canter (eds.) *Children of Character: Leading Your Children to Ethical Choices in Everyday Life*, Santa Monica, CA: Canter and Associates.

Rink, J. (2014) *Teaching Physical Education for Learning* (7th edn), Boston, MA: McGraw-Hill.

Rink, J. and Hall, T.J. (2008) 'Research on effective teaching in elementary school physical education', *The Elementary School Journal*, 108 (3), 207–218.

Saphier, J., Haley-Speca, M.A. and Gower, R. (2008) *The Skilful Teacher: Building Your Teaching Skills* (6th edn), Acton, MA: RBT Research for Better Teaching Inc.

Stenzel, E.J. (2006) 'A rubric for assessing in the affective domain for retention purposes', *Assessment Update*, 18 (3), 9–11.

Theodoulides, A. and Armour, K. (2001) 'Personal, social and moral development through team games: Some critical questions', *European Physical Education Review*, 7, 5–23.

Vidoni, C. and Ward, P. (2009) 'Effects of fair play instruction on student social skills during a middle school sport education unit', *Physical Education and Sport Pedagogy*, 14, 285–310.

Weare, K. and Gray, G. (2003) *What Works in Developing Children's Emotional and Social Competence and Wellbeing?* viewed 31 January 2021, http://webarchive.nationalarchives.gov.uk/20130401151715/http://education.gov.uk/publications/eorderingdownload/rr456.pdf

Developing as a Teacher

9 You as the Teacher

Teacher Identity and How It Relates to Your Philosophy of Teaching

Teng Tse Sheng

Introduction

The recent disruption caused by the COVID-19 pandemic turned what teachers know about teaching and learning upside down. Teaching remotely over a long period of time was unheard of before 2020. Remote teaching requires a skill set that was alien to many. The change in context also required teachers to rethink what physical education meant, and re-strategise how to effectively reach out to students. Did you remember feeling unease or frustration as you planned remote lessons? While planning the revised Scheme of Work, were there disagreements with your colleagues over what content to select, or how it should be taught? What could be the reason for the discomfort and frustration you felt, and the source of the disagreements? Pause and reflect for a moment.

Could the discomfort and frustration you felt be a result of how teaching and learning of physical education remotely, goes against everything you believe about the subject? Similarly, was the disagreement between you and your colleagues when discussing the content for remote learning a result of a difference in the beliefs you hold on the teaching, learning, and the nature of the subject? Such disagreements are not new and were relatively common even before the pandemic, as those of you who had those kinds of conversations would probably agree. Each of you may believe you are right because of your beliefs. These beliefs are usually hidden deep within each person. They are abstract and not very accessible to you, as very few people have really thought of or talked about them (Pratt, Smulders and Associates, 2016). Unaware of a hidden force manipulating your thoughts (and that of others), you may sometimes wonder why others do not understand your point of view.

This highlights several important questions that you need to ask yourself. For example,

1 What are your beliefs on teaching, learning, students, and content?
2 How have these beliefs been formed?

DOI: 10.4324/9781003171973-11

3   Are the beliefs you hold valid?
4   Are these beliefs making you reject new ideas or giving you fixed views about certain groups of students or ways of teaching?

Critical as these questions may be in your continual growth as a teacher, research has consistently shown that teachers are not aware of their own teaching beliefs (Pratt, Smulders and Associates, 2016). Knowing who you are and why you teach the way you do is integral to good teaching. As Palmer (1998) wrote, "Good teaching cannot be reduced to techniques; good teaching comes from the identity and integrity of the teacher" (p.10). So where should you start?

This chapter explores the importance of your teaching beliefs to you as a teacher and to your teaching, and consequently, to student learning. It examines ways that could encourage you to start reflecting on who you are and why you teach the way you do. Throughout the chapter, you are encouraged to relate your reading and the tasks to your own teaching and to reflect on the four questions posed previously.

OBJECTIVES

At the end of the chapter, you should be able to:

- articulate the importance of knowing your beliefs about teaching, learning, students, and content
- explain how your beliefs influence the way you plan and teach, and your development as a teacher
- use the Teaching Perspective Inventory (TPI) (2020) (Pratt, Smulders and Associates, 2016) and see learning through the eyes of students to examine and reflect on your teaching beliefs.

Why Are Teacher Beliefs Important?

The chapter begins by examining four questions:

1   What are beliefs?
2   How are beliefs formed?
3   Why is it important for you to know your beliefs about teaching, learning, students, and content?
4   How do your teaching beliefs influence the way you plan and teach, and your involvement in continuing professional development?

Defining beliefs is difficult. As explained by Pajares (1992), the term beliefs has a variety of meanings as they have been studied in diverse fields and researchers are not able to agree on a working definition. Similarly, in their comprehensive review of the literature on beliefs, Fives and Buehl (2012) highlighted how beliefs have been defined inconsistently by authors within and across fields. For the purpose of this chapter, beliefs are defined as "mental constructions of experience – often condensed and integrated into schemata or concepts that are held to be true and that guide behaviour" (Sigel, 1985, p. 351). While some may argue that knowledge is the driving force of teacher thought and decision, Lewis (1990) argues that the origin of all knowledge is rooted in beliefs. Belief is the invisible force that shapes what you see, how you think and drives what you do. This includes your lesson planning, your interaction with students, and your engagement in professional learning experiences (Fives and Buehl, 2012). How you view teaching, learning, students, and content is, thus, influenced by this lens that you put on. In short, beliefs are the "filter through which new phenomena are interpreted" (Pajares, 1992, p. 325). So how are beliefs formed?

Nespor (1987) argues that beliefs draw their power from previous episodes or events that colour the comprehension of subsequent events. They are formed early and tend to self-perpetuate, persevering even against contradictions caused by reason, time, schooling, or experience. In other words, you may not even be aware that a certain experience has shaped your beliefs about teaching, learning, students, and content. Those influences can come from a range of experiences, through a process of enculturation and social construction (Pajares, 1992). Examples of influences include your own schooling experience (Calderhead, 1996; Pajares, 1992), opportunities for, and type of, professional development (Organisation for Economic Cooperation and Development (OECD), 2009), teaching environment and culture of the school (Hardy, 1999; OECD, 2009), religion (Macdonald and Kirk, 1999; Mansour, 2008), and your life philosophy (Mansour, 2008; Pajares, 1992; Rokeach, 1968). What other factors could have shaped your beliefs about teaching, learning, students, and content?

All teachers hold beliefs about teaching, learning, students, and content. Understanding your belief structures is essential to improving your teaching practices, as the beliefs you hold influence your perception, judgement, and behaviour in the classroom (Butler, 2005, 2014; Calderhead, 1996; Ennis, 1996; Nespor, 1987; Pajares, 1992). As a result, your attitudes, beliefs, and practices also play a critical role in enabling you to support students' learning (Wacker and Olson, 2019). Before continuing, Task 9.1 is designed to help you to know yourself.

 Task 9.1 Knowing yourself

The importance of knowing yourself is, perhaps, best summed up by Palmer (1998) in his book, *Courage to Teach*,

> Teaching holds a mirror to the soul. If I am willing to look in that mirror, and not run away from what I see, I have a chance to gain self-knowledge – and knowing myself is as crucial to good teaching as knowing my students and my subject.
>
> (p. 2)

> Take a moment to reflect on the quote. When was the last time (if ever) you had a conversation with yourself on why you do what you do? What prompted you to have that conversation? How much do you agree that self-knowledge is critical to good teaching? What makes you say that? If you have not started this journey, read on and participate in the tasks. I am certain there will be many meaningful takeaways.

In order to know yourself, you must know the forces within that influence your thoughts and actions (i.e. your beliefs). But when asked about your beliefs on teaching, learning, students, or content, you may find that you struggle to articulate them. Teachers do not usually talk about or discuss their beliefs. Beliefs are often taken for granted, and as a result, you are not conscious of them. As beliefs are not examined, many of your beliefs are taken as truths even if they are based on incorrect or incomplete knowledge or are in conflict with personal and social realities (Pajares, 1992). In many cases, you continue to hold on to these beliefs even after evidence or scientifically correct explanations are presented to you (Pajares, 1992; Pratt, Smulders and Associates, 2016). Overtime, beliefs become so personal that they define a teacher's identity. When that happens, beliefs often become very resistant to change (Nisbett and Ross, 1980; Pajares, 1992). Let me share with you an example to illustrate this point. A former colleague of mine had served in the army before making the switch to become a physical education teacher. He believed that to instil discipline, the best way was to punish the whole class if someone stepped out of line, army style. His class could be seen doing several push-ups while he shouted at them (both boys and girls) like a drill sergeant because a number of students came late for the class. He believed that this worked all the time he was serving in the army. To him, discipline was key to success and it was his duty to make sure his students understood that. Feedback on this practice could not change him as he would defend his ways. By admitting that there was a better way to teach students about discipline would mean that he was wrong all this while and that he was not a good teacher.

Pratt, Smulders and Associates (2016) warned that:

> some of our beliefs are so rooted in core values that they represent long-held and significant aspects of who we are and how we see ourselves in relation to the world. With these deep-rooted beliefs, we sometimes assume that our values should be everyone's values.
>
> (p.14)

This may have implications for how you teach and your own personal growth (Saphier, Haley-Speca and Gower, 2008). For example, a teacher who holds strong beliefs that students are empty vessels and teachers are the fount of all knowledge filling up these empty vessels will favour more teacher-directed teaching styles and reject a more constructivist way of teaching games (e.g. Teaching Games for Understanding, Nonlinear Pedagogy). This teacher may also reject any continuing professional development opportunities that are constructivist in nature.

To change practice, you will need to honestly review your beliefs in their entirety by bringing these hidden beliefs to light, discussing them, and testing their validity (Tsangridou, 2006). In order to do that, it is sometimes necessary to look back at their origin: when the beliefs were formed. Examining beliefs that have been lying in the sub-conscious mind for a long time and that define who you are is not an easy, but a very necessary exercise (see Task 9.2).

No amount of lesson observations or professional development courses will change practice if teachers do not look within themselves to examine the unseen forces that guide what they do and how they view teaching and learning. But this self-reflective process cannot be done within a day or two. It is an ongoing exercise, a journey that teachers must embark upon and stay committed to. But, as you all know, time is a precious commodity for teachers. It may not be easy to convince them to start this process of self-discovery. Any tool or process that is introduced would, thus, need to be easy to use and impactful at the same time (see, for example, the following TPI section). The self-reflective process runs on autopilot when teachers see meaning in the exercise. For example, if it creates a dissonance that makes a teacher want to investigate further. While you may know the important role teaching beliefs play in the quality of teaching and learning, Doolittle, Dodds, and Placek (1993) pointed out that "few of us are yet sufficiently skilled in helping recruits articulate, share, discuss, or debate – much less change – their beliefs" (p. 364). In his book *Courage to Teach*, Palmer (1998) explained that it is important for teachers to have both identity and integrity (i.e. to know who they are, and the integrity to accept who they are). Having the courage to embrace their limitations and fear (for example, the fear of losing control in class and the fear of using technology), Palmer argues, is an important step towards change. But how many people truly know who they are? Do you know who you are? How do you begin this conversation, this soul-searching process?

Task 9.2 asks you to examine your beliefs.

 Task 9.2 Your beliefs

Before you continue, spend a moment reflecting on the following questions:

- What are your beliefs on the purpose of physical education, the role of teachers, how students learn, and the content of physical education? What makes you say that?
- How were these beliefs formed?
- Do you have any beliefs that you feel are holding you back in your teaching? For example, boys do not like to dance; students do not like teachers to ask questions as it interrupts their play. If yes, what are they? How were they formed?

> As you continue reading this chapter, review these beliefs constantly. Be honest when you interact with your inner thoughts and dig deep as you attempt to connect the beliefs to how they were formed to examine their validity.

The use of the TPI (Pratt, Smulders and Associates, 2016) and students' voice are two of the ways that this process of inward looking can begin. The TPI is discussed in the next section, followed by students' voice.

How Can You Uncover and Reflect Upon Your Beliefs?

The TPI

One of the ways of uncovering and reflecting on your beliefs is using an online tool known as the Teaching Perspectives Inventory (TPI) (see www.teachingperspectives.com/tpi). This was developed by a team led by Professor Daniel Pratt and Professor John Collins from the University of British Columbia in the late 1990s. The TPI measures teachers' profiles on five contrasting views of what it means to teach. The five perspectives are Transmission, Apprenticeship, Developmental, Nurturing, and Social Reform. Perspectives are not beliefs. Rather, "They are philosophical orientation of knowledge, learning and the role and responsibility of being a teacher" (Pratt, 2002, p.14). They comprise your belief, intention, and action (Table 9.2). Thus, a perspective is a lens through which you view teaching and learning and is neither good nor bad. No one perspective is superior over another. It does not necessarily mean that a teacher who has a dominant Developmental perspective is a better teacher than another teacher who has a dominant Transmission perspective. It just means that they view teaching and learning differently. Their teaching can be equally good, or bad, depending on how they enact the perspectives, and whether the beliefs and assumptions they hold are valid (Pratt, 2002). Table 9.1 gives more information about the five perspectives.

Table 9.1 Summary of five perspectives on teaching

Transmission (TRANS)	Teachers who see Transmission as their dominant perspective believe that: ■ Effective teaching requires teachers to have content mastery ■ Content is a well-defined and stable body of knowledge and skills ■ The instructional process is shaped and guided by the content ■ Teachers are responsible for effectively presenting the content to students and ■ Students are responsible for mastering that content

Apprenticeship (APPREN)	Teachers who see Apprenticeship as their dominant perspective believe that: ■ Effective teaching requires teachers to be experienced practitioners of what they are teaching ■ Students learn by observing them in action ■ Teaching and learning are most effective when people are working on authentic tasks in real settings of application or practice and ■ The instructional process should combine demonstration, observation, and guided practice, with students gradually doing more of the work
Developmental (DEVEL)	Teachers who see Developmental as their dominant perspective believe that: ■ Effective teaching begins with the students' prior knowledge of the content and skills to be learned ■ It is important to restructure how people think about the content ■ Increasingly complex and sophisticated cognitive structures emerge when thinking about content and ■ Effective questioning and 'bridging' knowledge challenges students to move from relatively simple to more complex forms of thinking
Nurturing (NURTUR)	Teachers who see Nurturing as their dominant perspective believe that: ■ Effective teaching must respect the student's self-concept and self-efficacy ■ Teachers should be committed to the whole person and not just the intellect of the student ■ It is important to support effort as much as achievement ■ Anything that threatens the student's self-concept interferes with learning and ■ There should be a balance between challenging students to do their best, while supporting their efforts to be successful
Social Reform (SOC REF)	Teachers who see Social Reform as their dominant perspective believe that: ■ Effective teaching should go beyond content or individual learning and lead to social change ■ Social issues and structural changes in society are necessary ■ It is important for teachers to be clear about what changes should take place in society and ■ Teaching is an instrument of social change

Source: Adapted from Pratt and Collins (2000)

The tool is both reliable and valid (Collins and Pratt, 2010), and has been widely used by researchers in their research on teaching beliefs over the years. The TPI is easy to use. It takes about ten minutes to complete the self-scoring 45-question survey. It reflects the teacher's dominant and recessive perspectives. The TPI identifies the level of belief, intention, and action within each perspective (Table 9.2 and Figure 9.1) and can detect conflicts within each perspective (i.e. when the score difference between belief, intention, and action is 3 or more). These features of the TPI make it a very useful reflective tool as the indicators provide an entry point for the conversation to begin.

Task 9.3 asks you to complete the TPI.

Table 9.2 Beliefs, intention, action

Beliefs (B)	Beliefs represent underlying values which are held to varying degrees of meaning by teachers. It is the most stable and least flexible aspect of a perspective on teaching.
Intentions (I)	Intentions of the teacher are general statements that point toward an overall agenda of purpose. It is the teacher's statement of purpose, responsibility, and commitment directed toward students, content, context, ideals, or some combination of these.
Actions (A)	Actions are described as the routines and techniques which are used to engage students in content. It is the most concrete and accessible aspect of a perspective on teaching and are the means through which you activate intentions and beliefs to help students learn.

Source: Pratt, Smulders, and Associates (2016)

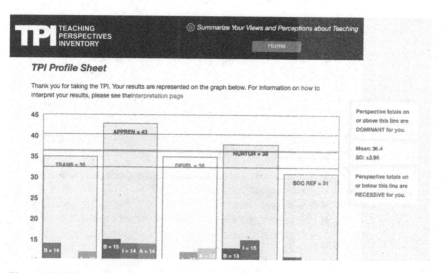

Figure 9.1 TPI results of Teacher X

 Task 9.3   Completing the TPI

Before reading further, please complete the TPI by visiting the website www.teachingperspectives.com/tpi. When answering the questions, have in mind a class that is most representative of the students you are teaching. After completing the survey, the result is shown in the form of a chart (see Figure 9.1). The chart by itself means nothing if there is no accompanying reflection or conversation. But if you analyse the result carefully, it will tell a thousand stories and enable you to uncover underlying subconscious beliefs. The website has a video that guides users on how they may go about analysing the result. Do take some time to watch it.

By reflecting on your results on the TPI, there is a possibility that you may start to uncover hidden beliefs and assumptions that you have held over many years. Only when you are conscious of these beliefs and assumptions can you start to examine them. This reflective process provides opportunities for you to gain greater clarity about why you teach the way you do, and embrace who you are, including acknowledging your own fears (i.e. what Palmer refers to as integrity). This importance was highlighted by Butler (2014):

Effective teaching practice cannot be separated from the beliefs and intentions that lie at its heart, even though these are not always easy to articulate. Teaching involves both the chicken and the egg, in that the ways we plan, teach and assess reveals what we believe about knowledge and learning, and what we believe about knowledge and learning inevitably influences what we offer our students in the way of learning experiences.... It is thus important that teachers delve into their tacit knowledge and understanding of teaching and learning in order to identify their beliefs and intentions and to investigate their congruency with their pedagogical actions.

(p.17)

Case study 9.1 looks at how the TPI was used to help one teacher uncover the underlying forces that influenced the way she taught. The process not only helped her know herself better; it also helped her become a better teacher as she resolved her internal conflicts.

Case study 9.1 Teacher X

The TPI in Figure 9.1 belongs to Teacher X, with whom I have been working with for the past three years. She is an experienced teacher, having taught in a secondary school (i.e. 13- to 16-year-olds) for 17 years. Teacher X embraces the game-centred approach while teaching games in her physical education classes but struggles with some unexplained discomfort when using it. As we worked through her TPI, we discovered many interesting things. The game-centred approach focuses on student inquiry, with the teacher acting as a facilitator of learning. Students are empowered to learn through playing well-designed games or practice tasks. The teacher supports student inquiry with a variety of questions to activate their thinking. Students are encouraged to collaborate with their teammates to experiment, explore, and problem solve. Through the process, students make meaning of their learning, and develop a sense of self-efficacy. As such, teachers who are proponents of game-centred approach would be expected to have higher scores in the Developmental and Nurturing perspectives (Butler, 2014).

Teacher X's TPI showed otherwise (refer to Figure 9.1). Her TPI scores suggested that she was still grappling with the value of using questions and giving time and space for students to make meaning of their own learning (as suggested by the low belief score (B=10) for the Developmental (DEVEL) perspective. While she had clarity in her sense of purpose when planning her lesson from the Nurturing (NURTUR) perspective (her intention score (I=15) for the Nurturing perspective was the highest among the five perspectives), the nurturing disposition was not apparent in her actual teaching (her action <A> score for the Nurturing Perspective was 10, joint lowest with Social Reform <SOC REF> perspective). In addition, her high belief score (B=14) for the Transmission (TRANS) perspective suggested that deep inside her, she still believed strongly in the value of direct instruction.

The findings initially surprised Teacher X. She had always thought that, as a game-centred approach practitioner, she would be high in Developmental and Nurturing perspectives, and low in the Transmission perspective. Upon reflection, she realised that these conflicts were not conscious to her. They may even have been be the cause of the discomfort and struggle she had been facing internally whenever she implemented the game-centred approach. As we analysed, interpreted, and made meaning of the results, we uncovered some possible reasons behind the conflicts and low scores for the Developmental and Nurturing perspectives (i.e. short lesson time, lack of the right learning culture for game-centred learning, and student's readiness to learn through a game-centred approach). The failure to get an appropriate response from students (i.e. students not responding to questions and not actively solving a tactical problem in the game) caused Teacher X to doubt the value of using inquiry to teach games. Unconsciously, Teacher X's belief in a more direct instruction approach to teaching games further contributed to the internal conflict and struggle. Upon reflection, she attributed that situation to how she herself was taught and coached by her teachers and coaches when she was a student.

The conversation on her high belief score for the Transmission (TRANS) perspective (B=14) also led to an interesting discovery; her fear of losing control of the class. To Teacher X, losing control was a sign of poor teaching. Before completing the TPI, she had not acknowledged this fear of losing control as she did not, in her words, wish to show her vulnerability. So rather than embracing this fear, she tucked it away. This prevented her from working on her fears and resulted in the conflicts she was experiencing. So, what did Teacher X do?

Teacher X wanted to make game-centred approach work. With this in mind, and a better understanding of herself after analysing her TPI scores, the plan was to devise ways to increase her belief (B) score for the Developmental (DEVEL) perspective and the action score for the Nurturing (NURTUR) perspective. To do that, she decided to implement the game-centred approach slowly by first preparing the class. She focused on developing the right learning culture and preparing students through a more structured and measured approach. To make sure that she was more deliberate in affording time for her students to problem solve (a trait of a teacher high in the Nurturing perspective), she would invite a colleague to observe her lesson, or record her own lessons and review them afterwards. In addition, Teacher X also took the step to accept and work on her own fear. She acknowledged that good classroom management comes in many forms, and one could still have control of the class in a different way. With a good lesson environment, and students working independently and collaboratively, control can still be achieved with the ownership of learning passed to the students. To teach the game-centred approach well, Teacher X acknowledged that she needed to make changes to how she viewed the roles of teacher, students, and learning.

While this realisation could have been achieved without the use of TPI, there is no denying the usefulness of the tool in allowing Teacher X to journey into her past, present, and future in an attempt to know and embrace who she really is as a teacher.

Task 9.4 asks you to analyse your own TPI profile.

Task 9.4 Analysing your TPI profile

Analyse your own TPI profile. Use the following questions to guide you as you reflect on the scores. Be honest and truthful when answering the questions:

- What is/are your dominant/recessive perspective/s? What are the beliefs/assumptions that may have led to the result?
- Are there internal discrepancies (i.e. conflicts) within each perspective (i.e. a score difference of 3 or more between beliefs, intentions, and action)? What may have led to these differences?
- Are the scores consistent with how you see yourself? Do they make sense to you? Are there any unexpected insights?
- How well does other evidence (e.g. student evaluations or feedback from colleagues) corroborate your TPI profile?
- Does your TPI profile highlight how you want to be seen by your colleagues and students?
- What underlying beliefs, assumptions, or convictions emerge from your profile?
- After analysing your TPI, what is one thing you need to do to help you grow as a teacher?

As the purpose of TPI is to create a dissonance and start a conversation, creative use of the TPI helps you uncover things about yourself you may not be aware of. It can create a dissonance and trigger a series of internal reflection. The following list identifies some other ways you may use the TPI to reflect on who you are. Try them if you have the opportunity:

1. Ask a colleague or students to complete the TPI survey for you. You will then know how others perceive you as a teacher versus how you perceive yourself. Important questions need to be asked if the difference is significant. This may help you reflect on what you do and say that have led to others perceiving you in a way that may be different from how you perceive yourself as a teacher.
2. Complete the TPI survey with groups of students in mind. For example, complete one TPI survey with a group of students who are more athletic in mind and complete the other TPI survey with another group of students who are less athletic in mind. If the results are different, then you can ask yourself if the differences are due to unconscious stereotypes or biases that you may hold.
3. Complete the TPI survey every three to six months to track your own growth. You may see a change in the perspectives score and ask yourself what may have caused those changes (e.g. a professional development course that you have attended, an action research you have conducted, a series of experiences you have had in school, a colleague who has been assigned to coach you). If the reasons behind the shifts are not examined, it may lead to a change in beliefs, even if they are not valid or supported by evidence.

(Note: A change in perspective score may not be due to a change in beliefs. It can be due to a change in intention and action. In some cases, the shift may also lead to a conversation on the validity of the beliefs held. What results in the shift depends on the teacher's own individual journey.)

One of the limitations of the TPI is that it requires time for teachers to analyse and reflect on the many soul-searching questions raised. While you know there is no short cut if you want to have a meaningful reflective conversation, the reality is that time is a scarce commodity for teachers. Very often, teachers do not reflect deeply on their TPI results. In addition, some teachers' beliefs have become so deeply rooted that these beliefs have become part of their identity. For these teachers, the TPI alone may not be enough for them to open the doors to their inner world. If you believe that teachers teach because of their love for students, then perhaps, students' voice may provide a stronger nudge to start examining their own biases and assumptions regarding teaching, learning, students, and content, and to know who they truly are. We now look at student voice.

Challenging Teaching Beliefs Through Students' Voice

Teachers are designers of learning. In order to design quality learning experiences, knowing your students is key. But how well do you know your students and how they learn? Have you attempted to see physical education through the lens of your students? How do you know that the assumptions and beliefs you have about students and learning are accurate?

These questions are important as teachers. Consider the following comments made by some teachers. Have you heard similar comments before?

> Girls are not interested in sports like football
> The students in this class are not academically inclined, they do not like me to ask questions. They just want to play.
> Girls and boys do not like to be in the same group. Girls generally think that boys are too competitive, and boys generally think that girls slow the game down.
> Students in the graduating classes just want to play to de-stress. They are not interested in learning.

Your beliefs about your students and how they learn affect how you design learning experiences. For example, if you believe that girls do not like to be in the same group as boys, girls and boys will never get the opportunity to collaborate, or if you believe that certain groups of students are not able to self-regulate their learning, they will never be given the opportunity to learn independently.

Teachers play an important role in the social and emotional dimension of student learning. The subtle messages you send through your body language, what you say and do, and the experience you design shape students' experiences in school, their motivation to learn, and their achievement level (Wacker and Olson, 2019). In the earlier examples (i.e. the comments by teachers), students' learning will be compromised as a result of what you believe about how students learn.

Over time, students may take on the beliefs of their teacher, which may have long-lasting effects on how they see themselves and on their self-esteem. There is, thus, an urgent need for teachers to check their own hidden biases and mental stereotypes through an honest review of their own beliefs.

But if you insist that you are right, how can you be encouraged to revisit and review your teaching beliefs? As Prawat (1982) suggests, "getting people to change beliefs, especially intuitively reasonable ones, is a difficult proposition" (p. 357).

For teachers to change their beliefs, identifying what is problematic with their existing beliefs is an important first step (Prawat, 1982). So, you are asked this question: "What if you have been wrong all this while about your students?" (i.e. you have inaccurate beliefs based on experience not supported by research or evidence). If you can see teaching and learning through the lenses of your students, it can provide you with a mirror to check the validity and accuracy of your assumptions. Students are your teachers in many ways. Their voices can be powerful influences over teacher change. This is discussed in Case study 9.2.

Case study 9.2 Students' voice and its impact on teaching beliefs

In 2018, I collaborated with two teachers to study how 400 secondary school students aged 15 years in Singapore perceived their physical education experience. We conducted a survey to find out what made physical education enjoyable or not enjoyable to them. In addition, we conducted four focus group discussions with selected students. The impact the findings of the study had on the two teachers was immense. It made them reflect on the assumptions and beliefs they had held onto dearly prior to the study. It changed their practice and made them realise the importance of seeking the voice of students to co-construct the physical education learning experience. For instance, both teachers' belief that the teacher is the authority of knowledge was challenged. Students' view on teaching and learning created the cognitive dissonance that triggered the need to reflect and review the teachers' own assumptions and beliefs. This led to the teachers changing their perspective, to seeing themselves as co-participants of learning, and that they, too, are learning from the students.

Now take a closer look at two of the findings from the study and how they have caused a shift in the teachers' beliefs.

Finding 1: The opportunity to interact with their friends
The opportunity to interact, play, and learn with their friends was overwhelmingly the top reason given by students on why they enjoyed physical education lessons. Students reflected in the survey and in the focus

group discussions that they do not get many opportunities to interact and learn with their friends in other lessons. Friends play an important role in the lives of students, especially during their teenage years. This is best summed up by the following quotes from students during the focused group discussions:

> *During the lesson, everyone is having fun playing together, fully involved. That's when you really get to know your classmates well. During other classes, all we do is study.*
>
> *Getting to play as a class, doing something wrong but just laughing off our mistakes and having fun together.*
>
> *When I get to play with my friends and bond with them (during physical education), it makes me want to attend school.*

This revelation by students made both teachers rethink how they design learning experiences. While the teachers were aware that the opportunity to play and learn with friends is important, they did not expect it to be the major determinant as to whether physical education lessons become enjoyable. Upon reflection, the teachers agreed that they may have overlooked the social component of learning at times, as they prioritised content and performance standards. The findings prompted the teachers to review their long-held belief on the purpose of physical education, and how students learn. So how has this changed the way both teachers design their lessons? Collaboration is now a key feature in their lessons, and the grouping strategy they employ is more intentional and flexible to allow students to build relationships and learn together. For example, teachers may group students randomly to promote interaction, or group them based on skill level to better address their learning needs. Students are also given time to practise key skills with their friends independently before the start of the lessons.

Without this set of responses from students to encourage the teachers to review their long-held beliefs on teaching and learning, it is likely that they may have continued to teach the way they did and miss many opportunities to improve social cohesion and improve the quality of learning and the level of enjoyment in a physical education class.

Finding 2: Not enough time to play

A normal school day is long, and many students look forward to physical education not only as a time to interact and learn with their friends, but also a time when they get to exercise, engage in friendly competition, or simply to play or exercise to de-stress. The two, one-hour weekly physical education lessons they have each week are, thus, very precious to students. They get very upset when the time is used by teachers to, for example, discipline the whole class because of one recalcitrant student, or when teachers spend too much time explaining a task. It is little wonder that students in the study cited having insufficient time to play as the biggest turn-off in their physical education lessons. The following quotes from focus group discussions illustrate this point.

> The teacher talks too much. They take too long to explain the task!
> We only have two physical education periods per week. If the teacher spends half the time talking, we are left with very little time to play. We don't like it when our teacher spends half the session scolding us. Sometimes, the whole class was scolded because a small group of students was being disruptive. The teacher is wasting precious physical education time!

Such responses from students made the teachers rethink how they should approach teaching, and their role as teachers. Prior to the research, they believed that it is the role of teachers to make sure everyone understands the instructions. The teacher, who is the authority of knowledge in the class, has the responsibility to ensure that the learning is paced to the needs of the students. In addition, like many teachers, they believed that students learn best when there is order, and a good teacher is one who has complete control of the class. This often leads to over-instructing and stopping the class to address minor behavioural issues. Indeed, letting go of control has often been identified as one reason why teachers are uncomfortable with more constructivist way of teaching (e.g. Teaching Games for Understanding).

The overwhelming response from students on wanting more time to play and practise convinced both teachers in the project to critically review their beliefs about teaching and learning. When they were willing to review their belief, it opened the door to review the validity of their beliefs on the role of the teacher and how students learn. They began to realise that control can be achieved through established routines, and misbehaviour can be resolved through other means (e.g. making the task engaging, speaking to the students involved separately rather than disrupting the whole class). They also realised that learning can be equally effective when students are empowered to problem solve collaboratively, and not necessarily through step by step progression instructed by the teacher. To the untrained eye, such a lesson may seem chaotic, with different groups of students playing a slightly different game, seemingly without the guidance from the teacher. It is true that there may be times when disagreements among students may break out, but teachers have to take that into their stride if they see it as part of the learning process.

A few months after the study, we asked students what they liked about their lessons now. The following were a sample of their responses:

More opportunities to play and learn as a class.
I enjoy when my class splits into groups and pairs to teach each other.
We get to change some of the rules of the game to make it more playable and enjoyable for us.

The change in practice, which resulted from a review of the two teachers' teaching beliefs, led to a more positive learning environment and more engaged learning. Students appreciated the greater autonomy and more time given during lessons to allow them to explore and problem solve. They also enjoyed how they could now learn from, and with their friends through the many collaborative tasks that the teachers had planned.

When teachers open the doors to their "inner landscape" (Palmer, 1998) and accept who they are, they embrace their vulnerabilities and own their fears. When they accept the need to change, rather than build an invisible wall to protect their identity as teachers, possibilities present themselves and they begin to teach who they are. And in teaching who we are, we connect with our students and enable them to engage with the subject in an enjoyable and meaningful process of learning.

Closing Thoughts

As your beliefs shape the way you plan, teach, and learn, a better understanding of your beliefs and who you are is essential to improving teaching practices (Pajares, 1992). To encourage you to access and review you beliefs, this chapter suggested using the TPI and students' voices to start this self-discovery journey.

The assumption is that if you care about the well-being of your students, the realisation (e.g. from the TPI or from what your students tell you) that your beliefs about teaching and learning may be invalid or inaccurate, may create a cognitive dissonance within you. The wall that you have erected to defend your beliefs may start to weaken. While practice may not change immediately, especially if those beliefs have been left unexplored for many years, the dissonance created could spark you to start questioning the validity and accuracy of your beliefs. If used together with the TPI, students' voices provide you with a more structured approach to review your beliefs. The process could lead you to discover who you truly are and uncover the reason you teach the way you do. As we approach the end of this chapter, how much have you discovered about yourself and why you teach the way you do? Take a moment to complete Task 9.5 to consolidate your thoughts.

> **Task 9.5 Consolidating your thoughts on beliefs**
>
> *When I do not know myself, I cannot know who my students are. I will see them through a glass darkly, in the shadows of my unexamined life – and when I cannot see them clearly, I cannot teach them well.*
>
> (Palmer, 1998, p. 2)
>
> Take a moment to reflect on the quote and the following questions. This exercise will be more meaningful and less arduous if you have taken time to complete the first four suggested tasks in this chapter. When answering the questions, refer back to the response you have given in Task 9.2.
>
> - How well do you know yourself as a teacher?
> - How have your beliefs in teaching, learning, students, and content shaped the way you plan and teach physical education?
> - Are there beliefs that are hidden and taken to be truths?
> - Are there beliefs that may be holding you back in your professional development as a teacher?
> - Are there beliefs that you are refusing to review, and have unconsciously become a part of who you are?

As Butler (2005) pointed out, teachers need to be supported with the tools, time, and space to engage in reflection, discussion, and consideration of their views and beliefs. Change in belief is more likely if experiences offer opportunities for practice, reflection, and support (Fives and Buehl, 2012). Without the right support, this is a real challenge as you are all aware of the demands of teaching. To ask teachers to start reflecting on something that is abstract and implicit can be challenging (Pratt, 2002). While the TPI provides a structure to start this reflective process, you may still find the process demanding. While there is no easy solution to this challenge, you are encouraged to start small, and do it often enough to make it a habit. Reflection does not have to take a long time to be effective. For a start, find pockets of time in your daily routine for this purpose (e.g. on your way to work or home or during your daily run or walk). What is important is that the reflection must be sustainable and realistic. If you can only afford the time to do it weekly, start with a weekly reflection time. Once it has become a habit, you can then explore ways to increase the frequency.

As Pajares (1992) explains, early experiences have strong influences on beliefs. Such early beliefs lead to biased interpretations of your subsequent experiences and influence the processing of new information. In time, these beliefs become resistant to changes. Having said this, beliefs are at their most adaptable, and least stable, when they are newly acquired. It is thus of paramount importance that pre-service and beginning teachers form the habit of reviewing their educational beliefs to ensure that they are valid, and revise them in face of contradictions, before beliefs become too deeply rooted. This is especially so for beliefs that may interfere with good teaching and teachers' continuing professional development (Raths, 2001). Good teaching should not be just about the mastery of content, techniques, and knowing how your students learn. As Palmer (1998) wrote, "good teaching requires self-knowledge: it is a secret in plain sight" (p. 3).

SUMMARY AND KEY POINTS

The aim of this chapter was to develop your understanding on the important role teaching beliefs play in shaping students' learning experience and your own professional growth. We have explored, with the use of case studies, how you may start this journey of self-discovery using the TPI and students' voice.

If you have undertaken the tasks, and considered your own practice, you should be able to:

- articulate the importance of knowing your beliefs about teaching, learning, students, and content
- explain how your beliefs influence how you plan and teach, and your development as a teacher
- use the TPI and see learning through the eyes of students to examine and reflect on your teaching beliefs.

Moving forward, do not confine the conversation to yourself. You are encouraged to share your thoughts with your mentor, a colleague, or friend. Having someone to check your blind spots, ask difficult questions, or simply providing a listening ear helps make this journey more enriching, meaningful, and sustainable.

Note: A list of further resources to help you take your learning forward is available on the PESTA website: https://academyofsingaporeteachers.moe.edu.sg/pesta/professional-development/book-chapters-by-the-pesta-team

References

Butler, J. (2005) 'TGfU pet-agogy: Old dogs, new tricks and puppy school', *Physical Education and Sport Pedagogy*, 10 (3), 225-240.

Butler, J. (2014) 'TgfU – Would you know it if you saw it? Benchmarks from the tacit knowledge of the founders', *European Physical Education Review*, 20 (4), 465-488.

Calderhead, J. (1996) 'Teachers: Beliefs and knowledge', in D.C. Berliner and R.C. Calfee (eds.) *Handbook of Educational Psychology*, New York: Macmillan, pp. 709-725.

Collins, J. and Pratt, D. (2010) 'The Teaching Perspectives Inventory at 10 years and 100,000 respondents: Reliability and validity of a teacher self-report inventory', *Adult Education Quarterly*, 61 (4), 358-375.

Doolittle, S., Dodds, P. and Placek, J. (1993) 'Persistence of beliefs about teaching during formal training of preservice teachers', *Journal of Teaching in Physical Education*, 12 (4), 355-365.

Ennis, C. (1996) 'A model describing the influence of values and context on student learning', in S. Silverman and C. Ennis (eds.) *Student Learning in Physical Education: Applying Research to Enhance Instruction*, Champaign, IL: Human Kinetics, pp. 127-147.

Fives, H. and Buehl, M. (2012) 'Spring cleaning for the "messy" construct of teachers' beliefs: What are they? Which have been examined? What can they tell us?' in K.R. Harris, S. Graham and T. Urdan (eds.) *APA Educational Psychology Handbook*, Washington, DC: APA, pp. 471-499.

Hardy, C. (1999) 'Preservice teachers' perceptions of learning to teach in a predominantly school-based teacher education program', *Journal of Teaching in Physical Education*, 18, 175-198.

Lewis, H. (1990) *A Question of Values*, San Francisco: Harper and Row.

Macdonald, D. and Kirk, D. (1999) 'Pedagogy, the body and Christian identity', *Sport, Education and Society*, 4 (2), 131-142.

Mansour, N. (2008) 'The experiences and personal religious beliefs of Egyptian science teachers as a framework for understanding the shaping and reshaping of their beliefs and practices about science-technology-society (STS)', *International Journal of Science Education*, 30, 1605-1634.

Nespor, J. (1987) 'The role of beliefs in the practice of teaching', *Journal of Curriculum Studies*, 19, 317-328.

Nisbett, R. and Ross, L. (1980) *Human Inference: Strategies and Shortcomings of Social Judgment*, Englewood Cliffs, NJ: Prentice-Hall.

OECD (Organisation for Economic Cooperation and Development) (2009) 'Teaching practices, teachers' beliefs and attitudes', in OECD *Creating Effective Teaching and Learning Environments: First Results from TALIS*, Paris: OECD. pp. 88-135.

Pajares, F. (1992) 'Teachers' beliefs and educational research: Cleaning up a messy construct', *Review of Educational Research*, 62 (3), 307-332.

Palmer, P. (1998) *The Courage to Teach: Exploring the Inner Landscape of a Teacher's Life*, San Francisco, CA: John Wiley and Sons.

Pratt, D. (2002) 'Good teaching: One size fits all?' *New Directions for Adult and Continuing Education*, 93 (Spring), 5-15.

Pratt, D. and Collins, J. (2000) 'The Teaching Perspectives Inventory (TPI)', in *Proceedings of the Adult Education Research Conference*, Canada: Vancouver, viewed 27 July 2021, https://newprairiepress.org/aerc/2000/papers/68.

Pratt, D., Smulders, D. and Associates (2016) *Five Perspectives on Teaching: Mapping a Plurality of the Good* (2nd edn), Malabar, Florida: Krieger Publishing Company.

Prawat, R. (1982) 'Teachers' beliefs about teaching and learning: A constructivist perspective', *American Journal of Education*, 100 (2), 354-359.

Raths, J. (2001) 'Teachers' beliefs and teaching beliefs', *Early Childhood Research and Practice*, 3 (1), 1-10.

Rokeach, M. (1968) *Beliefs, Attitudes, and Values: A Theory of Organization and Change*, San Francisco, CA: Jossey-Bass.

Saphier, J., Haley-Speca, M.A. and Gower, R. (2008) *The Skillful Teacher: Building your Teaching Skills* (6th edn), Acton, MA: Research for Better Teaching.

Sigel, I.E. (1985) 'A conceptual analysis of beliefs', in I.E. Sigel (ed.) *Parental Belief Systems: The Psychological Consequences for Children*, Hillsdale, NJ: Erlbaum, pp. 345-371.

Teaching Perspective Inventory. (2020) *Teaching Perspective Inventory*, viewed 27 July 2021, www.teachingperspective.com/tpi.

Tsangridou, N. (2006) 'Teachers beliefs', in D. Kirk, D. Macdonald and M. O'Sullivan (eds.) *Handbook of Physical Education*, London: Sage Publications, pp. 486-502.

Wacker, C. and Olson, L. (2019) *Teacher Mindsets: How Educators' Perspectives Shape Student Success*, Georgetown University, Washington DC: FutureEd.

10 Teaching Approaches

Benjamin S.J. Tan

Introduction

The chapter starts with a quote by Cotton (1912), "Those who dare to teach should not be afraid to learn" (p. 55). In light of the ever-changing educational landscape, diverse students, and learning context, teachers have to possess and learn different teaching skills to promote student learning, participation, and achievement (Bailey, 2001). It is also important for teachers to be reflective of their own practice in lessons and, by doing that, embrace new ways of teaching through continuing professional development (CPD) to hone their teaching skills.

Teaching and learning are interconnected. The dynamic and complex relationship between students and the learning environment requires teachers to select the most appropriate teaching approach to cater for the varying needs of students in a lesson. The teacher has to consider contextual factors like subject matter content, student learning profiles, gender, culture, and environment. The teacher has to make meaning of curriculum documents and education initiatives given to the school by curriculum designers from the educational board (in Singapore, the Ministry of Education). The teacher then goes through a process of designing and planning the content to teach the students, including selecting the appropriate teaching approaches to suit the different content and students and enable learning outcomes to be achieved.

A teaching approach is the overall pedagogical behaviour of a teacher in a lesson (Blair and Beaumont, 2020, p. 129). It is based on the teacher's beliefs about the nature of teaching and learning. When appropriate teaching approaches are adopted, they enable specific learning outcomes to be achieved in a lesson. Hence, a skilful teacher needs to possess a repertoire of teaching approaches to meet the needs of the students and enable psychomotor, cognitive, and affective outcomes to be achieved. Approaches used by experienced teachers are often eclectic and based on tacit experiences. Hence, a framework of teaching approaches is needed that can help teachers codify

DOI: 10.4324/9781003171973-12

their practices in a lesson and provide them with a repertoire of approaches from which they can select those most appropriate for any lesson. These help teachers to understand their practices in a lesson better and participate more meaningfully in CPD opportunities like lesson observations, post-lesson discussions, and reflections.

In this chapter, the focus is on the use of different teaching approaches in physical education lessons, informed by Mosston's Spectrum of Teaching Styles framework. The Spectrum describes 11 interconnected teaching styles (what are called teaching approaches in this chapter), which systematically and progressively devolve decision-making to students. If you are already familiar with the Spectrum, the chapter will remind you of its value in selecting appropriate teaching approaches.

The styles (from A to K) are listed in Figure 10.1.

The first five teaching styles (A to E) form the *reproduction* cluster. In these styles, students learn by reproducing or replicating what the teacher expects them to do. For example, the teacher demonstrates a balance in a gymnastics lesson and the students follow exactly what the teacher does. The teacher expects the students to reproduce known knowledge/skills. Between the *reproduction* and *production* cluster, the discovery threshold demarcates the two clusters. Teaching styles (F–K) are in the *production* cluster of teaching styles. In these styles students are facilitated by the teacher to discover new knowledge/skills (e.g. produce a movement that is unknown to them) based on a question or problem posed to them. They engage in cognitive operations that evoke critical thinking, curiosity, exploration, and discovery of knowledge that they engage in on their own (Mosston and Ashworth, 2008). Using gymnastics balance as an example, the teacher poses a question, "explore different ways of balancing using three body parts." Students explore and experiment on their own with as many balance poses as they can.

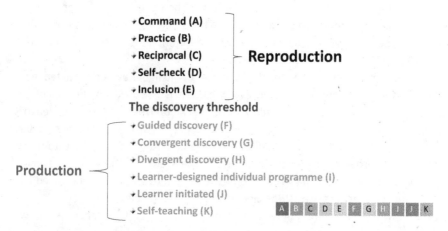

Figure 10.1 Mosston's Spectrum of Teaching Styles

■ ■ ■ ■ TEACHING APPROACHES 171

> **OBJECTIVES**
>
> At the end of the chapter, you should be able to:
>
> - have an overview of Mosston's Spectrum of Teaching Styles and its theoretical framework
> - understand how the Reproduction and Production Styles can be used in physical education lessons to meet specific psychomotor, cognitive, and affective learning outcomes
> - reflect on your use of Mosston's Spectrum of Teaching Styles in your lessons.

Why Mosston's Spectrum of Teaching Styles Was Developed

Mosston and Ashworth (2008) stated four reasons for developing the Spectrum. The first reason relates to teachers having a preferred way of teaching based on their own individual values and experiences (tacit and vicarious). Adopting one preferred style of teaching is problematic in that it limits the teacher's choices of teaching approaches and, consequently, limits the students' potential to achieve specific learning outcomes. Using the Spectrum, the teacher selects different styles to bring out the best in each student through designing varied learning experiences and opportunities which enable specific learning outcomes to be achieved. The second reason is that students are unique individuals. They have different learning dispositions (profiles), varied cultural backgrounds, and possess different physical skills and movement experiences. Hence, teachers need to use different styles to ensure inclusivity in their teaching. The third reason is that the spectrum relates to the wide array of learning outcomes associated with the delivery of the physical education curriculum in schools. Mosston and Ashworth (2008) aptly summarise the diverse nature of physical education outcomes:

> *Physical education encompasses objectives that range from uniformity and synchronization of performance in rowing or precise replication of models in gymnastics, to individual forms of freestyle swimming and modern dance performance. Objectives range from aesthetics in springboard diving to appreciation of nature during hiking, or from individual skills and tactics in fencing to group cooperation and strategy in team ball games.*
>
> (pp.16-17)

Hence, teachers need to equip themselves with different teaching styles (approaches) to meet the needs of diverse students and achieve diverse psychomotor, cognitive, and affective outcomes in physical education. The fourth reason for developing the Spectrum was the realisation that ideas about teaching seemed to be in opposition; one idea against another and that the 'versus' approach had limitations. A "coherent, comprehensive, and integrated framework for teaching" (Mosston and Ashworth, 2008, p.15) was needed. Hence, the Spectrum formulates a 'non-versus' approach to teaching. It aims to provide a common understanding of, and terminology for, teacher behaviours in the Spectrum. For instance, teacher A observing teacher B's lesson will be able to identify the teaching styles teacher B is using. During the post-lesson discourse, both teachers will be able to speak a common language to be able to discuss critically and perhaps come to similar conclusions on the lesson. This will allow concrete steps to be taken to improve the effectiveness of the teaching and learning in future lessons.

In the following section, eight of the 11 teaching styles (A-H) in the spectrum are highlighted and, wherever possible, the application of styles is illustrated with lesson examples and case studies. The last three teaching styles (I-K) are only mentioned briefly as they are not regularly used by teachers in schools.

In considering different styles in the spectrum, it is important to note that students are not able to adapt immediately to a style they have not encountered previously. For example, they may not be to make effective decisions, give feedback to a peer, or analyse their own performance if they were taught using the reproduction cluster of teaching styles. Hence, in adopting any of these styles in their lessons, teachers must give students time to adjust to the style by building in a 'Lesson Zero' into their unit plans. The writers of Chapter 11 of this book (Zhuo and Goh) explain the benefits of a 'Lesson Zero' where the first lesson's objective is to mainly familiarise the students with a new idea/strategy/digital tool. This will address the situation where teachers may want to abandon a style just because it has 'not worked' in the first lesson in which it was tried.

What Is Mosston's Spectrum of Teaching Styles?

In order to equip teachers with the fundamental knowledge for developing a repertoire of teaching approaches that enable learning outcomes in psychomotor, cognitive, and affective domains to be achieved in lessons, the Spectrum delineates a continuum of significantly different teaching styles, each style being defined by a specific decision-making pattern for both the teacher and student.

Mosston and Ashworth (2008) assert that the Spectrum is a set of decision-making processes made by the teacher and students. The decisions taken by teachers and students shift with different styles. For instance, in Command Style (A), the teacher makes all the decision in the lesson. Moving through the styles, students gradually take more decisions until, in the Divergent Discovery Style (H), students take most of the decisions to derive a solution to a given problem (note in styles I-K students take all decisions). Figure 10.2 depicts the decision-making by the teacher and the students across the Spectrum and Table 10.1 summarises the role of the teacher and students in each style.

TEACHING APPROACHES 173

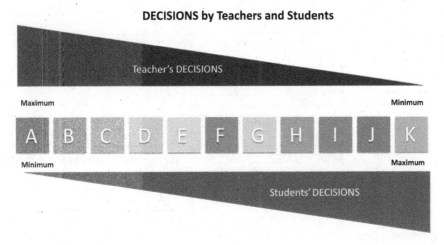

Figure 10.2 Decision-making by teachers and students in Mosston's Spectrum of Teaching Styles

Table 10.1 A summary of the key roles of teacher and students in the styles in the Spectrum

Teaching Style	Interaction Between Teacher and Students	Role of Teacher	Role of Student
Command (A)	Teacher makes all the decisions. Students copy and comply with decisions and instructions on cue (Precision).	Instructing	Copying, replication, modelling
Practice (B)	Teacher sets up opportunities and gives feedback to students who are working at own pace on tasks set.	Establishing	Repeating and improving through teacher feedback
Reciprocal (C)	Students work together, receiving feedback from each other. Teacher provides reference points for student observer to provide feedback to peers.	Supporting	Observing, performing, and peer feedback (assessing)
Self-Check (D)	Teacher sets criteria for success. Students check own performance against the criteria or standards.	Directing	Self-assessing
Inclusion (E)	Teacher sets out a variety of tasks/opportunities (from easy to complex). Students select which task most suits their abilities.	Facilitating	Selecting

(Continued)

Table 10.1 (Continued)

Teaching Style	Interaction Between Teacher and Students	Role of Teacher	Role of Student
Guided Discovery (F)	Teacher uses questions and tasks to gradually direct students towards a predetermined learning target.	Questioning	Uncovering
Convergent Discovery (G)	Teacher sets or frames problems. Students attempt to find out and explore the most appropriate solutions.	Guiding	Finding out
Divergent Discovery (H)	Teacher sets or frames problems. Students attempt to explore and create possible solutions.	Prompting	Creating
Student Designed (I)	Teacher decides on area of focus. Students develop within this area, drawing on teachers' experience and expertise.	Advising	Initiating
Student Initiated (J)	Students decide on how and what they are aiming for. Teacher provides support as needed.	Mentoring	Deciding
Self-Teach (K)	Students engage in development on their own.	N/A	Self-determined

Source: Adapted from Mosston and Ashworth (2008)

The next part of the chapter highlights some key tenets of the reproduction and production clusters in the spectrum and share some examples of how the styles are enacted to achieve specific learning outcomes.

Reproduction Cluster (Styles A-E)

Style A: Command Style

This style is used to enable students to learn and perform a task accurately (precision) as instructed by the teacher (Mosston and Ashworth, 2008). Consequently, the style enables students to perform actions by following specific cues, rhythm and pace (i.e. timing) provided by the teacher. When the style is enacted in a lesson, the teacher provides the movement command signal (i.e. exact movement cues, rhythms) and the students follow exactly according to the signal (cue) and timing of the actions. Students replicate the movement pattern by observing the actions and listening to the cues. It is in many ways like 'follow the leader'. The teacher makes *all* the decisions in relation to the task.

This style is well suited for students learning a new skill. For example, rolling a ball to a target. The teacher can first get the students to space themselves out, without the ball. They then walk through the actions step by step, replicating the teacher's demonstration and following the cues given. Once the teacher notices that students are competent with the actions, the next activity is to perform the rolling action with the ball again following the instructions given by the teacher. The teacher's role is to observe and provide feedback to individuals or groups. The actions are repeated for a few cycles to ensure that the students grasp the movement pattern.

The Command Style is widely used for content that involves safety and precision. In a javelin or shot putt lesson, for example, the teacher needs to make all the logistical arrangements (i.e. safety distance, equipment, designated throwing zones) as well as introduce 'rehearsals' without the equipment and/or with a foam javelin before introducing the actual implement. At the same time as demonstrating, the teacher can give cue commands like "Walk to the javelin, pick up the javelin, lift up the javelin and place it beside your ear, pull back the javelin and extend your throwing arm, throw the javelin and stay put, walk to pick up your javelin." It may come across as rather draconian, but the purpose is to ensure student safety. Other examples of content requiring this style could include dance set pieces (e.g. folk dance), synchronised swimming, marching bands, cheerleading, and team gymnastics. Some of the pitfalls of this style include too many instructions given by the teacher which may leave students disengaged. It is also "one size fits all" approach with little or no differentiation made to meet student needs/profiles and little or no individual feedback given to students.

Task 10.1 asks you to plan for a Command Style lesson activity.

 Task 10.1 Plan a Style A lesson activity and record students' behaviour

1 Refer to the content that you going to teach in one lesson in the following week;
2 Identify content and a learning outcome in which it is appropriate to use the Command Style to help students learn better;
3 Prepare and teach the lesson activity using the Command Style;
4 Reflect on the use of this style in the lesson, students learning and achievement of the learning outcome.

Style B: Practice Style

In this style, the teacher plans tasks (e.g. stationary and dynamic basketball dribbling), provides the instructions, and gives demonstrations at the start of the lesson and when required during the lesson. The students model and practise the tasks. The teacher moves around the class to give feedback to individuals and groups. In this style, there are opportunities for students to make some decisions such as where they locate themselves for the activity, when they start and stop, the order and duration of tasks. This is the beginning of student's independence in making some decisions. By allowing the students to make some decisions, the teacher is free to move around the students to help them with their practice and provide feedback. Also students begin to be empowered to take ownership of, and be accountable for, their decisions by purposefully planning decision-making opportunities in the lesson.

It takes time for younger students (or even older students who have not been used to making any decisions in lessons) to get used to making decisions. Use a 'Lesson Zero' and/or start with simple and manageable decisions like location and when to start/stop. Decisions that are more complex can then be layered in when the students show a readiness to embrace decision-making.

Task 10.2 asks you to identify some of the decisions that students can make in Practice Style task activities.

Table 10.2 Some examples of decisions that students can make in using the Practice Style in a basketball lesson on dribbling

Decision by Students	Examples
Location	Students select their practice area (which maybe within practice grids set up by the teacher).
Order of tasks	The teacher demonstrates a set of three practice tasks and the students decide which tasks to practise. For example, a student starts with stationary dribble (with dominant and non-dominant hand), moves on to practise a stationary crossover dribble, and ends with dribbling up and down the length of the grid. Another student chooses to start with stationary crossover dribble.
Starting time per task	The students listen and observe the teacher's instructions and demonstrations, then move on to practise on their own without waiting for the teacher to tell them to do so.
Pace and rhythm	Whilst practising the basketball dribble, the students choose the rhythm - speed and intensity of the bounce of the ball. For pacing, they choose to dribble at a pace that suits them.
Stopping time per task	Related to the order of tasks, the students regulate the duration of practice for each dribbling task.
Interval	In between tasks (inter-task), students can decide to take a break or rehydrate or they can practise a skill that is related to basketball. For example, dribbling combined with shooting a basket.

Decision by Students	Examples
Initiating questions for clarification	Students are encouraged to ask the teacher questions on the content they are learning. Alternatively, the teacher may pose questions to check on a student's understanding of the content.
Attire and appearance	Students decide on their attire for a basketball lesson. For example, put on a pair of basketball shoes or basketball jersey.

Task 10.2 Identify potential decision-making opportunities for students

1. Refer to the lesson plans you are going to teach in the next few lessons;
2. Identify potential decision-making opportunities for students to make in the lesson (refer to Table 10.2) and make a note of them in your plans;
3. During your lessons, create opportunities for your students to make their own decisions;
4. Observe how students make the decisions, assist those who may need your help and identify how you can support students to make more decisions.

Style C: Reciprocal Style

This style involves teachers inviting students to provide and receive specific task-related feedback from their peers who are observing each other and using a criteria worksheet that includes specific cues, illustrations, and a checklist designed by the teacher (an example of a peer observation worksheet is provided in Figure 10.3). The key roles for the students in this style are *doer and observer*. The doer performs the task and the observer watches the doer's actions using the criteria in the task worksheet. The teacher needs to specify the roles and functions clearly to the students. The students work collaboratively in pairs to perform the assigned tasks. The teacher designs the worksheet to complement the tasks. During the lesson, the teacher moves around to help the observers to hone their observational (e.g. positioning, angle of sight) and feedback skills to enable them to give feedback to the doer. In order for this style to be effective, the teacher must refrain from giving feedback directly to the doer to correct a performance as it negates the purpose of having a peer observer. The observer and doer switch roles during the lesson to enable each student to be observed by and receive feedback from a peer and to observe and give feedback to their peer. The peer observer needs to understand the critical learning points of the skill to enable them to compare and contrast the doer's performance with the

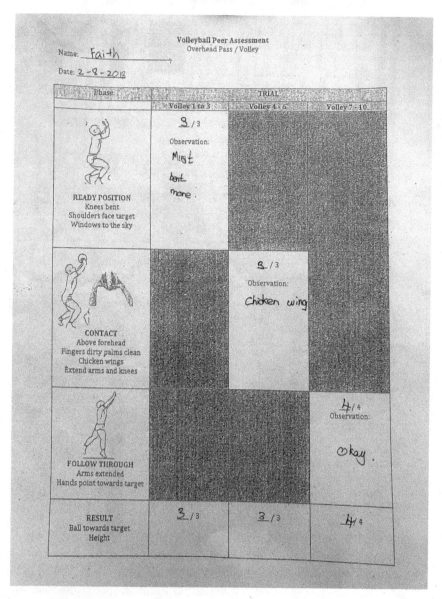

Figure 10.3 Sample criteria worksheet

model provided by the teacher. The observer communicates their observations through feedback to the doer. As the observer's main role is to be able to analyse and give feedback on the doer's performance, students expand their active role/decision-making in learning. Chapter 11 in this book also provides the reader with digital tools to support student peer observation.

Based on my own teaching practices, students gradually gravitate to this style of teaching, as long as they are given time to practise and develop the role of observer and their ability to give feedback. The students' confidence to help their peers improves over time with guidance and facilitation by the teacher.

TEACHING APPROACHES

In the Reciprocal Style, besides achieving a psychomotor outcome, the teacher also places emphasis on students developing cognitive and social outcomes through working collaboratively (Garn and Byra, 2002). In application, the teacher sets the tone and routines for a positive environment where students are empowered to help each other improve their physical, cognitive, and social skills. A primary school physical education teacher once told me, "I feel liberated as a teacher using this style, the social interaction between the students improved and they just have to focus and help the observers." See Chapter 11 for digital collaborative platforms to support this style.

Task 10.3 asks you to design a peer observation worksheet.

 Task 10.3   Design a peer observation worksheet

1. Select a topic in one of your physical education unit plans. For example, volleyball underarm pass, floorball shooting, or forward roll in gymnastics.
2. Design a peer observation worksheet that includes a short description of the task, teaching cues, and illustrations.
3. Ask some students to look at the worksheet and share with you their thoughts. By involving students in some decisions adds value to the experience.
4. Use the worksheet for a reciprocal teaching episode in the lesson.
5. Reflect on the process and share your experience with your colleagues.

Style D: Self-Check Style

Similar to the Reciprocal Style, in this style students perform a task and check on their performance based on a criteria worksheet designed by the teacher. The difference with this style is that the student uses the worksheet themselves to check their performance. The worksheet can be the same as the one used for Style D. The teacher's role is to provide the materials, task instructions and observe the students' performance. The teacher uses the criteria given in the worksheet to communicate with students and enable them to articulate their actions against the criteria on the worksheet. Students analyse their actions, reflect on the findings, and engage in further practice. The opportunity for students to assess their own performance is a step toward self-reliance. In this style, students make the decision to learn and give feedback to themselves.

The following example illustrates the use of Style D in a teaching episode in a football lesson:

Jane, a Secondary 1 student (13 years old) collected from the teacher a football criteria worksheet on 'kicking towards a goal'. She read the content to familiarise herself with the cues and task expectations. She proceeded to practise the skill with her peers. In order to acquire accurate information of her performance, she sought help from a peer to video record her kicking skills using a digital device. Jane then watched the video and analysed her technique based on the description in the criteria worksheet. The teacher observed Jane's performance and facilitated her analysis, and provided additional feedback and encouragement. In conversation with the teacher, Jane was able to describe the process of analysing her kicking technique and her actions to improve her technique.

As the example illustrates, the Self-Check Style focuses on the physical, cognitive, and affective domains. The process of self-analysis enables students to develop their ability to be critical of their own performance and promote self-awareness.

Task 10.4 focuses on applying the Self-Check Style in one of your lessons.

Task 10.4   Application of Self-Check Style

1. Try out the same criteria worksheet you designed for Task 10.3, with one class using Style D.
2. Encourage the students to video record each other's performance using a digital device. Alternatively, the teacher can set up a video-recording device to record students' performance and play back the video in the lesson. Students then review and analyse their performance (when videoing students in your lessons be sure to follow all school protocols and procedures).
3. Provide time for more individual practice.
4. At the end of the lesson, ask the students to reflect on how effective they were in reviewing their own performance and sharing their self-check experiences with a peer.
5. Invite the students to share their thoughts on the self-check experience.

Style E: Inclusion Style

Style E is the final style in the reproduction cluster. Physical education teachers sometimes affectionately call it the 'Slanting Rope' style. The teacher designs a criteria worksheet with a set of practice tasks with different levels (see Table 10.3). The worksheet guides students on how to perform the task, allowing them to assess their ability level and decide on the level of difficulty they want to work at. For example, a student assesses herself to be competent in kicking a football from a distance of 10 metres (Level 2) towards a target and decides to practise shooting at 15 metres (Level 3) away from the goal. Based on her own assessment, she decides to move up or down the levels.

Table 10.3 An example criteria worksheet

Name of Student:							
Class:							
Title of Activity: Underarm toss a beanbag to a low target							
Task	Task Description				Level		
A	Toss beanbag into a large-sized hula hoop placed 2 metres away				1 (Large target)		
B	Toss beanbag into a medium-sized hula hoop placed 2 metres away				2 (Medium-sized target)		
C	Toss beanbag into a spot marker placed 2 metres away				3 (Small target)		
Set	Task	Object	Prediction 1	1st Trial	Prediction 2	2nd Trial	
1			/10	/10	/10	/10	
2			/10	/10	/10	/10	
3			/10	/10	/10	/10	

Teaching cue:

- Hold beanbag, swing your arm backwards, eyes on the target, toss towards target, and point to the target
- Leading leg is opposite to tossing arm

Following are instructions for the students.

Task	Task Description	Level
A	Toss beanbag into a large sized hula hoop placed 2 metres away	1 (Large target)
B	Toss beanbag into a medium sized hula hoop placed 2 metres away	2 (Medium-sized target)
C	Toss beanbag into a spot marker placed 2 metres away	3 (Small target)

Instructions:

1 There are three sets of practices and for each set, there are two trials of ten tosses each;
2 Decide on a task (Task A–C) you want to work on;
3 Before attempting each set, record on the worksheet the predicted successful attempts at the target (e.g. Prediction 1: 8/10);
4 Perform the first trial and record the number of successful attempts. Repeat the process for second trial.

After Trial 2, refer to the worksheet and decide which task to practise for Set 2. Make your decision based on your performance recorded in the worksheet.

Example:
Based on the example, a student decides to attempt Task B, Level 2 (medium level) on the first practice set. Upon self-assessing, he realises that his performance falls short of his prediction. Hence, for Set 2, he decides to attempt an easier task, Task A.

(Continued)

Table 10.3 (Continued)

For Set 2, he was accurate in his prediction and, consequently, decided to move on to Set 3 to perform Task B.					
Set	Task	Prediction 1	1st Trial	Prediction 2	2nd Trial
1	B	9/10	5/10	7/10	4/10
2	A	8/10	7/10	9/10	8/10
3	B	8/10	8/10	9/10	8/10

During the practices, the teacher's main role is to ensure the accuracy of the student's self-assessment and the selection of appropriate difficulty in the levels of practice chosen. For younger students (or those using this style for the first time), the teacher needs to demonstrate the self-assessment process and monitor the students closely. The teacher should encourage the students to make their own decisions and refrain from prescribing which levels to practise. However, there may be instances where students choose to stay within the same level of practice. The teacher has to step in to encourage the students to try a different level. The Inclusion Style caters for student ability differences. Students learn to be aware of and accept their own level of achievement and perform the necessary actions to improve their level of achievement. The latter is a decision made by the student.

Task 10.5 asks you to design a task with different levels of difficulty/complexity.

Task 10.5 Design tasks with different levels of difficulties/complexities

1. Select a topic in which it is appropriate to use the Inclusion Style. Adapt the Inclusion Style criteria worksheet for the beanbag toss to suit the subject matter you are going to teach.
2. Try out the criteria worksheet with different classes (different student profiles) and record students' responses.
3. Keep a look out for students who are averse to moving on to a higher level of practice or refuse to move to a lower level. These students may experience lack of confidence, fear of failure or acceptance by their peers. Seize teachable moments to address their fears and encourage them without making a value judgement of their performance.
4. Reflect on the use of this style in the lesson.

The Production Cluster (Styles F– I)

The production cluster of styles in the Spectrum is based on the premise that a teacher's main role is to facilitate learning through creating a learning environment where students probe, explore, and experiment with the subject matter. In so doing, they derive their own conclusions and develop new knowledge related to the subject matter. In these styles, students make most decisions in a lesson.

Style F: Guided Discovery

In Style F, the teacher leads students to discover a predetermined response through a series of logically designed questions in a sequential order. Students actively seek out the answers to these questions (see Case study 10.1).

Case study 10.1 An example of the teacher guiding a student to discover the snapping of the wrist in the badminton overhead drive

T: After you have hit the shuttlecock with the overhead drive, what did you notice?
S: My shot was not able to reach the spot at the backcourt. There was no power when I hit the shuttlecock.
T: What do you think you can do to hit it with more power and accuracy?
S: I will use more strength.
(Student went on to practise, but did not achieve any success in sending the shuttlecock to the backcourt.)
T: Was using more strength effective?
S: No, it did not work.
T: What else can you explore to make your shots work better?
S: (took some time to think about the question). Maybe, I can use my wrist to help generate more power.
T: Let us try and see what happens.
(The student practised the overhead drive and this time round, he was successful in sending the shuttlecock to the backcourt.)
T: How did it go? I noticed you were successful in most of your drives to the backcourt.
S: Yes! I was more successful! I feel the power in the shots and my shots were accurate too. *I snapped my wrist to generate more power.* (A discovery by the student.)
T: Great! Continue to practise and get better at your overhead drives.

Prior to using this style, the teacher needs to identify the known fact (i.e. snapping of wrist improves the power of the overhead drive in badminton) and plan the questions that guide the student towards the right answer. The teacher also needs to list down possible answers students may give. This style is suited for guiding students to discover knowledge on their own. It is generally more

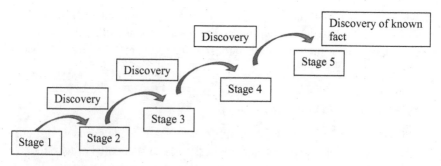

Figure 10.4 Guided questioning in stages

suitable for students who are at the same skill level. For example, for students with beginning level skills, the teacher asks a Stage 1 question whereas for a student with more advanced skill level, the teacher asks a Stage 3 question. So the teacher must be comfortable with the plan to address students of similar levels in different lessons throughout the course of the unit of work.

Figure 10.4 depicts a teacher guiding a student through a series of inquiry questions. At each stage, the student discovers new knowledge and the teacher leads the student to the next stage of discovery. At the final stage, the student arrives at a known fact.

Task 10.6 asks you to design a set of guided discovery questions that lead to a discovery of a known fact by a student.

Task 10.6 Design a set of questions and possible answers

1. Identify a skill that you will be teaching and the criteria related to what you want students to discover.
2. Devise five to seven questions in a sequential manner starting from a very basic question that suits a beginner student. Keep it to five to seven questions for a practical purpose.
3. Try out the questions with three-four students as a trial.
4. Analyse their responses and adjust the questions wherever necessary.

Style G: Convergent Discovery Style

In Style G, the teacher presents a single question or statement to students with the intention of leading them to discover a predetermined response. An example of a predetermined response is a gymnast having to tighten their muscles to perform and hold a balance for a duration of time. The teacher asks this question: "What must you do to keep a good balance for five seconds?" Individually or in small groups, students work independently to derive an answer (see Case study 10.2).

Case study 10.2 An example of the use of Style G for a netball lesson

Ms G's lesson was on netball shooting to a group of Secondary 2 students. Before this lesson, she taught the class the fundamentals of netball shooting. However, many students had problems trying to get the ball into the ring because they were not shooting the ball with a parabolic (rainbow shape) path. For this shooting lesson, Ms G prepared five netball posts for shooting practice. When the students gathered for the lesson, she said to them, "Try shooting into the ring as many times as possible and from different distances. Observe how the ball travels when it enters the ring. Share your answers with the class." Working in groups, students practised their shooting and discussed their findings. After ten minutes, they came back to share their findings. A girl exclaimed, "We discovered that the ball travels like a shape of a rainbow (arc, parabolic path) when it enters the ring." From that point onwards, students' shooting improved, as they understood how the ball must travel to increase their chances of scoring.

On another occasion, a teacher was teaching fundamental game concepts of volleyball to a class of Secondary 3 students. Most of the students were new to the game. Prior to this lesson, when students played 4 v 4 games, there were hardly any attacking set-ups by the teams – receive, set, and attack (three touches). Most would just send the ball over to their opponent's court. In the next lesson, the teacher gathered the students to watch a video of a volleyball game projected from a laptop to the wall and asked this question, "What do you notice about how each team played when the ball was on their side of the court?" After watching the video for a short duration, many students were able to articulate that in volleyball, a team were allowed to have up to three touches before sending the ball over the net. A bonus to this discovery was that they also noticed that the attacks were played mainly from the frontcourt. After this short activity, the teacher observed that the game play improved and with that, the students became more enthusiastic about their game.

The Convergent Discovery Style is a useful approach if the teacher wants students to work collaboratively or individually to discover knowledge through cognitive functions such as analysing, synthesising, and concluding. The teacher's role is to provide feedback, ask probing questions, and refrain from providing or hinting at answers. Ample time has to be planned for in the lesson for this style to be effective (Garn and Byra, 2002).

Task 10.7 asks you to develop a set of convergent discovery questions that leads to a discovery by the students.

> **Task 10.7 Questions and possible answers for the Convergent Discovery Style**
>
> 1 Refer to content you will be teaching for the next few weeks. Identify three-four topics you deem appropriate to use Style G.
> 2 Devise three to four questions and list down expected predetermined responses.
> 3 Try them out with different groups of students.
> 4 Reflect on the process of using this style in your lessons and share your thoughts with your colleagues.

Style H: Divergent Discovery

In Style H, the teacher poses a question or problem statement that leads students to discover multiple answers (divergent discovery). The teacher facilitates and encourages multiple solutions to a problem or question; there is no one right answer. For this style to be effective, students are empowered and provided with time to explore and derive new knowledge for themselves. This style is useful for content like creative dance, gymnastics, and outdoor education or exploring concepts like attacking and defending in games. It fosters an environment for students to be creative and accept multiple perspectives. For example, in a basketball lesson for Secondary 2 students, the teacher can ask the attacking team to "Work as a team to explore different strategies to attack the basket" and the defending team to "Find ways to keep the attacking team away from the basket." Time should be allowed for teams to communicate with each other by providing team talk time. In another example, a creative dance lesson for Primary 3 students, the teacher poses this statement, "Explore as many ways as you can to travel as smoothly as possible from a high point to a low point across the dance floor." Students work individually to choreograph their dance routines and perform for their peers. Like Style G, this style encourages students to activate their cognitive functions to derive multiple solutions to a problem statement. The teacher's role is to provide feedback and encouragement. Chapter 11 in this book will provide you with digital apps and platforms to support peer observation, feedback and group collaboration synchronously and even asynchronously if you intend for students to do pre-/post-lesson work.

Task 10.8 asks you to experiment with different subject matter using Style H.

> **Task 10.8 Experiment with different subject matter using Style H**
>
> 1 Select content you will be teaching, like attacking and defending in games, creative dance or gymnastics;

2. Devise three to four problem statements you want to pose to the students;
3. Try it out with different groups of students;
4. Interview some students and elicit their views on using this style;
5. Reflect on the process of using this style in your lessons and share your thoughts with your colleague.

Styles I, J, K: Learner-Designed Individual Programme, Learner-Initiated, Self-Teaching

Styles I, J, and K are at the end of the production cluster. They are rarely used by teachers in schools. They revolve around individualised learning in which teachers play a minimal role in the students' pursuit of learning. Students take on a self-directed role to explore and pursue learning on their own, making most (or all) of the decisions. The criteria for learning is not defined by the teacher but solely by the student's pursuit for self-learning. For example, many parkour practitioners learn the skills on their own, some with minimal formalised training in a related discipline like gymnastics.

SUMMARY AND KEY POINTS

Mosston's Spectrum is a very useful instructional framework for teachers as it guides them to select the styles that best suit the students to achieve specific psychomotor, cognitive, and affective learning outcomes. Several different styles may be used in a single lesson. For example, for a warm-up activity, a teacher may use the Command Style for physical fitness routines like jumping jacks. For skills practice, the teacher may use the Practice Style or Reciprocal Style. In game play, where game concepts are involved, the teacher can use the Divergent Discovery Style. The teacher must give students time to adjust to each style and not give up if it does not work the first time they use it in a lesson. It is useful to note that the processes of student peer observation, feedback, and group collaboration can be supported by digital technology as well as pre-/post-lesson tasks and follow-up activities. Chapter 11 of this book goes into detail of the applications and platforms that can be used by the teacher to make student learning more engaging and effective.

Note: A list of further resources to help you take your learning forward is available on the PESTA website: https://academyofsingaporeteachers.moe.edu.sg/pesta/professional-development/book-chapters-by-the-pesta-team

References

Bailey, R. (2001) *Teaching Physical Education: A Handbook for Primary and Secondary School Teachers*, London. Kogan Page.

Blair, R. and Beaumont, L.C. (2020) 'Designing teaching approaches to achieve intended learning outcomes, in S. Capel, J. Cliffe and J. Lawrence (eds.) *Learning to Teach Physical Education in the Secondary School: A Companion to School Experience* (5th edn), Abingdon: Routledge, pp. 128-143.

Cotton, J.D. (1912) Keen College of New Jersey motto, quoted in *The New York Times Book Review*, 5 March 1967, p. 55.

Garn, A. and Byra, M (2002) 'Psychomotor, cognitive, and social development spectrum style', *Teaching Elementary Physical Education*, 13 (2), 8-13, viewed 29 July 2021, https://spectrumofteachingstyles.org/assets/files/articles/Garn_Byra_2002_Psychomotor_Cognitive_and_Social_Development.pdf.

Mosston, M. and Ashworth, S. (2008) *Teaching Physical Education* (6th edn, First Online Edition) Spectrum Institute for Teaching and Learning, viewed 21 May 2021, www.spectrumofteachingstyles.org/e-book-download.php.

11 Enhancing Physical Education Using Digital Technologies

Jason Zhuo Gensheng and Goh Ming Ming Kelvin

Introduction

Some physical education teachers may envisage a typical physical education lesson as one that is intense, active and involving purposeful movement. To these teachers, the use of digital technologies in physical education may not invoke an image of students being active. They may perceive that lesson time might be sacrificed by technology-infused learning because it needs, for example, an elaborate set-up, time to instruct and scaffold the digital environment, and/or learning might be skewed to the cognitive domain – all of which could lead to hardly any physical activity in the lesson. As a result, some teachers are deterred from truly embracing all the possibilities of a technology-enabled lesson.

So, physical education teachers are not impartial when they engage in a conversation in which digital meets the physical in physical education. Any discourse about digital technologies in physical education would likely incorporate teachers' past experiences, beliefs, and perceptions.

There are a plethora of digital technologies already in the market, including, non-exhaustively:

- Hardware such as wearables like tracking devices, cameras, video-analysis applications to motivate, engage, and collect data on learning and
- Software that, for example, gamifies learning of physical literacy, dissects large student data, imbues virtual and augmented reality through smartphone applications, as well as web-based engines

The purpose of this chapter is to support you in your journey to discover what digital technologies you can use to enhance student learning in physical education, in the context in which you are teaching. It is important to stress that digital technologies should enhance pedagogical considerations – content, pedagogy, and assessment to support students' learning as they work towards achieving identified goals. It is also designed to enable you to consider your own readiness to take on whatever technologies are currently available to you and to take stock of the current technological landscape.

> **OBJECTIVES**
>
> At the end of this chapter, you should be able to:
>
> - evaluate your own pedagogical practices and consider how these can be augmented through the use of digital technologies to support student learning
> - examine the 'black box of learning' by using digital technologies to enhance formative assessment
> - develop strategies to support your learning in the implementation of digital technologies in physical education.

To address objective 1, we first explore how content and pedagogies to enable students to work towards achieving the lesson and unit of work objectives should be considered, followed by consideration of digital technologies to support the learning experience. This includes how setting the stage using the concept of a 'Lesson Zero' (Dyson and Casey, 2016, cited in Bodsworth and Goodyear, 2017) may help you prepare students in the skills and mentality to embrace a digital learning episode. 'Lesson Zero' is akin to a first draft. Experimentation with a new phenomenon/digital tool/idea in this first draft of a lesson helps your students be familiarised with the new phenomenon/tool/idea being introduced.

To address objective 2, we discuss how assessment practices can potentially be enhanced by digital technologies, exploring the capabilities/functionalities of different applications to further develop assessment processes.

Lastly, in relation to objective 3, we discuss some strategies to help consider digital technologies for teaching and learning in physical education, in view of some limitations it presents.

In totality, these objectives are designed to set the context for exploring technology-infused teaching and learning with your own students.

Objective 1: Pedagogy First, Digital Technology Supports

Incorporating digital technology into your teaching has been reported to have a wide variety of benefits, ranging from improving students' learning outcomes to increasing interactions and activity time (Hinojo et al., 2020). But this can only happen if digital technology is deliberately selected to enhance learning. It is important to avoid falling into the trap of forgetting about pedagogy and students' learning whilst chasing after the newest app, software, or hardware. Much of the latest digital technology has many interactive features which can be engaging for students. Some teachers may be tempted to dive right in and integrate this digital technology into their lessons without first considering the learning outcome and pedagogical approach, and how digital technology might support this. Without a clear outcome and pedagogy in mind, the digital technology with the latest features can be daunting and confusing for students to use, having a detrimental impact on their learning experiences. Pedagogy is still the core of learning and digital technology should be carefully selected to support and enhance this learning experience. This is illustrated in the three case studies (11.1, 11.2, and 11.3) from Jason and Kelvin (both physical education teachers teaching in a typical secondary school in Singapore with students aged 13–17 years) on the use of videos for group and peer discussions to help develop students' movement competencies, providing learning experiences beyond lesson time and many other affordances.

Case study 11.1   Use of Google Classroom for flipped learning

Jason was teaching a class of 40 14-year-old students. He realised that he often spent long periods of time demonstrating, addressing students' confusion with tasks set and providing support for students who needed more support in acquiring the skills. Periodically in his lessons (not every lesson), at junctures where he saw a good fit, he introduced Google Classroom as an online platform to post videos and practice tasks for his students to watch prior to the physical lesson in school. With clear learning outcomes and tasks for each lesson presented in Google Classroom, students could learn and practise at their own pace, space, and time. With the help of this online platform, his students could go straight into their practice tasks when they were in school, allowing Jason to reduce his time taken to explain the tasks to his students. As a result, he was able to afford more time to engage his students in discussions to address their learning needs. After a whole unit of 16 hours of lessons, he observed improvement in terms of students' psychomotor and cognitive skills. Further, students reported they found the online tasks enjoyable.

Case study 11.2   Using OnForm: Video Analysis App (formerly known as Hudl Technique) to support game-centred approach (GCA)

Kelvin taught a class of 40 13-year-old students through the game-centred approach (GCA), a common pedagogical approach used in physical education in Singapore schools. After teaching a few lessons, he observed that the students struggled to identify the tactical problem in the modified game. For those groups who were finding this difficult, he used an iPad to record a few minutes of game play using the OnForm: Video Analysis App. After recording, he gathered the group and showed them the video. He was able to annotate on the video as he was facilitating the discussion. This allowed the students to identify the tactical problem and to explore ways to work on it. With this approach, he was better able to support students' progress.

Case study 11.3   Enhancing cooperative learning with videos

During his lessons with a class of 38 15-year-old students, Kelvin decided to gather his students in their groups after a game to allow discussion about the game played and how they could improve on it. He observed that students were not engaged in discussions and were not able to give appropriate feedback to their peers. Rather, they relied on their gut feel of what they had observed. Their feedback were merely comments like: "You did well!" and "You need to run more!" To develop students' competencies on giving appropriate feedback, in his subsequent lessons, Kelvin gave each team an iPad from those available in the school. Students used this to record a short video of their peers performing the practice tasks or when they were playing a game. Teams were allocated time to gather and analyse the video with questions like "What did you observe?", "Based on the learning cues, what can be improved on?", and "How can you do that?" provided on a hardcopy poster given to them to scaffold the feedback process. With the recorded videos as a reference, he observed that the students were more engaged in their group discussions as they rewound, fast forwarded, and paused the videos to show their peers. They were also more motivated towards providing feedback to their peers as they reviewed their own videos.

These three case studies illustrate how the use of digital technologies can enhance the pedagogical approach and hence students' learning. Keep in mind that you are not doing anything special, but are reviewing how you can leverage the affordances of technology to enhance students' learning. This does not only apply to primary and secondary aged children. With deliberate planning, learning experiences for preschool children can also be enhanced through the integration of digital technology. With the widespread exposure of younger students to digital devices nowadays, Beschorner and Hutchison (2013) reported the use of iPads in preschools with children as young as 4 years old for learning. Task 11.1 asks you to reflect on the use of digital technology in lessons you observe.

> **Task 11.1 Reflecting on teaching and learning in lessons in which digital technology is integrated**
>
> Observe a lesson in which digital technology is integrated to support students' learning (this could be one of your own lessons which you have video recorded (following school guidelines for videoing lessons) or one taught by another teacher). Reflect on the following questions:
>
> - Did the students achieve the intended learning outcome/s?
> - Which pedagogical approach did you/the teacher use?
> - What digital technology was used? How did you/the teacher use it to support the pedagogy used? Why was it used?
> - How much did the students learn? What are the indicators?
> - What are some challenges you saw in the use of digital technology?
> - What would be the recommendations for future lessons?

Choosing the Right Digital Tool

As you can see from the case studies, choosing the right digital tool to support a specific pedagogy is crucial in being able to integrate digital technology effectively into your lessons. Through his collaboration with several schools, Kelvin developed the Outcome/s-Approach-Features-Plan-Evaluation (OAFPE) process (see Figure 11.1) to guide teachers in their lesson planning, based on placing the

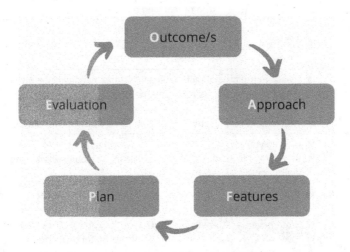

Figure 11.1 Outcome/s-Approach-Features-Plan-Evaluation (OAFPE) process

principle of pedagogy first before digital technology. This was developed from the Technology Implementation Planning Cycle (TIPC) by Hutchison and Woodward (2014). An example of some guiding questions is shown in Table 11.1. This cyclic approach allows you to review the digital technology used so that ongoing improvements can be made to cater for your students' needs and enhance their learning.

There are a wide variety of digital technologies on the market today. Knowing what is available is important to enable you to compare the features to select the right tool for your lessons. Table 11.2 provides a non-exhaustive list of apps and software which are used by some physical education teachers. You may know of others and/or you can keep a lookout for other apps and software through various online platforms such as Twitter, Facebook, or websites. If you are just starting to integrate digital technology into lessons, you can look at the list of apps and software your school or department has available currently before adopting a new app or software. This will allow you to have more support from your colleagues if necessary. However, this should not stop you from trying out a new app or software if it supports the pedagogy to enhance your students' learning.

With the speed at which advances are made in technology, this list of apps and software can go on forever and you will find yourself updating this list over and over again. Do not fall into the trap of force-feeding the latest digital tool into your lessons just because it gives you the latest features. When selecting a digital tool to integrate into a lesson, identifying the learning outcome and the pedagogy first is important. The selected digital tool should enhance the students' learning towards the identified learning outcome. Task 11.2 is designed to help you select an appropriate digital technology.

Table 11.1 Guiding questions for OAFPE process

Outcome/s	■ What is/are the lesson or learning outcome/s?
Approach	■ What is the pedagogical approach used? ■ What are some challenging pedagogical issues you need to minimise/solve?
Features	■ What are the crucial technological features needed to help you minimise/solve the issues mentioned earlier? ■ What are the digital tools available in the market? ■ Which digital tool is the most suitable and user-friendly? Why?
Plan	■ How do you plan to integrate the chosen digital tool? ■ What are some considerations to take into account when using this digital tool?
Evaluation	■ How well did the lesson/s go? Was the learning experience enhanced by the use of the digital technology? How do you know? ■ What have the students learned? ■ How effective was the integration of the digital technology? ■ Were there any issues with the integration? How can you improve on it?

Source: Adapted from Hutchison and Woodward (2014)

Table 11.2 Examples of apps and software for physical education

Video Technology		
Name of App/ Software	Features	Type of Pedagogy Tool Supports
OnForm: Video Analysis App (Known as Hudl on Android devices)	■ Playback in multiple slow motion speeds ■ Use of drawing tools to annotate video ■ Allows comparison of two videos side-by-side	■ Allows self- and peer assessment ■ Allows video annotation to help develop analytical skills ■ Allows students to deepen their discussions with reference to the video
Video Delay Instant Replay	■ Allows live video to be played after a delay (e.g. 10 or 20 seconds) ■ Replays actions using slow motion	■ Allows self- and peer assessment to identify areas of improvement ■ More effective for self-assessment as it reduces unnecessary stoppages to watch the video together
Data Collection		
Name of App/ Software	Features	Type of Pedagogy Tool Supports
Google Forms	■ Collects data in a quick and user-friendly manner ■ Data is presented with bars and charts ■ Data can be exported as a spreadsheet	■ Allows teachers to modify tasks based on students' needs and readiness level in a fuss-free manner
deck.toys	■ Gamifying online lessons ■ Students need to clear stages to earn points ■ Many interactive features such as puzzles, drawing, matching, etc. ■ Data can be exported as a PDF	■ Allows active learning and enhances engagement by gamifying the learning process
EdPuzzle	■ Allows questions to be inserted at different junctures of a video ■ Data can be exported as. csv files	■ Allows students to interact with videos asynchronously at their own pace and time to deepen their learning
Plickers	■ Uses QR codes to conduct polls readily ■ Only requires one mobile device to scan the QR codes ■ Data can be extracted into. csv files	■ Provides instant feedback from students to allow teachers to modify tasks based on students' needs and readiness level

(Continued)

Table 11.2 (Continued)

Collaboration Platform		
Name of App/Software	Features	Type of Pedagogy Tool Supports
Google Slides	■ Allows students to work on a slide or a deck of slides together	■ Enhances collaborative learning
Padlet	■ Allows students to share their comments, videos, images, files, and website links with others on a common board	■ Enhances collaborative learning
Flipgrid	■ Allows students to submit videos on a common platform ■ Students can add comments using videos	■ Enhances collaborative learning ■ Allows students to build self-confidence and presentation skills
Physical Health and Fitness		
Name of App/Software	Features	Type of Pedagogy Tool Supports
Sworkit Fitness	■ A repository of workout videos	■ Allows students to develop critical thinking by identifying appropriate workouts for different purposes
Relive: Run, Ride, Hike and More	■ Tracks your run, hike, or ride ■ Creates 3D video stories of your route ■ Photos and comments can be added in video stories	■ Allows students to work on their creativity in the creation of their own video stories ■ Tracks students' learning during the experience
Homecourt (only available on iOS – Apple devices)	■ Using Augmented Reality (AR) technology to practise agility and basketball and football skills ■ Videos can be recorded during the skills practice tasks ■ Data can be tracked over a period of time	■ Tracks students' learning over a period of time ■ Allows active learning and enhances engagement through novel effects from AR displays ■ Allows self- and peer assessment to identify areas of improvement

Task 11.2 Selecting an appropriate digital tool

Using the guiding questions in the OAFPE process (Figure 11.1), develop a plan to integrate a digital tool for one/some of your lessons in one unit of work. You do not have to work alone, gather some like-minded colleagues to collaborate on this journey with you.

Building a Set of Routines With 'Lesson Zero'

Hu and Garimella (2014) mentioned that it is important for students (as well as the teacher) to be familiar with the technical know-hows of the digital tool. Teachers often assume that their students, being digital natives, will be able to manage any digital tool that is given to them. However, research has debunked the myth of digital natives and you should avoid the assumption that all your students are proficient at using digital educational tools (Kirschner and De Bruyckere, 2017; Margaryan and LittleJohn, 2008). When a digital tool is being used in a lesson, some students will struggle to use it appropriately. As a result, both the teacher and students get frustrated with the learning experience and may eventually assess the use of digital technologies as ineffective.

To integrate digital technologies effectively, you first need to allocate sufficient time for students to explore and learn to use the digital tool. In order to do that, you can adopt the 'Lesson Zero' format suggested by Dyson and Casey (2016). Each unit can start with a 'Lesson Zero' in which students are able to explore the digital tool and familiarise themselves with the features you will be using in subsequent lessons. The rationale behind using this digital tool and a set of routines for students to follow should be conveyed in this 'Lesson Zero'. An example of a set of routines for video recording to be shared in Lesson Zero is shown in Figure 11.2.

Task 11.3 asks you to develop a set of routines for using digital technology in a lesson.

 Task 11.3 Routines for implementation of selected digital tool

Based on the digital tool you have selected in Task 11.2, develop a set of routines for your students to use it effectively. Limit your routines to a range of three to five points. You should also consider how you would check if your students have acquired the skills to use the tool.

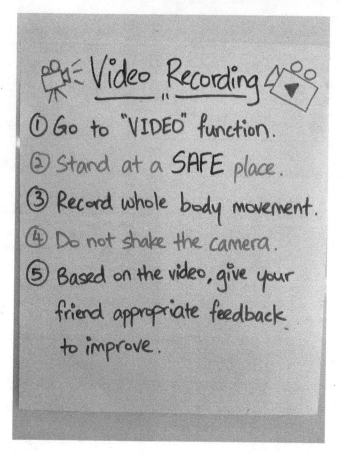

Figure 11.2 An example of a set of routines for video recording pasted on the wall to remind students when they are recording a video of their peers

Objective 2: Leverage Technology to Enact Effective Assessment

How do you know your students have learned, especially when you have just taught a technology-infused lesson? Can technology be used to find out if students have learned what you set out to teach?

It is pertinent to note again, as espoused in objective 1, that technology should be implemented in tandem with a good grasp of the teaching content, and the intended pedagogy in order to enable intended outcomes to be achieved (AIESEP, 2020).

After using digital technology to support your pedagogy to enhance learning, it is important to check if the students are progressing as you hope. In the 'OAFPE' process, technology can be used to find out if the content taught is well-learned. This closes the loop of the content-pedagogy-assessment cycle (Rink, 2010).

ENHANCING PHYSICAL EDUCATION 199

This section on enacting effective assessment outlines some possibilities to enhance assessment approaches through the capabilities of technology. Before proceeding, Task 11.4 presents a scenario and then asks you to reflect on one way of checking student progress.

> **Task 11.4 How do you assess every last student if there is only one mode of assessment?**
>
> This scenario aims to elucidate the point that technology has the potential to help you assess.
>
> You are teaching handball to a class of 14-year-olds. Students are playing a game of three versus two while attacking in a half-court with one goal-post. This is an exaggeration which often results in good success for the attacking side, as they have one free attacker who then has the space and time to attempt more passes and shots.
>
> After a few minutes, you gather the students together. You want to find out if they can articulate the importance of finding space through quick, accurate passes to the extra attacker who isn't marked. You ask the question:
>
> "Class, what did you learn about playing with one extra attacker?" And you wait. Wait time gives students the headspace needed to juxtapose what was asked and what they have just experienced, and that takes some waiting.
>
> Moments pass. You ask for answers. Only a few hands go up. They are from the usual vocal and physically inclined students who are waiting to answer any question asked. You look at the majority of the class who are avoiding your gaze, looking down and away. At this rate, the learning from the interaction will likely only reside with the selected few while the rest watch on.
>
> You wonder: Do the quiet ones really have nothing to contribute, or is this moment not quite right for them to give any form of answers?
>
> **Take a pause, and work through this scenario. Here are some questions to help.**
>
> 1 What have been your strategies for making sure you hear from every student?
> 2 How are you helping students learn about their progress?
> 3 Why is it important for every student to answer your questions?

The next section looks at one way of improving assessment.

The Power of Feedback (Hattie and Timperley, 2007)

Hattie and Timperley (2007) wrote about the power of assessment embedded in the learning process for effective student outcomes. They advocated the principles of feed-up (where is the student aiming towards?), feedback (how is the student doing now?), and feed forward (what are the steps ahead?). With these three principles as priorities, we look at how technology can afford more possibilities to support assessment.

These possibilities include:

1. Feed-up: Clarifying learning goals using blended learning platforms;
2. Feedback: Providing post-performance guidance to students; and
3. Feed forward: Using technological tools to design learning experiences supporting students' next steps.

(Hattie and Timperley, 2007)

Feed-Up: Clarifying Learning Goals Using Blended Learning Platforms

One of the key principles in enhancing learning through formative assessment is to make sure students are clear about what their end goals are (Black and Wiliam, 2010). Feed-up of learning goals is crucial to this. In order to feed-up accurately and consistently, you need to recognise various constraints that physical education teachers often face which hinder an easier feed-up process:

1. Unlike many classrooms, there is no information technology (IT) equipment (projector, computer screen, tablets) at physical education venues (sports hall, gymnasium, or field) to help project success criteria clearly. Physical education teachers may need to rely on verbal delivery of what students should achieve at the end of the lesson or unit. Students remain unclear if they are doing the task or skill right and how they are being assessed.
2. Performance of skills is fleeting; a demonstration by the teacher often takes only a few seconds. Students are likely to miss important details that may help them assess their own performances. Teachers who are observing the movement may also miss out on intricate details leading to reliability issues in assessment.

Looking at how crucial feed-up of learning goals is, we now examine how technology can help alleviate some issues mentioned earlier, as shown in Table 11.3.

Table 11.3 Seeing the affordance of technology through issues in assessment

S/NO	Issues	Technology Offers…
1	There is no IT equipment (projector, computer screen, tablets) at physical education venues. Success criteria are often shared verbally	Blended learning platforms,* allow sharing of success criteria prior to classes. These can be revisited during and post lesson to assess learning. Example of such platforms: ■ Google Classroom ■ Flipgrid ■ Google Drive sharing ■ Seesaw app ■ Classdojo
2	Performance of skills is fleeting; a demonstration by the teacher often takes only a few seconds to complete	Video-recording functionality, which may then be put together in blended learning platforms.* These videos of teacher demonstration and also of peer performances may help students assess their learning by leveraging slow-motion, focus-and-highlighting, and side-by-side comparison features of the video-editing tool. Examples of such video-recording tools: ■ Splice ■ OnForm: Video Analysis App ■ Any phone in-built software
3	There is no easy way to empower students to share their interpretation of learning goals. It is challenging to gather student voice to determine their understanding of learning objectives	Self-determination theory (Deci and Ryan, 2012) posits that one of the psychological needs of learners to be motivated is to be socially related to others when performing tasks. One of the key strategies of assessment is also to involve peers (schoolmates) in formative assessment routines to help each other track and chart progress in learning. It makes sense to then consider feed-up strategies in communities, in groups, and in pairs where students can learn in a social setting. With technology, you are looking at the capability to use social media, ring-fencing online communities to promote learning among peers, and subsequently, peers being collaborative in assessing each other through the course of learning. The objective of using technology in this feed-up process is for students to clarify with teachers and other students, the lesson's learning objectives, and address any doubts before proceeding into actual curricular time. Examples of such community-building tools: ■ Facebook closed groups ■ Google Classroom ■ Comment pages of blogs ■ Seesaw app

*Blended learning platforms refer to platforms with digital storage space for students to participate in a variety of digital activities, including uploading, commenting, and voting of video clips of performance on an activity.

Feedback: Providing Post-Performance Guidance to Students

The discussion thus far has highlighted considerations needed to enable students to utilise feed-up strategies to enact actual physical performance in games or tasks. Some considerations in giving feedback, and how pedagogically sound technological application can be used to circumvent these challenges, are now explored.

Feedback is information given to the learner or teacher about the learner's performance relative to learning goals or outcomes (Education Endowment Foundation (EEF), 2018). It is particularly effective in re-calibrating student's performance in relation to their attainment goals, using clear, encouraging language that helps students learn. See Table 11.4.

Table 11.4 Seeing the affordance of technology through issues in assessment

S/NO	Issues	Technology Offers...
1	Feedback is given verbally, and students forget what the learning cues are. Further, their corrections in relation to the cues have been forgotten by the start of the next lesson.	For retention of learning feedback and cues, digital documentation can be used. Many platforms offer free and easy solutions in letting students type in comments and, in this case, learning cues and feedback given for them to refer to as notes in the next lesson. You may also consider uploading student performance videos online (make sure you follow school requirements for use of video in learning, including using an online platform that provides secured uploading with password protection). Tagging videos to your feedback and student's reflection make for a powerful assessment-for-learning loop that will surely activate deep learning. Examples of such platforms include: ■ OneNote ■ Google Docs ■ Mentimeter.com ■ Seesaw app
2	Psychomotor feedback from past performance is not possible. Students who wish to review their actions on previous attempts are not able to. Given the complexities of movement, even with blow-by-blow replication of previous action, there can never be a	Video recording of movement performances as a form of assessment has long existed. You may have tried some form of video recording of performances to allow yourself or your students to review their movement, during or after their attempts. Some of the technology offerings may even be able to break down movement

S/NO	Issues	Technology Offers...
	complete copy of what just happened, and hence feedback without use of technology will be a fraction of its effectiveness in addressing and correcting skills or techniques based on what everyone can remember about the previous movement sequence.	patterns to mere seconds, showing clear visual scaffolding, empowering learners to understand more about, for example, dynamic biomechanics of the human in motion. Examples of affordances in using video technology in physical education include: ■ Clipstro ■ Video Delay Instant Replay ■ OnForm: Video Analysis App ■ Camera function in mobile devices
3	Only students involved in the movement are given feedback. And this feedback is not publicly available for others to also learn from others' experiences.	Where social learning is concerned, feedback is a great connector to involve peers to help each other learn. The nature of feedback, when documented, can form the conduit through which students collaborate and work with each other to improve. Leveraging technology, students can see each other's feedback, add in comments that represent their own interpretations, and co-construct meaning in the movement lesson with deeper understanding from multiple perspectives. Examples of such technology affordance are: ■ Padlet.com ■ Nearpod collaborative board ■ Facebook (use closed group)

Feed Forward: Using Technological Tools to Design Learning Experiences Supporting Students' Next Steps

Following up from feedback, in feeding forward, the learning information focuses on steps or tasks that students can take to get better in relation to the learning goal (feed-up). In this concept (as well as in feed-up and feedback) lies the potential to leverage personalised learning, because students are going to be at different stages of skill attainment at different junctures. Personalised learning refers to a holistic approach to determining learning progression, with scaffolding provided to individuals in relation to their own needs and pace (Redding, 2016). Harnessing data engines available in software, mobile, and web-based applications, there are many tools that can help teachers track each student's progress across weeks and months, and even visually represent these data in coherent charts for students and teachers alike to arrest learning gaps, or to see (and praise) learning growth. How then can teachers track students' progress and chart their learning over time?

Table 11.5 Seeing the affordance of technology through issues in assessment

S/NO	Issues	Technology Offers...
1	Students are progressing at different rates, and some are eager to get on with the lesson while certain groups are struggling.	There is no perfect solution, but technology offers you the option of differentiating learning by allowing for personalised learning paths to be built in through simple designs. The pedagogy enables each student to work on a certain task, and when completed, to self-assess their learning through knowledge quizzes or movement-form rubrics, or approach the teacher for information about the next task. This can be done through easily implementable 'quick response' (QR) codes pre-planned before a lesson to allow for easy access to teacher demonstration and the next tasks' instructions. Some technology offerings that can help support this pedagogy: ■ QR code generator ■ any Learning Management System (LMS) like Marshall Cavendish Online or Seesaw ■ Google Form with sections locked via passcodes

Table 11.5 identifies some issues with feed forward. If these issues resonate with you, some suggested approaches with technology to address them are included in the right-hand column.

Once you are comfortable with using technology for feed-up, feedback, and feed forward and are comfortable with the idea of tracking individualised progress of students, you can then work with students to enable them to follow the same process of feed-up/back and forward to assess and enhance their own learning.

Objective 3: Strategies to Support Learning in the Implementation of Digital Technologies in Physical Education

Although the examples shown earlier have illustrated the positive impact of integrating digital technologies to support both teaching and learning and assessment, there are some limitations which you may be familiar with that will affect the way you design your lessons. Not knowing these limitations may stifle your attempts to integrate digital technology into your lessons, and may eventually lead to you *not* using digital technologies that can enhance students' learning. In this section, the focus is on three limiting factors, teacher, student, and environment, in integrating digital technologies effectively into lessons, along with recommendations to overcome these.

In relation to the teacher, to enable digital technologies to be integrated effectively into lessons, Koehler et al. (2014) mentioned the importance of building technological knowledge (TK), technological content knowledge (TCK), and technological pedagogical knowledge (TPK) in addition to Shulman's (1986) pedagogical content knowledge (PCK). For teachers without prior experience in using digital technologies in lessons, Baek et al. (2018) recommended developing technological knowledge (TK) such as learning different technological functions of the digital tool first. A lack of understanding about how a digital tool works can limit its potential use in lessons. Besides technical know-how, having some hands-on experience in using the chosen digital tool before integrating it into your lesson provides you with insights when designing lessons which are engaging for your students and promote learning. Technological content knowledge (TCK) refers to a teacher's knowledge of how a certain digital tool can help deliver the subject matter better, for example, videos that show the biomechanics of a rapid movement in slow motion. Knowing a wide repertoire of digital tools and their features allows you to pick the most suitable tool to use. Even using the best tool, learning can be disrupted if you do not have sufficient technological pedagogical knowledge (TPK). When designing your lessons, pedagogical considerations, based on earlier sections in this chapter, should be thought through to maximise the potential of the chosen digital tool. To support your development of these knowledge bases, look out for relevant workshops, courses, or webinars you can attend. Consulting colleagues who have prior experience of using specific technologies can be helpful too. Alternatively, you can refer to social media (e.g. @PEgeeks, @connectedpe) for support in the use of technology.

Besides expanding your knowledge base, you need to understand that time has to be taken out from your busy work schedule to deliberately design meaningful learning activities supported by technology. To enhance students' learning, where relevant, these activities should be supplemented with relevant online resources for students to refer to in their own time and at their own pace. This is not an easy task, especially when you have limited time to prepare and create resources for a specific learning experience. However, remember that you are investing time now to save time later. Online resources can be stored on a platform for students to use asynchronously for self-directed learning and can be reused many times by different cohorts of students over a number of years. To save time and reduce stress, you can also collaborate with your colleagues to create these resources, called the power of collective teacher efficacy (Donohoo, Hattie and Eells, 2018).

In relation to students, digital competencies and the belief of not only the students, but also their parents, can limit the effectiveness of digital technologies in lessons. Table 11.6 summarises some possible limitations and recommendations.

Table 11.6 Possible limitations and recommendation of integrating digital technologies in relation to students

Possible Limitation	Recommendation
Bodsworth and Goodyear (2017) reported how learning was affected by the unfamiliarity of using a specific digital tool and digital competencies of students.	■ Adopt 'Lesson Zero' at the start of a unit to prepare students for the integration of a specific digital technology in lessons ■ Use a digital tool which has been used by students in other subjects for ease of transition
Students' perception of using digital technology in lessons. Not all students are ready to embrace digital technology.	■ Gather input from students and scaffold their learning to help them see the impact and benefits of learning with digital technology ■ Provide support to students who are struggling with the use of digital technology
Parental issues at home such as limited screen time and lack of parental guidance at home.	■ Find out about issues at home from parents ■ Collaborate with parents to devise a plan for their child ■ Provide support to parents

In relation to the environment, with most lessons being carried out in venues such as a field or gymnasium, poor or no internet connectivity can restrict the use of certain digital tools. If that is an issue, look for tools which can be used offline (e.g. video-recording function on iPad, Google Docs, Slides, or Sheets). For students who have no (or limited) access to the internet at home, you can engage them digitally during your lessons in school and identify alternative ways to engage them offline at home (e.g. hardcopy worksheets).

The maintenance of the hardware is important to prevent any technical difficulties during your lessons. A budget needs to be set aside for such maintenance.

Having sufficient hardware to support a lesson is equally important. If only one digital device can be afforded/is available for a lesson, think of single device solutions (e.g. having a laptop for students to work with by taking turns and a projector to share the screen for all students). In some countries, legal privacy issues such as the uploading of videos featuring students can be an issue limiting the use of digital technologies. For safeguarding students' privacy, make sure you adhere to your school's policy and ensure your devices are password protected. These environmental issues can significantly impact the effectiveness of the integration if not considered carefully. Task 11.5 asks you to consider limitations in integrating digital technologies in your lessons.

Task 11.5 Overcoming limitations in integrating digital technologies

With your colleagues, develop a plan to integrate technology readily in your lessons to enhance students' learning. Create a list of limitations in your current context and brainstorm with your colleagues various ways of overcoming these limitations. Go beyond your department to check with your colleagues teaching other subjects to find out what they have been using and what are the limitations and recommendations they have.

SUMMARY AND KEY POINTS

This chapter has aimed to provide you with an overview of how digital technology may be used in your lessons to support content and pedagogy to enhance students' learning. We hope the chapter has enabled you to:

- see the importance of focusing on the learning outcomes and pedagogy before deciding to utilise any digital technology
- apply the Outcome/s-Approach-Features-Plan-Evaluation (OAFPE) process to integrate digital technology effectively into learning experiences for your students
- give feed-up, feedback, and feed forward considerations to students more effectively
- develop strategies to overcome the challenges and limitations of digital technology.

If at first you do not succeed in integrating digital technologies into your lessons, keep trying – it takes time for both you and the students to adopt new ways of learning. As you embark on this journey, know that there are many teachers who will walk alongside you. Join your own school's digital technology discussion groups or community, or even organise one for yourself. Learning and professional development is richer when social relatedness is considered, so you may be more motivated to pursue excellence in your craft (Deci and Ryan, 2012).

Note: A list of further resources to help you take your learning forward is available on the PESTA website: https://academyofsingaporeteachers.moe.edu.sg/pesta/professional-development/book-chapters-by-the-pesta-team

References

AIESEP (Association Internationale des Écoles Supérieures d'Éducation Physique/International Association for Physical Education in Higher Education) (2020) *Position Statement on Physical Education Assessment*, viewed 9 March 2020, https://aiesep.org/scientific-meetings/position-statements/

Baek, J.H., Jones, E., Bulger, S. and Taliaferro, A. (2018) 'Physical education teacher perceptions of technology-related learning experiences: A qualitative investigation', *Journal of Teaching in Physical Education*, 37 (2), 175-185.

Beschorner, B. and Hutchison, A.C. (2013) 'iPads as a literacy teaching tool in early childhood', *International Journal of Education in Mathematics, Science and Technology*, 1 (1), 16-24.

Black, P. and Wiliam, D. (2010) 'Inside the black box: Raising standards through classroom assessment', *Phi Delta Kappan*, 92 (1), 81-90.

Bodsworth, H. and Goodyear, V.A. (2017) 'Barriers and facilitators to using digital technologies in the cooperative learning model in physical education', *Physical Education and Sport Pedagogy*, 22 (6), 563-579.

Deci, E.L. and Ryan, R.M. (2012) 'Motivation, personality, and development within embedded social contexts: An overview of self-determination theory', in R.M. Ryan (ed.) *Oxford Library of Psychology. The Oxford Handbook of Human Motivation*, Oxford: Oxford University Press, pp. 85-107.

Donohoo, J., Hattie, J. and Eells, R. (2018) 'The power of collective efficacy', *Educational Leadership*, 75 (6), 40-44.

Dyson, B. and Casey, A. (2016) *Cooperative Learning in Physical Education and Physical Activity: A Practical Introduction*, Abingdon: Routledge.

EEF (Education Endowment Foundation) (2018) *Teaching and Learning Toolkit: Feedback*, viewed 12 April 2021, https://educationendowmentfoundation.org.uk/pdf/generate/?u=https://educationendowmentfoundation.org.uk/pdf/toolkit/?id=131&t=Teaching%20and%20Learning%20Toolkit&e=131&s=

Hattie, J. and Timperley, H. (2007) 'The power of feedback', *Review of Educational Research*, 77 (1), 81-112.

Hinojo Lucena, F.J., López Belmonte, J., Fuentes Cabrera, A., Trujillo Torres, J.M. and Pozo Sánchez, S. (2020) 'Academic effects of the use of flipped learning in physical education', *International Journal of Environmental Research and Public Health*, 17 (1), 276.

Hu, H. and Garimella, U. (2014) 'iPads for STEM teachers: A case study on perceived usefulness, perceived proficiency, intention to adopt, and integration in K-12 instruction', *Journal of Educational Technology Development and Exchange (JETDE)*, 7 (1), 49-66.

Hutchison, A. and Woodward, L. (2014) 'A planning cycle for integrating digital technology into literacy instruction', *The Reading Teacher*, 67 (6), 455-464.

Kirschner, P.A. and De Bruyckere, P. (2017) 'The myths of the digital native and the multitasker', *Teaching and Teacher Education*, 67, 135-142.

Koehler, M.J., Mishra, P., Kereluik, K., Shin, T.S. and Graham, C.R. (2014) 'The technological pedagogical content knowledge framework' in J.M. Spector, M.D. Merrill, J. Elen and M.J. Bishop (eds.) *Handbook of Research on Educational Communications and Technology*, New York: Springer, pp. 101-111.

Margaryan, A. and Littlejohn, A. (2008) 'Are digital natives a myth or reality?: Students use of technologies for learning', *Computers & Education*, 56 (2), 429-440.

Redding, S. (2016) 'Competencies and personalized learning', in M. Murphy, S. Redding and J. Twyman (eds.) *Handbook on Personalized Learning for States, Districts, and Schools*, Charlotte, NC: Information Age Publishing, pp. 3-18.

Rink, J. (2010) *Teaching Physical Education for Learning*, Boston, MA: McGraw-Hill Higher Education.

Shulman, L.S. (1986) 'Those who understand: Knowledge growth in teaching', *Educational Researcher*, 15 (2), 4-14.

12

Being a Reflective Teacher

Using Narrative Inquiry as Professional Development in Physical Education

Nasrun Bin Mizzy

Introduction

The biggest struggle, and I know it starts with me, is the cultivation of a good teacher-student relationship. How do I love those so difficult to love? How do I speak kind words instead of 'following' students in the way they scream and shout at each other? I should be their role model; not learn from their bad habits. I find myself lacking in self-control and at times it is so tiring and frustrating, I don't feel like being kind to my students. But if this goes on, it affects my relationships with students. I don't want to appear as an angry, uncaring and unapproachable teacher. But I know I need an additional source of strength to shower love, care and concern for so many students of different characters, different needs. I am working on this but I do know that daily reminders to myself are important. Then students will be more willing to listen to me and more willing to learn.

(Nelly, 2nd-year PE teacher)

This excerpt reveals a tension that exists for some teachers in their relationship with some students. How do you feel reading the excerpt? What resonates with you? What thoughts, questions, and emotions were elicited? What impact do you think it could have on professional development and students' learning? How could the reflection improve the quality of your teaching? Have you embarked on such a reflective journey yourself? What stories of teaching, stories of students, and stories of school do you have? How have those stories of experience – *lived experiences* – shaped you into the teacher you are today? Finally, have you told those stories to others, and, if so, to whom and how was it done?

Narratives have the potential to uncover many hidden stories of teachers and teaching – stories of care, knowledge, and experience – that teachers carry with them throughout their careers. Teachers' reflections through narrative can uncover many intricacies and complexities of teachers' lives and the phenomenon of 'being a teacher'. What has shaped you into who you are? Why do you teach? Why do you teach the way you teach? How do you negotiate the demands of the curriculum amidst the changing educational landscape and student profiles?

How do you navigate the numerous competing priorities of the personal and the professional? How (often) do you reflect on your (daily) practice? How do those reflections impact your teaching? Or do they, at all?

My exposure to teachers' reflections through narrative inquiry brings a kaleidoscope of reflective stories of beginning physical education teachers (BPETs) who struggle with their identity as physical education teachers because they have to teach a second subject, experienced teachers who struggle with the daily grind of teaching and all the administrative work that comes with it, Heads of Departments balancing the 'acts of leading' with the 'acts of teaching', Teacher Leaders who struggle to uphold their beliefs and ideals of the profession against the realities of school and schooling, teachers who struggle to manage a wide range of special needs students, teachers who are anxious about using technology and many, many more. These are not mere stories. These are deep reflections which are written, analysed, re-written, and shared in various modes and with knowledgeable others. Ultimately, these reflections have impacted the teachers' beliefs, values, and practices. As they re-read and share their narratives, they discover their own strengths, uncover gaps and identify opportunities for growth. Through these analyses, they become more aware of who they are as teachers, how they have become who they are and how they resolve to work towards the ideals of who they want to be.

The purpose of this chapter is to help you understand how reflecting on classroom experience through a narrative approach allows you to get in touch with your own beliefs, (re)construct your knowledge, and (re)examine your practice. Reflection through a narrative approach highlights many trajectories as teachers journey along the *'narrative spaces'* of temporality (time), sociality (people), and place (context) (Connelly and Clandinin, 1990). Writing stories of practice (Rogers, 1954) allows teachers to make tacit knowledge explicit. In this chapter, the focus is on the narrative inquiry process, how narrative inquiry can be applied as a tool for continuing professional development, and the use of simple reflection tools that can supplement the narrative inquiry writing process. The excerpts used in this chapter are taken from an actual narrative inquiry project undertaken with physical education teachers from diverse backgrounds and experience. They are used as exemplars to illustrate critical features of narratives as a tool to support reflective practice.

OBJECTIVES

At the end of this chapter, you should be able to:

- understand the importance of being a reflective practitioner in order to enhance students' learning
- use narrative inquiry as a tool for reflective teaching to improve your knowledge and practice in PE

- use simple reflection tools and different modes of reflection to enhance your own reflective practice as a physical education teacher and
- start writing your own lived experiences as part of your continuing professional development endeavour.

Before reading further, Task 12.1 is designed to act as a trigger for you to start the narrative inquiry process. You will use the product from this task for the subsequent tasks in this chapter.

Task 12.1 A reflection on growth and change

Recall a physical education lesson (or a series of lessons) that prompted significant changes in your teaching practice.

- Write about that lesson.
- Include specific events and actions in your writing.
- How did that lesson (or those lessons) trigger the need to change your teaching practice?
- What was the change?
- How did you go about making that change? What was the process?
- What was the impact of that change?
- Write as much as you need to, enough to capture the essence of the change.
- Re-read what you have written. Feel free to add or take away details as you read it.

Reflective Practice

I cannot teach clearly unless I recognise my own ignorance, unless I identify what I do not know, what I have not mastered.

(Freire, 1996, p.2)

Busy physical education teachers are often conditioned by the drive to be productive and efficient. They tend to continue to practise what has worked for them before. As long as a strategy has worked, they tend to repeat it with different cohorts of students, year after year. Even when new problems arise, they sometimes use the same solutions with the hope of eradicating the new problems; or they may attribute problems mainly to a lack of student motivation or other external factors. This phenomena is exacerbated by the lack of deep reflective processes or a lack of meaningful feedback given over the years. In such a scenario, teachers are not able to identify their strengths or areas for growth effectively. In the long run, this is detrimental not only to their growth as teachers but also to students' learning. Argyris and Schon (1974) termed this phenomena 'single-loop' learning, whereby the symptoms of a problem are removed but the root causes still remain (Figure 12.1a). The learning process loop is localised between the action and the results and merely deals with the question *"What next?"*

Reflective practice is not only a professional development strategy, but also a problem-solving strategy. It entails teachers embarking on 'double-loop' learning (Argyris and Schon, 1974) (Figure 12.1b). Instead of stopping at the question *"What next?"* teachers should also ask *"What am I doing now?"* and, most importantly, *"Why?"*

For this purpose, Schon (1983, 1987) identified two processes that reflective teachers must engage in – *reflection-in-action* and *reflection-on-action*. *Reflection-in-action* involves dealing with on-the-spot problems as they arise. It involves teachers absorbing 'real-time' data or phenomena (for example, students' engagement or disengagement) to make immediate decisions based on their past or current knowledge of practice. This act of *'thinking on your feet'* does not necessarily lead to a critical evaluation of practice (and, therefore, learning) but involves continuous adjustments to overcome immediate problems.

Reflection-on-action, on the other hand, takes place after the action. It involves a deeper evaluation which is not bounded by the action alone. It is a

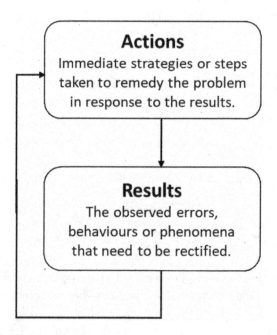

Figure 12.1a Single-loop learning

Source: Adapted from Argyris and Schon (1974)

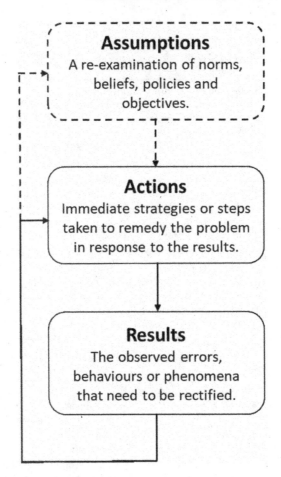

Figure 12.1b Double-loop learning

Source: Adapted from Argyris and Schon (1974)

more structured process of deliberation in which teachers think about the impact of an action on themselves and others (Schon, 1983). In this process, teachers can engage knowledgeable or trusted others for a deeper discourse based on, and around, the main action of a particular teaching episode. This is a process in which teachers give meaning to their teaching and gain deeper insights into their practices as a teacher. Analysis and dialogue are critical as they allow for the reconstruction of experience and invite multiple perspectives from peers or knowledgeable others. When teachers engage in dialogue, they make public their thoughts, beliefs, and knowledge about their practice of teaching based on their own authentic experiences. This, in turn, can elicit stories of experience and provoke deeper discussions on the theory-practice nexus of teaching. By sharing tensions and resonance, a strong collegial connection can be forged among teachers in a learning community. Table 12.1 summarises the two types of reflection and what they may look like in relation to a physical education teacher.

Table 12.1 Types of reflection

Reflection Type	Features or Nature of Reflection	Physical Education Exemplars
Reflection-in-action	■ Dealing with on-the-spot problems and issues as they emerge ■ Decision-making or response depends on past experiences and current knowledge, based on the immediate stimulus (may be personal, emotional, and environmental information) gathered in that particular time or event (for example, during a lesson) ■ On its own, may or may not lead to professional learning or growth	Students are to toss and catch a beanbag ten times. After ten successful catches, students are to sit. The teacher observes that within less than a minute, more than half the class have sat down while a few others are still trying to meet the target. Some students toss the beanbag all the way up to the ceiling and this becomes a competition among a few of them. Those seated are starting to get restless. Feeling frustrated, the teacher blows the whistle and addresses their behaviour. He also realises that he needs to change the task. He then asks students to increase the target by five each time they are successful. Immediately, he sees increased engagement and motivation in his class.
Reflection-on-action	■ After-event analysis of actions ■ Considers the action from multiple viewpoints (personal and professional) ■ More cognitive in nature and can be done alone or with others ■ Dialogue enhances this process as it takes into account social, political, and/or cultural forces	After the lesson, the teacher recalls what he observed and why he made the decision to change the task. He realises that he did not consider students' different abilities and profiles; he expected all students to finish the task at the same time. He notes that the off-task behaviours were down to him not making the task challenging enough for some students. Upon sharing this with a colleague, he is affirmed for his ability to 'read' his students' responses to the task and make on-the-spot decisions to modify the task to be more self-directed. He also listened to suggestions on how to improve his task progressions. For the next lesson, he decides to plan differentiated tasks to meet the different needs of the students. He also analyses the different profiles of his students and prepares the tasks to be more progressive and self-directed. He also plans to be more specific in his instructions.

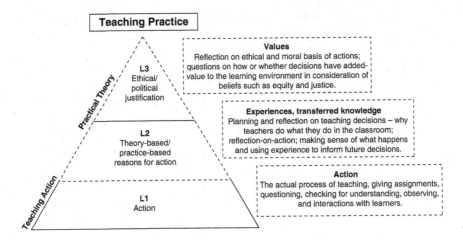

Figure 12.2 Practical theory

Source: Adapted from Handal and Lauvas (1987)

But how do teachers know the 'depth' of their reflections? What is 'deep' enough, and what is 'just scratching the surface'? Handal and Lauvas (1987) organised the concept of reflective practice into three different levels to encourage reflective teaching (Figure 12.2). They contended that to be truly reflective practitioners, teachers must go beyond talking about their actions (L1), to talking about the reasons for their actions (L2), and to considering the ethical, political, and moral justifications for those actions (L3). To move beyond L1, teachers must be given the space, time, and environment to be engaged in higher levels of complexity in thinking.

What Is Narrative Inquiry? Why Narrative Inquiry?

According to Dewey (1938), experience is both individual and social. He stressed that experience has an inherent continuity; it does not exist on its own. Current experiences are borne out of past experiences and lead to future experiences. Narrative inquiry is a way of understanding and inquiring into that experience through a three-dimensional narrative space (Connelly and Clandinin, 2000), namely, temporality (*when* the experience takes place), sociality (*who* is involved in that experience), and place (*where*, or the context in which the experience occurs). Several renowned thinkers have concluded that humans think narratively in order to make sense of a world full of chaos and unstructured events and experiences (Bruner, 1986; Coles, 1989; Rosen, 1988). Bruer (1993), in particular, suggests that our brain operates in stories of experience. Attesting to the power of narrative, British author Barbara Hardy (1977, p.12) writes:

> We dream in narrative, daydream in narrative, remember, anticipate, hope, despair, believe, doubt, plan, revise, criticise, construct, gossip, learn, hate and love by

narrative. In order really to live, we make up stories about ourselves and others, about the personal as well as the social past and future.

Although narrative inquiry is frequently used as a research tool, it is not reserved for researchers. It is a tool that physical education teachers can use to make sense of their teaching, their 'being' as teachers, their students' learning, and their students' being. It can be done "*by* teachers, *for* teachers" (Johnson and Golombek, 2002, p. 6) and *with* teachers. It is about making meaning of life experiences using the process of telling stories. When teachers merely describe, for example, the success or failure of a physical education lesson, or a challenging or disruptive student, they attach their emotions such as anger, frustration, dilemma, or joy – "classroom dilemmas" (Noddings, 1991, p. 4) to that recollection of experience. However, when teachers inquire or reflect on these experiences, they can analyse factors that contributed to those classroom dilemmas. Depending on their convictions and moral beliefs about teaching, teachers confront those emotions and examine the consequences of their teaching practices on their students, and students' perceptions of the subject matter. Thus, when teachers reflect on their experiences through a narrative approach, they are able to act with better foresight, more thoughtfulness and mindfulness (Johnson and Golombek, 2002).

However, narrative inquiry is not mere storytelling. Polkinghorne (1988) highlights three key features of narratives:

1. Attributing meaning to time-bound experiences and personal actions;
2. Arranging daily actions and events into brief episodes; and, lastly,
3. Structuring past events and planning for future events.

Furthermore, Barkhuizen (2020) contends that the narrative must indicate clearly the protagonists in the story (*who*) – the narrator, others, and their relationships – and what happened or what will happen together. Next, it must identify the places and sequences of places (*where*) in the story and what happened or will happen there. Lastly, stories must contain clear descriptions and analysis that indicate *when* those experiences occurred or will occur – in the past, the present, and the future. Using the metaphor of a school building, the "who", "where", and "when" are represented by the rooftop that provides shelter to the various rooms of the building (see Figure 12.3).

Barkhuizen elaborates that there are three different types of stories. The first story is, simply, *story* (spelled with a small letter). These are personal experiences of the narrator and his/her close social interactions with students and other teachers which are most likely to take place in lessons, with short time scales. The second story is *Story* (with a capital S). These take place in mesospaces in the school such as the staffroom, the canteen, the neighbourhood, and the community, with medium-term time scales. Lastly, there is STORY (all in capital letters). These take place in the broader ideological context of teaching

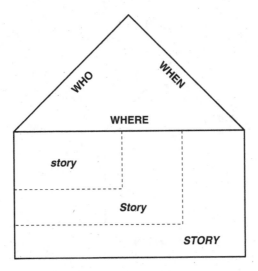

Figure 12.3 A three-dimensional narrative space
Source: Adapted from Barkhuizen (2020)

and include the sociocultural, political, historical, and economic domains. It is a macro context that requires longer time scales. Thus, individual stories in micro-spaces can move out and expand into stories in macro-spaces. These are represented by the different rooms of the school building constructed with dashed lines to indicate the porosity of each type of story.

Placed together, the content and context form the three-dimensional narrative space to give the full picture of any phenomenon in each narrative as represented by the entire school building. When this space is replicated and multiplied with stories from more individuals (via, for example, collaborative professional development spaces with other teachers, and with other schools), a larger picture is painted from sieving out common (or uncommon) threads on any phenomenon that surfaces from them. The different sizes of the school building can represent the size of each context, which further emphasises the differences that exist, even as a common educational space is shared (see Figure 12.4).

How Do Narratives Contribute to Professional Growth?

The more I teach, the more I realise that we teachers are nothing but our anecdotes, our reflections on experience.

(Ohanian, 1989, p. 542)

The nature of teachers' narratives, and thus, their reflections, speak a lot about their beliefs and values as teachers because teachers "become the stories we choose to tell" (Jalongo, Isenberg and Gerbracht, 1995, p. 142). Through

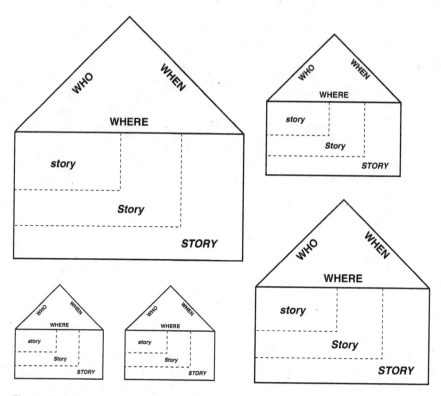

Figure 12.4 A shared educational space

Source: Adapted from Barkhuizen (2020)

narratives, teachers can articulate, synthesise, and communicate their beliefs about teaching and students. Narratives of beginning teachers, for example, focus largely on themselves navigating the many challenges they face in trying to assimilate into the physical education community, 'surviving' from lesson to lesson or balancing the demands of teaching with other administrative duties. Experienced teachers, on the other hand, may focus more on the celebration of student learning or specific stories of students that they have impacted (or have been impacted by). The tone of the narratives may also shed some light on teachers' current state of motivation and commitment in the profession.

How, then, can narratives be used for professional growth?

Jalongo, Isenberg, and Gerbracht (1995) identify five ways that narratives can contribute to professional development and professional growth. Excerpts of narratives, taken from an actual narrative inquiry project with Singapore physical education teachers, are added to illustrate each of the five points.

1. **Narratives invite reflective practice.** Teachers' narratives reveal not just the professional phenomena of teaching, but also uncover deep-seated personal beliefs that influence the act of teaching. No two experiences are the same. Through narratives, teachers are able to articulate multi-dimensional

perspectives surrounding their teaching actions and uncover some of their beliefs that may have hindered their growth as teachers. For example,

> The lesson was highly energised and there was a lot of excitement. Mainly because now they had a voice and they could 'see' their voice when they commented on one another's work... they were also mostly enjoying themselves and engaged, evident from their smiles and the constant need to remind them to look at me.... I think technology has had a big impact. It opened my eyes to the possibilities and also made me reconsider the use of technology in physical education and how much potential there is. Yes, there's still planning but the focus is mainly on me as a facilitator and the learner as well.
>
> (Jaslyn, experienced teacher)

2. **Narratives chronicle growth and change.** As stories are built up from many years' experience, they present teachers with invaluable data on how their knowledge and practice have (or have not) evolved. New meanings, via new lenses, can give teachers more insights into their past, present, and future experience. For example,

> I am a beginning physical education teacher, a newbie to this school. But from the moment I stepped into this school, I didn't feel like a beginning teacher at all. I took on roles to develop learning packages the moment I came in due to my past experience before becoming a teacher. My first year in this school was a rollercoaster ride and definitely a steep learning curve.... I want to be a contributor. But I feel like the busiest beginning teacher in the school. Most peers think I've been around for a long time but I've been here barely 2.5 years. But I feel a bit more calm and in control now. Still busy, but a bit calmer.
>
> (Hayley, 3rd year teacher)

3. **Narratives promote the 'ethic of caring'.** Teachers keep many acts of care and love within them. These are 'secrets to be brought to the grave' without any expectations of reward or recognition. However, sharing some of these stories may inspire more acts of kindness among other teachers and affirm why they answered the calling in the first place. For example,

> So on that first day of school, I told the class sternly that everyone must have a water bottle for physical education lessons. I was confident of students meeting this requirement as most of them already had one. In the next lesson, one student had no water bottle. As he approached me, I noticed his fear. Suddenly, a voice inside tells me, hey, maybe he doesn't have one at home because he just can't afford it. And true enough, that was it. He was close to tears! And it broke me. That very day, I bought some bottles and passed one to him secretly. He looked like that's the best present he had ever had in his

life! It made me more aware of who my students are outside school. Where they are from. I shared this with a colleague and she shared a similar story too! I felt good, but guilty for assuming that all students have these things.

(Lia, 3rd year teacher)

4. **Narratives reveal teachers' 'voice'.** Like students, teachers have their own inhibitions when standing in front of an audience. The fear of being judged or showing up their vulnerabilities is paramount in many teachers' minds. Narratives help teachers to find their 'voice' as they can be themselves. They are the story. To be reflective, teachers must be able to articulate themselves openly, especially when experiencing tensions in having to implement practices that are counter to their beliefs and values or when faced with morale-depleting incidents with colleagues or students. For example,

On a side note, I do feel super-tired these days. The phrase 'Don't get burned out too early' that the other teachers kept saying tends to ring in my head now and again. But that usually happens on really low, tiring days. I do not feel that I am burning out, but I do feel really tired on some days. And it doesn't help that some non-physical education colleagues have this misconception that we physical education teachers that do 100% physical education have it easy. But it really takes a lot out of me especially when there are meetings or PD workshops after school.

(Kareem, 3rd year teacher)

5. **Narratives can develop cross-cultural understandings.** In multicultural settings, it is important for teachers to be sensitive to the different cultures and belief systems of their students and colleagues. Narratives can serve as a platform to articulate, bridge, develop, or strengthen their understanding of their students and how best to connect with them in the classroom. Sharing those narratives can then create a culture of community as differences can be understood and appreciated. For example,

It was the 'Bridge Tag' Game. Two students had to build a bridge with their hands and the frozen students had to just walk under that bridge to be unfrozen. Right after I blew the whistle to start, a boy ran to me and said, 'Teacher, my religion says its bad luck to walk under two hands like that. So I can't play this game.' That shocked me a little. I almost agreed to his request to stay out but I wanted him to be involved. So I told him that he could just run one round around the bridge to be unfrozen. It looked like a simple solution, but it taught me to consider these differences as well when I plan my lessons. Or, at least, ask if anyone is not comfortable doing that. Right after that game, I caught his attention and just gestured with a thumbs up. He reciprocated and I knew everything was good.

(Nelly, 2nd year teacher)

Consider the following excerpt from an experienced teacher's narrative as she describes her struggle to use information and communication technology (ICT) in her physical education lessons. The brief analysis that follows summarises the earlier discussions on using narratives as a tool for reflective practice and professional growth.

> *I tried using ICT in my physical education lesson but I don't think it really turned out well because not all students are on task when they have iPads with them. Therefore, I had to step in to correct some misinterpretations about the movement pattern in sending and receiving the ball. The iPads really helped with the peer evaluations, as students could review their friends' movement patterns several times before deciding on their 'grade'. But quite a number of students do not know how to video record their friends effectively, and thus, are unable to observe the movement pattern accurately... logging in took half an hour as some passwords expired and I had to help students change them (they didn't know how to). So that was quite a struggle. I did complete the lesson in the end but not everyone got to do their own quiz so the data collection process was flawed... in the end, it took away too much physical activity time... so I really need to know how to use ICT more effectively without compromising the amount of activity time.*
>
> (Yenny, experienced teacher)

In her narrative, Yenny included elements of reflection-in-action. She describes her in-lesson actions and the thoughts and emotions that were involved throughout her lesson. Her intention of infusing ICT to enhance student feedback and collaboration was hampered by technical issues that she did not anticipate. As she reflected in narrative form, she applied reflection-on-action as well. She realised gaps in her knowledge and skill in infusing ICT effectively. Her ideal of not "compromising the amount of physical activity time" pushed her to resolve to learn how to do so. This was made explicit in her narrative and could serve as a professional development plan for her to pursue.

When Handal and Lauvas' (1987) practical theory model (Figure 12.2) is layered in over her narrative, you can see that Yenny's reflection is situated at L1 and L2. Besides describing the tasks, her actions, and the problems that came with it, she also described the impact her planning (or lack of planning) had on the flow of the lesson. She considered her role in contributing to that problem (lack of knowledge in infusing ICT) and professed her desire to plug that gap as part of her professional growth. For Yenny to reach L3, she could include the wider purpose of why she felt that she needed to infuse ICT in her PE lessons in the first place. Was it an expectation placed upon her? Or was it something that she merely wanted to explore? What was the higher political, educational, or ethical justification in wanting to infuse ICT for student learning in physical education? The question of 'why' was not addressed in her narrative.

With the previous brief analysis and the preceding excerpts, attempt Task 12.2, which is a continuation of Task 12.1.

> ### ✏️ Task 12.2 Am I reflective enough?
>
> Re-read your reflections in Task 12.1. As you read them, refer to Table 12.1 (Types of reflections) and Figure 12.2 (Handal and Lauvas's practical theory hierarchy). Consider the following prompts:
>
> - Evaluation of your narrative:
>   - ☐ Are there elements of reflection-in-action and reflection-on action (see Table 12.1)?
>   - ☐ Which type of reflection is dominant?
>   - ☐ Where would you place your narrative, based on Figure 12.2 – L1, L2, or L3?
>   - ☐ Are there elements of each level in your narrative?
> - Re-writing your narrative (do not discard your first draft!)
>   - ☐ Enhance your narrative based on the earlier evaluation
>   - ☐ What details are missing?
>   - ☐ What other perspectives could you include in order to reach the L3 level?
>   - ☐ If you are merely describing events or actions, consider finding out the reasons behind those events or actions
>   - ☐ Re-read your revised version
> - Reflecting on the process
>   - ☐ Place your first and second drafts side by side
>   - ☐ Look at all the revisions you have made
>   - ☐ How different are the two drafts? Are they significantly different? How?
>
> Has the writing process benefitted you? How?

Supplementing the Narrative Process

Not everyone can write, or likes to write. For some, it takes a lot of time and effort just to start penning down simple thoughts, let alone engage in deep reflection, and then to analyse it through different lenses. However, there are some supplementary tools that you can use to initiate the narrative process. View these pre-writing processes as cognitive strategies that support or supplement the actual writing process; not as step-by-step directives. They can also be viewed as a data collection process to identify key events or milestones – a 'parking lot' – before expanding and unpacking them in the main writing process.

Mood Graphs

Mood graphs allow critical milestones in your teaching career or teaching episode to be captured. The milestones identified give a visual of your trajectory over a self-defined period of time (see Figure 12.5). It serves as a trigger to identify important events you feel are significant enough for you to reflect on. The time frame can be within a lesson or a day, week, month, term, semester, a year, or even over a few years.

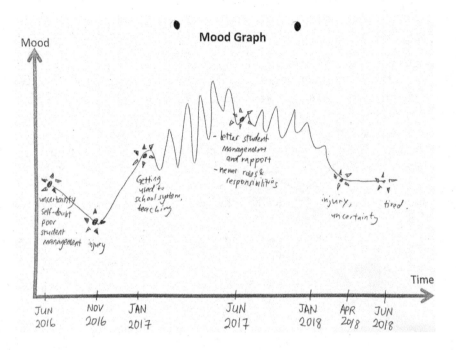

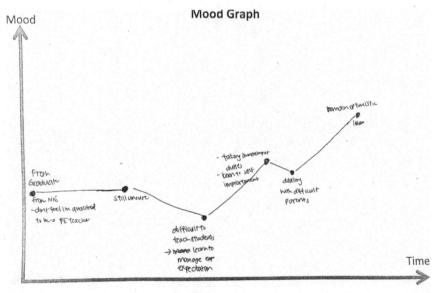

Figure 12.5 Samples of mood graphs (reproduced with permission)

Before you embark on your narrative, use a mood graph to quickly identify the key events of a lesson, or a series of lessons. It could also be used to reflect on the highs and lows of your classroom experiences with your students. You can annotate each milestone with short notes and emojis and then expand it further when you start your narrative writing process.

Metaphors

Metaphors are used to conceptualise individuals' thinking and beliefs (Lakoff and Johnson, 1980). Metaphors enable you to paint a picture of your thoughts, emotions, and experiences. Through metaphors, you can understand better your tacit beliefs, values, and cognitive constructs. For example, beginning teachers use metaphors of resilience - a Cylon roller coaster, fire, a kite, a skinny person trying to buff up, wild weather, onions, or a stubborn never-say-die cockroach (Figure 12.6). These are a strong indication of their positive capacity to maintain effective functioning in their practice despite difficult circumstances and to develop increased productivity through consistent achievement in the classroom (Day et al., 2007; Gu and Day, 2013).

The following excerpt illustrates how metaphors can be used to represent an experience or a state of mind.

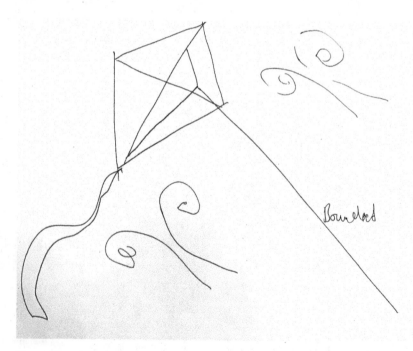

Figure 12.6 Examples of metaphors - kite, onion, weather (reproduced with permission)

BEING A REFLECTIVE TEACHER

Figure 12.6 (Continued)

Truthfully, I thought, as a new teacher, I am doing a lot more and am even busier than any of my peers in this school. I am not complaining about the workload, mostly, as I am willing to do it as long as it is for students. And that leads to my strength. In Chinese, there is a saying: 'A cockroach won't die regardless of how many beatings'. My endurance and tolerance can be quite high. Though it saps my patience dry at times. Things do not always go my way. And it's alright, I accept and I continue. There's really no point whining and complaining about something but still stay put. The moment you decide to just stay put, you lose sight of what you are truly battling for.

(Hayley)

Hayley had to dig deep and be resilient in the first few years of her teaching career simply because she found meaning in every aspect of her work, although she found it overwhelming at most times. The 'beatings' have not fazed her. She is one strong 'cockroach'.

Journaling

Keeping a journal of teaching experiences allows you to "dip into (it) again and again as a reservoir for narrative" (Jalongo, Isenberg and Gerbracht, 1995, p 183). Journaling allows you to re-read and relive recent past experiences with perhaps a different set of lenses. The issues may not be apparent at the time of the journal entry, but can be revisited, further considered and analysed for common themes or significant events that could alter your teaching stances or beliefs. As you read and re-read your journals, you may find yourselves amending some of those stories as you gain more light or recall more details that were not considered before.

Journaling should be a medium- or long-term endeavour. For example, if you are starting a new pedagogical strategy such as cooperative learning that spans a few weeks, you could start journaling even during the planning stage. Include your thought processes, rationale for using the new strategy, and what you already know about it. As you embark on the day-to-day lessons applying that strategy, include some details about what happened, what you did, and what the students did. At this point in time, these could be written in bulleted form or even in audio format and may or may not include your analysis of the events. The analysis could take place at the end of the day, or key time periods, for you to effectively modify your strategies based on what you have experienced. It should also include teacher-student and student-student interactions and the outcomes of the lesson. More importantly, include the emotions you felt during those teaching episodes. Then, re-read all your entries in the journal. What themes stand out? What did you write mostly about? Your actions or your students? What were the dominant emotions felt? Did your enactment of teaching align with your intended plans? These questions ultimately help you make sense of your experiences and contribute to your professional growth as a reflective practitioner.

4Ws – What I Learned, What I Wonder, What I Wish, What I Need

Jalongo, Isenberg, and Gerbracht (1995) formulated a simple 4W structure to encourage teachers to "chronicle and examine their stories of practice" (p. 191). This strategy can also be embedded as part of journaling when reflecting on a teaching episode. The strategy includes components which do not have to be done in sequence and can be used multiple times:

- *What I learned* – What you have learned through the observations of yourself and your students during a teaching episode
- *What I wonder* – What nagging questions you have from the experience
- *What I wish* – What your goals are in relation to the experience; what you wish you knew, or had done during that experience
- *What I need* – A strong statement about your role as a professional borne out of the experience that you have just gone through

An example to illustrate the use of the 4Ws in a physical education context:

> *From today's dance lesson,* **I wonder** *how I could better balance giving students space and time to explore and covering the lesson objectives. Surprisingly, contrary to my perception of them as 'hating dance lessons',* **I learned** *that the students were willing to do it if they could choose their group members.* **I learned** *that they are very creative in modifying the dance steps.* **I wish** *I could make the decision to make adjustments to the unit plans and modes of assessment.* **I need** *to convince my colleagues that we need more time in this unit. Plus,* **I need** *to learn about more student-centric strategies, especially in dance.*

This section has identified some tools to help you kick-start or enhance the narrative process. Use these tools (and others) with discretion and modify them to suit your needs. Using such tools makes the narrative process simpler as they are meant to help you gather concrete evidence at specific points of time. This evidence is then expanded and unpacked in greater detail during the writing process. Ultimately, such tools should help you be more reflective in your narrative by considering multiple perspectives. Now, attempt Task 12.3.

 Task 12.3 Enhancing your narrative

Look again at the second draft of your narrative from Task 12.2. Use one of the following tools to enhance your narrative.

- Mood graph
  - ☐ Construct a mood graph based on the time period of your narrative (a week, month, term, etc.)

- ☐ Annotate each milestone as a reminder of that particular incident
- ☐ Attach evocative memories or emotions to those events
- ☐ Use the completed mood graph and check if you have indicated each milestone in your narrative
- ☐ If you can, reflect on why you have left out some events and included others
- **Metaphors**
  - ☐ Based on what you have written, think of a specific event or a series of events that is/are significant
  - ☐ Think of a metaphor that can aptly represent that part of your experience
  - ☐ You may also look at your writing holistically and select a metaphor to represent your entire trajectory of events
  - ☐ Share in detail why you have chosen that metaphor
  - ☐ Relate that metaphor to your story
- **Journaling**

Some suggested steps and guiding questions (adapted from Johnson and Golombek, 2002):

- Keep a reflective journal for at least two weeks in which you focus on your daily practices for a class (or a few classes, or all of your classes). It could also be at the start of a new pedagogical strategy that you are embarking on such as cooperative learning strategies.
- Describe the activities within each class and the rationale behind the decisions that you made in those classes.
- In your reflections, describe
  - ☐ how you felt about each class
  - ☐ your interactions with students and their interactions with one another
  - ☐ aspects of your practice that were in conflict with one another
  - ☐ individual or institutional constraints and moral issues that affect your teaching
- Re-read your journal; identify themes or patterns.
  - ☐ Do these themes reflect who you are as a learner and as a teacher?
  - ☐ What tensions do these themes represent in your current teaching practice?
- Identify a "problem" – this is your area of inquiry.
  - ☐ Define and scope the main question
  - ☐ Plan how to collect data seamlessly in your classes
  - ☐ Analyse the data – what does it tell you?
  - ☐ Do you need to adopt alternative teaching methods?

- ☐ Plan for interventions
- ☐ What worked? What did not? Why?
■ Video record your lessons (if possible, from the beginning of the inquiry).
- ☐ What do you see?
- ☐ What are the critical incidents?
- ☐ Describe how your pedagogy is aligned to your knowledge, beliefs, and values about teaching and learning, and about your students
■ Lastly, include these in your narratives where appropriate. You could also reflect on the journaling process in your narrative and include excerpts from the journal in your narrative.

From Narratives to Professional Insight

An important part of the process in using narrative inquiry to develop as a reflective practitioner is the process of professional conversations or dialogues. This is when teachers can validate and affirm one another's experiences, find common themes, challenge assumptions, and, to some extent, re-examine their beliefs and value systems. Written narratives, if kept to the narrator, are still of value, but only to the narrator themself. However, Yonemura (1986) strongly advocates dialogue as teachers can reflect upon their practice; articulate tensions, frustrations, and feelings; and examine the alignment between their professional beliefs and teaching enactment.

Sharing your stories with knowledgeable others, trusted colleagues, or in a professional learning community invites multiple perspectives of your experience. When common themes arise, these experiences become shared experiences which increase professional collegiality and promote collaborative professional development. When you tell and re-tell your stories, you invite support for yourself, and, at the same time, open up an opportunity to give support to peers and colleagues. This elevates the status of the teaching profession as you situate yourself in "intellectual communities of teacher-researchers, or networks of individuals who enter with other teachers into a collective search for meaning in their work lives" (Cochran-Smith and Lytle, 1990, p. 9).

SUMMARY AND KEY POINTS

As a reflective teacher, you can gain insights about yourself, your beliefs, values, teaching, students, and the curriculum by leveraging the strengths of your stories – your own products (Jalongo, Isenberg and Gerbracht, 1995). You think about the acts of teaching, are responsible for making decisions on those actions, and are enthusiastic and open as you go about the duties of educating students (Grant and Zeichner, 1984). The amount and regularity of introspection done ultimately changes teaching practices as you become more aware of issues in the classroom and the beliefs you hold about teaching and your students. This step is critical in your journey towards being a reflective practitioner and, essentially, in contributing towards your own professional growth and development.

The power of narrative extends beyond the narrator. It 'pulls' readers to interpret the shared stories in such a way that it resonates with their own life history to the point that the "lifelikeness, the verisimilitude, of narrative allows for multiple interpretations, and multiple interpretations render multiple educational possibilities" (Oliver, 1998, p. 249). You can then better understand yourself as a teacher, your students, your colleagues, and the complex learning environments that you are operating in so that your students can truly flourish and realise the ideals that education has to offer to each of them.

Note: A list of further resources to help you take your learning forward is available on the PESTA website: https://academyofsingaporeteachers.moe.edu.sg/pesta/professional-development/book-chapters-by-the-pesta-team

References

Argyris, C. and Schon, D.A. (1974) *Theory in Practice: Increasing Professional Effectiveness*, San Francisco: Jossey-Bass.

Barkhuizen, G. (2020) 'Core dimensions of narrative inquiry', in J. McKinley and H. Rose (eds.) *The Routledge Handbook of Research Methods in Applied Linguistics*, New York: Routledge, pp. 188-198.

Bruer, J.T. (1993) 'The mind's journey from novice to expert', *American Educator*, 17 (2), 6-15.

Bruner, J. (1986) *Actual Minds, Possible Worlds*, Cambridge, MA: Harvard University Press.

Cochran-Smith, M. and Lytle, S.L. (1990) 'Research on teachers and teacher research: The issues that divide', *Educational Researcher*, 19 (2), 2-11.

Coles, R. (1989) *The Call of Stories*, Boston: Houghton Mifflin.

Connelly, F.M. and Clandinin, D.J. (1990) 'Stories of experience and narrative inquiry', *Educational Researcher*, 19 (5), 2-14.

Connelly, F.M. and Clandinin, D.J. (2000) *Narrative Inquiry: Experience and Story in Educational Research*, San Francisco: Jossey-Bass.

Day, C., Sammons, P., Stobart, G., Kington, A. and Gu, Q. (2007) *Teachers Matter: Connecting Lives, Work and Effectiveness*, New York: McGraw-Hill.

Dewey, J. (1938) *Experience and Education*, New York: Collier Books.

Freire, P. (1996) *Letters to Cristina*, New York: Routledge.

Grant, C. and Zeichner, K. (1984) 'On becoming a reflective teacher', in C. Grant (ed.) *Preparing for Reflective Teaching*, MA: Allyn & Bacon.

Gu, Q. and Day, C. (2013) 'Challenges to teacher resilience: Conditions count', *British Educational Research Journal*, 39 (1), 22-44.

Handal, G. and Lauvas, P. (1987) *Promoting Reflective Teaching: Supervision in Practice*, Milton Keynes: Open University Education Enterprises.

Hardy, B. (1977) 'Towards a poetics of fiction', in M. Meek and others (eds.) *The Cool Web*, London: The Bodley Head.

Jalongo, M.R., Isenberg, J.P. and Gerbracht, G. (1995) *Teachers' Stories: From Personal Narrative to Professional Insight*, San Francisco: Jossey-Bass.

Johnson, K.E. and Golombek, P.R. (eds.) (2002) *Teachers' Narrative Inquiry as Professional Development*, New York: Cambridge University Press.

Lakoff, G. and Johnson, M. (1980) *Metaphors We Live by*, Chicago, IL: University of Chicago Press.

Noddings, N. (1991) 'Stories in dialogue', in C. Witherell and N. Noddings (eds.) *Stories Lives Tell: Narrative and Dialogue in Education*, New York: Teachers College Press.

Oliver, K.L. (1998) 'A journey into narrative analysis: A methodology for discovering meaning', *Journal of Teaching in Physical Education*, 17 (2), 244-259.

Ohanian, S. (1989) Quoted in Schuster, E. in 'Pursuit of cultural literacy', *Phi Delta Kappan*, 70, 539-542.

Polkinghorne, D.E. (1988) *Narrative Knowing and the Human Sciences*, Albany: State University of New York Press.

Rogers, C. (1954) 'Towards a theory of creativity', *ETC: A Review of General Semantics*, 11, 249-260.

Rosen, B. (1988) *And None of it was Nonsense: The Power of Storytelling in School*, London: Mary Glasgow Publications.

Schon, D.A. (1983) *The Reflective Practitioner: How Professionals Think in Action*, New York: Basic Books.

Schon, D.A. (1987) *Educating the Reflective Practitioner*, San Francisco: Jossey-Bass.

Yonemura, M.V. (1986) *A Teacher at Work*, New York: Teachers College Press.

 **Organising Continuing Professional Development**

13 Professional Development

What Is It and How Can It Work for Me?

Joanna Phan Swee Lee

Introduction

The purpose of this chapter is not to convince you that professional development is important and necessary. It is. Period. Especially if you remain in the teaching profession and are entrusted with the responsibility to impact positively and effectively the many lives that pass through your hands. Indeed, "Unless physical education teachers undertake challenging and effective professional learning throughout their long careers, they are unfit to be trusted with responsibility for children and young people in education, physical education, wellness, health, or anything else" (Armour, Makopoulou and Chambers, 2009, p.213). This strongly worded statement underscores the important role professional development plays in a teacher's career, and also implies it has an impact on improving teaching and learning. Teaching is a complex and demanding skill, requiring a teacher to design appropriate lesson activities by taking into consideration a myriad of factors that impact the success of a lesson and students' learning. During the act of teaching, experienced teachers are constantly making adjustments to their plans in response to students' learning, behaviour, and to the environment. Researchers and practitioners are in constant pursuit of teaching and learning excellence, which means that knowledge and practice in teaching is constantly evolving. Teachers need to continually engage in professional development to ensure that the knowledge underlying their practice remains current as advances are made in the theory and practice of teaching.

This chapter goes beyond beliefs and attitudes towards professional development. It assumes that as a teacher you have a growth mindset (Dweck, 2016) and that you see learning as a lifelong endeavour. With this assumption in mind, this chapter focuses on how professional development can impact your practice and factors at your school that enable or restrict your professional development. This is not to say that your professional development is not impacted by other factors like family or interests beyond work. This chapter, however, focuses on the professional aspects of your professional development as a physical education teacher. The professional development journeys of three Singapore physical education teachers are shared with you to help you relate

DOI: 10.4324/9781003171973-16

better to the principles referenced in this chapter which are related to adult learning and professional development. The three journeys, though different, have enabled each of these teachers to become successful in their careers. Throughout the chapter, you are invited to reflect on the content covered to help you review your own professional journey and how you might apply the learning to your own practice so that you continue to develop into the physical education teacher you aim to be.

> **OBJECTIVES**
>
> At the end of the chapter, you should be able to:
>
> - determine the type or types of professional development you think would be effective for your development
> - identify factors that can support your professional development and
> - design an appropriate professional development plan for yourself given your needs and the support or constraints at your school.

What Is Professional Development?

Life as a physical education teacher in Singapore begins after a trainee teacher graduates from the National Institute of Education (NIE) following two to four years of teacher preparation, depending on whether they followed a diploma or degree programme. New graduates of NIE can expect to have the necessary knowledge and skills to competently "meet the demands and challenges of a dynamic teaching career" (NIE, 2021). The adjective "dynamic" implies that the teaching landscape is not always going to stay the same and that it will be shaped by contemporary events. It also implies that the knowledge and skills that teachers graduate with from NIE need to be constantly updated and developed as they progress through their teaching career. Such updates and developments normally occur through professional development.

Guskey (2000) describes professional development as any undertaking that contributes to the advancement of professional knowledge, skills, and attitudes of teachers that results in an improvement in teaching and, hence, students' learning. According to Eraut (2004), types of professional development can be placed along a continuum ranging from informal to formal. He describes learning in the informal context as "implicit, unintended, opportunistic and unstructured learning and the absence of a teacher" (p. 250). At the other end of the continuum, formal professional development includes planned and structured learning activities where learning outcomes are specified and targeted in the learning activities. In the ensuing discussion, professional development is taken to mean learning activities in both informal and formal contexts as well as anything in between. Task 13.1 asks you to consider types of professional development you have been involved in.

PROFESSIONAL DEVELOPMENT 237

 Task 13.1 What kind of professional development have I been involved with?

Looking back at your own professional development since you became a teacher, what professional development activities (formal, in between, and informal) have you participated in? Make a list of these activities in the table. The descriptors can guide you in your listing and the examples given are non-exhaustive.

Formal	In Between	Informal
Planned and structured learning activities where learning outcomes are specified and targeted in advance, for example, workshops, conferences, etc.	*Somewhat planned but also including ad hoc learning experiences. The learning occurred through structured and unstructured activities, for example, a coaching engagement.*	*Unplanned, ad hoc and unstructured learning. Often, learning was not the intention in these activities, for example, being assigned a project at school that was new to you.*

The Professional Learning Journeys of Three Singapore Physical Education Teachers

At this point in the chapter, three Singapore physical education teachers are introduced and their professional learning stories shared. They are successful teachers at their respective schools and have made professional development work for them. Reference to their journeys is made throughout the chapter to help you better understand the principles covered.

Case study 13.1   Aarifa's professional development journey

Aarifa started her career being deployed to teach physical education and another academic subject. She was also part of the school's discipline committee. While she was interested in honing her craft in teaching physical education, she found it challenging to do so because her attention was divided between physical education, the other subject, and the demands of the discipline committee. While she attended workshops conducted by the Physical Education and Sports Teacher Academy (PESTA) in the Ministry of Education (MOE), she could not find other like-minded physical education teachers that she could get support from, and collaborate with, beyond the workshops to learn and improve her craft. In the early years of her career, she was given the opportunity to conduct action research on learners with varied needs. As her knowledge and experience in this area grew, so too did her achievements and, hence, her confidence and interest in this area. With the support of the principal at her school, she went on to pursue a full-time master's degree in curriculum and teaching. She found the learning relevant and rich.

After graduating from the master's course, Aarifa was posted to another school. At this school, she was deployed to only teach physical education. This rekindled her interest in advancing her knowledge and skills to improve her practice. She could also give physical education more focus. However, once again, she found it difficult to find other teachers who shared the same interest and who wanted to create a learning community to support one another. Nevertheless, she continued to learn and improve on her own and did well enough to be appointed a Teacher Leader.[1]

The role opened up the opportunity for her to collaborate with a physical education Continuing Professional Development (CPD) officer from PESTA. Through this partnership, she embarked on a continuing professional development journey that enabled her to deepen her knowledge and skills in teaching the subject. Aarifa still attended workshops and the collaboration with the CPD officer provided her with the professional support she had been looking for in the past. She had a knowledgeable other (Chapter 14 gives insight on how to be a mentor and be that knowledgeable other) who could guide her in her practice, and the professional conversations they had were enlightening and invigorating. As her practice improved, she began to see a positive impact on her students' learning. Apart from having the opportunity to collaborate with a CPD officer, being a Teacher Leader also gave Aarifa access to a network of physical education Teacher Leaders in Singapore. It became easier for her to find like-minded professionals to collaborate and learn with. (Chapter 16 lays out the principles and approach taken by the CPD provider, PESTA, to design, support, and sustain teachers' learning, application, and reinforcement of new knowledge and skills gained.)

Case study 13.2 Banu's professional development journey

Banu taught physical education and mathematics when she started teaching. She found it challenging to give both subjects equal attention and felt that the teaching of mathematics demanded more of her in terms of planning, teaching, and grading. The other physical education teachers at the school also taught a second subject, and found themselves in the same predicament. This changed when a directive from the MOE was issued that physical education lessons had to be taught by trained physical education teachers (physical education lessons had previously been taught by several non-trained physical education teachers at her school). Thus, the physical education teachers no longer taught a second subject.

Banu's professional development in physical education was largely self-initiated and took the form of attending workshops. She found opportunities to explore teaching strategies during her lessons and learned from those experiences. She had many opportunities to share her learning and experiences with others at her school and beyond. Through sharing, Banu was also able to get affirmation of her practices when the teachers told her that they would try out her ideas or share them with other physical education teachers. As she progressed through her career, her supervising colleague recognised her potential to excel in her craft and encouraged her to develop and hone her teaching further. He made numerous opportunities available to her over the years to attend workshops and to share her expertise and experience with other teachers to help them be more effective in teaching physical education. She was recognised for her competence and was appointed a Teacher Leader. Through this role, more professional development opportunities opened up to her. She attended masterclasses conducted by experts, shared at conferences and teachers' networks and even took the role of a facilitator at workshops.

Banu attributed the success of her own professional development to the supportive environment she worked in. Physical education at the school was given due importance and recognition and the physical education teachers worked very closely together to share ideas and practices with one another. Her supervisor was very supportive of the professional development of the department members and did not limit the number of professional development opportunities the physical education teachers participated in as long as their involvement did not compromise their abilities to see to the school's needs first. In Chapter 16, this would be the structural motivator and enabler to sustain teachers' learning, application, and reinforcement from their PD programmes.

Case study 13.3   Chris's professional development journey

Chris took to teaching physical education like fish to water. Professionally, he knew how he wanted to develop himself and he had a supportive school environment that allowed him to determine the type of professional development he wanted to engage in and the method of engagement. Chris regarded professional development for himself as important because it helped him remain current in his practice, and assured that he was delivering quality physical education to his students to enhance their learning. In the first half of his career (approximately ten years), there was an absence of professional development through traditional means; therefore he sought professional development mainly through informal avenues through his network of physical education teacher colleagues and friends (e.g. conversations with colleagues and friends or observing lessons taught by other teachers). He preferred informal learning to formal learning as the latter would mean that he had to sit through segments of a course which did not appeal to him.

He excelled at what he did and was eventually appointed a Teacher Leader. He was also nominated for a prestigious teaching award in recognition of his commitment to delivering effective lessons and for being a role model for other teachers.

He recognised that as a Teacher Leader he was able to work with and learn from CPD officers who made themselves readily available to support his learning and development. He was also afforded more opportunities to interact with more teachers, to learn and share at various platforms. Being obligated to open his classroom to other teachers, he began to realise the need to deepen his pedagogical knowledge even further. Teaching had been very natural to him, but now that he had to share his knowledge and practice with others, he needed to communicate his practice and his tacit knowledge with others more objectively and effectively. He therefore began to codify his teaching practices so that he could gain a deeper understanding of why he was doing what he was doing.

He had found a community of like-minded professionals who could engage with him in meaningful dialogues and help him improve his theory and practice. He also found, in this community, role models who could give him the assurance and affirmation to be a pedagogical leader for other physical education teachers.

The Role of Professional Development and the Adult Learner

As teachers start out on their careers, they are in the "survival stage" (Rovegno and Bandhauer, 2017). At this stage, novice teachers typically focus on lesson management and discipline during their lessons. As they become more confident and move out of the "survival stage", they are able to manage typical challenges that arise during lessons and begin to focus more on students' learning, establishing good routines that facilitate learning. The final stage is the expert stage, at which the teacher is able to assimilate the range of factors that impact teaching and learning and plan and conduct effective lessons for student learning. Rovegno and Bandhauer (2017) were quick to point out that arriving at the expert stage is not necessarily the result of years of experience but, rather, a combination of experience and learning. This is where professional development, formal or informal or anything in between, can help a teacher to become an expert. We see this in the professional journeys of Aarifa, Banu, and Chris. While their journeys were quite different, they all engaged with professional development to help them become better teachers. The mix of formal and informal professional development was different for each of them and yet they each became successful at what they did.

Before getting too excited about having found an elixir to help teachers move from "survival" to expert stage, where learning is concerned, it is important to remember that you must first be ready and willing to learn. A teacher's *Readiness to learn* is one of the six key principles of adult learning (Knowles, 1990) that undergirds the adult learning model. Readiness to learn describes a learner as someone who is open to new knowledge and experiences. Considering the professional journeys of Aarifa, Banu, and Chris, each of them was very keen to learn and improve their practices. They were proactive in looking for and taking full advantage of professional development opportunities. The adult learner also needs to see the relevance of the learning. This brings in another key principle, *Orientation to learning*, which emphasises the importance of the content for

Table 13.1 Knowles (1990) principles of adult learning

> **1 The learner's need to know;**
> Adult learners have the need to understand why they are learning what they are learning. Sometimes this might not be immediately obvious and might need to be explained to them.
>
> **2 The learner's self-concept;**
> Learners direct their own learning, determine the learning outcomes and the pathways to achieving these outcomes.
>
> **3 The role of the learner's experiences;**
> Life experiences shape an adult's knowledge and perspectives and cannot be discounted or ignored in the learning process. The learning process should involve building on these valuable and varied experiences.
>
> **4 Readiness to learn;**
> An adult's readiness to learn can be affected by the relevance of the learning to work performance needs. At times, the relevance might not be immediately obvious in which case readiness to learn can be nurtured by sharing examples of best practices, mentoring, or coaching, or other ways that can help the learner realise the need for professional development.
>
> **5 Orientation to learning;**
> Adult learners learn more willingly and effectively when they are presented with authentic problems to solve. This helps to contextualise the solution to a situation they are more familiar with and increase the applicability of the solution in their own contexts.
>
> **6 Motivation.**
> According to Knowles, while "external motivators" like monetary rewards or a rise in status in the organisation can serve to encourage adults to learn and grow professionally, "internal motivators" like personal desires, satisfaction, and the perception of self in relation to one's work influence one's level of motivation even more.

learning being centred around real-life problems so that the learner can see the usefulness of the learning and its practical applications (referred to in Chapter 16 as the "day-to-day complexities"). Table 13.1 provides a summary of Knowles's six principles of adult learning. Task 13.2 asks you to reflect on yourself as a learner.

> **Task 13.2 Reflecting on my own professional development experiences and learning in relation to the six principles for adult learning**
>
> In the list you have created in Task 13.1, select one professional development activity that you attended that you felt
>
> 1 You benefitted greatly from;
> 2 Was not very useful to you.

PROFESSIONAL DEVELOPMENT

> Using the following questions as a guide, reflect on your learning experiences from these two professional development activities and explore possible reasons why there were differences in the learning experiences and outcome for you:
>
> - How clear was my understanding of why I was participating in this professional development activity?
> - To what extent was I able to determine how I accessed the learning content and interacted with it?
> - How much of what I learned was built on my prior knowledge and experiences?
> - How willing and ready was I for the learning?
> - To what extent was my learning relevant to my work?
> - What was my real reason for engaging in this professional development activity?
>
> Are there differences in your responses to each question for each professional development activity? The differences could help explain why the level of learning was different for both activities, but let us not be too quick to come to a conclusion here. Do note that there could also be other factors that could impact the effectiveness of a professional development activity which are discussed in the ensuing sections of this chapter.

Effective Professional Development

For professional development to be considered effective, learning must have taken place. Knowles's (1990) six principles alone do not guarantee that any professional development activity you participate in will effectively lead to learning. Attention now shifts to the way professional development is conducted. Merrill (2002) identifies five essential principles for professional development to be effective (summarised in Table 13.2). He argues that these five principles can be

Table 13.2 Five essential principles for professional development to be effective

---

Problem-centred
Instruction needs to involve real-world problems which are relevant to learners.

Activation
Learners' prior knowledge and experiences are activated and used as a foundation for new knowledge to be built on.

Demonstration
Learning is enhanced when it is demonstrated to learners instead of learners being told the information.

Application
Learners get to apply their new knowledge or skills to solve the problem.

Integration
Learners get to use their new knowledge or skills in their work context.

Source: Merrill (2002)

found in all effective instructional strategies for professional development and if any one or more of these principles are not included, learning is compromised.

The principle *Integration* might not feature in every professional development activity, even those that learners found to be very beneficial to their learning. This principle will be elaborated on in the next section of this chapter.

Although the five principles are about effective instructional strategies, they also work hand in hand with the six principles for adult learning. The principle of *Problem-centred* helps learners have a better *Orientation to learning* and *Activation* supports *The role of the learner's experiences*. Hence, learning from any professional development activity depends on the learner and the instructor. With this in mind, Task 13.3 asks you to reflect on the effectiveness of the instructional strategies used in the professional development activities you identified in Task 13.2.

Task 13.3   Reflecting on my own professional experiences and level of learning in relation to the five principles for effective instructional strategies

With the reflections from Task 13.2, recall the way the two professional development activities were conducted.

1. For the professional development activity that you benefitted greatly from, were all five principles featured in the instructional strategy? To what extent did this impact your learning? Why?
2. For the professional development activity that you did not find very useful, were any of the five principles missing from the instructional strategy? To what extent did this impact your learning? Why?

Continued Learning After the Professional Development Session – Integration of Learning

Four of five of Merrill's (2002) principles for effective instructional strategies are commonly found in most traditional professional development sessions. *Integration* rarely gets the attention required for you to consolidate your learning and apply it in an authentic setting. This section focuses on Merrill's (2002) principle of *Integration* which requires you to apply the new learning from the professional development activity in your own work context, reflect on the experience and adapt and personalise the learning. *Integration* enhances the *Orientation to learning*.

Integration is perhaps where the secret to making professional development work for you lies. The crux of effective professional development is when practice improves and positively impacts students' learning. Garet et al. (2001) opined that the traditional method of professional development, typically a one-off session with little follow-up support for integration of learning, is not optimal. This is not to say that traditional professional development is totally ineffective and should be discouraged; rather, what follows after the professional development session can make the difference to the quality of learning and, importantly, change in practice. If you think about Aarifa's and Banu's professional development journeys, both included traditional professional development elements in their routes and together with a mix of the non-traditional, this worked very well for each of them. The National Partnership for Excellence and Accountability in Teaching (NPEAT, 1998, cited in Armour and Yelling, 2004) argue that effective professional development "is continuous and ongoing with follow up and support for further learning". You can see this happening in the three teachers' journeys. None of them stopped their learning when the professional development activity ended. Their learning from formal or informal professional development was integrated into their lessons and, with the feedback they received from teachers they shared their lessons with, they continued to learn and grow. This is essentially referring to the *Integration* principle.

So now that *Integration* seems like the next logical and necessary progression in the learning journey, you need to understand the factors that support or inhibit *Integration* at your school. Eraut (2004) identifies six factors that affect learning at work and categorised these into two groups: *Learning Factors* and *Context Factors*. *Learning Factors* pertain to the level of challenge in, and the value of, the work assigned to the teacher, the level of confidence and commitment the teacher has in completing the work assignment, and the quality of feedback and amount of support the teacher receives during the teacher's management of the assignment. *Context Factors* refer to the larger picture of the organisation's structure like deployment, expectations of performance, and interactions with others at work (seen in Chapter 16 as the "structural enabler"). These factors do not work in isolation but are in a synchronous relationship that serves to enhance the support for learning at work. These six factors are listed in Table 13.3.

Table 13.3 Six factors that affect learning at the workplace

Learning Factors
These consist of

- Challenge and value of the work
- Feedback and support and
- Confidence and commitment

Context Factors
These consist of

- Allocation and structuring of work
- Encounters and relationships with people at work and
- Expectations of each person's role, performance, and progress

The six factors interplay with one another to impact your learning at your school.

Source: Eraut (2004)

How did *Learning Factors* and *Context Factors* play a part in Aarifa's, Banu's, and Chris's professional development journeys? At the start of Aarifa's career, her route seemed to largely be shaped by *allocation and structuring of work* and *encounters and relationships with people at work*. In her development as a physical education teacher, the two factors played more of an inhibitive role. At the same time, *Learning Factors* were working to encourage her to deepen her knowledge in teaching learners with varied needs. At her second school, the two factors that played an inhibitive role at her first school now served to direct her attention towards physical education. *Expectations of each person's role, performance, and progress* began to feature more prominently in guiding her development when she became a Teacher Leader, a role that came with a higher professional performance demand. In Banu's journey, the *allocation and structuring of work* also seemed to inhibit professional development in physical education initially. Like Aarifa, when Banu was given only physical education to teach, she was able to focus more on the subject. Fortunately for her, *encounters and relationships with people at work* combined with *feedback and support* from her department members helped her grow her *confidence and commitment*. Chris did not encounter the same inhibitors as Aarifa and Banu and had the good fortune to focus on physical education early in his career. For him, the *Learning Factors* motivated him to keep learning and growing. As he became good at what he did and was rewarded for this through the appointment as Teacher Leader and an award, *expectations of each person's role, performance, and progress* imposed on him an obligation to ensure that his knowledge and skills were current and that he had the depth of understanding needed to be able to effectively and meaningfully share with others. Both Chapters 15 and 16 underscore the importance of a key structural enabler in effective PD of teachers – that of school leadership, specifically, the school principal.

In your own journey, are you able to identify the *Learning Factors* and *Context Factors* that support or inhibit your growth and development as a physical education teacher? Task 13.4 asks you to identify these supporters and inhibitors at your school.

Task 13.4 Identifying school supporters and inhibitors of professional development

- What makes you feel supported or inhibited in your own professional development at your school? You may wish to use the six factors that affect learning at the workplace in Table 13.3 to help you organise your thoughts.
- Which of these factors are within your means to improve on or to seek alternatives/support for your own professional development?

Your Professional Development Journey

The three case studies are examples of different professional development journeys. However, they do not represent the only kinds of journeys a physical education teacher can take to develop their practice. In fact, no two journeys can be entirely the same since there are a myriad of factors that interplay to shape the journey and the learning. Would their stories be very different if they were in a less conducive professional development environment? We cannot say for sure, but there is one common trait among all three of the teachers that probably helped them gain access to learning: they had a growth mindset (Dweck, 2016). They all regarded professional development as important in continually ensuring that they provided quality teaching to enable quality learning by students. Furthermore, they also displayed a high level of *self-concept* in that they took the initiative to continually seek professional development to improve their practice. They capitalised on the opportunities and support made available to them to learn and grow as a professional. They did not just depend on formal professional development workshops to improve their knowledge and skills. They continued their development beyond this by engaging in professional collaborations and conversations to further hone their craft. As they engaged in these professional development opportunities, more opportunities opened up to them and the learning and improving continued.

Now that you know about Aarifa's, Banu's, and Chris's professional development journeys, and have reflected on your own journey so far, what do you think yours can look like in the future in order to become the best physical education teacher you can be? Task 13.5 asks you to make a plan for your own professional development.

 Task 13.5 My professional development journey as a physical education teacher

You may wish to use the following questions to help with your planning.

- How important are formal, informal, or in-between types of professional development for you? Is there any one type that you think is more effective for you as a learner?
- Consider your responses to the questions in Task 13.4. Which factors can you leverage or improve to help with your professional development? Are there alternatives you can consider if your school is not able to support your professional development?
- What does your professional development journey look like in this coming year? How about over the next three years?

SUMMARY AND KEY POINTS

Professional development plays an important role in your development as a teacher. Learning does not stop once a workshop is finished. It continues as you apply the new learning in your own teaching context, receive feedback about it, and refine your teaching practice. In this chapter, the following were discussed:

- Professional development can happen in a range of events from formal (planned and scheduled) to informal (ad hoc in which learning is incidental)
- Both the learner and instructor can impact the quality of learning that results from a professional development activity
- There are *Learning Factors* and *Context Factors* that can support or restrict your continued learning at your school
- There can be many ways you can have a meaningful professional development journey

How professional development can work for you is now in your hands. As you embark or continue on your own professional learning journey, expect that the ride can be smooth at times and bumpy at others. Regardless, our relentless pursuit to improve ourselves professionally can be aptly explained by (1856-1929) who said "Who dares to TEACH must never cease to LEARN", because through our hands passes a generation of young people who deserve our best selves.

Note: A list of further resources to help you take your learning forward is available on the PESTA website: https://academyofsingaporeteachers.moe.edu.sg/pesta/professional-development/book-chapters-by-the-pesta-team

References

Armour, K., Makopoulou, K. and Chambers, F. (2009) 'The learning teacher in physical education', in L.D. Housner, M.W. Metzler, P.G. Schempp and T.J. Templin (eds.) *Historic Traditions and Future Directions of Research on Teaching and Teacher Education in Physical Education*, Morgantown, WV: Fitness Information Technology, pp. 213-220.

Armour, K.M. and Yelling, M.R. (2004) 'Continuing professional development for experienced physical education teachers: Towards effective provision', *Sport, Education and Society*, 9 (1), 95-114.

Dweck, C. (2016) 'What having a "growth mindset" actually means', *Harvard Business Review*, 13, 213-226.

Eraut, M. (2004) 'Informal learning in the workplace', *Studies in Continuing Education*, 26 (2), 247-273.

Garet, S.M., Porter, C.A., Desimone, L., Birman, B.F. and Suk Yoon, K. (2001) 'What makes professional development effective? Results from a national sample of teachers', *American Educational Research Journal*, 38, 915-945.

Guskey, T.R. (2000) Quoted in K. Van Veen, R. Zwart and J. Meirink (2012) 'What makes teacher professional development effective? A literature review', in M. Kooy and K.V. Veen (eds.) *Teacher Learning that Matters: International Perspectives* (Vol. 62), New York and Abingdon: Routledge, p. 4.

Knowles, M.S. (1990) *The Adult Learner: A Neglected Species* (4th edn), Houston, TX: Gulf.

Merrill, M.D. (2002) 'First principles of instruction', *Educational Technology Research and Development*, 50 (3), 43–59.

Ministry of Education MOE (Ministry of Education) (2021) *Professional Development and Career Tracks*, Singapore: Ministry of Education, viewed 29 May 2021, www.moe.gov.sg/careers/become-teachers/pri-sec-jc-ci/professional-development.

National Institute of Education (2021) *Teacher Education*, Singapore: National Institute of Education, viewed 22 May 2021, https://nie.edu.sg/teacher-education.

National Partnership for Excellence and Accountability in Teaching (NPEAT) (1998) *Improving Professional Development: Eight Research-based Principles*, New York: Teachers College Columbia University.

Rovegno, I. and Bandhauer, D. (2017) *Elementary Physical Education*, Burlington, MA: Jones and Bartlett Learning.

Note

1 In Singapore, a Teacher Leader is a teacher who is entrusted with the responsibility to "develop the pedagogical capability of the teaching force" (MOE, 2021). A Teacher Leader can be designated as a Senior Teacher, Lead Teacher, or Master Teacher depending on their depth of expertise, their experience, and their ability to lead others in professional learning.

14 Being a Mentor

Fazlin Jaya Indra

Introduction

Structured and continual professional development (PD) is essential and rewarding as it supports teachers' growth and development. Professional learning after initial teacher education keeps teachers current with teaching practices and supports them to become more effective in enhancing students' learning and achievement of learning outcomes. While PD opportunities across countries are not consistent, Armour and Yelling (2007) highlighted two common types of PD.

- *Out-of-school* PD opportunities like courses, workshops, conferences and
- *In-school* PD platforms such as networked learning and 'in-house workshops' that are conducted by experienced colleagues

Out-of-school PD opportunities are prestigious but high in cost (Hudson, 2013). Limited finance and an undesirable loss of teaching time prevent teachers from attending them regularly, if at all. Thus, many schools offer in-house PD opportunities, including mentoring, as a cost-effective and high-yielding approach to support teachers' PD.

In recent years, teacher mentors in schools have become a valuable personnel resource. Mentors have been empowered and trusted to exhibit their teacher leadership to have an impact and influence that extends beyond their own lessons, including supporting the development of teachers they mentor. Mentoring is valuable at many different levels, for example to:

- Induct beginning teachers or newly posted teachers (Wright and Smith, 2000)
- Induct teachers who are trusted with a new portfolio, higher role, or responsibility (Tolhurst, 2010) and
- Support the professional learning of experienced teachers to advance their pedagogical content knowledge (Hudson, 2013; Ng, 2004; Sempowicz and Hudson, 2011)

However, much mentoring supports beginning teachers. Hence, many of the examples in this chapter relate to mentoring beginning teachers. Where no examples are given for more experienced teachers, if you are mentoring a more experienced teacher, you will need to adapt the examples. Whilst the chapter looks at mentoring generally it is also important to remember that mentoring needs to be tailored to meet the needs of each individual mentee.

Throughout the chapter a case study is developed which explores a mentor's experiences in developing knowledge, skills, and understanding in mentoring.

> **OBJECTIVES**
>
> At the end of this chapter, you should be able to
>
> - define mentoring and appreciate its benefits (*the what of mentoring*)
> - understand roles and responsibilities of being a mentor (*the who of mentoring*)
> - mentor other physical education teachers in a structured approach (*the why, when, and how of mentoring*).

What Do You Need to Know Before You Start Mentoring?

It is important to be clear what mentoring is and why a teacher should consider becoming a mentor. Case study 14.1a looks at how one mentor (Kenny) started thinking about mentoring more deeply.

> **Case study 14.1a   What's the difference?**
>
> The year, 2012.
>
> Kenny was conversing with his former mentor. He proudly shared how coaching a beginning teacher in 2009 and guiding a younger colleague in 2010 had contributed to his mentoring experience and enhanced his professional growth. Kenny was asked, "Kenny, how do you differentiate between mentoring and coaching?" It set Kenny thinking more deeply about the definition of being a mentor.

Definition of Mentoring

Kenny, being an inexperienced mentor, used the terms mentoring and coaching interchangeably and loosely. It made sense to him that since the work of a mentor and a coach were similar, *mentoring* and *coaching* were synonymous.

He wasn't aware of differences between mentoring and coaching. To help Kenny uncover what mentoring is, a good starting point is to define what mentoring is.

The Oxford Learner's Dictionary (n.d.) defines mentoring as "the practice of helping and advising a less experienced person over a period of time, especially as part of a formal programme". The Centre for the Use of Research and Evidence in Education (CUREE) (2014) includes a professional growth benefit in the definition; the processes of supporting and developing others. Similarly, for Parsloe (1992) mentoring supports others' (mentees') growth by developing their skills and performance. Finally, for Megginson and Clutterbuck (1995), mentoring supports mentees to develop knowledge, skills, work, or thinking. From these definitions, it can be seen that mentoring is a support-based activity aimed at helping a mentee to develop/improve in a specific way.

Kram (1985) highlights a psychosocial function to mentoring that enhances the connection between two people: the mentor and mentee. In order to build this connection, mentoring must include role modelling good attitudes, values, behaviour, and practices; creating trust, mutual respect, and genuine appreciation of the mentor-mentee dynamics; and encouraging a mentee as they work to get established in the school. Connor and Pokora (2007) build on this by suggesting that mentoring is a learning relationship, in which mentors help mentees to take charge of their own development. In practice, Feiman-Nemser (2012) highlight the establishment of a trusting pedagogical relationship to support mentees' professional growth. Thus, trust is a bedrock of a mentoring relationship; it influences how the mentor and mentee regard and behave towards each other. More recently Clutterbuck (2014) suggests that listening to mentees with empathy, sharing mutual experiences, and encouraging mentees to realise their potential also form part of mentoring.

So, what does mentoring mean to you? Task 14.1 will help you to start thinking about how you define mentoring.

Task 14.1 What does mentoring mean to you?

Reflecting on your practice:

1 How would you define mentoring?
2 What mentoring practices would you include in the definition?
3 Why are these mentoring practices important for supporting mentees?

In this chapter, mentoring is viewed as developmental and empowering; a flourishing relationship that supports mentees' learning and gives them the autonomy to own their professional growth and development. These aspects of mentoring support a mentee in becoming the person (in this case, teacher) they want to be (Parsloe, 1992) and to take charge of their own development (Connor and Pokora, 2007). Thus, mentoring is defined as "a professionalised practice of supporting others in a trusting relationship". Within this definition, three key aspects are identified:

- A 'professionalised practice': an empowering process to support teachers' growth and development
- A 'support': a holistic approach of guiding, providing advice on content, pedagogy, and school administration matters, and taking due regard of the mentees' general well-being, for example, settling into a new school environment and
- A 'trusting relationship': a relationship that is based on trust and professional respect, and from which the mentoring relationship flourishes

Returning to Kenny's thoughts from the start of the chapter, what is the difference between mentoring and coaching?

Mentoring Versus Coaching

While both mentoring and coaching are PD practices in schools to provide support to less experienced teachers (Clutterbuck and Ragins, 2002), there are subtle differences between the two. Mentoring is a broader concept than coaching. It has a developmental focus and has a different structure and goals from coaching. Mentoring focuses on the holistic development of the mentee that leads to career advancement, whereas coaching focuses on enhancing specific teaching practices. Table 14.1 summarises the differences in the role focus, type, and duration of support to mentees.

Table 14.1 Differences between mentoring and coaching in physical education

	Mentoring	Coaching
Focus	Teacher's holistic growth and development (e.g. becoming a full-pledge physical education teacher in a school).	Teacher's capability to demonstrate a particular teaching skill (e.g. how to implement a peer feedback strategy in a gymnastics lesson)
Types of Support	Psychosocial and teaching-related; holistic development of the mentee as a professional and a person.	Teaching-related (e.g. on subject content, pedagogy, assessment, or lesson management)
Duration of Support	Long term; a school-based mentoring programme occurring over a period of time.	Short to medium term; performance-based or based on an ad hoc request

Source: Adapted from Douglas (1997); Craig (1996); Gray (1988)

Having defined mentoring and differentiated it from coaching, consideration is given to Kenny's view that mentoring had enhanced his professional growth. The next section focuses on the benefits of mentoring.

Benefits of Mentoring

Mentoring has become widespread within schools (Ewing et al., 2008) to support a mentee's professional development and advancement at various points in the mentee's teaching career (Huberman, 1989). Its importance leads to a conscious effort to establish a structured mentoring programme in schools.

But why is mentoring such an important part of supporting teachers' PD? The next section elaborates the benefits of effective mentoring under three categories of outcomes – teacher, student, and school.

Benefits of Effective Mentoring for Teachers – Mentors and Mentees

Effective mentoring promotes a concept of mutual growth for both mentor and mentee. As both parties are engaged in a pedagogical discourse and reflective thinking about their own practice, it can develop and enhance both mentors' and mentees' teaching practices. Further, a mentor is more committed and enthusiastic and a mentee becomes more confident and capable (Hobson et al., 2009; Wright and Smith, 2000).

A well-conceptualised and implemented mentoring programme, with a well-qualified mentor, can support professional learning and development, for example, in co-planning meaningful learning experiences, in helping design implementable assessment strategies or addressing disruptive behaviours. Effective conversations between a mentor and mentee can build the mentee's confidence to teach and develop problem-solving skills. This leads to less teaching-related stress (Hobson et al., 2009).

Mentoring provides a safety net for a mentee. For example, a mentor can act as a go-to person for a mentee when trying a new teaching practice, then to seek further pedagogical advice and re-try teaching the lesson. Mentoring may lead to a beginning teacher acquiring a more positive attitude towards teaching as the learning environment that is afforded by mentoring is supportive and enables a teacher to flourish. This positive attitude towards teaching sowed in the early days may lead to a beginning teacher overcoming the challenging initial years of teaching. With an experienced teacher taking on a new leadership portfolio or pedagogical approach, this positive support can be the difference between thriving and career burnout.

Mentors also benefit from mentoring, for example, by becoming more reflective of their own teaching practice (Sempowicz and Hudson, 2011). During the early phase of the mentoring period, a beginning teacher is given the opportunity to observe a mentor's lesson. Mentors make visible to mentees the teaching practices they find to be effective. In most mentoring practices, mentors 'walk the talk' by modelling to mentees a range of teaching practices that promote meaningful learning. It is also common for mentors to 'talk the walk', to articulate their pedagogical knowledge; sharing with their mentee the theories underpinning the practices that address various learning needs. Due to the nature of the trusting relationship, mentors may invite constructive feedback from mentees in a reciprocal learning arrangement. The parallel process of learning, from critical self-reflection and through feedback from mentees, helps mentors to further refine their teaching and advance their own pedagogical knowledge. The increase in pedagogical knowledge, effectiveness of teaching, and lesson management practices provide mentors with a sense of renewal and rejuvenation in their own teaching (Hudson, 2013).

Finally, mentors will be able to express their personal and professional satisfaction in contributing significantly to the profession (Wright and Smith, 2000) through some of their mentoring practices. Validating mentees' teaching practices offers mentors a greater responsibility to ensure that their feedback and suggestions lead to enhanced student learning. Facilitating mentees to explore and reconsider other teaching practice options enables mentors to demonstrate leadership capabilities of problem-solving and communication skills. Witnessing growth in mentees produces a feeling of achievement and satisfaction in mentors.

Benefits of Effective Mentoring for Students

Effective mentoring contributes positively to students' learning outcomes through more effective teaching. For example, mentees, in particular beginning teachers, will receive guidance from mentors to adapt to norms, standards, and expectations of teaching, which leads to mentees' increased capabilities in pedagogy and lesson management skills (Hobson et al., 2009). The cyclic process of constructing and deconstructing of mentors' and mentees' learning allows them to continually revisit their teaching styles and make refinements to them. They may also openly inform their classes about trialling a new teaching strategy with them as it was successfully implemented in other classes. Improved lesson management skills may include better planning, resulting in both engaging lessons to address various learning needs in the class and in students' learning being enhanced.

Mentoring also helps a teacher to strengthen and improve their relationship with students (Hobson, 2012), again, leading to better student outcomes. A teacher's openness in communication may lead to an enhanced teacher-student relationship and an optimal learning environment.

Benefits of Effective Mentoring for Schools

Mentoring develops the human capital within a school and is widely acknowledged as critical to enhancing teaching and students' learning. A structured mentoring programme promotes an increased retention of teachers in the service, and helps stabilise staffing requirements in school. Teachers who are given structured mentoring are less likely to leave teaching, or in the context of Singapore, request a transfer out of the school (Chong and Tan, 2006; Hobson et al., 2009; Ng et al., 2018; Teng, 2016; Wright and Smith, 2000).

An established mentoring culture in a school generally results in a collegial social environment where teachers know each other better, have a collaborative and enjoyable working relationship, and benefit from an enhanced PD programme to support their professional learning (Aslan and Ocal, 2012). Mentees display ownership of their growth and development and an informal mentoring relationship may develop when beginning teachers approach other experienced teachers for guidance to implement a specific teaching strategy for which the experienced teacher is known.

Task 14.2 asks you to reflect on how mentoring can benefit you and your students.

 Task 14.2 What benefits have you and your students gained from being mentored?

1 Recall a PD practice in your school in which there was any of the element(s) of mentoring presented earlier in this chapter;
   a How have you personally benefitted in terms of your teaching practices?
   b How did your teaching practices change?
   c What impact did this have on how you teach and on your students' progress?
2 How would you transfer this knowledge into your own mentoring practice?

The next section focuses on how you can develop your knowledge and skills as a mentor. Start by reading Case study 14.1b.

Case study 14.1b Preparing, being, and developing as a mentor

The year, 2020.

Kenny has amassed a wealth of mentoring experience since 2009. He enjoys his mentoring role and looks forward to mentoring his colleagues. His experiences have increased his mentoring knowledge and skills and has led to greater self-confidence and efficacy. In his school, Kenny is

> trusted to develop other colleagues to be effective mentors. In one of his mentoring conversations, a mentee asked him how she could become a mentor. Kenny starts to consider what skills he has developed over the time he has been mentoring.

Developing Your Knowledge and Skills as a Mentor

This section focuses on how a teacher can develop as a mentor. It identifies four aspects that every mentor should minimally develop (pedagogical knowledge, interest to develop others, effective interpersonal skills, and mentoring knowledge and skills). It then draws out the expectations of being a mentor through identifying its roles and responsibilities.

Build Your Pedagogical Knowledge and Your Ability to Articulate It

A teacher's understanding of physical education, alongside the skills necessary to be an effective teacher, should provide a sound basis for them to be able to facilitate mentees' learning and development as a teacher. However, being effective in doing this cannot be taken for granted. Not only does a teacher need to demonstrate and model a range of teaching methods and pedagogies that promote learning, they also need to be able articulate this to mentees. For example, a mentor should be able to model the effectiveness of teaching games concepts using the Teaching Games for Understanding (TGfU) approach and articulate how the thematic approach enables students to develop tactical knowledge and skills associated with playing games.

Show a Genuine Interest to Develop Others Around You

Effective mentoring requires willingness to support other teachers. Where does this willingness come from? Its source is most likely derived from the mentor's clarity about their purpose in life and the choices they have made to fulfil that. A mentor should always ask why they have chosen teaching as a career. If the answers revolve around a desire to have a positive impact on the learning and lives of young people, then the likelihood of them becoming a successful mentor increases. This desire then becomes a compelling force to focus a mentor's efforts to grow and develop the quality of the teaching students receive from the teachers they mentor.

Because of this purpose, this desire, a mentor will be prepared to embrace colleagues who may have heard of the mentor's pedagogical expertise and seek their guidance to improve themselves. The mentor will be able to empathise with their own purpose and desire to become better teachers. The mentor will understand how much it takes for some teachers to ask others for help. A mentor's purpose, manifested in their willingness to help others, is the first step towards a successful mentoring journey.

Develop Effective Interpersonal and Communication Skills

Mentoring requires regular interaction with the mentee and others. It is thus imperative as a mentor to draw upon their interpersonal and communication skills to establish a relationship that is based on trust and respect.

One way to achieve this is through active listening. Active listening increase mentees' engagement, facilitates discussions, and can enhance a relationship (Schechter, 2014). For example, a mentor might use paraphrasing questions to show that they have listened to, and interpreted what a mentee has said. Such skills may allow the mentor to provide feedback that assists the mentee in reflecting on their practice to enrich their professional learning.

During a conversation, the mentor should afford greater agency to mentees to speak. The mentor has to allow mentees to elaborate in detail without interrupting before responding. The mentor also has to think carefully about the types of questions to ask to deepen the discussion.

Showing empathy allows a mentor to create a safe and trustworthy environment. When a mentor demonstrates the ability to understand and share a mentee's feelings, the communication is based on respect and openness. A mentor may, for example, ask clarifying questions to understand a mentee's feelings, thoughts, and emotions better. What is important is that a sense of safety is provided for the mentee to be able to share their experiences.

Develop Mentoring Knowledge and Skills

Mentors cannot set people up for success if they do not know how to do it. All mentors have learned to teach during their initial teacher education and subsequent PD. However, this cannot be assumed to have been adequate preparation for mentoring others. Attending training that introduces key mentoring knowledge and skills is fundamental to mentorship. This includes ongoing PD support to develop their professional identity as a mentor. This may include networking with other mentors within or beyond your school. Awareness of the ethical aspects of mentoring and developing an understanding of strategies to handle difficult mentoring situations is also important. Other ways of developing mentoring knowledge and skill can be through reading, conversing with experienced mentors, or being an apprentice to a mentor in practice.

Before elaborating on the roles and responsibilities of a mentor further, Task 14.3 helps you to recall what you have developed over time that may equip you to be a mentor in relation to the four areas identified earlier that a teacher needs to consider in preparing for, being, and developing as a mentor.

> **Task 14.3   How have you developed as a mentor?**
>
> - What strong pedagogical practices can you model to your mentees? How can you articulate these?
> - In terms of personal attributes, what are you known for among your colleagues? How can you develop these – and also the attributes in which you are less strong?
> - How have you improved your mentoring knowledge and skills?
> - What further knowledge and skills do you need to develop and how can you go about doing this?

Understanding the Roles and Responsibilities of a Mentor

Mentors model effective practices, provide advice, guidance, and constructive feedback to mentees on many aspects of teaching to support student learning. Mentors also look into mentees' holistic development like settling into the school system. An understanding of such roles allows you to provide necessary interventions to address your mentees' learning needs. Next are some mentoring roles which mentors can, minimally, expect to take on.

A Pedagogical Leader

In addition to strong interpersonal relationship skills, mentors are often identified for their pedagogical leadership – individuals who shape, form, and influence others about teaching and learning (Male and Palailogou, 2013). A mentor needs to demonstrate pedagogical leadership to mentees on, for example, effective lesson management to better engage students in meaningful learning experiences, planning safe task progressions, and establishing teacher 'withit-ness' (Kounin, 1977; Rink, 2014, p. 134) to have peripheral vision of all students and be aware of all situations and events taking place in a physical education lesson. Other pedagogical expertise includes implementing effective assessment and feedback practices to inform teachers' instructions or modelling an effective teaching strategy.

A Resourceful Colleague

Mentors often provide or share resources with mentees. As an experienced colleague, a mentor may undertake the role of a resource person for a beginning teacher by modelling effective teaching strategies and directing a mentee to available teaching resources and reading materials. In mentoring an experienced teacher to prepare them for the next step in their teaching career, a mentor may share additional resources such as information about the career path, or materials that broaden their mentee's views of themselves and the teaching profession, or even guiding them to mentor others effectively.

An Advisor

A role that is in tandem with being a resourceful colleague, is that of a mentor providing advice on professional matters, teaching, PD activities, or career pathways. The advice may be directive, for example, "this is what you need to do" or at times in the form of questioning to facilitate mentees to think deeper about the situation they are in and consider another perspective. The mentor becomes a trusted listener and advisor; someone who facilitates mentees in attaining stability in the school, and helping mentees progress in their teaching practices. Should an experienced teacher/mentee intend to pursue more challenging school or teaching responsibilities, a mentor may accelerate personal growth (Kram, 1985; Tolhurst, 2010).

A Nurturer, Not a Judge

Mentors facilitate a nurturing process that leads to mentees' professional and personal growth. The process may include an aspect of guidance that influences behaviour in such a way that the mentee can function effectively in class and in school. For example, expecting a certain standard in teaching quality or sharing and advising a mentee not to repeat mistakes that they might have made in at the beginning of their teaching career.

Mentors take on a developmental role, rather than an evaluative one throughout the entire mentoring process (Clutterbuck, 2004; Hobson and Malderez, 2013). As a person who possesses much wisdom (Sempowicz and Hudson, 2011), a mentor communicates and demonstrates hope and optimism (Association for Supervision and Curriculum Development (ASCD), 1999) by their willingness to nurture others to discover the same joy, sense of renewal, and rejuvenation in teaching (Wright and Smith, 2000).

Developing an understanding of these roles will enable mentors to provide interventions to support their mentees' professional learning. A developmental-focused mentoring style suits the characteristics of adult learners and addresses a mentee's learning needs better. (Adult learners are considered in Chapter 13.) Mentees need to feel emotionally and socially safe in a learning environment where they believe discussions are kept confidential, the relationship is based on trust and respect, and promotes self-efficacy and empowerment.

Task 14.4 asks you to identify different roles of a mentor.

> **Task 14.4 Identify roles of a mentor**
>
> Reflecting on your practice, think of a moment when you mentored a colleague.
>
> - What did you do or say that facilitated the mentee's learning?
> - What mentoring role(s) did you undertake and why?

So far, the chapter has explored what mentoring is and the different roles a mentor might undertake. The next section moves on to look at how mentors can address learning gaps of their mentees. Case study 14.1c revisits Kenny and his experience of identifying a learning gap to support the development of the subject knowledge.

> **Case study 14.1c Identifying learning gaps in the mentoring process**
>
> The year, 2015.
>
> Kenny was co-planning a lesson on Volleyball concepts with his mentee, Yoel. Kenny realised that Yoel planned a setting skill as a defence strategy. However, Kenny was very sure that setting is used in a volleyball game, either to send the ball over to an undefended opponent's court or to set the ball into a position that allows hitter to spike over. Both skills are used in attacking situations, an offence strategy. Before he put forward his view on it, Kenny thought deeply about Yoel's learning gap and how he was going to support Yoel to address it.

The chapter now takes a closer look at learning gaps.

Learning Gaps

Mentors need to understand how mentees learn as adults. Mentors advise, guide, and make recommendations to mentees with the sole purpose of addressing their learning needs. The interventions are meant to bridge the gap between mentees' current level of understanding or knowledge and the goal(s) of mentoring. An inexperienced mentor may tend, for example, to engage in a more 'instructive and direct stance' in mentoring others with a mindset that they are more knowledgeable than their mentees. This is evident in, for example, a lesson observation, when an inexperienced mentor intervenes in the mentee's lesson management and teaching when things do not go well (Jaspers et al., 2014).

A mentee who experiences this situation where a mentor steps in may feel powerless and, at times, useless, perceiving that someone else has had to step in to clear the mess. Alternatively, the mentee may feel glad and relieved that somebody else is doing the difficult part of the job, which in turn does not bode well for the mentee's confidence and empowerment.

On the other hand, experienced mentors take a step back to reflect and identify what could be the cause of the learning gap, before facilitating and raising the mentees' awareness to do something, stop doing something, or to even do something totally different.

In the example of Kenny, his first impulse might be to go in and tell Yoel what was wrong with his lesson. But he has now to reconsider how to have this conversation with Yoel bearing in mind the feedback he is going to give has to get Yoel to come to this assessment himself.

Adapting Aguilar's (2013) 'Mind the Gap' framework, a mentor can analyse why mentees are not doing what a mentor thinks they should be doing, by understanding the 'gap' between current performance and desired performance. The framework identifies six learning gaps that provide insights and perspectives for a mentor to ponder before exploring for solutions. This framework is shown in Table 14.2.

Table 14.2 The Mind the Gap framework

Gap	Example of What a Mentor Can Do
Skill Gap: Lacks the technical skills of teaching. For example, a mentee's lesson management skill is not sound enough to implement differentiated learning of how to throw using an underarm movement pattern.	Facilitate the learning of the skill using Pearson and Gallagher's (1983) Gradual Release of Responsibility model; 'I do it – We do it together – You Do it, I observe – You do it alone'.
Knowledge Gap: Lacks pedagogical content knowledge (i.e. gaps in content, pedagogy, and assessment). For example, a mentee does not know the inclusive physical education practice of modification by adaptation to engage students with special learning needs.	Become the resource person, by providing reading materials on 'adapted physical education', or collaborate with other teachers whom the mentee can learn from.
Capacity Gap: Lacks the mental, emotional, physical ability, or time to do something. For example, a beginning teacher who is struggling to meet a deadline could be facing overwhelming expectations and requirements of a qualified teacher, like planning and teaching engaging lessons, fulfilling administration duties like updating students' progress to parents, settling disciplinary issues, or running a sports event or programme.	Assist mentee to prioritise workload, based on its urgency and importance, and within what is pragmatically manageable for the mentee, based on their professional experience.

Gap	Example of What a Mentor Can Do
Emotional Intelligence Gap: Lacks the capability to identify own strengths and limitations, manage and express emotions, and evaluate benefits and consequence of their own actions. For example, a mentee feels fearful of failing in front of the mentor during trialling of a games-based approach to teach attacking concepts in a territorial game.	Facilitate discussion in which mentee feels safe to share feelings of anxiety. Focus on mentee's strengths more and show how it can address limitations.
Cultural Competency Gap: Lacks the ability to understand, appreciate, and interact with people from different cultures or belief systems. Demonstrates prejudice against a specific group of students who are from a different cultural background. This may affect understanding of instructions and hence, learning.	Guide mentee to look at factors that might influence the students' ability to learn. This knowledge enables a mentee to question their own personal assumptions and possible bias, and thereafter to plan a lesson to engage all students effectively.
Will Gap: Lacks the desire, passion, and motivation to learn from others. For example, a mentee who is not ready or willing to be mentored may demonstrate poor acceptance towards feedback. At times, mentees may mistakenly be assessed as displaying the 'will' gap but are actually too embarrassed to admit that they do not know how to do something.	Collaborate or facilitate a goal-setting process for mentee to identify their 'real self' against their 'ideal self'. Invite suggestions how mentor can help to bridge the gap. If necessary, as a final resort, the mentor may suggest an alternative mentor-mentee pairing to school leaders if the current partnership is not productive.

Source: Adapted from Aguilar (2013)

At the same time, mentors should also undergo a parallel process of initiating self-awareness and understanding of their own gaps so that they can address them with appropriate interventions. This will augment the mentor's ability to suggest appropriate interventions to address a mentee's learning gap. Task 14.5 is designed to help you do this.

 Task 14.5   What is your process of identifying your mentee's learning gap?

If you are currently a mentor, recall a recent mentoring conversation you had with a mentee.

- Did that mentee have a particular learning gap?
- What course of action did you take or advise the mentee to take to address this gap? Was it effective?
- How could you have done better?

> If you are currently not a mentor, recall a recent conversation you had with a colleague who was seeking professional help from you. Similarly, identify any learning gap(s) and course of actions for that colleague.
> Case Study 14.1d looks at addressing a learning gap.

Case study 14.1d   Addressing a learning gap

Kenny identified Yoel's learning gap as a lack of knowledge in volleyball offence and defence concepts. Yoel informed Kenny that he thought it was a defence skill because it seemed that the setter passes the ball to the spiker. Kenny addressed the learning gap by watching videos on volleyball together with Yoel to direct his attention to the application of the setting skill during an attack move. He also pointed Yoel to a few books on volleyball. The guidance by Kenny was part of his mentoring work.

In considering Kenny's advice to address the learning gap, it is important to consider that mentoring approaches may differ based on the experience of the person being mentored. The next section offers a guide to help you commence or develop your mentoring work.

Case study 14.1e looks at mentoring at different phases of the relationship.

Case study 14.1e   Performing mentoring work in phases

One of Kenny's mentoring tasks is to address Yoel's learning gap to develop his subject content knowledge. His other tasks include, but are not limited to, early in the mentoring process assimilating Yoel to the school environment and towards the end of the mentoring process to plan a strategic exit, to allow Yoel to experience independence and autonomy at earlier and later phases of the mentoring relationship, respectively.

In the next section, a cycle of mentoring is elaborated to allow mentors to appreciate various mentoring work that addresses mentees' personal and professional needs at different phases of the mentoring relationship.

Commencing the Mentoring Cycle

One way of operationalising your mentoring work is in a three-phase cycle of *Orientation*, *Development*, and *Separation* (see Figure 14.1), and within an agreed time between mentor and mentee. Adapted from Kram's (1985) sequence of

BEING A MENTOR 265

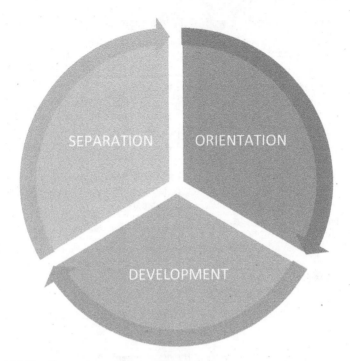

Figure 14.1 The three phases of mentoring cycle

Source: Adapted from Kram (1985); Clutterbuck (2014)

mentoring relationship phases and drawing upon Clutterbuck's (2014) developmental mentoring model, where the focus is on empowerment and personal accountability, mentoring at each phase of the cycle is progressive, intentional, and unique to your school setting and individual mentee.

Phase 1: Orientation Phase

At this phase (see Table 14.3), for a newly qualified or student teacher, the immediate work of a mentor is to assimilate and enculturate the teacher to the school environment.

At this phase, the mentee should be orientated to the professional work of a physical education teacher to enable them to operate effectively in the school context. The mentor and mentee should discuss their respective roles in, and commitment to the mentoring relationship, details of how the mentoring process will work, and its deliverables. They should also hold regular conversations about students and lessons. Table 14.3 provides examples of how this is done.

Phase 2: Development Phase

This is the crux of the mentoring process. A great deal of time and energy are spent in this phase. The purpose of this phase is to accustom the mentee to the authentic setting of teaching physical education, replete with its daily

Table 14.3 Examples of mentoring work at the orientation phase for mentoring beginning teachers

Examples of Immediate Work	Examples of Longer-Term Work
■ Briefing about school's standard operating procedures (e.g. reporting time, dress code, staff meeting schedule, and venue) ■ Physical orientation to locate physical education teaching resources (e.g. books, equipment room, venue to conduct lessons) ■ Set-up of personal workspace environment ■ Conversation on the work context, including teaching assignment and extra-curricular work ■ Understand roles and responsibilities of being a teacher in the school ■ Induct into staff community	■ Clarify the intent of the mentoring, its outcomes, and deliverables ■ Understand the school's physical education curriculum ■ Clarify expectations of a physical education teacher ■ Be cognisant of individual role and responsibility in a physical education department

Table 14.4 Examples of mentoring work at the development phase

Examples of Career Support Work	Examples of Psychosocial Support Work
■ Analyse mentee's learning needs ■ Set, revisit, and advance initial mentoring goals ■ Attend planned mentoring meetings ■ Guide/model a teaching cycle of lesson planning, enactment, and evaluation ■ Conduct two-way lesson observation to model and demonstrate learning	■ Praise mentees for job well done and provide further challenge ■ Provide assurance and encouragement when mentees are discouraged ■ Perform co-teaching sessions to motivate mentees in trialling discussed teaching strategies

complexities and unpredictability which require a physical education teacher to be nimble and flexible to adapt to a continuously changing learning environment in class.

At this phase (see Table 14.4), as well as career support towards teaching duties, which takes centre stage, psychosocial support is also needed (Kram, 1983, 1985; Chao, 1997; Ensher and Murphy, 2011). The mentee gains, for example, planning skills or the ability to develop tasks due to mentor intervention. For psychosocial support, the mentor's work includes developing a sense of competence, confidence, and effectiveness in the mentee. A beginning teacher mentee may face challenging situations that can cause anxiety. For example, a failed attempt to engage students with special educational needs who may not be able to perform the same physical tasks as the rest of the class can lead to increased stress. In this situation, a mentor may take a co-teaching approach to model an inclusive practice in the class.

Phase 3: Separation Phase

The last phase of the mentoring cycle (see Table 14.5) is when mentoring tapers to its end. The end of the mentoring cycle usually occurs through a *structural separation*, for example, at the end of the agreed mentoring duration, or prematurely, for example, when either the mentor or mentee is deployed out of school. Another separation type, a *psychological separation*, occurs when, for example, the mentoring relationship can no longer address the changing needs of the mentee.

Timely separation eases the transition of the mentoring relationship to the next stage and affords the mentees more independence. An unexpected or premature separation may cause anxiety and negative emotions as the mentee may be 'forced' by circumstance to function independently before feeling ready to do so.

Both mentor and mentee should anticipate the end of the mentoring relationship, be mentally prepared, and accept the impending separation. Most discussion now revolves around reflection on the learning, an appreciation of the mutual learning gained from each other and the preparation to move on. Feelings may be mixed as both may feel relieved at coming to the end of an intense mentoring relationship, yet facing anxiety at the impending separation of a close relationship (Kram, 1983).

While the actual mentoring responsibility ends at this stage, where appropriate, a mentor may provide a mentee with an assurance that they will be around to provide support if and when needed. A mentee may seek help from the mentor after the official mentoring process ends but such occurrences are likely to reduce as the mentee develops increasing self-confidence, a sense of autonomy, and greater independence (Chao, 1997; Kram, 1983, 1985).

Success, in the form of learning accomplishment, is celebrated by both individuals. Mentees develop and improve their teaching knowledge and skills and

Table 14.5 Examples of mentoring work at the separation phase

Examples of Timely Separation	Examples of Premature Separation
■ Facilitate mentees' reflection of learning gained ■ Encourage mentee to function effectively with a sense of confidence and autonomy ■ Assure mentee that while the mentoring relationship may end, a friendship that has developed over time can be maintained ■ If appropriate, the mentor may continue to monitor mentee's performance from a distance	■ Should both parties agree to continue the mentoring relationship in a different form, they need to revisit and refine goals of mentoring. ■ Address mentee's potential feeling of abandonment and unpreparedness to meet new challenges without a mentor; should this happen, departing mentor may need to suggest a new mentor to take over the task

develop positive attitudes towards teaching while mentors experience a sense of renewal and rejuvenation, and may express personal and professional satisfaction in contributing significantly to mentees' learning (Wright and Smith, 2000). Task 14.6 asks you to reflect on your best mentoring moment which provided you a sense of satisfaction from knowing that you have helped another teacher.

> **Task 14.6 Reflect on your best mentoring moment**
>
> Recall a moment when a former mentee made a contact with you to express their gratitude and indebtedness.
>
> - What did you do or say that made the mentee show gratitude?
> - What strong emotion was evoked by the act of gratitude? Does it make you want to mentor others again? Why is it so?
> - What was the most important thing that you learned about yourself in the mentoring process?

Case study 14.1f identifies a challenge in mentoring.

> **Case study 14.1f A challenge of mentoring**
>
> Kenny's mentoring of Yoel was enriching and satisfying, albeit with some difficult moments. There were instances when they could not meet or converse for up to four weeks due to both being busy with school events. There were times when Kenny had to put in much effort to convince Yoel of his suggestion.

In the next section, a few challenges which a mentor may face during mentoring practice are identified.

Challenges of Mentoring

The task of mentoring offers many challenges to a mentor. The challenges are real, authentic, and could tip the work-life balance if a mentor is caught off guard and is unable to manage the balance.

Unique to specific school settings, the challenges are categorised based on

- The workplace context in which the mentoring takes place (see Table 14.6)
- The conflict in personal philosophy where the mentor and mentee hold different teaching and/or mentoring beliefs (see Table 14.7)

Table 14.6 Examples of mentoring challenges for the mentor in the workplace

Untrained mentors	Mentors who have not received requisite training, especially in engaging adult learners, or training has not been in time to guide mentees' growth and development (Podsen and Denmark, 2000) will struggle, which will impact not just the mentoring process but undermine the trust mentees would have in their mentor.
Limited teaching knowledge and skills	The lack of practical physical education knowledge influences the mentor's ability to teach, and mentors' competency in mentoring (Smith and Ingersoll, 2004). For example, if a mentor lacked prior involvement in/knowledge about football, it would prevent the mentor from modelling the planning and teaching of progressive learning tasks in teaching football effectively. The outcome would be the same if the mentee lacked the knowledge and skills to teach a particular skill or concept or movement.
Time constraint	The struggle to find time in school to observe lessons, engage in lesson observation conferencing, and hold mentoring conversations (Wilkins, 2015) leads to limited collaborative learning opportunities between mentors and mentees.
Assignment of more mentees	This situation arises when the physical education department lacks capable mentors, but the school insists on same subject mentoring pairing. It is more likely that an experienced physical education teacher in the department is then assigned more than one mentee. Catering for the learning needs of two or more mentees is complex (Hudson and Hudson, 2016).
Mentors have no mentors	As mentoring is emotionally draining and energy-sapping, mentors also need help, at times. However, mentors receive no mentoring support. It is important that mentors, especially new ones, are provided with psychosocial support, mentored or coached by other experienced mentors, if any, in the school to help them be more effective in their mentoring responsibility (Holbeche, 1996).

Table 14.7 Examples of mentoring challenges due to conflicting beliefs between mentor and mentee

Teaching Beliefs	A tussle between two beliefs that are held strongly by mentor and mentee. For example, it would seem meaningless for a mentor and mentee to spend time and effort in endless debate trying to convince each other of the superiority of skills-based versus games-centred teaching approach.
Mentoring Beliefs	The chosen mentoring stance does not suit mentee's readiness to learn (Bechtel and O'Sullivan, 2006). For example, a mentor adopts a facilitative stance, but the mentee prefers the assistance to be more direct and instructive.

In the truest sense of learning organisations, mentoring allows teachers in schools to recognise the need for ongoing learning. Mentors need to anticipate and navigate around the challenges to make mentoring successful and effective in supporting teachers' professional learning.

SUMMARY AND KEY POINTS

This chapter has aimed to develop your understanding of the values and functions of mentoring to support teachers' PD to enhance students learning, and how you can equip yourself to fulfil a mentoring task successfully in school.

The chapter started by identifying what a teacher needs need to know before they embark on mentoring another. It explored what mentoring is; how it can be defined and how it is different from coaching; provided clarification on the multiple roles of a mentor, and the benefits that mentoring would bring to teachers, students, and schools.

It then focused on the preparation needed to mentor others, the four aspects of personal development needed to become a mentor, and gave insights into the roles and responsibilities of being a mentor.

Lastly the chapter focused on the Mind the Gap framework to identify mentees' learning gap(s) and an adapted three phases mentoring cycle to guide mentoring work.

Finally, it identified some challenges for mentors, or soon to-be mentors, to be aware of during their mentoring experience.

In summary, if you have undertaken the chapter tasks, and reflected on your own mentoring practices, you should have been able to

- define mentoring and appreciate its benefits (*the what of mentoring*)
- understand role and responsibilities of being a mentor (*the who of mentoring*)
- mentor others in a structured approach (*the why, when, and how of mentoring*).

Note: A list of further resources to help you take your learning forward is available on the PESTA website: https://academyofsingaporeteachers.moe.edu.sg/pesta/professional-development/book-chapters-by-the-pesta-team

References

Aguilar, E. (2013) *The Art of Coaching: Effective Strategies for School*, San Francisco: Jossey-Bass.

Armour, K.M. and Yelling, M. (2007) 'Effective professional development for physical education teachers: The role of informal, collaborative learning', *Journal of Teaching in Physical Education*, 26, 177-200.

Aslan, B. and Ocal, S.D. (2012) 'A case study on mentoring in a teacher development program', *Journal of Education and Future*, 2, 31-48.
ASCD (Association for Supervision and Curriculum Development) (1999) *The Good Mentor*, ASCD, viewed 22 August 2021, www.ascd.org/publications/educational-leadership/may99/vol56/num08/The-Good-Mentor.aspx
Bechtel, P.A. and O'Sullivan, M. (2006) 'Effective professional development – What we know now', *Journal of Teaching in Physical Education*, 25 (4), 363-378.
Chao, G.T. (1997) 'Mentoring phases and outcomes', *Journal of Vocational Behavior*, 51, 15-28.
Chong, S. and Tan, Y.K. (2006, November) 'Supporting the beginning teacher in Singapore schools: The structured mentoring programme (SMP)', Paper presented at the *APERA Conference*.
Clutterbuck, D. (2014) *Everyone Needs a Mentor* (5th edn), London: Chartered Institute of Personnel and Development.
Clutterbuck, D.C. (2004) *Everyone Needs a Mentor: Fostering Talent in Your Organisation*, London: Chartered Institute of Personnel and Development.
Clutterbuck, D. and Ragins, B.R. (2002) *Mentoring and Diversity*, Oxford: Heinemann.
Connor, M. and Pokora, J. (2007) 'Coaching and mentoring at work: Developing effective practice', *Industrial and Commercial Training*, 39 (5), 288-289.
Craig, R.L. (1996) *The ASTD Training and Development Handbook. A Guide to Human Resource Development*, New York: McGraw-Hill.
(CUREE) Centre for the Use of Research and Evidence in Education (2014) *National Framework for Mentoring and Coaching*, viewed 22 August 2021, www.curee.co.uk/files/publication/1219925968/National-framework-for-mentoring-and-coaching.pdf
Douglas, C.A. (1997) *Formal Mentoring Programs in Organizations*, Greensboro, NC: Center for Creative Leadership.
Ensher, E.A. and Murphy, S.E. (2011) 'The mentoring relationship challenges scale: The impact of mentoring stage, type and gender', *Journal of Vocational Behavior*, 79, 253-266.
Ewing, R., Freeman, M.A., Barrie, S., Bell, A., O'Connor, D., Waugh, F. and Sykes, C.S. (2008) 'Building community in academic settings: The importance of flexibility in a structured mentoring program', *Mentoring and Tutoring: Partnership in Learning*, 16 (3), 294-310, http://dx.doi.org/10.1080/13611260802231690
Feiman-Nemser, S. (2012) *Teachers as Learners*, Cambridge, MA: Harvard Education Press.
Gray, W.A. (1988) 'Developing a planned mentoring program to facilitate career development', *Career Planning and Adult Development Journal*, 4 (2), 9-16.
Hobson, A.J. (2012) 'Fostering face-to-face mentoring and coaching', in S. Fletcher and C. Mullen (eds.) *The SAGE Handbook of Mentoring and Coaching in Education*, London: SAGE, pp. 59-73.
Hobson, A.J., Ashby, P., Malderez, A. and Tomlinson, P.D. (2009) 'Mentoring beginning teachers: What we know and what we don't', *Teaching and Teacher Education*, 25, 207-216.
Hobson, A.J. and Malderez, A. (2013) 'Judgementoring and other threats to realizing the potential of school-based mentoring in teacher education', *International Journal of Mentoring and Tutoring in Education*, 2 (2), 89-108.
Holbeche, L. (1996) 'Peer mentoring: The challenges and opportunities', *Career Development International*, 1 (7), 24-27.
Huberman, M. (1989) 'The professional life cycle of teachers', *Teachers College Record*, 91 (1), 31-57.
Hudson, P. (2013) 'Mentoring as professional development: Growth for both mentor and mentee', *Professional Development in Education*, 39 (5), 771-783.
Hudson, P. and Hudson, S. (2016) 'Mentoring beginning teachers and goal setting', *Australian Journal of Teacher Education*, 41 (10), 48-62.
Jaspers, W.M., Meijer, P.C., Prins, F. and Wubbels, T. (2014) 'Mentor teachers: Their perceived possibilities and challenges as mentor and teacher', *Teaching and Teacher Education*, 44, 106-116.

Kounin, J.S. (1977) *Discipline and Group Management in Classrooms*, New York: Holt, Rinehart and Winston.

Kram, K.E. (1983) 'Phases of the mentor relationship', *Academy of Management Journal*, 26 (4), 608-625.

Kram, K.E. (1985) *Mentoring at Work: Developmental Relationships in Organizational Life*, Glenview, IL: Scott Foresman

Male, T. and Palailogou, I. (2013) 'Pedagogical leadership in the 21st Century: Evidence from the field', *Educational Management, Administration and Leadership*, 43 (2), 214-231.

Megginson, D. and Clutterbuck, D. (1995) *Mentoring in Action: A Practical Guide for Managers*, London: Kogan Page.

Ng, P.T. (2004) *Grow Me! Coaching for Schools*, Singapore: Pearson.

Ng, P.T., Lim, K.M., Low, E.L. and Hui, C. (2018) 'Provision of early field experiences for teacher candidates in Singapore and how it can contribute to teacher resilience and retention', *Teacher Development*, 22 (5), 632-650.

Oxford Learners' Dictionaries (n.d.) *Mentoring*, viewed August 22 2021, www.oxfordlearnersdictionaries.com/definition/english/mentoring?q=mentoring

Parsloe, E. (1992) *Coaching, Mentoring and Assessing*, London: Kogan Page.

Pearson, P.D. and Gallagher, M.C. (1983) 'The instruction of reading comprehension', *Contemporary Educational Psychology*, 8, 317-344.

Podsen, I.J. and Denmark, V.M. (2000) *Coaching and Mentoring First Year and Student Teachers*, Larchmont, NY: Eye on Education.

Rink, J. (2014) *Teaching Physical Education for Learning* (7th edn), New York: McGraw Hill.

Sempowicz, T. and Hudson, P. (2011) 'How can a mentor's personal attributes and pedagogical knowledge develop a preservice teacher's behaviour management?', *International Journal of Learning*, 18 (1), 303-314.

Schechter, C. (2014) 'Mentoring prospective principals: Determinants of productive mentor-mentee relationship', *International Journal of Educational Reform*, 23 (1), 52-65.

Smith, T.M. and Ingersoll, R.M. (2004) 'What are the effects of induction and mentoring on beginning teacher turnover?', *American Educational Research Journal*, 41, 68-714.

Teng, A. (2016) 'Helping teachers to manage their workload', Straights Times 23 October 2016, viewed 25 August 2021, www.straitstimes.com/singapore/education/helping-teachers-to-manage-their-workload

Tolhurst, J. (2010) *The Essential Guide to Coaching and Mentoring: Practical Skills for Teachers* (2nd edn), New York: Pearson Education.

Wilkins, E.A. (2015) 'The impact of mentors as teacher leaders in induction programs', in N. Bond (ed.) *The Power of Teacher Leaders: Their Roles, Influence and Impact*, New York: Routledge, pp. 223-235.

Wright, S.C. and Smith, D.E. (2000) 'A case for formalized mentoring', *Quest -Illinois- National Association for Physical Education in Higher Education*, 52 (2), 200-213.

15 Leading and Managing for Effective Continuing Professional Development in Physical Education

Mark Chan and Kiran Kumar Gosian

Introduction

School principals have a critical role to play in ensuring that continuing professional development (CPD) of teachers is effective and sustained. Leadership is essential for the creation of a learning community. It is noted that "a learning mode only occurs when an organisation's top leaders understand the process, see learning as something to be valued, and are prepared to personally commit themselves to it" (Beckhard and Pritchard, 1992, p. 14, in Boyd and Hord, 1994). While the articulation of the growing importance and impact of distributed leadership in school improvement and teaching and learning effectiveness has been well noted in recent decades (Hairon, 2017; Spillane, Halverson and Diamond, 2004; Stoll et al., 2006; Timperley, 2005), this chapter is focused on what and how principals, as heads of schools entrusted with the responsibility to make critical decisions on school matters, should give dedicated attention to and act on, to build effective and sustaining CPD.

This chapter takes a closer look at CPD from an organisational perspective. Although the chapter is particularly relevant for principals and, to some extent, possibly teachers who have administrative and leadership roles related to the planning and implementation of teachers' CPD, it is also useful for physical education teachers to consider CPD from a principal's viewpoint. If you are a principal or a teacher entrusted with the leadership role for CPD for physical education in the school, this chapter informs you on what effective CPD in schools looks like from a leadership perspective. With this perspective, some key roles in planning and implementation of effective CPD in your schools are explored. The focus then turns to monitoring and evaluating CPD for progress and sustainability. In addition to sharing literature and research, which informs CPD, we also corroborate the theory with what is being practised at the schools, in the form of narratives gathered from interviews conducted with four principals of local public schools, namely Ivan, Nancy, Terry, and Don (fictitious names). These four principals were not randomly chosen, but were intentionally approached. They share a similar background in that they all started their teaching careers as physical education

DOI: 10.4324/9781003171973-18

teachers before eventually being appointed as principals. The rationale for this is simple. Since this chapter is premised on leading and managing for effective CPD in physical education, we decided that it is perhaps most apt to take the perspective from these principals. We hope that in gathering useful insights on teacher CPD, they are able to provide examples of effective CPD for physical education teachers. This information can help physical education teachers to understand reasons behind some practices and decisions made. Throughout the chapter, you are encouraged to reflect on the content and apply your understanding of the learning via the tasks.

> **OBJECTIVES**
>
> At the end of this chapter you should be able to:
>
> - know what effective CPD is from a principal's perspective
> - be aware of key roles a principal plays in planning and implementing effective CPD in physical education and
> - monitor and evaluate CPD in physical education for progress and sustainability.

Defining Effective Continuing Professional Development

What defines effective CPD? This is certainly not a trick question. The definition of CPD has been comprehensively covered in Chapter 13 from the perspective of teachers. However, the same cannot be said for *effective* CPD as adding the word 'effective' before CPD brings in a considerable amount of subjectivity. From whose perspective is it effective? Do principals and teachers have a common understanding of effectiveness? It is not easy to define CPD effectiveness in general or with respect to CPD in physical education. However, due to professional learning communities (PLCs) being increasingly adopted as an integral part of CPD for teachers in schools in recent years, effective CPD of teachers has increasingly been linked with student learning outcomes. In some cases, CPD effectiveness is also linked to teacher evaluation (Bechtel and O'Sullivan, 2006; Derrington and Kirk, 2017; Jensen et al., 2016; Ministry of Education, 2011; Stoll et al., 2006).

From our interviews with the principals, similar connections between teacher's CPD and student learning can be identified, and specifically the connecting of teacher CPD effectiveness to student learning outcomes and teacher evaluation is fairly evident. When asked about what effective CPD looks like, Ivan explained that,

> *We have to be very clear that student centricity is actually central to the theme of CPD. Without the sort of clear constructive alignment, how are you developing*

yourself? So it's not just you attending, for example, a course, or a programme to get a certificate in football coaching, if related to physical education. It is, if you get a certificate in coaching, how you are going to translate that to the students' learning and improvement. So, I would say, go back to the key results areas of staff (tied to teacher evaluation and appraisal) and ask teachers how is that contribution impacting the students (learning and improvement)? So, when we talk about CPD (effectiveness), it has to be definitely connected to the students.

Don had a similar perspective:

> To me, CPD is effective when it leads to a change in (teachers') practice, which in turn leads to an improvement in outcomes aligned to school and national directions. Some of the possible success criteria may include (i) teachers adopting a common professional language, (ii) teachers being able to apply what they have learnt and (iii) teachers being able to explain why they are doing what they are doing during lessons. The school CPD system should also be aligned to teacher appraisal.

As you can see, the Ivan and Don suggest the connecting of effective staff CPD to evidence of student learning outcomes. The bottom line for schools, being organisations whose many functions include good teaching and learning, is ultimately educational success. How does CPD impact the students? It simply means that the principals' perception of effective CPD not only entails positive outcomes arising from the teacher as a learner and beneficiary of the CPD he or she has received, but also corresponding expectations that the teacher concerned is able to apply the learning to improve his or her teaching practices, which in turn lead to improved student learning outcomes. This should not be a surprise as this is identified in the literature. For example, Darling-Hammond, Hyler, and Gardner (2017) cited changes in teachers' practices and students' learning outcomes as key contributing factors to CPD effectiveness.

In addition, what Ivan and Don perceive as effective CPD in physical education also resonates with the work of Guskey (2016) in *Gauge Impact with Five Levels of Data*, in particular the more complex upper Levels 3 to 5. At these levels, Guskey argued that evaluation of the effectiveness of CPD is required to provide evidence of "organizational support and change" (Level 3) (Guskey, 2016, p. 7); teachers making a difference to their teaching practice with their "new knowledge and skills" (Level 4) (Guskey, 2016, p. 8); and finally on "students' learning outcomes" (Level 5) (Guskey, 2016, p. 9). Table 15.1 depicts the five levels suggested by Guskey (2016). More of Guskey's work is discussed in a later section of the chapter.

From the interviews and what the literature has documented, we define a principal's perspective of effective CPD as any form of CPD that teachers have undertaken that leads to changes in teacher knowledge, skills, and teaching practices, and also improvement in student learning outcomes, in alignment with school teaching and learning goals. Task 15.1 asks you to reflect on effective CPD from a principal's perspective.

Table 15.1 Professional development evaluation model involving five levels of data

Key CPD Evaluation Consideration for Each Level				
Level 1	Level 2	Level 3	Level 4	Level 5
Initial reactions that participants have of the CPD session that they have just attended.	**Amount of learning, such as knowledge and skills acquired from the CPD session.**	**Organisational backing and commitment.**	**Impact on participants' professional practice.**	**Translation to student-related outcomes.**
Evaluation at this level may include choice of learning venue, learning content and activities, trainer's effectiveness, immediate assessment of the extent of usefulness and meaningfulness of the CPD to the participants.	Evaluation at this level focuses on the extent to which a participant demonstrates a set of skills or/ and knowledge through CPD activities such as simulations or demonstrations with clear success criteria.	Evaluation at this level focuses on the extent to which organisational ethos, mission, policies, structures, processes, or/ and changes facilitate the actualisation of intended improvements or outcomes set upon successful completion of the CPD session.	Evaluation at this level focuses on the extent to which a participant has, over time, adopted new professional practices through a continuous period of conscious application of the newly acquired knowledge and skills from the CPD session.	Evaluation at this level is premised on the end in mind in terms of educating pupils, therefore it focuses on the extent to which positive changes in participants' professional practice translate to positive student-related outcomes in various domains, such as physical, cognitive, and affective.

Source: Adapted from Guskey (2016)

 Task 15.1 Effective CPD from a principal's perspective

Putting on the lens of a principal, take some time to reflect on the following questions:

1 What is effective CPD to me?
2 What are some features or characteristics of effective CPD in physical education?

The Role of the Principal

With greater clarity in what effective CPD means from the principal's perspective, we now discuss the principal's roles in ensuring that the CPD taking place in a school is effective. What are critical considerations in planning and implementing teacher CPD for it to be effective, and translate into positive and improved student learning outcomes in physical education?

Scanning the existing literature surfaced a myriad of roles for principals (Bechtel and O'Sullivan, 2006; Boyd and Hord, 1994; Bredeson, 2000; Croft et al., 2010; Deal and Peterson, 1991; Payne and Wolfson, 2000). Rather than list all these roles in this section, we have adopted a theory-practice nexus approach to highlight a few key roles a principal needs to play for effective CPD. In order to provide a richer and more authentic context to this, we start by taking into consideration what we gleaned from our interviews and then illustrate how such practices are supported by research and literature.

The Principal Sets Directions, Role Models Learning, and Takes a Personal Interest in Staff CPD

Don started by stressing that as the principal, it rests on his shoulders to:

> set directions in staff CPD in my school. This includes communicating the importance and significance of CPD for staff in relation to the school vision, values and goals. This requires the principal to communicate clearly how the school CPD direction is set.

From his account, Don set the stage by outlining a few important CPD decisions for a principal. What CPD should teachers undertake? Why is this CPD critical, relevant, and useful to teachers? How does the principal decide on the school's CPD direction? Don then explained that he established the direction of CPD for his school by taking into consideration organisational CPD needs vis-à-vis the Ministry of Education's (MOE) directions in terms of what knowledge, skills, and attitudes students need to acquire in the current educational landscape, how learning could be delivered in view of the students' profiles, the ever-changing landscape, and future workplace demands. Don also considered the school's own future directions in terms of the school vision, values, and goals and what the school hoped to become in the end. He then communicated to the teachers how the identified organisational CPD needs are relevant and significant in supporting the school to achieve the desired students' outcomes that it has set. CPD needs and programmes determined at the school level are meant for teachers to address and undertake.

Ivan highlighted the importance of role-modelling as a principal in CPD-related endeavours:

> For example, as a school, we focus on embedding a positive classroom culture with an emphasis on good social skills and developing student leadership to build a healthy school community. This hinges on two approaches:
>
> a. The use of the Restorative Practice approach that builds social capital and achieve social discipline through participatory learning and decision making; and
> b. Student Leadership Challenge model by Jim Kouzes and Barry Posner as our main training philosophy. This model works on the basis that any student can be a leader.
>
> And, I am personally involved in it as well. In fact, I am also a qualified facilitator for the latter. There is strategic deployment of experts in the school, at every level. There are also teacher experts in these particular areas. It is to my advantage that I can role model continual learning in the school.

Ivan demonstrated the importance of principals being role models of CPD aligned to school goals. In leading by example, Ivan is able to journey alongside his teachers with stronger conviction and better relate to the challenges that his teachers face. Don also described how he felt about taking a personal interest in teachers' CPD as an important role of the principal:

> I think it is important to take a personal interest in staff CPD; to have that leadership presence in CPD. In recent years, the MOE has intensified its focus on assessment literacy... about assessment for learning, and I find this concept lends itself well to support better teaching and learning. It is a concept, not a specific teaching method, you know. It is about a certain mode of thinking on how you make use of assessment to inform how you are going to plug learning gaps. So, that becomes a way I look at things (when) driving CPD at the school level. I get involved more in the CPD. There are a few things that I will do first, I want to understand first whether teaching and learning is actually happening in the class, whatever pedagogy the physical education teachers adopt. It sounds like a simple thing. But in a physical education lesson, it can be very deceiving. If you see students being happy, they are running, they are cheering and participating actively, is the teacher teaching well and the students learning well? Let's go a little bit deeper into assessment in physical education. Let's say, passing and receiving in Ultimate Frisbee, for example. This is the focus of the lesson, right? What I then look at is how the teacher delivers the lesson such that they can confidently say at the end of the lesson that the students have improved in terms of their passing and receiving. Does the teacher have any form of assessment in the lesson? For example, at the start of the lesson, through some pre activity, the teacher realises that when students are doing the passing and receiving in one minute, maybe the Frisbee dropped to the ground 50 times, and at the end of the lesson, this has reduced to 15 to 20 times, that's an improvement right? So, is the teacher conscious of having some form of assessment or measurement to inform himself or herself? My question is always: Is there teaching and learning happening? How can I come in to provide CPD support to the physical education teachers to help them address this better? And based on that, then I think we can identify and recommend relevant CPD for the teachers. Actually, the physical education teachers also want to do well. So, when they realise that, hey, having a principal who comes from

> a physical education background is actually a good thing, right? Because he (the principal) understands the challenges we (the physical education teachers) face, he understands the importance of the subject.

What Don has shared describes his keenness to be personally involved with the physical education department in identifying exactly what their CPD needs might be in the area of assessment literacy; how he would approach the physical education teachers to find out more what they are doing, and then work with them to identify possible CPD areas for the teachers to move forward and improve in this area. In her example, Nancy also cited how a principal should always take a personal interest in staff CPD and support his or her staff in their CPD journey:

> For example, in our physical education department, it started out as a push factor when the physical education teachers came up with the physical education Buzz, a protected period of time where they would come together on a regular basis to share good teaching practices. They bounced ideas off each other (and took off). Why we did that here was because back then, not everyone in the department was physical education trained. So, we needed to help those who were not fully physical education trained; to give them some just-in-time skills so that they could conduct a decent physical education lesson. But after a while, even though we had more physical education trained teachers, they still continued to come together and share. Physical education Buzz has become an online sharing platform now. As a principal, I am so thankful when people take initiative like this and we support them, and affirm them or give them airtime in the school to share. So, like this example, I always encourage my department heads or teachers, if they want to do anything, to come and talk to me. If someone has any CPD idea, come share with me. I take an interest, and at the same time, I share with you some of my thoughts, I give you my input. I am part of your plan. I then know that the ownership is shared. Ownership is shared when you get support.

Terry shared how he was personally involved in facilitating staff CPD:

> I learned some things and ways that we could change how assessment can be done in the school. So right from the start, our school has been focussing on assessment, as part of the school goals. Perhaps because of my links, I talked a lot with curriculum officers from MOE headquarters and we bounced ideas off one another as we talked a lot about moving assessment forward. So, that becomes a strategic advantage in a way, as my school happened to be looking into self-assessment. Hence, (our) CPD for that part is pretty strong (now).

The practices identified in these interview accounts are supported by literature. For example, Bredeson (2000) described how the principal is an instructional leader and learner; and the willingness of the principal to be directly involved in the design and delivery of CPD may impact teachers' CPD in a positive way. To a considerable extent, the practices of role modelling and active advocacy towards continual CPD, motivating and inspiring staff to pursue professional growth, and supporting and facilitating CPD activities are also highlighted by Payne and Wolfson (2000) as critical roles principals play in the CPD of teachers.

The Principal Creates an Environment for CPD

Besides displaying the appropriate dispositions and attitudes towards CPD, and leading and supporting by example, the principal also needs to put in place key structures and processes, including creating a culture of learning and sharing within the organisation. To this end, several key broad areas a principal needs to look into carefully when creating an environment that is conducive for staff CPD are considered next.

We start with Don's account, as he shared how the principal can identify and prioritise CPD needs in the school in a timely manner:

> *Whether in my previous school or my current school, I always structure CPD to three levels of learning needs. One is of course, the school level. We reference MOE's general direction and latest emphasis and then determine as a school CPD priorities. We identify any possible learning gaps that we need to address, looking at our school and staff profile so that we can better focus on certain key learning we want to drive (as a school-wide approach). For example, if classroom management is lacking, then you know that this must be one big piece that as a school you want to drive. So, at school level, (key) learning needs have to be determined and set. Secondly, we also respect and acknowledge the needs at departmental level. They may also have key learning needs unique to their subject. It could be (due to) a change of syllabus, or it could be some specific pedagogy that they need to develop due to the nature of the teaching and learning process. Finally, there are, of course also individual teacher learning needs. An individual teacher will also surface professional needs at a more personal level. So, we certainly have to do some planning and coordination, and make sure our structures can (prioritise and) support these learning needs.*

The importance of coordinating and prioritising CPD needs and undertakings is also echoed by both Ivan and Nancy. In Ivan's opinion:

> *Autonomy must be given to the departments to decide whether there are certain areas they want to focus on, to improve certain outcomes. As a principal, your job becomes more crucial in the sense that you need to curate those CPD opportunities out there, and curation comes in (different) forms. The first is that you want to identify whether this will benefit the teachers, to the extent that this will also benefit the students. The second, is to manage the flow of CPD opportunities. For example, curation can be based on time. Let's say you have five people in the physical education department. You do not want all of them to go away for CPD at the time, right? So you need to prioritise and schedule their CPD at different times, based on certain prioritisation principles. I think one of the key roles of a principal, in terms of CPD for everyone, is to curate the timeline for all of the teachers.*

Nancy shared that in her school, CPD can be defined as either 'internal' or 'external':

> Internal will be something the school can plan, implement and facilitate. Then there is the external; some of us will have external (courses), because we have a specific (CPD) need which the school is not able to provide. The next thing is prioritising. So while we can aggregate our CPD needs, we must also be sensitive to the pace. Teachers who work in one department may find it easier to manage their CPD, as compared to teachers who work in more than one department. So, as principals, since we have the most comprehensive information (about CPD), I think this is where we can do sense-making, we can scaffold and we can prioritise (for our teachers).

Besides putting in place key structures, processes, and support mechanisms to provide teachers with opportunities to access CPD, schools also make available to staff the time and space to participate in CPD. But there is more to be done. Nancy added:

> Along the way, we celebrate, I mean that is what we are doing for CPD too. We have a learning festival. You know, all these encourage (and motivate) people, so that we make learning enjoyable. We make CPD easy.

Further to having celebrations of learning, Don also stressed the need to build a culture of sharing the learning:

> We create internal (school) platforms to learn and share among the teachers. This helps to build a culture of open sharing and learning. We also identify external platforms for learning and sharing. Actually, I encourage my teachers to go for conferences and things like that. Not just to attend as participants, but also to present. In a way, it is a motivation thing that I'm also working on. There's a feel-good factor (about presenting), you know. And, it also contributes to the overall community culture of sharing. With a positive culture of sharing, I hope that becomes a mindset thing too, that teachers can share and learn from one another.

From this series of accounts from interviews, we are able to surface some key structures and processes principals need to plan and implement when creating an environment that is conducive for CPD. First, adopting a holistic approach to addressing teachers' learning needs is an important process to ensure that CPD needs at the school, departmental, and individual levels can be met. Articulating the school's prioritisation plans to the staff so that they are aware that the needs of everyone are being looked into. They also need to understand that not everyone can be away for CPD at the same time. Providing the appropriate resources, such as protected time, scheduling support, physical facilities, and affordances of technology are also essential ingredients to creating the desired environment for CPD. Bredeson (2000, p. 393) outlined the principal's role in "creating a learning environment" as one area where the principal may impact teacher CPD. This requires the principal to "communicate, support and manage" (Bredeson, 2000, p. 393). By communicating, the principal engages teachers in meaningful dialogue about CPD, clarifies doubts about CPD, such as its direction, implementation, and expectation. The principal also plays key roles in providing "professional, psychological and emotional support" (Bredeson, 2000, p. 395) so that staff feel safe and secure in embracing CPD, willing to take risks and attempting new innovative practices to improve student learning. Through the action of managing, the principal strategises a myriad of resources, manpower deployment, time and scheduling, facilities and equipment to create the environment for teacher CPD.

Second, principals articulated the need to build a culture of learning and sharing within the learning environment. Payne and Wolfson (2000) highlighted the emphasis on professional growth by engendering a lifelong learning culture. Similarly, they also highlighted the principal's role as a "motivator and supporter", which requires the principal to be "communicating with enthusiasm and sincere interest, encouraging staff to share, promoting risk-taking and supporting innovation like trying new initiatives in teaching" (Payne and Wolfson, 2000, p. 18).

Third, the interview highlighted that all four principals adopted the Professional Learning Community (PLC) approach as an integral part of their staff CPD efforts, in particular job-embedded CPD, sharing and learning platforms that are provided for internally (within the school). PLCs constitute a significant portion of in-service teacher professional development within Singapore schools (MOE, 2011), by facilitating job-embedded CPD among teachers in a collaborative learning setting within schools. Since the late 1990s, research and literature have been published that highlight effective planning and implementation of PLCs as well as the roles that principals play (Brown, Horn and King, 2018; Hipp and Huffman, 2010; Hord, 1997; Huffman et al., 2001; Jones, Stall and Yarbrough, 2013). Thus, the adoption of PLCs is a key component in principals' overall plans to create a positive environment for CPD.

From the practices shared during the interview sessions, it is evident again that the roles played and actions taken by the four principals to create an environment for staff CPD are supported by the literature.

The Principal Advocates for Reflective Practice

The interview accounts showed that some principals place a high premium on teacher reflection, specifically on reflective practice that supports deeper learning. Terry described the journey his school took in relation to teacher reflection:

> In the past, teachers used to submit weekly lesson plans. Now, we get them to write reflections. We encourage them to deepen their thoughts, to look into who they are, and how they can improve their craft. In our school, we use Google Classroom (digital collaboration tool) as a learning management system for students. We also use it

for teachers. (As the principal) I am given the (access) rights to read all my teachers' reflections. We space the reflections apart. We don't do it weekly, as it is too intensive. We space it out, fortnightly. We encourage teachers to be more intentional in their reflections on teaching and learning. Does it have a component where they reflect on what they may be trying to apply? Yes, and you can see the analytical type of evidence that they are indeed trying to... you can see the transfer... an attempt to transfer and apply the learning. We have been practicing teacher reflection for about five years. I am quite surprised at some of the quality of teachers' reflections which are pretty good. The teachers take pride in completing their reflections. They take pictures of students learning and they also illustrate how they can improve on their previous lessons. It is heartening.

Nancy also echoed the importance of teacher reflection for better and deeper learning:

My Cluster Superintendent (equivalent to a district leader) once shared with me that experience is not learning. Rather, reflecting on experience is learning. Same thing for staff CPD. When I attend a CPD course, only when I reflect on what I have learnt, can I then apply in context. This is very important and critical for staff. It is not just focusing on applying short term learning but also providing the space and time to reflect deep enough to look at how the learning could possibly transform what they are doing in the longer term. As you know, we want to see how teachers can change their mindset. And if teachers can reach a deep impact, it means a lot more for our CPD effectiveness.

Both Terry and Nancy presented themselves as strong advocates of reflective practice, as they put staff reflection structures into their overall CPD plans. They are able to recognise that reflective practice is a key element in ensuring a continual learning process. Such actions are supported by the works of Moon (2002), who suggested that structuring reflection into various key stages of school CPD processes allows a teacher to inquire into their own practice and enables deeper learning to occur. According to Moon (2002, p.156), key roles of "reflection in learning are reflection in initial learning; reflection in the process of representation of learning and the reflection in the upgrading of learning". We are glad to note that aspects of these have been documented in the interview accounts of Terry and Nancy. Task 15.2 looks at the roles of a principal in CPD.

 Task 15.2   Reflecting on roles of a principal in CPD

Consider the key roles a principal has to play in planning and implementing effective CPD. Putting on the lens of a principal, take some time to reflect on your school's CPD efforts and list your top five roles as a principal that you would need to work on. Provide a brief rationale for each of the undertakings identified:

No.	Top Five Roles of the Principal in the Planning and Implementation of Effective CPD	Rationale
1		
2		
3		
4		
5		

Monitoring and Evaluating Continuing Professional Development for Progress and Sustainability

This section takes a closer look at how principals monitor and evaluate the effectiveness of their school's CCPD plans. What data and information do principals use to help them evaluate CPD for progress and sustainability? How do principals carry out the evaluation in their schools? And, what does the literature say about the evaluation of the effectiveness of CPD?

When asked about evaluation of the effectiveness of CPD, Don was quick to stress that this is certainly one component that needs to be included into any CPD endeavour in schools.

> CPD process should have a Learn, Apply, Evaluate and Review cycle. There is no point learning without opportunities to apply. Evaluation and review will lead to further improvement (and for sustainability).

Ivan shared similar views with Don:

> The official approach that is communicated to staff from me is that when you come back (from CPD), you need to be able to apply. But the next challenge is how do you know that they have applied? So, what you want as a school leader is the capacity to do two things. One is that you know what you are going to look out for when you come in to monitor. This can be, for example, through lesson observations. Secondly, you can then connect what you are looking for to the CPD opportunity that you know the teacher has actually attended or is currently doing.

Terry also reminded us how evidence gleaned from his teachers' reflection has helped him to monitor the extent of application of learning of his teachers each time they have completed their CPD. From the information gathered on student learning, there is some information that can be linked to student outcomes.

Guskey (2016) recommended that evaluation of the effectiveness and impact of CPD can be carried out using five levels (also refer to Table 15.1). Of these five levels, we focus on three that are of interest to us and the principals. They are Levels 3 to 5, namely "Organisational Support and Change" (Level 3) (Guskey, 2016, p.7), "Participants' Use of New Knowledge and Skills" (Level 4) (p.7), and, "Student Learning Outcomes" (Level 5) (p.7). In addition, Guskey (2014) also suggested a backward planning approach when it comes to planning CPD. In other words, Guskey opined for the order of levels to be reversed when it comes to planning considerations considering first the monitoring and evaluation aspects of the overall plan (i.e. starting with the end in mind). Following Guskey's suggestion, we now discuss the levels in the reverse order with you.

Level 5 "Student Learning Outcomes" (Guskey, 2016, p.9) is premised on the eventual impact of CPD on students. Does the CPD of teachers benefit the students, who essentially represent the end-of-line customers? Guskey (2016) proposed several indicators as possible measures to support evaluation, such as lesson observations, student assessments (both formative and summative); student learning portfolios; student surveys to gather information on self-efficacy, and confidence towards new learning approach (p.9). Sharing a similar viewpoint that student learning outcomes are key considerations and therefore identified as key measures of CPD effectiveness is the PLC approach towards professional learning (Bechtel and O'Sullivan, 2006; Derrington and Kirk, 2017; Jensen et al., 2016; MOE, 2011; Stoll et al., 2006).

Level 4 "Participant's Use of New Knowledge and Skills" (Guskey, 2016, p.8) emphasises the importance of principals monitoring teachers' ability to apply their learning from the CPD they have completed. Besides the need to demonstrate how they have made use of the new knowledge and skills, it is critical to also question whether the improvement or changes made have caused a difference in teachers' attitudes and mindset towards embracing learning. Guskey (2016) cautioned that sufficient time needs to be set aside for teachers to allow them to adapt to the new ideas, knowledge, and skills. Guskey identified some common evaluation and monitoring measures for Level 4 including lesson observations, and teachers' reflections (oral and/or written) of their application of learning.

Level 3 "Organisational Support and Change" (Guskey, 2016, p.7) focuses on what the school, as an organisation, has put in place, to support the teachers in applying their learning and managing mindset shifts as a result of CPD. To this end, Guskey (2014) suggests checks on the alignment of school policies with the new teaching practices, if necessary, to minimise staff tension and implementation issues at the fundamental level; evaluating various forms of resources (time for reflection, space, flexible schedule, facilities, equipment, and manpower deployment) for their effectiveness to support CPD processes; and the gathering of staff feedback on CPD matters via different platforms and multiple sources, such as formal and informal interaction channels, staff surveys, and minutes of department meetings.

While the principals' interviews do not surface the specific indicators and evaluation measures proposed by Guskey (2014, 2016), there are examples in the interviews of practice spread across the three levels that are supported by literature. This suggests to some extent, the existence of a theory-practice nexus in this aspect. While we are pleased to note this observation, we also wish to reiterate that evaluation of the effectiveness of CPD remains a very complex and complicated endeavour for future inquiry into CPD and leadership in CPD practices and its enactment, including in the context of physical education. Task 15.3 focuses on a school's efforts to monitor and evaluate progress and sustainability of CPD.

Task 15.3 School's efforts to monitor and evaluate CPD

Putting on the lens of a principal, take some time to reflect on your school's existing efforts to monitor and evaluate progress and sustainability of CPD. You may use the following questions to guide your thoughts in this reflection task:

1. What are the current efforts to monitor CPD progress and sustainability in your school?
2. What evaluation data is used to monitor CPD progress and sustainability?
3. What does the data tell you about the effectiveness of CPD in your school?
4. With reference to the CPD Evaluation Model (refer to Table 15.2), what can you keep, improve on, start or stop doing as you review the overall evaluation of CPD progress and sustainability?

Table 15.2 CPD evaluation model

Keep	Improve	Start	Stop

SUMMARY AND KEY POINTS

The aim of this chapter was to develop your understanding of what some principals perceive as effective CPD in schools, and how a principal can play key roles in the planning and implementation of CPD for physical education teachers. In so doing, we looked at how the principal can monitor and evaluate teachers' CPD for progress and sustainability.

The interview accounts of four principals who were formerly physical education teachers, shows their abilities to role model, connect with, and be a resource person for external CPD opportunities. Their background also allows them to help frame and direct physical education CPD in alignment with overarching CPD directions of the MOE as they have the deeper knowledge of the subject matter.

If you have undertaken the tasks presented in this chapter, and reflected on your own or school's current practice, you should be able to:

- know what effective CPD is from a principal's perspective
- be aware of key roles a principal plays in planning and implementing effective CPD in physical education and
- monitor and evaluate CPD in physical education for progress and sustainability.

Leading and managing CPD at the school level is a complex undertaking, with numerous considerations that require important decision-making from the principal. What has been covered in this chapter is but just a tip of the iceberg. You are encouraged to read more widely if you are keen to find out more about leading and managing CPD in schools, as a principal, as a teacher who has administrative and leadership roles related to the planning and implementation of teachers' CPD or as a physical education teacher who wants to understand reasons behind some practices and decisions which affect their experiences of CPD.

Note: A list of further resources to help you take your learning forward is available on the PESTA website: https://academyofsingaporeteachers.moe.edu.sg/pesta/professional-development/book-chapters-by-the-pesta-team

References

Bechtel, P.A. and O'Sullivan, M. (2006) 'Effective professional development – What we now know', *Journal of Teaching in Physical Education*, 25, 363-378.

Beckhard, R. and Pritchard, W. (1992) *Changing the Essence*, San Francisco: Jossey-Bass, Inc.

Boyd, V. and Hord, S.M. (1994) *Principals and the New Paradigm: Schools as Learning Communities*, Paper presented at the Annual Meeting of the American Educational Research Association, New Orleans, LA, April 4-8, 1994.

Bredeson, P.V. (2000) 'The school principal's role in teacher professional development', *Journal of In-service Education*, 26 (2), 385-401.

Brown, B.D., Horn, R.S. and King, G. (2018) 'The effective implementation of professional learning communities', *Alabama Journal of Educational Leadership*, 5, 53-59.

Croft, A., Coggshall, J.G., Dolan, M. and Powers, E. (2010) *Job-Embedded Professional Development: What It Is, Who Is Responsible, and How to Get It Done Well. Issue Brief*, Washington, DC: National Comprehensive Center for Teacher Quality.

Darling-Hammond, L., Hyler, M.E. and Gardner, M. (2017) *Effective Teacher Professional Development*, Palo Alto, CA and Washington, DC: Learning Policy Institute, viewed 22 June 2021, https://learningpolicyinstitute.org/sites/default/files/product-files/Effective_Teacher_Professional_Development_REPORT.CPDf.

Deal, T.E. and Peterson, K.D. (1991) *The Principal's Role in Shaping School Culture*, Washington, DC: US Department of Education, Office of Educational Research and Improvement, Programs for the Improvement of Practice.

Derrington, M.L. and Kirk, J. (2017) 'Linking job-embedded professional development and mandated teacher evaluation: Teacher as learner', *Professional Development in Education*, 43 (4), 630-644.

Guskey, T.R. (2014) 'Planning professional learning', *Educational Leadership*, 71 (8), 10.

Guskey, T.R. (2016) 'Gauge impact with 5 levels of data', *SMEC2016 Organising Committee*, 6. *Learning Forward*, 37 (1), 32-37.

Hairon, S. (2017) 'Teacher leadership in Singapore: The next wave of effective leadership', *Research in Educational Administration and Leadership (REAL)*, 2 (2), 170-194.

Hipp, K. and Huffman, J. (2010) *Demystifying Professional Learning Communities: School Leadership at its Best*, Lanham, MD: Rowman and Littlefield Education.

Hord, S.M. (1997) *Professional Learning Communities: Communities of Continuous Inquiry and Improvement*, Washington DC: US Department of Education, viewed 22 June 2021, https://files.eric.ed.gov/fulltext/ED410659.CPDf

Huffman, J.B., Hipp, K.A., Pankake, A.M. and Moller, G.A.Y.L.E. (2001) 'Professional learning communities: Leadership, purposeful decision making, and job-embedded staff development', *Journal of School Leadership*, 11 (5), 448-463.

Jensen, B., Sonnemann, J., Roberts-Hull, K. and Hunter, A. (2016) *Beyond CPD: Teacher Professional Learning in High-Performing Systems. Teacher Quality Systems in Top Performing Countries*, Washington DC: National Center on Education and the Economy, viewed 22 June 2021, www.ncee.org/wp-content/uploads/2015/08/BeyondCPDWeb.CPDf

Jones, L., Stall, G. and Yarbrough, D. (2013) 'The importance of professional learning communities for school improvement', *Creative Education*, 40 (5), 357.

Ministry of Education MOE (Ministry of Education) (2011) 'Supporting teachers in their strive towards professional excellence', *Contact: The Teachers' Digest*, July, 11, viewed 21 June 2021, www.moe.gov.sg/-/media/files/publications/contact_jul11.CPDf

Moon, J.A. (2002) *Reflection in Learning and Professional Development: Theory and Practice*, Abingdon: Routledge.

Payne, D. and Wolfson, T. (2000) 'Teacher professional development - the principal's critical role', *Nassp Bulletin*, 84 (618), 13-21.

Spillane, J.P., Halverson, R. and Diamond, J.B. (2004) 'Towards a theory of leadership practice: A distributed perspective', *Journal of Curriculum Studies*, 36 (1), 3-34.

Stoll, L., Bolam, R., McMahon, A., Wallace, M. and Thomas, S. (2006) 'Professional learning communities: A review of the literature', *Journal of Educational Change*, 7 (4), 221-258.

Timperley, H.S. (2005) 'Distributed leadership: Developing theory from practice', *Journal of Curriculum Studies*, 37 (4), 395-420.

16 Continuing Professional Development (CPD)

Supporting the Delivery of Quality Teaching in Physical Education

Wendy Koh

Introduction

This chapter focuses on how organisations can provide effective CPD for physical education teachers. It draws on the Physical education and Sports Teachers Academy's (PESTA) experiences of improving the effectiveness of CPD for physical education teachers in Singapore. What PESTA has learned in the last ten years of providing CPD in physical education is that the effectiveness of the CPD provided is critical in sparking teachers' desire to engage in professional learning. This chapter shows how this can happen.

> **OBJECTIVES**
>
> By the end of this chapter you should be able to:
>
> - gain insights into how to influence change in perceptions on the importance of CPD for physical education teacher effectiveness
> - formulate an approach to conduct effective CPD for physical education teacher development to enhance students' learning.

What the Research Says About Effective CPD

At PESTA, the CPD programme has been built on what the research has indicated about effective CPD. Research (e.g. King, 2009; Thorburn, 2017) states that to make CPD effective and produce sustainable change in physical education teacher behaviour for the benefit of student learning, organisations must consider bringing about transformative learning in teachers. Mezirow (2009) defined transformative learning as the process by which "problematic frames of reference", for example habits of mind, perspectives, and sets of assumptions and expectations, are transformed and made "inclusive, discriminating, open, reflective and emotionally able to change" (p. 92). Habits of mind, as defined by Mezirow (2009), are the "broad, abstract, orienting, habitual ways of thinking, feeling and acting, influenced by assumptions that constitute a set of codes" of an individual (p. 92). According to Moon (1999), teachers who are enlightened through transformative learning have reached the point where they can formulate new ideas of their own through a critical overview at a metacognitive level. Thus, ensuring transformative learning in teachers takes place, is key to making sustainable changed behaviour happen for the benefit of all students.

To provide effective and impactful CPD that transforms learning and sustains changed behaviour, the Academy of Singapore Teachers (AST) of the Ministry of Education (MOE) identifies five key principles (MOE, 2015) which form the cornerstone of PESTA's CPD provision.

1. Coherence, which is the meaningful alignment to the standards and outcomes of education in a specific context, teachers' personal goals, and professional beliefs (Lumpe, Heny and Czerniak, 2000);
2. Focus on subject content knowledge (SCK) and pedagogical content knowledge (PCK) which are the critical knowledge bases for teaching (Shulman, 1987);
3. Effective CPD should have activities that allow teachers to cognitively engage in professional discourse, planning, and practice. This means that there should be learning experiences within CPD that allow teachers "to observe, listen and experiment in relation to the content" (MOE, 2015, p. 3);
4. Collaborative learning where teachers learn in teams with common goals enabling them to co-construct ideas, challenge assumptions, and extend thinking about effective teaching (Penuel et al., 2009);
5. Ensuring that sustained learning happens. This is the provision of adequate time for teachers to effect change on personal and professional levels as they engage in the content related to PCK and SCK (Bybee, 1993; Crawford, 2000).

An Overview of Singapore's CPD for Physical Education

In 2011, PESTA was established to oversee CPD for all physical education teachers in Singapore schools. PESTA personnel went on study trips to learn about how CPD organisations in other countries (notably the US, UK, and Hungary) provided CPD for their physical education teachers. Based on the observations made during these trips, PESTA designed its CPD using the first three principles of effective CPD described earlier. Workshops were aligned to the Singapore standards and outcomes for physical education, focused on SCK and PCK, and provided learning experiences that allowed teachers "to observe, listen and experiment in relation to the content" (MOE, 2015, p. 3). Workshop learning experiences were carried out using theory and practical activities.

Workshops

To design and conduct the workshops, PESTA recruited (and continues to recruit) experienced school physical education teachers and/or Heads of Departments as Academy Training Officers (AOs) or Master Teachers (MTTs) (called CPD officers in this chapter) depending on their level of expertise in PCK and SCK, their years of experience, and their effectiveness as physical education teachers in their respective schools. AOs are appointed after an interview process and submission of a lesson plan and video of a lesson that they have taught that best showcases their SCK and PCK. MTTs are appointed after a stringent selection process of interviews, portfolio submissions, lesson observations, and a final assessment by a panel of the MOE's senior management. AOs serve a term of three years before returning to school whereas MTTs are permanently based at PESTA.

To generate interest and motivation to attend workshops, it is important that the CPD officers selected are recognised in the physical education community for being passionate advocates of CPD and experts in a specific content area of the physical education syllabus. Even in corporate training provision, Grenny, Patterson, Maxfield, McMillan and Switzler (Grenny et al., 2013) identify this role modelling of desired behaviour and values as a vital source of influence that can bring about sustainable changed behaviour. At least once a year, PESTA also brings in internationally recognised academics and practitioners) to run workshops and provide consultancy to schools to bolster this objective. Online consultancy has also been adopted using digital platforms like Zoom (see Chapter 11 for more examples) to adapt to the current COVID-19 situation.

School Support

PESTA realised, through surveys, focus group discussions (FGDs), its annual end-of-year reviews, and lesson observations of workshop participants, that the traditional format of one-off workshops would be unlikely to result in significant changes in teachers' pedagogies or practices if they were not "rooted in day-to-day complexities of teaching" (Armour and Yelling, 2003, p. 2). Armour and Yelling (2003) also noted that traditional structures of CPD such as one-off and off-site workshops were not effective and the key to improving standards and raising educational outcomes was providing high quality CPD which was sustained, progressive, and coherent.

From the reviews and lesson observations, PESTA learned that, for physical education teachers to learn best, the learning needed to be related to what they could connect with, the work they did in schools and the challenges they faced as they taught their students, the "day-to-day complexities" that Armour and Yelling (2003) highlighted. PESTA needed to provide further support for workshop participants *in their schools*. Thus, CPD officers visited participants' schools on short work attachments to observe and co-teach lessons with teachers to guide and give feedback to them as they applied what they learned from workshops in lessons. This approach underscored the principles of collaborative and sustained learning. With access to a knowledgeable or expert other (in the form of the CPD officer), teachers could co-construct and apply ideas and extend the thinking process on learning they gained at the workshops. Access to a knowledgeable other and collaboration among like-minded others has also been identified as crucial to sustain desired change in behaviour (Grenny et al., 2013).

Networked Learning

PESTA also leveraged networked learning, a process by which "individuals from different schools engage in purposeful and sustained developmental activities together" (Jackson and Temperly). This broader level of collaborative and sustained learning is based on the 4th and 5th principles for effective CPD and has also been categorised as a key social motivator and enabler of sustainable changed behaviour by Grenny, Patterson, Maxfield, McMillan and Switzler. (Grenny et al, 2007). Feedback from surveys and FGDs indicated that conducting workshops with teachers from schools in the same geographical area (which in Singapore are called 'school clusters') or with the same profile and needs, would result in more "authenticity", that is, the "day-to-day complexities" (Armour and Yelling, 2003, p.9). PESTA supported teams of physical education teachers from different schools as they established networked learning communities (NLCs) where teachers from different schools came together to work and learn collaboratively "to examine and reflect on their practice… to learn from one another, with one another, and on behalf of others" (Jackson and Temperly) with the support of school leaders. This support is a crucial structural enabler identified by Grenny, Patterson, Maxfield, McMillan and Switzler (Grenny et al, 2007) as it is another key source of influence to sustain desired changed behaviour in people.

PESTA established network groups for different categories of teachers, such as the Beginning Physical Education Teachers (BPET) Network for teachers in their first to third year of service, the Teacher Leaders (TL) Network for experienced teachers who have been appointed as senior teachers or lead teachers within a school or clusters of schools, and the PESTA Champions Network comprising Heads of Department and Subject Heads of physical education. The PESTA Club was established and brought together physical education teachers who wanted to deepen their understanding and application of research tools to work together on projects they were passionate about in physical education within their specific range of expertise. Members of these different networks would have a set of concerns and needs different to those of teachers in other networks. Such networks allowed for discussions and projects to be grounded in the needs of the specific group and the five principles to be applied in relation to what each network group needed (AST, n.d.). PESTA identified teachers within

CONTINUING PROFESSIONAL DEVELOPMENT (CPD) 293

each network group with the potential to motivate and lead others. These identified teachers were offered personalised support and learning opportunities in the form of collaboration on PESTA-led projects, invitations to closed sessions with visiting overseas academics, and other opportunities to develop into pedagogical leaders (who are called Senior, Lead, or Master Teachers in the Singapore context).

Task 16.1 is designed to give some insights into how planning for effective CPD could be done.

Task 16.1 Planning for CPD

With the strategies that PESTA put in place for CPD, school support, and networked learning, take some time to consider how this could be done in your organisation/in your context.

Consider your current environment and policies for physical education and CPD. Ask yourself some critical questions and reflect on what your response would mean for current or future practice.

1	What is the current environment for physical education and CPD in your context?
2	In your view, how effective is this? What can be done to improve the effectiveness of your current CPD programmes and processes?
3	What does the individual physical education teacher need – so that they develop a desire for continual self-development and quality teaching of physical education to enhance students' learning?
4	What kind of peer support is needed to improve knowledge, skills, and attitudes (KSA) of physical education teachers?
5	What kind of structural processes and recognition schemes are needed to enable and strengthen efforts for effective CPD that will support the quality teaching of physical education to enhance students' learning?
6	What is needed to make this happen? And what is the feasibility of your ideas?

Idea Description	Feasible/Not Feasible	Reasons Why

With the ideas in your list, it is possible to begin planning for effective CPD for physical education teachers in your context. These questions could also be used for surveys and FGD to find out what your physical education teachers believe in, and need (Chapter 9 in this book provides more insight into teacher beliefs and their influence on quality teaching and learning in physical education and may help you formulate questions). The responses from these surveys and FGDs would provide some information on what physical education teachers' needs and challenges are, and the current environment for physical education and CPD in your context.

The Nuts and Bolts of Delivering the CPD

At PESTA, the five principles were utilised to design the approach to implement CPD. This approach is called the *LeARN Approach*. The LeARN Approach comprises a four-stage structured format to deliver CPD starting with workshops, which are intensive hands-on training experiences that can last a half a day, a whole day, or two days and are designed to enhance the knowledge, skills, and competencies of participants.

Figure16.1 gives you a brief definition of what the four-stage LeARN Approach is. This is then explained further.

Stage 1 of LeARN is the planning, preparation, and conduct stage (Le).

In the *planning* part of Stage 1, it is important to decide on what form a workshop will take. For example, should it be conducted using a solely digital platform, a face-to-face session where participants are physically present or using a blended version with both online and face-to-face activities for participants? Once the decision is made about how the workshop is to be conducted, these are some critical questions to consider.

- What is the topic and focus of the workshop?
- How does this align with the CPD organisation's key strategic plans? This question is key as it allows the CPD organisation to remain focused on its

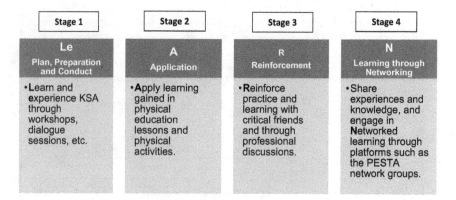

Figure 16.1 The LeARN Approach

core business of providing PD. There can be times when a CPD provider might be tempted to be involved in a curriculum overhaul or run morale boosting events, which may put a strain on resources.
- How do the topic and focus bring about coherence to educational standards and outcomes as well as address the PCK and SCK needs of the participants?

These questions help CPD officers plan how to incorporate the five principles into workshops. Currently all workshops use the blended form and in cases of unexpected situations like the COVID-19 pandemic, digital technology is utilised for online workshops through applications such as Google Classrooms, the Padlet App, and Zoom. (See Chapter 11 for a deeper discussion on digital application use in physical education teaching and learning contexts.)

In the planning stage it is also important to consider using *video enhanced observation (VEO) tools* (see Rodríguez, 2016) when CPD cannot be conducted face to face. Such tools are platforms for online collaboration, and facilitate online lesson viewing and discussion. Users can time-stamp live videos of lessons with tags relating to the activity in the classroom based on a range of categories and sub-categories that are customised to teachers' needs and contexts. For instance, a teacher can create tags to identify how much talk time versus activity time there is in a physical education lesson. Tagging/annotations can be made to the video synchronously and asynchronously. They provide opportunity for the workshop leader or participants to initiate discussion and dialogue. Participants are able to respond at times convenient to them, either before the start of the workshop or after it ends (i.e. as a pre- or post-workshop activity). The flexibility of response allows the participants to create more time for their learning.

The *preparation* part of this stage involves more than the preparation of training activities, equipment, and resources. Pre-workshop activities such as providing participants with articles to read or participating in a Zoom-enabled online discussion are conducted to give participants a brief awareness of what they will be learning. It is also important to consider the amount of time it will take to complete pre-workshop activities and hence, manage the amount of pre-workshop reading materials, preparatory tasks/assignments, bearing in mind the schedules of teachers who will be involved in preparing and teaching lessons during the week.

Pre-workshop activities can also include a short participant survey to give a better understanding of what participants know prior to their attendance and what their learning needs are, and why they want to attend the workshop. It allows for more practical activities to take place and helps customise the workshop to better suit the needs of participants.

The final part in Stage 1 is to *conduct* the workshop. There are theory and practical individual and group activities in a workshop which will allow participants to actualise the SCK and PCK being delivered, allowing for collaborative learning to occur. At the end of a theory or practical segment, time is set aside for participants to reflect on their learning through trainer-guided reflective questions. At the end of each workshop, feedback is gathered through a survey to determine participants' commitment to apply the new knowledge they have gained.

Stage 2 of LeARN is where application of learning begins (A).

Through planning tasks for physical education lessons to be conducted when back in school, participants can *apply* their learning from the workshop to the context of their students and eventually allow sustained learning to happen. This is where CPD officers ensure sustained learning by observing participants' teaching lessons when back in their schools. They provide feedback on delivery of the lesson and the impact on student learning. They can also co-teach and conduct demonstration lessons. In addition to lesson observations, CPD officers also encourage participants to show application of their learning through the following means:

- Submission of a video snippet of a lesson for analysis and discussion by/with the workshop leader
- Participant reflection of a lesson they have conducted using recently acquired workshop knowledge
- Submission of a lesson or unit of work plan by participants based on the workshop content for analysis and discussion by the workshop leader
- A presentation by participants of their learning to department colleagues OR a plan of how their department will implement the learning
- A literature review of the workshop topic and/or reflection on application of the workshop content in lessons
- Or a combination of options listed

Stage 3 of LeARN is when reinforcement of learning takes place (R).

Workshops also include an additional half-day session where participants can share the impact of their application of learning with the others in their workshop and *reinforce* their understanding of what they have learned. This professional discussion with peers in the same workshop facilitates collaborative and sustained learning. Sharing knowledge and experiences with a larger group of like-minded learners broadens inquiry and the exchange of knowledge, and in the process innovates and enhances a teacher-led culture of professional excellence. Such sessions also take place online and this has gained support of teachers as much treasured teacher time and energy are conserved.

Stage 4 of LeARN is where participation in networked learning occurs (N).

Workshop participants are also provided with opportunities to network by the creation and support of different groups of participants in the BPET Network and the TL Network. CPD officers also facilitate participant collaboration on research projects and study trips abroad to the US, UK, and Australia for collaboration with international colleagues. Networked learning opportunities are also provided through professional learning community sessions, seminars and conferences, and using social media platforms like Facebook Live for professional discussions.

Once CPD strategies, processes, and programmes have been established, conducting a review of these strategies, processes, and programmes provides a means to finding out their impact on the quality delivery of physical education and the impact on student learning in schools.

Evaluating CPD for Physical Education

In its ongoing efforts to improve its practices and processes to ensure effective CPD, PESTA constantly reviews the impact of the CPD it provides for physical education. To achieve this, PESTA has developed a framework as a blueprint for evaluating the effectiveness of its CPD efforts.

PESTA administers feedback surveys at the end of each workshop to gather data on participants' satisfaction and learning. This is done using a quantitative and qualitative format. For the quantitative part, a 4-point Likert scale with a range from Strongly Agree (4 points) to Strongly Disagree (1 point) is used. A calculation of the numbers for each statement in the survey determines the Mean Rating Index (MRI) of participants' satisfaction level and the usefulness of the learning they have gained. The qualitative portion evaluates participants' reflective statements on the key learning they have gained and how they intend to apply their learning. One point to note is that the time frame for the administration of surveys impacts the depth of reflection received. To ensure quality responses, positive or negative, sufficient time needs to be provided for learners to conceptualise their thoughts. In PESTA workshops, at least 20 minutes is set aside at the end of a workshop for this to take place. This time must be included in the overall workshop duration.

An example of questions and statements in the surveys, taken from a concurrent session with 38 participants at one of its conferences, is shown in Table 16.1. Please note that SA is Strongly Agree (4 points), A is Agree (3 points), D is Disagree (2 points), and SD is Strongly Disagree (1 point). Our target for the MRI is 3.4 or better and we have been scoring between a range of 3.3 to 4.

Table 16.1 Sample analysis of data from CPD

Statement	SA (4 pts)	A (3 pts)	D (2 pts)	SD (1 pt)	Total	MRI
Q1. I am satisfied with the concurrent session/learning journey	17 (64 pts)	21 (63 pts)	0	0	127 pts ÷ 38 = 3.34	3.3
Q2. I can apply the ideas/knowledge/skills learned from the concurrent session/learning journey.	21 (84 pts)	17 (51 pts)	0	0	135 pts ÷ 38 = 3.55	3.6

Other examples of statements that were included in these surveys are:

- Opportunities to network and learn from colleagues were supported
- The content in this workshop/seminar is related to my school/cluster improvement goals
- The trainer prepared me to implement new ideas or strategies from the workshop/seminar

Two sample questions used to gather qualitative data are:

- How did this workshop/seminar relate to your work, and in what way(s) has it caused you to review your professional learning activities?
- What new ideas have you gained and how do you plan to implement these new ideas in your work?

Apart from the quantitative and qualitative surveys conducted at the end of workshops, qualitative comments are also collected via survey forms and FGDs on the effectiveness of the school support provided by its CPD officers.

PESTA has developed a set of rubrics (Table 16.2) to analyse the qualitative feedback collected. The *Rubrics for Level of Change: Orientation of Reflection* (see Table 16.2), which PESTA developed, is based on merging the theories and practices of Moon (1999), Guskey (2000), and Valli (1997). Moon's levels of transformation learning provides simple descriptors of the depth of participants' reflections, which informs PESTA of the depth of its CPD in enabling participants to progress. Guskey's (2000) five levels of CPD provide a more comprehensive picture of the end goals of any CPD (i.e. the application of the knowledge and/or skills acquired by teachers from the CPD and how this application eventually translates into increased student learning). PESTA selected the three of the five levels of CPD as classified by Guskey (2000) which pertained to participants: participants' reactions (Level 1); participants' learning (Level 2); and participants' use of knowledge and skills (Level 3). Valli's five levels of reflection identifies the impact of learning through the manner and language of participants' reflection.

PESTA also needed to identify the key components of participants' reflection to focus on. Three key components were selected for this:

- Perspectives which encompass participants' professional attitudes that describe their values and beliefs that guide their decisions and actions taken
- Teacher knowledge which encompass new learning and SCK gained and
- Application which focuses on the intent and actual application of learning

Task 16.2 is designed to provide a way to consider how to evaluate CPD.

Task 16.2 Evaluating the impact of CPD

1	How would you determine the impact of your CPD on changing the behaviour in the practices of your teacher participants?
2	How would you assess your teacher participants to gauge if they are motivated and ready to change their practice?
3	What questions would you ask teacher participants to gather critical information to understand their learning needs, their CPD experiences, and how they have transferred key learning into practice and sustainable changed behaviour?

Improvements to CPD for Physical Education

Between 2018 and 2019, PESTA conducted an internal review of the effectiveness of its CPD processes and programmes for physical education. Feedback surveys, interviews, and observations of learning application were conducted on three selected workshops with a sample size of 156 participants across different categories such as beginning physical education teachers, Teacher Leaders, and physical education Heads of Department.

Findings from participants' reflections and interviews showed that training was well-received by participants. Changes were evident in participants' thinking and lesson delivery as a result of learning from PESTA's programmes and school support processes. Participants indicated that their application of learning gained from workshops and school support produced a higher level of student engagement and changes in student achievement of learning outcomes in their lessons. Participants also stated that their learning became embedded within lesson planning. These were corroborated by specific examples of changes in their practices. Participants identified the use of co-teaching and lesson demonstrations by CPD officers, and workshops based in schools as positive factors in the effectiveness of CPD.

Findings also reiterated their support for workshops that started after school hours. They felt that going for whole-day workshops meant that a replacement teacher had to be found to teach their classes; the absence of whom inevitably resulted in the physical education class not being conducted, hence depriving students of much needed psychomotor, socio-emotional, and cognitive experiences for the day.

Table 16.2 Rubrics for Level of Change: Orientation of Reflection

		Guskey (2000)	Level 1	Level 2		Level 4	
			Learners' Reactions	Learners' Learning		Learners' Use of New Knowledge and Skills	
Aspects		Types	Level of Change (J Moon, 1999)				
			Noticing Notice/know/recall	Making Sense Aware/conscious/attentive/mindful	Making Meaning	Working With Meaning	Transformative Learning
Key Components of Professional Learning Impact	Perspectives	Attitudes Compliance Identification Internalisation	Able to articulate clearly personal attitudes and perspectives appropriate for the content 1.1	Able to identify personal attitude and differing viewpoints from others and making effort to clarify differing viewpoints 1.2	Displays an open-minded mindset and is willing to consider a deeper understanding of other viewpoints 1.3	Embraces diversity of opinions and can relate to them – also identifies with them – also attempts to experiment with new ideas 1.4	Internalises and infuses the diverse viewpoints – Is enabled and self-directed in how change is approached and implemented 1.5
		Beliefs	Able to articulate personal beliefs and remain steadfast in the consistent display of these beliefs 2.1	Personal beliefs are strong but displays willingness to consider (be aware of) the alternative views 2.2	Conscious and has awareness of others' beliefs and engages in dialogue with others to better understand these premises 2.3	Is open to immerse personal beliefs into how others view the approach to teaching and learning 2.4	Critically questions personal and others' premises and beliefs to move forward with new direction and knowledge 2.5

Knowledge	New Learning				
		Aware of and can recall/describe the new material being taught (recognise, describes identifies, aware of)	Mimics the teaching mode approaches and the idea of lesson conduct from others	Displays ability and intent to grasp the meaning of the new material and making attempts to look into possible application and interpretation of previous situations (comparing deconstructing, structuring)	Can break down new material into its parts and is able to appreciate inter-relationships between the parts (checking, critiquing, experimentation, integrating)	Shows ability to reflect on and question the use of the information, evidently using them in new patterns and situations (designing, constructing)
		3.1	3.2	3.3	3.4	3.5
	SCK	Attention is focused on within class management processes and control (focuses on the traditional approach where mastery of content is of utmost importance)	Able to consider contextual factors influencing the operational mode of class management processes and control (involves synthesising concepts and attempting to apply some of the knowledge)	Expresses interest and adapts new knowledge/approach aligned to the expected institutional requirements into existing lessons (becomes more student-centred in approach)	Infuses required institutional required teaching approaches into the personal approach to teaching conduct (student-centred approach and moves towards a more holistic approach to teaching)	Effective implementation and conduct of personal and institutional aligned teaching strategies Looks to influence others with the new perspectives (student-centred and holistic approach with alignment to goals of PE curriculum)
		4.1	4.2	4.3	4.4	4.5

(Continued)

Table 16.2 (Continued)

	Guskey (2000)	Level 1	Level 2		Level 4	
Aspects	Types	Learners' Reactions	Learners' Learning		Learners' Use of New Knowledge and Skills	
		Level of Change (J Moon, 1999)				
Application	Intent	Able to identify the needs of the students' learning needs but may not be able to intervene or strategise ways to support them appropriately 5.1	Aware of and acknowledges the need to consider various approaches to attend to differing needs for teaching approaches 5.2	Articulates and questions the norms connecting cause and effect thinking between learner needs, context, and teaching 5.3	Conscious of own role in the development of the students Understands that there is a need to take cognizance of learners' needs 5.4	Anticipates learning needs, encapsulates new learning into approaches and strategies for teaching and support 5.5
	Actual	Classroom practice/ strategies are inconsistent with the intended plan or teaching beliefs/ philosophy 6.1	Articulates the possible application of new ideas and concepts but not able to infuse them into the action plan 6.2	Trying new ideas and concepts and infusing them into the action plan 6.3	Categorising and organising relevant content to support new perspectives and new context 6.4	Critically reflects on present situation and challenges and adapts for change and implementation in teaching new knowledge and approach May also influence others and work with them to integrate new learning experiences 6.5
Five Ways or Orientation to Teaching Practice (Valli, 1997)		Technical Reflection	Reflection-in and on-action	Deliberative Reflection	Personalistic Reflection	Critical Reflection

Findings from an impact study conducted in 2020 with a sample size of 764 physical education teachers reconfirmed that participants value CPD and recognise its efficacy in their teaching.

Findings from the 2020 study also raised two key considerations for PESTA to address:

- Firstly, teachers want greater 'authenticity'. For them, they wanted more authenticity in the workshops. They did not wish to see a 'perfect' lesson. They wanted to be able to discuss what happens when a lesson doesn't go as planned. They wished for their fellow participants to give input and share experiences of how they have met the challenges or failures that an 'authentic' workshop lesson demonstration would unveil. They wished for this discussion to continue online using Video Enhanced Observation tools or social media platforms like Facebook/Instagram so that they could participate asynchronously according to their tight schedules.
- Secondly, teachers wanted time to attend CPD, plan and apply learning and longer support time with CPD officers. To meet this need, PESTA now conducts online learning and blended learning formats more frequently and has made efforts to bring face-to-face workshops to school clusters. PESTA has begun to identify and develop knowledgeable others among the physical education teachers within school clusters who can deliver CPD for their school cluster, with PESTA providing any guiding support needed.

The use of video enhanced collaborative tools for online discussions of lessons also received positive feedback, especially during unforeseen circumstances such as the COVID-19 pandemic where safe distancing measures did not allow or restricted face-to-face interactions.

Participants raised the need for support from school leadership to attend CPD, apply learning gained, and participate in opportunities to share learning. The work of Grenny et al. (2013) highlights the need for this as a structural motivator and enabler for sustaining changed behaviour. PESTA has always tried to gain the support for CDP from school leadership at school cluster meetings by highlighting schools in which there was quality delivery of physical education under the guidance of CPD officers. PESTA has established a series of programmes and recognition schemes to inspire and motivate school leaders and the teachers' immediate supervisors to provide further support for physical education. This has proven to be effective based on the increase in school leaders requesting PESTA's support for their physical education departments and teachers. Chapter 15 in this book aims to help school leaders understand the administrative and leadership demands of implementing effective CPD in schools and some of the key roles school leaders must play in sustaining the transformation in teaching and learning as a result.

SUMMARY AND KEY POINTS

The success of providing effective CPD to the physical education lies in a CPD provider's ability to plan and implement programmes and processes that are aligned to the five principles for effective CPD:

- coherence to the standards and outcomes of education in Singapore
- focus on SCK and PCK
- provision of opportunities for active learning
- ensuring collaborative learning
- supporting sustained learning.

It is important to understand teachers' needs in relation to the first two principles. This can be done through conducting surveys and FGDs. Engaging teachers in active and collaborative learning through interactive CPD with both theory and practical activities that are authentic situations that teachers face in their schools exemplifies principles 3 and 4. Additional school support provided by CPD officers reinforces and sustains learning gained from CPD through guidance, feedback, and co-teaching, as stated in principle 5.

Establishing links with physical education teachers to determine their needs and build trust and rapport with them is another factor in sustaining desired behaviour change in teaching. This trust and rapport can be enhanced by selection of CPD officers who are known role models for their expertise, experience, and commitment to CPD. Creating opportunities for like-minded teacher participants to come together after the PD to discuss and share practices and points of view, and at the same time providing them access to knowledgeable others is also vital to sustaining changed teaching practices. Structural motivators like providing teacher participants with incentives and recognition schemes to continue learning, and structural enablers like engaging school leaders to support CPD of their teachers by providing and protecting time for teachers to engage in CPD are the cornerstones of successful CPD programmes.

For effective CPD to happen, organisations must have a willingness to critically review and improve on their programmes and processes. Quantitative and qualitative feedback surveys conducted at the end of each workshop enable this to happen. To gauge the impact of CPD on teacher practice, developing a set of rubrics such as PESTA's *Rubrics for Level of Change: Orientation of Reflection* will allow for a qualitative analysis of teachers' reflection of the learning they gained at workshops and their application of their learning.

Finally, to deliver effective CPD, it is crucial to constantly ask "What happened?", "Why did it happen?", and "How can it be made better?"

Note: A list of further resources to help you take your learning forward is available on the PESTA website: www. https://academyofsingaporeteachers.moe.edu.sg/pesta/professional-development/book-chapters-by-the-pesta-team

References

Armour, K.M. and Yelling, M. (2003) 'Physical education departments as learning organisations: The foundation for effective professional development', Paper presented at the annual meeting of the British Education Research Association, Edinburgh, September 2003.

AST (Academy of Singapore Teachers). (n.d.) 'AST professional learning communities: 3 big ideas, 4 critical questions and 5 dimensions', viewed 31 August 2021, https://academyofsingaporeteachers.moe.edu.sg/professional-excellence/professional-learning-communities/3-big-ideas-4-critical-questions-5-dimensions

Bybee, R. (1993) 'Leadership, responsibility, and reform in science education', *Science Educator*, 2 (1), 1-9.

Crawford, B. (2000) 'Embracing the essence of inquiry: New roles for science teachers', *Journal of Research in Science Teaching*, 37 (9), 916-937.

Grenny, J., Patterson, K., Maxfield, D., McMillan, R. and Switzler, A. (2007) *Influencer: The Power to Change Anything*, Uttar Pradesh, India: McGraw-Hill Education (India) Pvt Ltd.

Grenny, J., Patterson, K., Maxfield, D., McMillan, R. and Switzler, A. (2013) *Influencer: The New Science of Leading Change*, New York, NY: McGraw-Hill Education.

Guskey, T.R. (2000) *Evaluating Professional Development*, Thousand Oaks, CA: Corwin Press.

Jackson, D. and Temperly, J. (2007) 'From professional learning community to networked learning community, in L. Stoll and K.S. Louis (eds.) *Professional Learning Communities: Divergence, Depth and Dilemmas*, Maidenhead, Berks: Open University Press, pp. 45-62.

King, K.P. (2009) *Handbook of the Evolving Research of Transformative Learning*, Charlotte, NC: Information Age Publishing Inc.

Lumpe, T.A., Heny, J.J. and Czerniak, C.M. (2000) 'Assessing teachers' beliefs about their science teaching context', *Journal of Research in Science Teaching*, 37 (3), 275-292, doi:10.1002/(SICI)1098-2736(200003)37:3<275::AID-TE4>3.0.CO;2-2

Mezirow, J. (2009) 'An overview on transformative learning', in K. Illeris (ed.) *Contemporary Theories of Learning*, New York: Routledge, pp. 90-105.

MOE (Ministry of Education) (2015) *Guide to Effective Professional Development – Workshops and Learning Programmes*, Volume 1, Singapore: Ministry of Education.

Moon, J.A. (1999) *Reflection in Learning and Professional Development Theory and Practice*, London: Kagan Page Limited.

Penuel, W., Riel, M., Krause, A. and Frank, K. (2009) 'Analysingt Teachers' professional interactions in a school as social capital: A social network approach', *Teachers College Record*, 111 (1), 124-163.

Rodríguez, J.B. (2016) 'An interview with Paul Seedhouse on video enhanced observation (VEO): A new tool for teacher training, professional development and classroom research', *Bellaterra Journal of Teaching & Learning Language & Literature*, 9 (3), 90-97.

Shulman, L. (1987) 'Knowledge and teaching: Foundations of new reform', *Harvard Educational Review*, 51 (1), 1-22.

Thorburn, M. (2017) *Transformative Learning and Teaching in Physical Education*, Abingdon and New York: Routledge.

Valli, L. (1997) 'Listening to other voices: A description of teacher reflection in the United States', *Peabody Journal of Education*, 72 (1), 67-88, https//doi.org/10.1207/s15327930pje7201_4

17 And Finally... Would You Like to Be Taught by You?

Hanif Abdul Rahman

Would you like to be taught by you?
If you put yourself in the shoes of your students, would you learn in, and enjoy, your physical education lessons? Would you be meaningfully engaged in the lesson? The meaningfulness and the level of engagement of a lesson is often a result of the pedagogy employed and enacted. Looking at the word pedagogy, where '*peda*' means child and '*gogy*' means the art and science of teaching, pedagogy thus refers to the effectiveness of the teacher to put together effective and appropriate teaching approaches and strategies, based on sound theories and concepts, to best connect and engage each student, to learn and develop holistically. While you would have been inspired by the teaching approaches and strategies presented in the book, and motivated by the structures and processes of continuing professional development, let us not forget the student. We exist as teachers because our students exist. Inevitably, we must be student-centric by putting our students at the centre of learning.

The book started by reminding you that biological differences in psychomotor, cognitive, emotional, and social development play a part in learning. The physical and socio-emotional environment also play an important role in providing a context for interaction, as does a student's prior experience, both of which impact learning. Once you recognise these elements, you are then able to identify the knowledge, skills, and understanding that you should have as a teacher, to better create that meaningfully engaging learning experience. Pedagogical models and teaching approaches and styles are in abundance, each with their key characteristics and considerations. What is then imperative for you as a teacher, based on your intent in terms of the learning outcomes, is to decide on the most appropriate pedagogy for the content, and for your students in their specific context. It is critical that the pedagogy employed empowers students to take ownership of their learning and actualise their greatest potential. You empower them with the disposition to be able to manage themselves in their complex physical and socio-emotional environment, for them to be able to navigate and thrive in the future.

DOI: 10.4324/9781003171973-20

The question next is, have you been the best teacher that you can be in engaging your students, for them to actualise this premise? There are many junctures in the book where you would have been prompted to reflect on your beliefs, practices, personal development, life journey, and the enabling factors in your own educational system. The tasks presented serve as pit stops for you to re-calibrate and re-evaluate your identity as a physical education teacher. Viewing teaching, and your role as a teacher from the perspective of the student as the learner, helps you see what they need. This will then make you more conscious of how best to engage your students. The science of teaching provides all the theories and concepts, and the art of teaching is about the enactment of these theories and concepts into practice in the physical education lesson. But what makes teachers effective is when they have the craft of teaching where they are armed with strong knowledge in content, pedagogy, and assessment. These teachers are then able to select the most fitting teaching strategies from among their repertoire of tools to best connect to their students – this, in essence, is the teachers' exhibition of strong pedagogical content knowledge.

What the book had provided you are many tenets of quality physical education, quality teaching of physical education, and quality professional development for physical education teachers. Some are seminal knowledge and institutional understandings that have stood the test of time serving as reminders to us, while others are slightly more contemporary. Regardless, they have been inquired and practised in Singapore schools with reasonable success. There are also many accounts of teachers narrating their journeys and reflections of their shortcomings and growth by overcoming their challenges.

Context, however, is key. The authors recognised that what works in their own schools in Singapore might yield different outcomes when implemented in other systems, schools, or contexts. You would have, too. The critical thing is that you understand the principles and considerations behind these enactments or implementations. The key theories and concepts remain the same, but your considerations should be on who your students are and what their learning needs are. Can you apply the same approach, or should you adapt and modify to better suit your context? For example, certain teaching approaches will only work when the accompanying routines have already been pre-established. Do you have appropriate routines for the teaching approach to work? If not, can you possibly develop that first? Or, should you consider another teaching approach to better suit the learning outcomes that you have envisioned for your class? Are you also able to manage the various sophisticated components of a complex teaching approach? Your considerations should also include the type of school and educational ecosystem you are in. For example, do you have the same enablers as identified in the chapters, or do you have other prohibitors in your system? Or, are your seemingly perceived prohibitors, in fact, opportunities for you to identify and leverage your own unique enablers? The book shares the answers to these questions as lessons from the Singapore experience. Lessons that you can draw upon and make a part of your own professional learning.

So, now what? What can you do now, and where do you go from here? As a physical education teacher, you have the power to set your own destiny. You are who you are. To be a better teacher who can better design learning experiences, and better teach and engage your students, for them to learn better, we urge you to be ever reflective of your practices. There is a need to look inwards to know and understand yourself. Keep questioning your assumptions and mental models. Keep questioning why certain things happened, and inquire into what really made them happen. At times, take a step back, take a few more maybe, and see the issue from a broader and even different perspective. See from the students' perspective. Draw personal meanings from what you sense from the situation. Build your own narratives surrounding the things that make you the teacher teaching the way you are, and ever striving to be a better self.

The book begins by stating that continuing professional development (CPD) is central to teaching and learning. Professional development doesn't just happen to you. You have to take the initiative and seize any opportunity: formal and informal, structured and unstructured, off-site as well as on-site, top-down directives, as well as bottom-up initiatives. These are all part of the compendium of continuing to engage in professional development throughout your teaching career. Again, context is key, where some professional development approaches work better in some situation for some adult learners, depending on the needs. With that, to finally close the book, we now leave you with this thought, with the hope to inspire you to go forth on your own professional development journey and be the best physical education teacher that you can be.

You cannot stop now and change how and where you started, but you can definitely start from where you are and decide on how and where you would like to go in the future.

BIOGRAPHIES

Hanif Abdul Rahman is the Principal Master Teacher at Singapore Ministry of Education Physical Education and Sports Teacher Academy, where he conceptualises and facilitates continual professional development of physical education teachers. Always striving to seek new frontiers, his current interest is inquiring into neurocognitive perspectives in physical education. On the sporting field, Hanif was a national representative in rugby, an international referee, an accredited coach, and also an inductee to the Singapore Olympic Academy Roll of Honour for his contribution to the Singapore physical education and sports fraternity.

Susan Capel is Emeritus Professor of Physical Education at Brunel University, London. A former physical education teacher, she has been involved in both initial teacher education and continuing professional development of physical education teachers for over 35 years. She is editor/co-editor of many books, including *Learning to Teach in the Secondary School: A Companion to School Experience*, *Learning to Teach Physical Education in the Secondary School: A Companion to School Experience*, a *Practical Guide to Teaching Physical Education*, *Debates in Physical Education*, and *Surviving and Thriving in the Secondary School: The NQT's Essential Companion*.

BIOGRAPHIES

Mark Chan is currently based in the Physical Education and Sports Teacher Academy as Deputy Director for Special Projects. His main scope of work focuses on providing physical education teachers with professional development opportunities for improved lesson delivery in schools through quality workshops, schools support, and networks support.

Goh Ming Ming Kelvin is currently teaching students aged 13 to 17 at Beatty Secondary School. He has been exploring the effective use of digital technology in physical education as he strongly believes in its affordances in enhancing our students' learning experiences. He enjoys collaborating with teachers to explore new and innovative pedagogies as he believes that "one alone cannot change the world, but one can cast a stone across the waters to create many ripples".

Kiran Kumar Gosian is a recently retired principal. He has helmed two primary schools and was involved in the development of sports through his roles as the zonal chairman of the Singapore Primary Schools Sports Council. Prior to that, he was also involved in reframing the physical education curriculum and introducing the Games Concept Approach in the Singapore national curriculum in his capacity as senior curriculum officer. On the sporting front, Kiran is an avid sportsperson and is still involved in competitive sports. He continues his involvement in education and coaching as a consultant, lecturer, and mentor at Sport Singapore and institutions of higher learning.

Fazlin Jaya Indra is passionate about professional and personal growth. Currently, he specialises in teaching physical education at the primary level. Armed with a growth philosophy of "iron sharpens iron", he has keen interests in enhancing teachers' professional learning and growth, especially through mentoring.

Fathul Rahman Kamsani is the Deputy Director at the Physical Education and Sports Teacher Academy, Ministry of Education, Singapore. He oversees the delivery of professional development opportunities for physical education and sports teachers for improved physical and sports education delivery in schools through quality workshops, schools and networks support. In his free time, Fathul loves to spend time outdoors exploring nature, and playing football and rugby. He has been in the Singapore education service since 1997.

Wendy Koh has been a mainstream school physical education teacher for 35 years before her secondment to Woodlands Gardens School in 2019 to develop the physical education curriculum for the Movement for the Intellectually Disabled of Singapore schools. Her work on the Mediated Learning Experience approach has spread from mainstream to special education schools.

Hui Min Kwok is Senior Academy Officer at the Physical Education and Sports Teacher Academy by day, habitual introvert by dusk – running, reading, writing poetry, or sketching. Originally an English Language teacher to children aged 9 to 12 years old, her interest in early childhood has led her to delve into its secrets and mysteries. Hui Min enjoys creating interdisciplinary opportunities for children to learn and grow in. She believes that "All endings are also beginnings, so love what you do and you'll do what you love".

Dr Julia Lawrence is Senior Lecturer in Education at Northumbria University. Julia has written on a number of subjects including physical education, mentoring, reflective practice, and becoming a teacher educator. She has worked closely with the Academy of Singapore Teachers since 2015.

Karen Low Lai Fong is a school-based Master Teacher for physical education at Punggol View Primary School. Her current areas of interest include early childhood and movement education. She teaches children 5 to 12 years old, and enjoys the opportunities to work with both children and teachers to build the young learners' foundations and interests in physical activities and sports.

Melanie Martens is currently the Academy Principal at the Physical Education and Sports Teacher Academy at the Academy of Singapore Teachers, Ministry of Education. She leads a team of 25 Professional Development Officers in forging a culture of professional excellence among the fraternity of physical education and sports teachers in Singapore. She has been in the Singapore education service since 1984. She used to play elite level field hockey but now enjoys the outdoors on her bicycle or whatever her battered knees allow her to do.

Nasrun Bin Mizzy is Head of Department for Physical Education and Co-Curricular Activities at Teck Whye Primary School, Singapore. He believes in the power of narratives to elicit teachers' knowledge and experience and to impact student learning and professional growth. His mentors include Mr Hanif Abdul Rahman (Principal Master Teacher, PESTA) and Dr Fang Yanping (Associate Professor, NIE, NTU). Lifelong #Liverpool supporter. Trying-his-best-father-of-5. Husband of 1. #YNWA.

Joanna Phan Swee Lee is Master Teacher for physical education, specialising in inclusive physical education, the teaching of softball and the teaching of dance in physical education. She has a keen interest in adult learning and recently graduated from a Master of Arts in Professional Education course, equipping her with tools to deepen her knowledge and skills in providing and facilitating professional development. "Learning never stops!"

Benjamin S.J. Tan is currently Master Teacher for Physical Education at the Physical Education and Sports Teacher Academy. He has taught at the primary, secondary, and tertiary levels. His areas of professional interest are physical education assessment and Mosston's Spectrum of Teaching Styles. As a keen sports and outdoorsman, Benjamin enjoys basketball, volleyball, hiking, and nature photography.

Tan Seck Heong was a physical education teacher and Head of Department for more than 18 years before becoming a Master Teacher at the Physical Education and Sports Teacher Academy. He is a certified Instructional Mentor and has been working with physical educators to apply learner-centred pedagogies to nurture lifelong learners.

Dr Tan Wee Keat Clara taught at the National Institute of Education, Singapore for 14 years, specialising in physical education and sports pedagogy. She joined the Physical Education and Sports Teacher Academy as a Master Teacher in 2015. Her teaching and research interests include physical education and sport pedagogy, Teaching Games for Understanding, children's perceptions of physical education and nonlinear pedagogy.

Teng Tse Sheng is Master Teacher at the Physical Education and Sports Teacher Academy. Other than teaching beliefs, his other research interests include Game-Based Approaches, the Inventing Games Model, and Students' Voice. It is his belief that as educators, we need to see learning through our students' lenses in order to create a more meaningful and fun learning experience.

Justin Wakefield is a senior leader based at a secondary school in England. Having trained as a teacher of physical education, he has held multiple teaching and learning responsibilities through both middle and senior leadership roles. Through his director of teaching school role, he has successfully led regional professional development provision across a number of schools within the East of England. He is still actively teaching, has contributed to national research projects and written texts within teacher education.

Mabel Yong is Master Teacher at the Physical Education and Sports Teacher Academy. She has been teaching physical education for more than 25 years. She believes that every child is an individual and should have access to knowledge, skills, and concepts. She has as a keen interest inquiring into the various ways to know if student learning has taken place.

Jason Zhuo Gensheng is currently teaching 13- to 17-year-olds at a secondary school and oversees the physical education curriculum in the school. He is deeply passionate in innovative practices in physical education, through the use of technology or implementation of exciting pedagogies. He believes every teacher can teach, and wants to teach effectively.

AUTHOR INDEX

Abdul Rahman, H. 130, 134-135, 140-141, 146
Adkins, S. 131, 145
Aguilar, E. 262-263, 270
AIESEP (Association Internationale des Écoles Supérieures d'Éducation Physique/International Association for Physical Education in Higher Education) 198, 208
Ainscow, M. 86, 106-107
Almond, L. 48, 60
Ames, C. 75, 84
Anderson, M.C. 80, 85
Ang, L. 94, 106-107
Araujo, D. 52, 56, 61, 63
Argyris, C. 212-213, 230
Armour, K.M. 130-146; Makopoulou, K. and Chambers, F. 235, 248; and Yelling, M. 244-245, 248, 250, 270, 291-293, 305
ASCD (Association for Supervision and Curriculum Development) 260, 271
Ashworth, S. 170-174, 188
Aslan, B. 256, 271
AST (Academy of Singapore Teachers) 290, 292, 305
Atencio, M. 52, 54, 59, 61
Atkinson, R. 73, 84

Baek, J.H. 205, 208
Bailey, R. 130, 145, 169, 188; Armour, K., Kirk, D., Jess, M., Pickup, I.,
Sanford, R. and BERA Physical Education and Sport Pedagogy Special Interest Group 39, 43
Barkhuizen, G. 216-218, 230
Barrie, S. 254, 271
Bates, B. 68, 84
Beaumont, L.C. 169, 188
Bechtel, P.A. 269, 271, 274, 277, 285, 287
Beckhard, R. 273, 287
Bell, A. 254, 271
Bennett, T. 72, 84
Bernstein, N.A. 54, 61
Beschorner, B. 192, 208
Birman, B.F. 244, 248
Black, K. 99, 107; and Stevenson, P. 94, 98-101, 107
Black, P. 200, 208
Blair, R. 169, 188
Block, M.E. 89, 106-107, 108
Bloom, B. 126-127, 129
Bodsworth, H. 190, 206, 208
Bokhove, C. 65, 80, 85
Bolam, R. 273-274, 285, 288
Booth, T. 86, 106-107
Bootsma, R.J. 59, 61
Boyd, V. 273, 277, 287
Brady, K. 106, 109
Bredeson, P.V. 277, 279, 281-282, 287
Bremen, K. 144-145
Bronfenbrenner, U. 5-6, 90-91, 93, 96, 100, 107
Brown, B.D. 282, 287

AUTHOR INDEX

Brown, L. 89, 109
Bruce, P. 144-145
Bruer, J.T. 215, 230
Bruner, J. 34, 43, 215, 230
Buehl, M. 150-151, 166-167
Bulger, S. 205, 208
Bunker, D. 35, 43, 45, 49, 61, 63
Bunker, L.K. 89, 107
Butler, J. 151, 157-158, 165, 167; Griffin, L., Lombardo, B. and Nastasi, R. 49, 61; and Robson, C. 48-49, 61
Button, C. 52, 61
Bybee, R. 290, 305
Byra, M. 179, 185, 188

Calderhead, J. 151, 167
Cardon, G. 40, 44
Carrett, R. 86, 109
Carvalho, J. 52, 61
Casel (Collaborative for Academic Social and Emotional Learning) 131-132, 134-135, 145
Cavigioli, O. 74, 84
Cepeda, N.J. 82, 84
Casey, A. 190, 197, 208
Chao, G.T. 266-267, 271
Chen, A. 11, 25, 41, 43
Chong, S. 256, 271
Chong, W. 88, 90, 94, 109
Chow, J.Y. 49, 52-56, 59-61, 63; and Atencio, M. 54-55, 61; Davids, K., Button, C. and Rein, R. 59, 61; Davids, K., Button, C. and Renshaw, I. 45-46, 51, 53, 59, 61; Davids, K.W., Button, C., Renshaw, I., Shuttleworth, R. and Uehara, L.A. 51-56, 59-61; Davids, K., Button, C., Shuttleworth, R., Renshaw, I. and Araújo, D. 45, 53, 61; Davids, K., Hristovski, R., Araújo, D. and Passos, P. 51, 54, 61; Davids, K.W., Shuttleworth, R., Button, C., Renshaw, I. and Araújo, D. 51, 53, 61; Komar, J., Davids, K., and Tan, C.W.K. 59, 61; Renshaw, I., Button, C., Davids, K. and Tan, C.W.K. 51-55, 61

Church, M. 122, 129
Clandinin, D.J. 210, 215, 230
Clutterbuck, D.C. 252, 260, 265, 271, 272; and Ragins, B.R. 253, 271
Coates, J. 90, 108
Cochran-Smith, M. 229-230
Coggshall, J.G. 277, 287
Coles, R. 215, 230
Collier, D. 89, 109
Collins, J. 155, 167
Connelly, F.M. 210, 215, 230
Connor, M. 252-253, 271
Correia, V. 52, 61
Cotton, J.D. 169, 188, 248
Craig, R.L. 253, 271
Crawford, B. 290, 305
Croft, A. 277, 287
CUREE (Centre for the Use of Research and Evidence in Education) 252, 271
Czerniak, C.M. 290, 305

Darling-Hammond, L. 275, 287
Davids, K. 49, 52-56, 60-61, 63; Bennett, S. and Newell, K.M. 54, 61; Button, C. and Bennett, S.J. 53-55, 62; Chow, J.Y. and Shuttleworth, R. 45, 61
Day, C. 224, 230
De Boer, A.A. 95, 108
De Bruijn, A.G.M. 40, 43
De Bruyckere, P. 197, 208
Deal, T.E. 277, 288
Deci, E.L. 39-40, 43, 201, 207-208
den Duyn, N. 35, 43
Denmark, V.M. 269, 272
Derrington, M.L. 274, 285, 288
DES (Department of Education and Science) 9, 25
Desimone, L. 244, 248
Dewey, J. 6, 215, 230
Diamond, J.B. 273, 288
Dodds, P. 153, 167
Dolan, M. 277, 287
Donohoo, J. 205, 208
Doolittle S. 153, 167

Douglas, C.A. 253, 271
Driscoll, M.P. 34, 43
Dweck, C. 75, 77, 78, 84, 85, 235, 247-248
Dyson, B. 190, 197, 208

Eccles, J.S. 132, 145
EEF (Education Endowment Foundation) 202, 208
Eells, R. 205, 208
Ekkekakis, P. 39, 43
Ellis, M. 48, 62
Ennis, C. 11, 25, 151, 167
Ensher, E.A. 266, 271
Eraut, M. 236, 245, 248
Erikson, E.H. 35-36, 43
Ewing, R. 254, 271

Feiman-Nemser, S. 252, 271
Fives, H. 150-151, 166-167
Fogarty, R. 80, 85
Foley, M. 94, 106, 108
Forlin, C. 94, 108
Frank, K. 290, 305
Freeman, M.A. 254, 271
Freire, P. 211, 230
French, R. 90, 108
Fry, J.M. 35, 43, 44, 47, 50, 62, 63
Fuentes Cabrera, A. 190

Gagne, R.M. 65, 67, 84-85
Gallagher, M.C. 262, 272
Gallahue, D.L. 29-30, 35, 42-43
Gallimore, R. 91, 109
Gardner, M. 275, 287
Garet, S.M. 244, 248
Garimella, U. 197, 208
Garn, A. 179, 185, 188
Gärtner, M. 59, 63
Gerbracht, G. 217-218, 226-227, 229, 231
Gibbons, S.L. 144-145
Godbout, P. 46, 62
Golombek, P.R. 216, 228, 231

Good, C. 77, 85
Goodway, J. 29-30, 35, 42-43
Goodyear, V.A. 190, 206, 208
Gouveia, L., 56, 63
Gower, R. 89, 109, 134, 146, 152, 168
Graff, C. 94, 106, 108
Graham, C.R. 205, 208
Graham, G. 31-32, 43
Grant, C. 230
Gray, G. 134, 146
Gray, W.A. 253, 271
Greenberg, M.T. 133, 146
Gréhaigne, J.F. 46, 62
Grenny, J. 291-292, 303, 305
Griffin, L.L. 35, 43, 46, 62
Gu, Q. 224, 230
Guskey, T.R. 236, 249, 275-276, 284-285, 288, 298, 300, 302, 305

Haerens, L. 40, 44
Hairon, S. 273, 288
Haley-Speca, M.A. 89, 109, 134, 146, 152, 168
Halverson, R. 273, 288
Handal, G. 215, 221-222, 231
Hansen, K. 130, 145
Hardin, B. 107-108
Hardy, B. 215, 230
Hardy, C. 151, 167
Harvey, S. 46, 62
Hastie, P. 46, 62
Hattie, J. 200, 205, 208
Hellison, D. 130, 134, 145
Henderson, H. 90, 108
Heny, J.J. 290, 305
Hinojo Lucena, F.J. 190
Hipp, K. 282, 288
Hobson, A.J. 254-255, 271; and Malderez, A. 260, 271; Ashby, P., Malderez, A. and Tomlinson, P.D. 254-256, 271
Holbeche, L. 269, 271
Holt/Hale, S.A. 31-32, 43

AUTHOR INDEX

Hopper, T. 47, 49-50, 62, 63; Butler, J. and Storey, B. 54. 62; Sanford, K. and Clarke, A. 47, 49, 62
Hoque, M.E. 130, 145
Hord, S.M. 273, 277, 282, 287, 288
Horn, R.S. 282, 287
Hu, H. 197, 208
Huan, V. 88, 90, 94, 109
Huberman, M. 254, 271
Hudson, P. 250, 254, 255, 260, 271, 272; and Hudson, S. 269, 271
Huffman, J.B. 282, 288
Hughes, M. 114, 129
Hunter, A. 274, 285, 288
Hutchison, A. 192, 194, 208
Hyler, M.E. 275, 287

Imbeau, M.B. 16, 18, 26
Ingersoll, R.M. 269, 272
Isaacs, L.D. 33, 43
Isen, A.M. 25-26
Isenberg, J.P. 217-218, 226-227, 229, 231

Jackson, D. 292, 305
Jalongo, M.R. 217-218, 226-227, 229, 231
Jarrett, K. 46, 62
Jaspers, W.M. 261, 271
Jennings, P.A. 133, 146
Jensen, A.R. 64-65, 75, 85
Jensen, B. 274, 285, 288
Johnson, K.E. 216, 228, 231
Johnson, M. 224, 231
Jones, E. 205, 208
Jones, L. 282, 288
Jones, R. 50, 62

Kaur, S. 87, 90, 94, 95, 108, 109
Kereluik, K. 205, 208
King, G. 282, 287
King, K.P. 289, 305
Kington, A. 224, 230
Kirk, D. 40, 44, 151, 167
Kirk, J. 274, 285, 288

Kirschner, P.A. 197, 208
Knowles, M.S. 241-243, 249
Koehler, M.J. 205, 208
Koh, G.W. 130, 134-135, 140-141, 146
Kounin, J.S. 259, 272
Kram, K.E. 252, 260, 264-267, 276
Krathwohl, D. 126-127, 129
Krause, A. 290, 305

Ladwig, M.A. 39, 43
Laker, A. 38, 43
Lakoff, G. 224, 231
Launder, A.G. 35, 43, 46, 62; and Piltz, W. 50, 62
Lauvas, P. 215, 221-222, 231
Lavay, B. 90, 108
Lawrence, J. 67, 85
Lee, A.M. 45, 62
Lee, C.Y.M. 52, 54, 59, 61
Lee, M.C.Y.: Chow, J.Y., Button, C. and Tan, C.W.K. 54-55, 59, 62; Chow, J.Y., Komar, J., Tan, C.W.K. and Button, C. 59, 62
Lemos, M.S. 25-26
Leow, A. 130, 134-135, 140-141, 146
Lew, K.E.M. 60, 62
Lewis, H. 151, 167
Lieberman, L.J.: Arndt, K.L. and Daggett, S. 89, 108; and Houston-Wilson, C. 106, 108; Lytle, R. and Clarcq, J. 96, 108
Liersch, S. 39, 43
Lim, L. 90-91, 109
Lim, S. 87-88, 106, 108
Lipponen, L. 94, 106-107
Littlejohn, A. 197, 208
López Belmonte, J. 190
Loreman, T. 94, 108
Lumpe, T.A. 290, 305
Lund J.: and Tannehill D. 11, 26; and Veal, M.L. 117, 129
Lundeen, L. 144-145
Lytle, S.L. 229-230

Maatta, K. 25-26
Macdonald, D. 151, 167
Male, T. 259, 272
Mandigo, J.: Francis, N., Lodewyk, K. and Lopez, R. 110, 129; Holt, N., Anderson, A. and Sheppard, J. 50, 62
Mansour, N. 151, 167
Margaryan, A. 197, 208
Marshall, S. 50, 62
Martin, J. 89, 108
Martin, R.J. 11, 25, 50, 62
Marzano, J.S. 133, 146
Marzano, R.J. 133, 146
Masia, B. 126-127, 129
Maxfield, D. 291-292, 303, 305
May Yin, S. 94, 106-107
McConnel, N., 59, 63
McMahon, A. 273-274, 285, 288
McMillan, R. 291-292, 303, 305
McNabb, J. 90, 108
McNeill, M. 35, 43, 44, 47, 50, 62, 63
Megginson, D. 252, 272
Meijer, P.C. 261, 271
Merrill, M.D. 243-244, 249
Mesquita, I. 46, 62
Meyer, A. 96, 108
Mezirow, J. 289-290, 305
Milho, J. 56, 63
Ministry of Community Development, Youth and Sports 88, 108
Minnaert, A. 95, 108
Mishra, P. 205, 208
Mitchell, S. 35, 43, 46, 62, 63
Mitchell, S.A. and Oslin, J.L. 50, 62; Oslin, J. and Griffin, L. 49-50, 62
MOE (Ministry of Education) 1, 3, 6, 10-11, 13-15, 26, 30, 43, 88, 94, 104, 108, 238, 249, 274, 282, 285, 288, 290-292, 305
Moller, G.A.Y.L.E. 282, 288
Mombarg, R. 40, 43
Moon, J.A. 283, 288, 290, 298, 300, 302, 305
Moon, T.R. 16, 18, 26

Morris, P.A. 5-6, 90-91, 93, 96, 100, 107
Morrison, K. 122, 129
Mosston, M. 170-174, 188
Mouritzen, J. 144-145
Mueller, C.M. 75, 78, 84
Muijs, D. 65-67, 70, 80, 85
Murphy, S.E. 266, 271

National Institute of Education (NIE) 236, 249
National Partnership for Excellence and Accountability in Teaching (NPEAT) 245, 249
Neihart, M. 88, 90, 94, 109
Nespor, J. 151, 167
Nevin, A.I. 96, 109
Newcombe, D.J. 52, 59, 63
Newell, K. 51-52, 63
Ng, P.T. 250, 272; Lim, K.M., Low, E.L. and Hui, C. 256, 272
Ng, Z. 87, 90, 94, 95, 108, 109
Nietfeld, J.L. 80, 85
Nisbett, R. 152, 167
Noddings, N. 216, 231
Nuthall, G. 110, 129

Obrusnikova, I. 89, 108
Ocal, S.D. 256, 271
O'Connor, D. 254, 271
O'Connor, U. 90, 108
OECD (Organisation for Economic Cooperation and Development) 2, 151, 167
Ohanian, S. 217, 231
Oliver, K.L. 230-231
Olson, L. 151, 161, 168
O'Neill, L.M. 96, 108
Oslin, J.L. 35, 43, 46, 62, 63
O'Sullivan, M. 269, 271, 274, 277, 285, 287
Oxford Learners' Dictionaries 252, 272
Ozmun, J.C. 29-30, 35, 42-43

Pajares, F. 150-152, 165-167
Palailogou, I. 259, 272

Palmer, P. 150-151, 153, 157, 164-166, 168
Pankake, A.M. 282, 288
Parker, M. 31-32, 43
Parsloe, E. 252, 272
Pashler, H. 82, 84
Passos, P. 56, 63
Patterson, K. 291-292, 303, 305
Payne, D. 277, 280, 282, 288
Payne, V.G. 33, 43
Pearson, P.D. 262, 272
Peh, S.Y.C. 56, 63
Penuel, W. 290, 305
Pereira, E. 52, 61
Perkins, J. 144-145
Peters, D.M. 50, 62
Peterson, K.D. 277, 288
Piaget, J. 33, 34, 43; and Inhelder, B. 34, 43
Pickering, D.J. 133, 146
Pijl, S.J. 95, 108
Pill, S. 47, 63
Placek, J. 153, 167
Podsen, I.J. 269, 272
Pokora, J. 252-253, 271
Polkinghorne, D.E. 216, 231
Poon, K.K. 87, 90, 94, 95, 108, 109
Pope, S. 131, 146
Porter, C.A. 244, 248
Powers, E. 277, 287
Pozo Sánchez, S. 190
Pratt, D. 154-155, 166-168; and Collins, J. 155, 168; Smulders D. and Associates 149-150, 152, 154, 156, 168
Prawat, R. 161-162, 168
Prins, F. 261, 271
Pritchard, W. 273, 287
Prochaska, J.J. 39, 43

Quigley, A. 65-67, 70, 85

Rantala, T. 25-26
Raths, J. 166, 168
Rattan, A. 77, 85

Raymond 79, 85
Redding, S. 203, 208
Reeve, J. 25-26
Renshaw, I.: Araújo, D., Button, C., Chow, J.Y., Davids, K. and Moy, B. 53, 60, 63; Chow, J.Y., Davids, K. and Hammond, J. 51, 54, 63
Reuben, S.C. 137, 146
Richard, J.F. 45, 63
Richardson, K.P. 50, 63
Riel, M. 290, 305
Rink, J. 15, 18, 26, 130, 134, 146, 198, 208, 259, 272; and Hall, T.J. 134, 146
Ritchhart, R. 122, 129
Roberts, W.M. 52, 59, 63
Roberts-Hull, K. 274, 285, 288
Robinson, B. 144-145
Rodríguez, J.B. 295, 305
Roeser, R. 132, 145
Rogers, C. 210, 231
Rohrer, D. 82, 84
Rokeach, M. 151, 168
Rosen, B. 215, 231
Rosenshine, B. 65, 67-68, 71-72, 85
Rosenthal, R. and Babad, E.Y 72, 85; and Jacobson, L. 72, 85
Ross, L. 152, 167
Rovegno, I.: and Bandhauer, D. 11, 24, 26, 113, 129, 241, 249; and Dolly, J.P. 45, 63
Ryan, R.M. 39-40, 43, 201, 207-208

Sallis, J.F. 39, 43
Sammons, P. 224, 230
Saphier, J., 89, 109, 134, 146, 152, 168
Schechter, C. 258, 272
Schiemer, S. 111, 113, 129
Schindler, A.W. 64, 65, 85
Schon, D.A. 212-213, 230-231
Schwarz, A. 59, 63
Seifert, L. 52, 61
Sempowicz, T. 250, 254, 260, 272
Serpa, S. 56, 63

Shanklin, J. 118, 129
Sharma, U. 94, 108
Sheehy, D. 50, 63
Sherrington, T. 65, 85
Shiffrin, R. 73, 84
Shin, T.S. 205, 208
Shraw, G. 80, 85
Shulman, L.S. 205, 208, 290, 306
Siedentop, D. 41, 43
Sigel, I.E. 151, 168
Siraj-Blatchford, I. 10, 26
Smith, D.E. 250, 254-256, 260, 268, 272
Smith, J. 76, 85
Smith, K. 89, 108
Smith, T.M. 269, 272
Sonnemann, J. 274, 285, 288
Spillane, J.P. 273, 288
Sport Australia 98, 109
Stall, G. 282, 288
Stenzel, E.J. 145-146
Sterdt, E. 39, 43
Stobart, G. 224, 230
Stogre, T. 144-145
Stoll, L. 273-274, 285, 288
Stolz, S. 47, 63
Stringer, E. 65-67, 70, 85
Suk Yoon, K. 244, 248
Sun, H. 11, 25, 41, 43
Suomi, J. 89, 109
Switzler, A. 291-292, 303, 305
Sykes, C.S. 254, 271

Taliaferro, A. 205, 208
Tan, C. 35, 44, 47, 60, 62, 63
Tan, C.W.K. 35, 43, 49, 50, 53-55, 60, 62, 63
Tan, D. 87-88, 106, 108
Tan, S. 89-90, 94, 106
Tan, S.K.S. 35, 44, 47, 63
Tan, W.K.C. 52, 54, 59, 61
Tan, Y.K. 256, 271
Tapasak, R. 89, 109

Taylor, W.C. 39, 43
Teaching Perspective Inventory (TPI) 150, 154-156, 168
Temperly, J. 292, 305
Teng, A. 256, 272
Tharp, R.G. 91, 109
Thaver, T. 90-91, 109
Theodoulides, A. 130-146
Therriault, D. 80, 85
The Straits Times 94, 109
Thiede, K.W. 80, 85
Thomas, S. 273-274, 285, 288
Thompson, M. 65, 85
Thorburn, M. 289, 306
Thorpe, R. 35, 43, 45, 49, 61, 63; and Bunker, D. 45-49, 63; Bunker, D. and Almond, L. 45-49, 63
Thousand, J.S. 96, 109
Timmermans, A.C. 40, 43
Timperley, H.S. 200, 208, 273, 288
Tolhurst, J. 250, 260, 271
Tomlinson, C.A. 16, 18, 26
Training and Development Agency for Schools 98, 109
Trujillo Torres, J.M. 190
Tsangridou, N. 153, 168

UNESCO (United Nations Educational Scientific and Cultural Organization) 86, 88, 109

Valkova, H. 89, 108
Valli, L. 298, 302, 306
Van den Berghe, L. 40, 44
Vansteenkiste, M. 40, 44
van Wieringen, P.C. 59, 61
Vazou, S. 39, 43
Veríssimo, L. 25-26
Vickerman, P. 90, 108, 109
Vidoni, C. 145-146
Villa, R.A. 96, 109
Vul, E. 82, 84
Vygotsky, L.S. 27, 34, 44, 79, 85

Wacker, C. 151, 161, 168
Wallace, M. 273-274, 285, 288
Wallian, N. 45, 46, 62, 63
Walter, U. 39, 43
Walther-Thomas, C. 89, 109
Ward, P. 145-146
Warnock, M. 106, 109
Waugh, F. 254, 271
Weare, K. 134, 146
Wejr, C. 144-145
Wentzel, K.R. 41, 44; and Watkins, D.E. 41, 44
Werner, P. 49, 63
Whitehead, M. 17, 26
Wiliam, D. 65, 85, 200, 208
Wilkins, E.A. 269, 272
Wixted, J.T. 82, 84

Wolfson, T. 277, 280, 282, 288
Wong, M. 87-88, 90, 94, 95, 106, 108, 109
Woodward, L. 194, 208
Woolfson, L.M. 106, 109
Wrench, A. 86, 109
Wright, S.C. 35, 43, 44, 47, 50, 62, 63, 250, 254-256, 260, 268, 272
Wubbels, T. 261, 271
Wulf, G. 59, 63

Yarbrough, D. 282, 288
Yeo, L. 88-90, 94, 106, 109
Yonemura, M. 229, 231
YST (Youth Sport Trust) 2, 2622

Zeichner, K. 230

SUBJECT INDEX

ability: cognitive 88, 262; groups 48, 100; intellectual 87-88, 97; of students 13, 29-32, 34, 36-37, 41, 47, 49-50, 65, 70, 75, 80, 87, 110, 126, 131-136, 179-180, 182, 263; of teacher 72, 90, 136, 138, 257-258, 266, 269, 285, 301

access/accessible 4; to CPD 281, 292; to learning 96, 123, 156, 247; of all students to physical education 96, 104; to technology 206; see also inclusion

accommodation(s) (to teaching for students with SEND) 9, 34, 81, 96, 99, 110

achievement 118, 135-136, 140, 145, 169, 182, 224, 250; barriers to 31; evidence of 33-34; of learning outcome 175; levels of 17, 22, 112, 161; of students 13-14, 18, 40, 75, 299; see also progress

activation/activate(d) 186, 202, 243; of learning) 243-244

active 34, 53, 114, 189; learners 5, 45; learning 3, 178, 195-196, 304; listening 258; participants 51; physically 11; recall 82

activity (ies) 30, 52, 115; areas of 31, 36, 53, 71, 82, 114; assessment 115, 122; benefits of 122; classroom 136, 295; differentiated 22, 94, 99-101, 103, 118; physical 1, 11, 13, 17, 38-39, 104, 117, 120, 138, 189, 221; professional development 242-245; time 190, 221, 295; types of 118, 120, 138, 142, 175; see also athletics; dance; differentiation; games; gymnastics; inclusion; outdoor; swimming

adapt/adaptation: of behaviours 51, 54; of the curriculum 9; of mentoring 255; of skills 24, 285; of teaching 1, 27, 46, 60, 64, 98-99, 172, 244, 266; see also approaches, teaching; differentiation; inclusion

advisor 260

advocate (s)/advocacy 14, 229, 279, 282-283, 291

affective: competence 11; development 35-39, 130-144; domain 21, 27-29, 35, 38-39, 88, 110, 126-128, 130-144, 172, 180, 276; learning 130-144; outcomes 14, 130, 169, 171

affordance of technology 192, 201-204, 281

agency 258

aims of physical education 10, 12, 14, 17; see also goals; objectives

analogies use of 56, 58, 60

apps 186, 194-195; see also digital, technologies

application: of learning 4, 141, 154, 240, 276, 284, 296, 298-299, 302;

SUBJECT INDEX

of mindset 75-76; of pedagogies 50, 57-60, 90, 122, 172, 179, 202; in professional development 243, 294; of research 292; of skills 13
appraisal of teacher 275
approaches: assessment 121, 199; constructivist 34, 45-46; games centred 45-46; learning 84, 141; teaching 5, 22, 34, 45, 77, 169-187, 301-302, 307-308; see also Mosston's spectrum of teaching; pedagogy
assessment 110-129; application of 278-279; approaches to 121, 199; criteria 76; of CPD 276; differentiated 110, 118, 125; formative 5, 22, 110-114; for learning (AFL) 17-18, 111-124; rubric 112; self 16, 20, 24; summative 285; use of 5; tiered 121; tool 113, 118
asynchronous(ly) 186, 195, 295, 303; learning 4, 205; see also learning
athletics 15, 30, 35, 54, 82; see also activities
attainment (of students) 15, 75, 137, 202-203; grades 114; see also assessment
Attention Deficit Hyperactivity Disorder (ADHD) 87; see also special education
attention(al) 52 301; as behaviour 104, 141; external focus 56; focus 55-56; internal focus 55-56; of student 18, 55-56, 68; of teacher 131
Attention Deficit Hyperactivity Disorder (ADHD) 87
attitudes 9, 114, 126, 130, 151, 246; towards inclusion 89, 91, 94; towards mentoring 252, 268; towards physical education 29, 29; towards professional development 235-236, 226, 280, 285, 300; of students 29, 29, 89, 126, 130, 277; of teachers 91, 94, 114, 151, 236, 252, 268, 280, 285, 298; see also beliefs; values
Autism Spectrum Disorder (ASD) 87, 93, 95, 104; see also special education
automatic: behaviour 104-105; movement 32
autonomy 45, 47, 134, 140; of mentees 252, 267; of students 38. 40-41, 51, 59, 136, 138, 164

beginning teacher (s) 166, 218, 224, 250-252, 254-256, 259, 262, 266
behaviour(al) 38-40, 51, 56, 66-67, 87-88, 94, 105, 126-127, 131-132, 134, 164, 252; adapted 54, 65, 106; causes of 104-105; disruptive 64, 74, 92-93, 133-134, 254; expected 72, 75, 135, 138, 140-141; functional analysis (FBA) 104-105; management of 106, 133, 141, 151, 214; movement 41, 51, 55; social 11, 41, 130, 138; of teacher 65, 106, 289-292; see also management
beliefs: of mentoring 268-269; professional 290, 298; of students 75, 77, 161-162; of teachers 3, 86, 106, 149-167, 169, 189, 210, 213, 215, 224, 226, 235, 269, 294, 300, 302, 308
belonging: sense of 41, 89, 98, 106
benefits: of activity 122, 132; of inclusion 89; of mentoring 251, 254-256; of technology 190, 206
Blogs 201
boys 21, 39, 92, 1520153, 161; see also gender; girls

camera(s) 4, 189, 203; see also digital, technologies
challenge(s) 55, 69, 76, 99, 143, 266; levels of 10, 22, 24, 27, 32, 40, 47, 49, 50, 78, 80, 96, 100, 135, 166, 245; of mentoring 266, 268-269; models 278; and stretch 78-80

328 SUBJECT INDEX

changing rooms 67, 73-74
classroom 3-4, 41, 114, 126, 151, 159, 210, 215-216, 220, 224, 295, 302; culture 278; dilemmas 216; management 22, 159, 280; see also Google
coaching 133, 137; and mentoring 242, 251-254; style 98
cognitive xxiv, 11, 14, 21, 27-29, 33-35, 38-39, 65-66, 73-73, 88, 110, 121-122, 125-126, 130, 137, 141, 155, 165, 169-172, 179-180, 185-186, 189, 214, 222, 224, 276; load theory 73-74, 82 see also development; domains of learning
collaborative 4, 140, 201, 217, 229, 256; learning 3, 229, 269, 282, 290, 292, 295-296; tools 132, 179, 196, 203, 303
command style of teaching 170, 172-175; see also Mosston's spectrum of teaching
communication (by the teacher) 81, 133-134, 136, 255, 258; clarity of 11; with students 91; styles 140; see also language; talk
community 2, 216, 218, 220, 266, 291; learning 213, 229, 273, 282, 296
competencies 2, 5, 130, 140, 294; digital 205-206; movement 13, 49, 57, 191; social and emotional 130-134, 142
confidence 12, 57, 266-267, 288, 245; self 267, 131, 196, 254, 262; student 36, 79-80, 83, 110, 179
constraints 51-52, 54, 56, 200, 228, 236; environmental 51-52; led 51; performer 51-52, 54, 57; task 51-52, 54-55, 57, 60
constructivist 152, 164; approaches 34, 45; see also knowledgeable other; teaching, approaches; zone of proximal development (ZPD)
content: knowledge 3, 46, 133, 155, 169, 205, 250, 262, 290, 308;

learning 11, 122, 150, 154, 177, 242, 276, 291; lesson 22, 27, 35, 68, 72, 76, 83, 124-125, 127, 151-152, 156, 163, 166, 175, 186, 189-190, 198, 253, 296, 307; setting 140; see also knowledge
context: factors 245-246; learning 24, 82, 169; physical education 82, 89, 131, 227, 286; place 210, 215; teaching 189-190, 216; Singapore 2, 5, 256, 293; work 265-266, 268
cooperative 36, 41, 142-143; learning 143, 226, 228
criteria 173, 184; assessment 76, 115, 118; for learning 187; success 16-20, 24, 112-113, 118-119, 200-201, 275-276; worksheets 176, 178-182; see also worksheet
critical 53, 180, 280; evaluation 280, 212; reflection 255, 302; thinking 45, 47, 170, 196; see also evaluation; reflection
cues 74, 87, 137; learning 19-20, 35, 114, 120-121, 135, 137, 192, 202; teaching 55-56, 58, 174-176, 179; see also learning; teaching
culture(al) 169; classroom 278; community 220, 281; learning 158-159, 280-282, 296; mentoring 256; mindset 78; school 151
curriculum 9, 41; adapted 9, 24, 91, 96, 98-99; aims 12, 17; goals 11-12, 15, 17; models 46, 64, 111; policies 9, 169; progression 12, 21, 24; purpose 11, 17; quality 16; see also adapt; design; models

dance 14-15, 30, 35, 114, 153, 175, 186, 227
decision making: by students 46, 49, 51, 132-134, 138, 170, 172-172, 176, 178; by teachers 172-173, 214, 278
definition: of effective CPD 275; of LeARN approach 294; mentoring

251-252; metacognition 80; self-regulation 80; *see also* LeARN; mentoring; metacognition
demonstration 96, 154, 243, 276; lessons 296, 299, 303; student 97, 177; teacher 74, 175, 200-201, 204
design: learning 22, 47, 161, 163, 200, 205, 301; lesson 17, 27, 51, 138, 204, 238; principles 52, 294; programme 239, 279, 291; task 51, 53, 58, 138, 140; *see also* curriculum
dedicated improvement and reflection time (DIRT) 70, 115, 117
development (student) 1, 4-5, 9-12, 14-15, 17, 21-22, 27-43, 46, 60, 66-67, 69, 71, 75-76, 79, 81-82, 88-90, 95, 121, 126, 174; affective 35-38, 66, 95, 130-138, 142, 144; cognitive 33-35, 65; holistic 21, 27-29, 39, 88, 130; psychomotor 21, 29-32, 69, 121, 130-131; of skills 14-15, 21, 28, 32; stages of 22, 28, 35-38 42; *see also* affective; cognitive; psychomotor
device(s) 195, 203, 206; digital 180, 192, 195; electronic 4; tracking 189; *see also* digital, technologies
differentiation(ed) 22, 118 175; assessments 110, 125; instruction 3; tasks 22, 135-136, 138, 214; *see also* inclusion; STEP
digital: competencies 205-206; devices 180, 192, 195; environment 189, 204, 206; hardware 4, 189-190, 206; natives 197; platforms 4, 291, 294-295; technologies 189-208, 295; tools 190-207, 282
DIRT *see* dedicated improvement; reflection time
discovery 184; convergent 174, 184-186; divergent 172, 174, 186; guided 174, 183-184; self 153, 165; threshold 170; *see also* approaches, to teaching; Mosston's spectrum of teaching

disability 88; *see also* special education
domains of learning xxii, 27; *see also* affective; cognitive; psychomotor

ecological framework 5, 90
efficacy 303; self 13, 131, 155, 158, 260, 285; teacher 205
effective: assessment 198-199; communication 134, 136; learning 25, 51, 64, 67, 83, 118, 145, 164; learning environment 64, 72-74, 77, 83; mentoring 254, 257, 259, 269; pedagogy 64, 130; professional development xxii, xxiv, 3, 5, 243-245, 250, 273-287, 289-305; teaching 1, 24, 27, 51, 56, 67, 154-155, 177, 185-186, 239-241, 257; *see also* assessment; mentoring; professional development
effort: levels of 24, 64, 67, 75, 78, 95, 134; towards learning 76, 106, 136, 155, 300; *see also* mindset; motivation
emotions 35, 130-132, 209, 216, 221, 224, 226, 258, 263, 267
emotional 29, 64, 66, 86-88, 94-95, 161, 214, 262, competencies 11, 130-134, 142; intelligence 263; socio 27, 29, 229, 307; *see also* affective; development
empathy 132, 252, 258
empower(ing)(ment) 1, 12, 134, 138, 201, 203, 252, 260, 262, 265, 307
engage(ment) 67-68, 75; active 45; with CPD 3, 151, 241, 247; in learning 135, 137, 164, 192, 215; levels of 29, 65, 192, 195-196, 215, 307; of students 42, 64, 74, 76, 79-80, 124, 195-196, 214
enthusiastic/enthusiasm 59, 185, 230, 254
environment(al) 11, 21, 28, 32, 89, 206; constraints 51-52; for CPD

280-282, 293-294; digital 189, 204, 206; learning 22, 39, 41-42, 45, 53-55, 59, 64, 72, 75, 78, 81, 83, 88, 94, 106, 134-140, 164, 169, 179, 186, 215, 235, 254255, 260, 266
equipment 16, 22, 27, 41, 50, 52-53, 55, 59, 94, 96, 98-100, 103, 106, 135-136, 138, 175, 200-201, 266, 282, 285, 295
ethic (al) 215, 221, 258; of caring 219; standards 132; work 75
evaluation 80-81, 193-194, 212, 274-276, 284-286, 298; student 17, 24, 36, 81, 118, 263; self 263, 308; teacher 110, 118, 132, 266, 274
evidence of learning see achievement; progress
expectations 12, 14, 27, 72-73, 75, 135, 138, 180, 219, 245; of individuals 245-246, 275; of mentors 257, 266; of students 74, 80; see also behaviour
experience(s) 13, 35, 53, 111, 151, 174, 189, 241, 262, 268, 299, 294; learning 2, 4-5, 14, 16, 27-28, 32, 36, 38, 40-41, 47, 50, 52, 91-96, 112, 116, 135, 137, 151, 161, 163, 166, 171, 182, 190-192, 196-197, 200, 203, 205, 210, 224, 229, 237, 290-291, 294, 302, 307, 309; lived 209, 215-216, 219, 227, 242-244; success 27, 36, 98, 106, 135, 138-139
expert(s) 239, 241, 278, 291, 292
exploratory learning 51-52, 54, 57; see also learning
explicit: control of movement 56; instruction/teaching 55, 73, 82, 140
external: CPD 287; factors 90-92, 211; focus 56, 58; motivation 40, 242; organization 2

facilities 281-282, 285
feed 66; forward 200, 203-204, 207; up 200-205, 207

feedback 39, 58, 69, 75-77, 112, 134, 172-172, 200, 202-204; and mentoring 255, 258-259, 263; peer 18, 24, 66, 81, 95, 135, 137, 143, 177-178, 192, 253; strategies 77, 82, 142, 173, 176, 179, 192; to students 36, 58, 66, 69-70, 115, 245; in teaching 51, 56, 137, 140, 175-176, 185-186, 195, 245; see also assessment
flipped learning 191
formative 285; assessment 5, 22, 110-113, 115, 119, 124, 190, 200-201; see also assessment
foundations: for learning 10, 14, 64, 130, 133, 243
fundamental: concepts 185; knowledge 172; level of CPD 285; movement skills 12-14, 29-31, 36, 60; skills 124

game(s): -as-teacher 50; -based learning 49; categories 49; -centred approaches (GCA) 45-51; classification 50; -concept approach 46; invasion 13, 19, 48-49, 53-60; net-barrier 41, 49, 59, 123-125; striking and fielding 49, 59; Teaching Games for Understanding (TGfU) 45-51; types 47-48; see also activities, approaches, to teaching; Mosston's spectrum of teaching; teaching, approaches; teaching, strategies
gender 103, 169; see also boys; girls
girls 39, 92, 103, 161; see also boys; gender
goals: achieve 132; behavioural 51; clear 112; coaching 253; collective 132; curriculum 11-12, 15, 17; educational; end 200, 298; identified 189; learning 38, 96, 145, 200-202, 275; mentoring 253, 266-267; personal 290; physical education

SUBJECT INDEX 331

10-12, 25; school 277-279; set 17, 20, 95, 121, 136; tactical 49; task 55; *see also* learning outcomes; objectives; purpose
Google: classroom 191, 201, 282, 295; docs 202, 206; drive 201; form 195, 204; slides 196
guidance: adult 79; from mentors 255-257, 259-260; parental 206; sheets 97; for students 36, 68, 73, 75, 77, 143, 164, 179, 200, 202; visual 69; *see also* cues; mentoring
gymnastics 14-16, 23, 30, 35, 97, 112, 114, 119-120, 134, 170-171, 175, 179, 186, 253; *see also* activities

hardware 4, 189-190, 206; *see also* digital, technologies
holistic 29, 96, 307; approach 203, 253, 281; development of mentees 253, 259; development of students 21, 27-29, 39, 88, 130; education xxvi, 88-89; writing 228
human capital 255

impairment (student) 100; *see also* differentiation; inclusion; special education
implementation of: CPD 273, 282, 284, 286-287; digital technologies 190, 197, 204; guidelines 113; lesson 51-52; Professional Learning Community (PLC) 282; target 83
inclusion/inclusive 11, 86-109, 125, 290; behaviour 106; education 88, 90; environment 89; lesson 89, 104; perception towards 94-95, 106; policy 88; practice 5, 86-90, 107, 266; spectrum 94, 98-101; style 170, 173, 180, 182; in teaching 86, 88-90
individual differences 21, 28, 54, 89, 106
individualised: learning 187; movement solution 51, 56; progress 204; target 118

information-movement couplings 53-55
intelligence: emotional 263; quotient 97
intentional 1, 86, 142, 144, 163, 265, 283; Intentionality 40, 130, 141, 145
interaction: didactic 141; dynamic 51; with mentee 258; social 41, 100, 130, 132, 163, 179, 226, 228; with students 151, 173, 215-216, 226, 228
internet 206; *see also* digital, technologies
instruction(s): clear 74, 77, 134-137; direct 158; explicit 55, 73, 83; in inclusive physical education (IPE) 97-98; in Mosston's spectrum of teaching styles 173-179; in non-linear pedagogy (NLP) 51, 55-58; principles 67-71, 82; theory 67; video 101; *see also* approaches, to teaching; guidance; Mosston's spectrum of teaching
instructional: decisions 111; framework 187; leader 279; learner 279; materials 96; methods xxiv; needs 111; process 154; strategies 88, 94, 244
interpersonal 132, 257-259
iPad 103, 192, 206

knowledge: mentoring 256-259; pedagogical (PK) xxii, 133, 240, 255, 257; pedagogical content (PCK) xxvii, 3, 205, 250, 262, 290, 308; subject content (SCK) xxii, xxvi, 3, 133, 253, 264, 290; technological (TK) 205; technological content (TCK) 205; technological pedagogical (TPK) 205
knowledgeable other 4, 238, 292; *see also* constructivist

language 27, 29, 33, 73, 94, 106, 120, 127, 140, 298; age-appropriate 35; body 161; common 172; for learning 76, 78; and literacy 86-88; people

first 94-95, 106; positive 95, 202; professional 275; see also communication
leader(s)/leadership: classroom 22; demand 303; distributed 273; instructional 279; pedagogical 241, 259, 293; perspective 273; presence 278; roles 254, 273, 287; school 5, 246, 263, 273, 284, 292, 303-4; skills 81, 132, 255; student 89, 278; teacher xxiii, 1, 210, 238-240, 246, 250, 292, 299; track 2
LeARN approach to CPD 294-296
learner: adult 241-244, 247-248; -centred 34, 46; designed 170, 187; -initiated 170, 187; lead 80-81; student as 52, 308; teacher as iii, 5, 219, 228, 275; principal as 279
learning: activation of 243-244; collaborative 3, 196, 269, 282, 290, 295, 304; conditions for 67; cooperative 143, 192, 226, 228; deep 202; deeper 282-283; double-loop 212-213; environment 22, 39, 41-42, 45, 55, 58-59, 64, 72, 75, 78, 81, 83, 88, 94-97, 101, 106, 134-143, 164, 169, 215, 254-255, 260, 266, 281-282; exploratory 51-52, 54, 57; flipped 191; gaps 261-264, 270; management systems (LMS) 204, 282; needs (students) 22, 77, 88, 90, 96, 106, 111-112, 118, 130, 163, 191, 255, 308; needs (teachers) 6, 255, 259-261, 266, 269, 280-281, 295, 299; outcomes 10, 15-21, 40, 88, 125, 131, 135-136, 144, 169-174, 187, 190-191, 207, 236-237, 242, 250, 255, 274-277, 285, 299, 307-308; personalised 203-204; relationship 252; self-directed 205; single-loop 212; transfer of 138-140; see also collaborative; environment; inclusion; objectives

lesson: observation 4, 153, 170, 261, 266, 269, 284-285, 291, 296; zero 172, 176, 190, 197, 206
lesson plan(ning) 38-39, 51, 57, 84, 142, 144, 151, 193, 266, 299
limitations: of mentoring 263; students 131, 153; of TPI 160; of technology 204-206; see also approaches, to teaching; digital, technologies; mentoring; teaching perspectives inventory (TPI)
listening: active 258
literacy 86-88; assessment 3, 278-279; physical 189

management see behaviour; classroom; learning; self
meaningful: feedback 18, 211; learning experiences 21, 56, 72, 86, 107, 164, 205, 254, 259; relationships 77, 86; tasks 38, 54, 64; see also learning, environment; lesson planning
metacognition 65, 78, 80-81, 83; definition of 80
metaphors 216, 224-225, 228
mentoring 250-272; approaches to 264; culture 256; cycle 264-267, 270; definition of 251-252; function of 270; phases of 265; process 260-261, 264-269
mindset: fixed 75-76; growth 75-78, 83-84, 131, 235, 247
models see curriculum; teaching approaches
modification: by adaptation 47, 49-50, 94, 1100, 102; for pupils with SEN 86, 99-100, 103; see also differentiation; inclusion; special education
monitor (ing) effectiveness 273, 284-285; and evaluate CPD 273-274, 284-287; performance 267; progress 286; by students 80-81; by teachers 39, 69, 80, 182

SUBJECT INDEX 333

mood graph 222-223, 227-228
Mosston's spectrum of teaching 169-188
motivation 39-40; definition 67; external 40; intrinsic 39-40, 133 to learn (mentees) 263; to learn (students) 10-11, 161; self determination theory 39-40, 75; self motivation 132; students 22, 41, 65, 70, 82, 96, 211, 214; teachers 5, 41, 218, 242; *see also* effort; theory, self-determination
motivator (s): external 242; social 292; structural 240, 303-304
movement: form 55-58, 204; outcome 55-56

narrative(s): approach 210, 216; features of 210, 216; inquiry 209-229; power of 215, 230; spaces 210

observation: lesson 261, 266, 269; peer 176-179, 186-187; skills 21, 81; by students 21, 54; tools 295, 303; *see also* lesson, observation; Video Enhanced Observation tool
objective(s) 213; learning 38, 54, 68, 99, 201; lesson 17, 59, 134, 143, 190; *see also* learning, outcomes
organisational: CPD 277; level 5; routines 138; skills 132; support and change 276, 285; *see also* management; routines
organise (ation) 14, 34, 280, 283; of learning 80, 294; of self 40-41; of students 140
orientation: to learning 241-244; phase for mentoring 264-266; of reflection 298-300, 304
outdoor education 15, 24, 30, 156; *see also* activities
ownership: student 9, 12, 14, 17-20, 24, 34, 40, 65, 80, 88, 134-138, 159, 176, 307; teacher xxiii, 1-2, 256, 279

parents 41, 91, 93, 95, 97-98, 205-206, 262
pedagogy/pedagogical: approaches 46, 191-194, 254; behaviour 169; linear 59; nonlinear (NLP) 5, 45, 51-60, 152; principles (affective learning) 134-140; principles (NLP) 51-60; principles (TGfU) 47-51
peer *see* feedback; observation
performer constraints 51-57
perspective(s) of teacher: developmental 27; multiple 186, 203, 213, 219, 222, 227, 229, 309; Teaching Perspective Inventory (TPI) 150-166; *see also* philosophy of teaching
philosophy of teaching 149-169
portfolio: leadership 254; student 67, 97, 285; teacher 250
practical theory model 215, 221-222
practice: change in 164, 245; variability in 51, 54
principal(s) 273-287
principles *see* design; effective; instruction; pedagogical; readiness; STEP
privacy 206
problem (solving) 24, 55, 59; independent 79; in professional development 243; as reflection 212-213; skill 47, 254-255; by students 22, 55, 113, 132, 164, 170, 172, 186; tactical 48, 55, 158, 192; *see also* approaches, to teaching; Mosston's spectrum of teaching
professional: conversations 229, 239; growth 166, 217-218, 221, 226, 230, 251-254, 282; learning 2, 6, 151, 214, 235, 237-238, 248-250, 254-260, 270, 285, 289, 298-300; practice 3, 144, 276
progress: assessment of student 20, 55, 70, 75, 82, 97, 110-129, 199, 201, 203-204; definition of 9;

planning for 21-25, 72, 79, 99; in skill development 29-43, 50, 71; supporting student 9-25, 77, 92, 192, 199; and sustainability 274, 284, 286; *see also* assessment

projector 200-201, 206; *see also* digital, technologies

psychosocial 140, 252-253, 266, 269; *see also* affective; social, and emotional competencies

psychomotor: development 21, 29-32, 69, 121, 130-131; domain 27, 29-30, 38-39, 110, 117, 130, 138-137, 141, 172; feedback 202; objectives 143; outcomes 140, 145, 169, 171, 179, 187; skills 30, 191; tasks 135; *see also* domains

purpose: of an activity 76, 160; of the curriculum 9; of physical education 10-12, 17, 130, 153, 163; sense of 131; of teacher 156, 257; *see also* aims of physical education; goals

question(s) 6, 14, 20, 56, 123-124, 150, 157, 161; example/sample 69, 75, 79, 82, 141, 192, 199, 226-227, 247, 297-298; questioning 46, 56, 58, 69-71, 81-82, 135, 155, 174, 184, 260, 309; guiding 93, 114, 159, 174, 194, 228, 243, 286; for reflection 14, 94-95, 111, 149, 153, 165, 193, 276, 293-294, 299; types 81, 89, 90, 177, 183-185, 258

QR codes 195, 204; *see also* digital, technologies

readiness: to learn 64-65, 67, 71-75, 77, 79-80, 83-84, 158; staff/teacher 90, 241-242, 269; of students 5, 16, 64, 75, 97, 99, 118, 125

reciprocal 170, 179; relationship 33, 255; teaching strategy 170, 173

reflection (s) 1, 20, 57-58, 71, 81, 157-158, 287, 299; in action 212-214, 221-222, 302; on action 212-214, 221-222, 302; depth of 297-298; in learning 66, 70, 75, 111, 113, 128, 135, 138, 141, 202, 267, 283; by staff 160, 163, 165-166, 209-210, 215, 217, 228, 244, 267, 282-285; structure of 78, 128, 283, 287; tools 115, 117, 210-211, 222-227, 286, 298, 300, 302, 304; *see also* evaluation; observation; reflective

reflective 137, 160, 220, 222, 227, 254, 290, 295, 297, 309; practice 5, 153, 157, 166, 209-212, 215, 218, 282-283; practitioner 169, 209-210, 212, 215, 220, 226, 229-230; teaching 210, 215; tool 156, 221, 228; *see also* learner; learning; reflection(s)

relationship 16, 24, 60, 134, 169, 216, 245-246, 301; learning 53; mentoring 252-253, 255-256, 258, 260, 264-265, 267; positive 132; skills 132, 138, 142, 259; student to student 41, 67, 86-87, 93, 141, 163; supportive 1, 132; teacher student 41, 77, 91, 94, 133-134, 136, 139, 141, 209, 255

repetition: of action 54, 58; *see also* practice

representation 47-48, 73, 92, 283; representativeness 52-53

resources 91; types of 6, 205, 259-260, 266, 285

respect (ful)/respecting 95, 127-128, 133, 135-137, 155, 252-253, 258, 260, 280

responsibility(ies): of leaders 273; of mentor 250, 255, 257-270; of student 12, 37, 81-82, 126: of teacher 154, 156, 164, 235

retention: of learning 73, 202; of teachers 2, 256

risk(s) 124, 282; taking 38, 282

roles and responsibilities 82; in mentoring 251, 257-259, 266, 270

SUBJECT INDEX

role model/modelling: age appropriate 89; mentor (as) 252; principal (as) 277-279, 286, 291; student (as) 95, 106; teacher (as) 136, 140, 209, 240, 252, 304

routines 72-75, 83-84, 87, 129, 135, 138, 156, 164, 179, 186-187, 197-198, 201, 241, 308; thinking 122

rules 13-14, 19, 34, 46-49, 52-53, 55, 57-58, 73, 81-82, 94, 98-100, 103, 123, 125, 128, 164

sampling 47-48, 50 see also pedagogical: principles

scaffold (s) 20, 69-70, 77, 99, 114, 135, 139, 189, 192 206, 281; scaffolding 79-80, 84, 203

Scheme of work see unit of work

self: -assessment 16, 18, 20; awareness 131, 134, 135, 137, 180, 263; determination theory 39-40, 42, 75, 201; directed learning 75, 84, 118, 187, 205, 214, 300; efficacy 13, 131, 155, 158, 260, 285; management 132, 137; regulation 78, 80, 83, 105, 111, 138

sensory 86-88, 94, 104; processing disorder 92, 101

skill(s) students: academic 131, 191, 195-196; acquisition 35, 51, 76, 97; adapted 100; affective 131, 142; application 12; decision making 51; development 30-31, 41, 60, 66, 71, 76-78, 95, 131; execution 46, 54; fundamental movement 11-14, 29034, 36; level 19, 41, 50, 53, 97, 117-119, 123, 163, 184; mastery 77; motor 14-15, 29, 31, 117, 130; movement 31, 60; physical 16, 46, 171; portfolio 67; practice 47, 104; problem solving 45, 47, 51, 58; proficiency 31-32, 98, 114, 200, 203; rehearsal 70; social 36, 38, 89, 105-106, 171; sport specific 13-14, 16, 69-70, 76-77, 82, 110, 123, 131,

177; see also affective; cognitive; psychomotor

skill(s) teacher xxii, 10, 20, 64, 66, 86, 133, 163, 169-170, 221, 235-236, 243, 253, 262, 269; mentoring 250-272; set 149; see also teaching

social: and emotional learning 131; and emotional competencies 27, 29, 86, 130-134; problems 87-88; see also affective; psychosocial

software 4, 189-190, 194-196, 201, 203; see also digital, technologies

space 13, 19-20, 22-24, 48-50, 55-58, 73, 98-99, 122-123, 125, 175, 191, 199; narrative 210, 215, 217; and time 18, 92, 158, 165, 215, 227, 281, 283; see also differentiation; environment; inclusion

special education 86-109; accommodation for 50, 88, 96; needs 3, 86-87; see also inclusion

speech 86-88

STEP principles (space, task, equipment, people) 22-23, 98-99; see also inclusion

story (ies) 104, 157, 196, 209-210, 213, 215-220, 226-228, 237, 247; storyboards 121

stretch: and challenge 78-80

structural 293; enabler 245-246, 292; motivator 240, 303-304

student: assessment 285; centred 34, 45, 51, 60, 301; development 5, 71, 134, 144; surveys 58, 285; voice 135, 154, 161-162, 201

subject content knowledge xxii, xxvi, 3, 133, 253, 261, 264, 290; see also knowledge

success: criteria 16-19, 24, 112-113, 115, 118-119, 129, 200-201, 275-276

summative assessment 285; see also assessment

support(ive): environment 1, 54, 60, 86, 134, 136, 240; materials

70; mentoring 254; relationships 132-133
swimming 15, 30, 171, 175; see also activities

tactical 32, 46-50, 53, 123, 158, 192; complexity 47, 49; decision learning 46; games approach 35, 46; knowledge 257
talk 18, 80, 95, 133, 186; mentor 255; student 80, 143, 186; teacher 152, 295; time 186, 295
target 23, 50, 175, 180-181; grade 83, 114; individualized 118; intended 66; learning 174; level 117-118; setting 17, 24, 214; zone 66; see also assessment
task 5, 10, 18, 21-22, 24-25, 32, 38, 40, 50, 52, 56-57, 64, 70, 112, 133; cards 19, 99; constraints 51-52, 54-55, 57-58, 60; decomposition 53-54; design 27, 32, 47, 53, 58-59, 69, 79, 96, 138; simplification 52-53, 55
teachable moments 137, 141, 182
teacher practice (s) 134-135, 140, 304; voice 220
teaching: approaches 22, 169-174, 179, 301-302, 307-308; cues 55-56, 58, 174-176, 179; strategies 28, 77, 144, 239, 259, 266, 301, 308; see also Mosston's spectrum of teaching; teaching games for understanding
teaching games for understanding (TGFU) 35, 45-46, 152, 164, 257; see also games, centred approaches
Teaching Perspective Inventory (TPI) 150-166
team(s) 58, 66-67, 77, 125, 185-186, 192, 290, 292; activities 24; captain 134; games 48, 171; gymnastics 175; players 128; teamwork 23, 53, 57-58, 132, 136-138, 186
technical: abilities 52; difficulties 206; instruction 56; know-how 197, 205; reflection 302; rules 66; skills 123, 262; see also rules; skills
technology/technological 4, 153, 187, 190, 194, 200, 203, 219; approaches to 204; apps/software 194-196, 203-204; in assessment 198-201; in learning 189-197, 204-207; in professional development 281, 295; see also digital, technologies
Technological 4, 190, 194, 200, 203; content knowledge (TCK) 205; knowledge (TK) 205; pedagogical knowledge (TPK) 205
theory 4, 42; cognitive-load 67, 73; of instruction 67; practical 215, 221; -practice xxii-xxiv, 1, 4-5, 45, 57, 59, 304; - practice nexus 213, 277, 286; practical theory model 215, 221-222; in real-life xxii; self-determination 39, 42, 75, 201; see also cognitive; constructivist; mindset motivation
think(ing) 33-34, 39, 155, 215, 224, 252, 290, 299; activities 122; critical 45, 47, 170, 196; processes 130; reflective 138, 254; routines 122; teachers 381; visible 124; see also critical
time 153, 161; curriculum 129, 201; as differentiation 99-100, 123; lesson 59, 158-159, 163-164, 156, 172, 177-178, 189-191, 195, 197, 221; planning 205; for reflection 20, 166, 212-215, 285, 295; thinking 35, 70, 135, 158, 165; see dedicated improvement and reflection time; space; wait
TREE (Teaching style, Rules and regulations, Equipment, and Environment) 94, 98, 100, 103

unit of work (scheme of work) 16, 70, 149, 184, 190, 296
Universal Design for Learning (UDL) 96; see also inclusion

values 10-12, 15, 72, 88, 91, 122, 126-127, 130-131, 140, 152, 156, 171, 210, 215, 217, 220, 224, 229, 252, 270, 277, 291, 298
variability in practice 51, 54
video 4, 16, 19, 36, 92, 101, 120-121, 127, 157, 185, 189, 191-192, 201-202, 205, 264, 291; gaming 49-50; recording 96, 142, 180, 193, 197-198, 201-202, 206, 221, 229, 296; technology 195-196, 201, 203, 295; see also digital, technologies
Video Enhanced Observation (tool) 295, 303 see also digital, technologies

virtual: and augmented reality 4, 189; platforms 4; see also digital, technologies
visual aids 74, 99, 103
voice: student 135, 154, 161-162, 201; teacher 220

wait: time 199; see also tine
web-based applications 203; see also digital, technologies
whiteboard 18, 82
workout 196
worksheet 176, 178-181, 206

Zone of Proximal Development (ZPD) (Vygotsky) 27, 79; see also constructivist